Adventurers and Exiles
The Great Scottish Exodus

Adventurers and Exiles

The Great Scottish Exodus

Marjory Harper

PROFILE BOOKS

First published in Great Britain in 2003 by
PROFILE BOOKS LTD
58A Hatton Garden
London EC1N 8LX
www.profilebooks.co.uk

Copyright © Marjory Harper, 2003
1 3 5 7 9 10 8 6 4 2

Typeset in Fournier by MacGuru
info@macguru.org.uk

Printed and bound in Great Britain by
Clays, Bungay, Suffolk

A CIP catalogue record for this book is available from the British Library.

ISBN 1 86197 304 7

CONTENTS

DARWIN

NORTHERN
TERRITORY

QUEENSLAND

WESTERN
AUSTRALIA

*Darling
Downs* • Brisbane

SOUTH
AUSTRALIA

NEW SOUTH
WALES

• Perth

Canberra • Sydney

Adelaide •

Bendigo
• Melbourne
Geelong • *Gippsland*
Port Phillip VICTORIA

AUSTRALIA

TASMANIA • Hobart

ORKNEY

Stromness • •Kirkwall

Thurso

CAITHNESS •Wick

SUTHERLAND •Dunbeath

Lerwick

SHETLAND

•Stornoway

LEWIS

•Lochinver

HARRIS

•Ullapool

NORTH
UIST

BENBECULA

SOUTH
UIST

BARRA

Skye

Rum

Eigg

Knoydart

ROSS AND
CROMARTY •Cromarty

MORAY BANFF •Fraserburgh

•Peterhead

NAIRN

Inverness

ABERDEEN

Old Rayne

Logie Coldstone •Aberdeen

Aboyne •Stonehaven

KINCARDINE

INVERNESS

•Fort William

Coll

Tiree

Mull

Colonsay *Jura*

ARGYLL

ANGUS

PERTH

Breadalbane KINROSS •Dundee

CLACKMANNAN

FIFE

DUNBARTON

STIRLING

Greenock
RENFREW Glasgow •Edinburgh
Bridge Paisley W. MID E. LOTHIAN
of LOTHIAN LOTHIAN
Weir
LANARK BERWICK

Arran

PEEBLES

SELKIRK ROXBURGH

AYR

DUMFRIES

KIRKCUDBRIGHT

WIGTOWN

S C O T L A N D

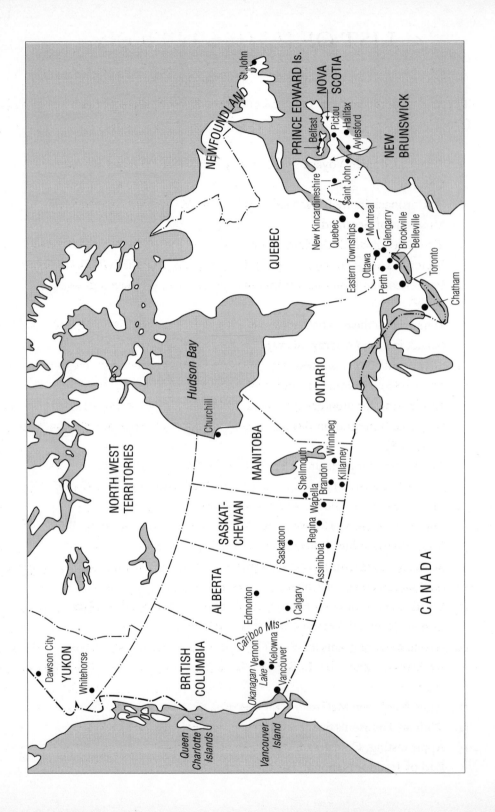

LIST OF ILLUSTRATIONS

The end papers show an emigration poster displayed in Arbroath in 1882 (Douglas MacKenzie)

TRADITIONS OF EMIGRATION

'When colonisation came into vogue, he [the Scot] was foremost among colonisers.'[1]

The Scots have always been a restless people, 'wonderful at living anywhere but in Scotland'.[2] In the nineteenth century their restlessness exploded into a sustained surge of emigration that carried Scotland almost to the top of a European league table of emigrant-exporting countries and created in the process a powerful, enduring image of a land of both exiles and adventurers. Yet the wanderlust that infected 2 million Scots in those years was no new phenomenon. Since the Middle Ages at least, Scots had habitually sought adventure or sanctuary in England and throughout Europe, before they began to turn their eyes westward, initially to Ulster in the seventeenth century, and then by the eighteenth century across the Atlantic to the Americas. The remarkable nineteenth-century diaspora at the hub of this book was therefore built on firm foundations and a variety of interlocking – and sometimes competing – traditions of demographic upheaval.

The statistics of emigration

On what statistical basis can we argue that the Scots were 'notoriously migratory'?[3] Reliable figures are impossible to come by until the 1850s, but it seems that in the first half of the seventeenth century Scotland probably lost about 2,000 people a year, mostly young men, out of an estimated total population of up to 1.2 million. Less is known about the period between 1650 and 1700, but while the overall loss was probably similar, the gender mix was more balanced, with young males accounting for perhaps a tenth (rather than a fifth) of the emigrants. Although 70 per cent of the haemorrhage of approximately 1 million people from the British Isles in the seventeenth century came from south of the border, the Scots – whose population base was four to five times smaller than that of their English neighbours – seem to have been proportionately more disposed to emigrate, perhaps not surprisingly given their more meagre domestic opportunities. Emigration statistics in the eighteenth century are even more elusive, with the exception of an eighteen-month period from 1773 to 1775, but the emphasis clearly shifted from England to Scotland and Ireland. Estimates suggest an overall Scottish exodus of 75,000 between 1700 and 1780, made up of 60,000 Lowlanders and 15,000 Highlanders. At the same time, it is reckoned that there were 80,000 emigrants from England and Wales and 115,000 from Ireland. In the last two decades of the century the biggest outflow was from Ireland, while 10,000 out of approximately 15,000 emigrants from Scotland now came from the Highlands.

All this activity laid a firm foundation for the nineteenth century, when emigration became a significant European phenomenon. Over 50 million Europeans went overseas between 1815 and 1914, mainly from Britain and Ireland in the first half of the century, from parts of Scandinavia and several German states in mid-century, and from Italy and other areas in southern and eastern Europe by the early 1900s. For all these emigrants the United States was the main destination. Information-gathering also improved gradually in the course of the nineteenth century, although there was probably a significant amount of under-recording in the early years, when shipping was still fairly decentralized, and passengers might be embarked at remote locations, unknown to the authorities. As far as the British Isles were concerned, from 1815 the Colonial Office published annual tables of emigrants who had left for various non-European destinations, then from 1825 details were given of emigration from the constituent parts of the British Isles to these destinations. After 1872 responsibility for collecting emigration and immigration data was taken over by the Board of Trade, and detailed passenger lists survive from 1895. Approximately 22 million emigrants left the British Isles between 1815 and 1914, the yearly exodus ranging from 33,222 in 1838 to 656,835 in 1912. The biggest departures proportionally were from Ireland, from where more than twice the number of the entire Irish population of 1801 had emigrated before the end of the century. Most of them left in the wake of the Great Famine in the 1840s, although this tends to be obscured in the statistics by the classification of emigrants according to port of departure before 1853. Since the majority of Irish emigrants took their transatlantic passage from Liverpool, they appeared in the English figures up to and including 1852.

In the same way, a large number of Scots who embarked at Liverpool were excluded from the Scottish returns for the first half of the century, while several Irish who embarked in Glasgow were registered as Scottish emigrants. Problems also occur when we try to identify the regional origins of emigrants, for although the records list a large number of ports until 1872, passengers often came from much further afield to embark or were picked up later at an unrecorded port. Between 1872 and the systematic retention of passenger lists from 1895, the task of identifying regional origins becomes well-nigh impossible, since Scottish emigrant departures are listed only under Glasgow, Greenock and 'other Scottish ports' at the same time as easier railway communication encouraged even more Scots to continue to embark at Liverpool, London and Southampton.

But partial information is better than no information at all. The records indicate that Scotland sent 1,841,534 citizens to non-European destinations in the years 1825–1914, an unknown but significant proportion of whom were probably first-generation Irish, especially by the twentieth century. Of the emigrants 44 per cent went to the United States, 28 per cent to Canada and 25 per cent to Australasia. But whereas the USA received most emigrants from Britain and Ireland in every single year from 1835 to 1909, the Scots' preference for Canada persisted until 1847, and was demonstrated in three subsequent years, before Canada reappeared as the favoured destination of all but Irish emigrants from 1910 to 1914. Scotland's overall contribution to emigration from the British Isles in the nineteenth century – just over 12 per cent – might at first glance seem like a drop in the ocean compared with the departure of around 8 million from England and Wales and over 5 million from Ireland, yet it represented a significant loss to a small country whose total population in 1911 was less than 5 million. The departure of almost 2 million emigrants in the nineteenth century was equal to 42 per cent of Scotland's population at the 1911 census, whereas emigration from England and Wales in the same period represented less than 25 per cent of the total population of 1911 – even less, if we take into account the false inflation of the English statistics before 1853. As in Ireland, emigration was always an essential part of the fabric of Scottish life, and a commonplace device for self-improvement, to a much greater extent than south of the border.

Internal migration

Migration and emigration are inextricably linked, and mobility within Scotland always constituted a significant, if statistically elusive, component of population change. Migrants, who were mainly young adults of both sexes, moved within rural areas and from rural to urban settlements, in an expanding pattern of relocation. Impartible inheritance among tenant farmers in the Lowlands clearly created a migratory climate, as did periodic bouts of famine and shortage. As farming became increasingly commercialized, tenant farmers were forced off the land by rising rents, consolidation of farms and the phasing out of sub-tenancies, particularly in the eighteenth century, although in some border counties the process had begun as early as the 1660s. The six-monthly or annual contracts under which farm servants were employed gave them no incentive to put down roots either; on the contrary, many changed employers at every biannual feeing market, steadily enlarging the area within which they circulated. Dispossessed farmers and farm servants also migrated to planned villages, eighty-five of which were planted across Lowland Scotland between 1700 and 1840, to function as market centres and embryonic industrial enterprises, as well as repositories for surplus agriculturists and tradesmen. For some, the move to planned villages paved the way for subsequent, longer-distance migration to urban centres, which began to develop dramatically in the second half of the eighteenth century, particularly around the River Clyde. All this had a major impact on the demographic map, for whereas Scotland in the seventeenth century had been one of the least urbanized countries in western Europe, by 1800 17.3 per cent of the Scottish population lived in towns, and Scotland had risen to fourth place in the league table of western Europe's most urbanized societies. Much of this urban growth was achieved by migration, not only from the towns' rural hinterlands but also from the Highlands, where migration to the Lowlands had been an integral part of the region's economic structure since at least the early eighteenth century. Commercialization had begun to affect parts of the Highlands even before the parliamentary union, particularly on the estates of Clan Campbell in Argyll, and in the eighteenth century buoyant southern markets for cattle, fish, timber, slate and later kelp, wool and mutton led to higher rents, competitive bidding for tenancies and a whole new socio-economic order that lined the chieftains' pockets at the expense of their clansmen. Temporary migration was a common response of young Highlanders who sought to contribute to their family's rental payment from wages earned in Lowland agriculture, industry and domestic service, as well as in the Clyde fisheries and in military service. John Knox, the traveller and writer, claimed in the 1780s that half the young women in the southern Highlands went south for harvest work, and most eighteenth-century Highland migrants came from Argyll, Easter Ross and the eastern part of Inverness-shire.

While evidence of eighteenth-century migration is difficult to quantify, contemporary sources leave us in no doubt that it was an integral part of Scotland's demographic make-up. The records of poorhouses, Gaelic churches and Gaelic societies reflect the substantial presence of Highlanders in the urban Lowlands. Throughout the country, the clerical contributors to the *Statistical Account of Scotland*, the indefatigable Sir John Sinclair's parish-by-parish chronicle of Scottish life at the end of the eighteenth century, made repeated references to the causes and effects of migration. In rural parishes across the country consolidation of farms was blamed for much depopulation, although the search for higher wages and better conditions was also a common cause of movement. Some ministers were highly critical of the attitudes of migrant Highlanders. The minister of the parish of Daviot and Dunlichty in Inverness-shire referred to them scathingly as 'partial emigrants', whose seasonal migration impeded agricultural improvements, was 'inimical to the general prosperity of the people', artificially raised local wages and encouraged the introduction of extravagant luxuries among the lower classes. The minister of the parish of Kincardine, in the same county, was more blunt in his criticism of lazy and avaricious migrants.

> Many of the young men and women move southward, when the day lengthens, and the weather becomes mild. By low living, and hard labour, they return with comfortable profits, great part of which they lend out at exorbitant interest, and, during the inclemency of the seasons, they live with, and are a burden on, their friends and acquaintances, especially such as necessity has obliged to borrow their money, and who are not punctual in paying either principal or interest. These are evils to be remedied only by finding proper employment for the people at home.[4]

The minister of Kilmallie, also in Inverness-shire, feared that the 'heroic spirit and martial ardour' of migrants to the Lowlands would soon be extinguished by 'debility and effeminacy', a problem which was presumably unlikely to afflict the large numbers from the Highlands in particular who were reported as having enlisted in the army. Migrants' attitudes were not uniform, for while some of Cromarty's seasonal migrants had failed to return from the south, the natives of Mortlach in Banffshire allegedly could not beat the homeward path quickly enough. As the minister observed, 'Such is the attachment to one's native soil, that it is seldom deserted but either from necessity or the gratification of an ambitious desire; and as soon as circumstances will permit, or the passion is cured, it is commonly resorted to again.'[5] Not far away, the people of Duffus in Morayshire had come to favour migration over emigration because of the reports of disappointed emigrants.

> About the end of [the] last war, some individuals went to North America, a few of whom returned and settled at home, bringing bad tidings of the country, which their imaginations had figured to be the *fairy-land* of wealth. Since that time, those who would have gone to America, had the prospect been favourable, have preferred a *home* emigration to the southern parts of Scotland, particularly Glasgow, Paisley &c. And from this part of the north, there is, and always has been, a constant succession of adventurers issuing forth to the British capital, the East and West Indies, and other parts of the empire.[6]

Ministers of urban parishes were more likely to record in-migration, as in the central-belt parish of Lanark, where 'a great proportion' of the people were Gaelic-speaking Highlanders from Caithness, Inverness and Argyllshire. They included 200 would-be emigrants from Skye, who, while their ship was storm-bound in Greenock in 1791, had been recruited by David Dale for his cotton-spinning mill at New Lanark. In order further to deflect the interest of restless Highlanders from America, Dale had subsequently provided houses for 200 Highland families. As a result 'a considerable number' had come to work at New Lanark in 1793, although some from Barra had apparently returned from New Lanark disillusioned, after Dale's terms had failed to match their expectations.[7] The Highland community at New Lanark is still commemorated, both in New Lanark's street names – notably Caithness Row – and in the little cemetery adjacent to the modern, and sensitively restored, heritage site.

The migratory trends set in the eighteenth century were confirmed and extended after 1800. They also become easier to quantify after 1851, when for the first time the Scottish census began to record places of birth by county, indicating that by mid-century a third of the population had crossed a county boundary or moved from a rural to an urban environment. The modernization of farming practices and changing levels of expectations in the countryside that were mentioned so frequently in the *Statistical Account of Scotland* as major causes of emigration from the rural Lowlands continued unabated throughout much of the nineteenth century, and by the 1870s had created labour shortages in areas such as Aberdeenshire. Agriculturists' mobility was provoked not only by the economic implications of farm consolidation, which dashed the hopes of many aspiring small tenant farmers, but also by the loss of status involved in such curtailment of opportunities, the threat and reality of permanent landlessness and changes in accommodation arrangements that saw farm workers housed in squalid bothies and chaumers. Many rolling stones stayed no longer than six months on any one farm. In the 1840s the contributor to the *New Statistical Account* for the parish of Kinellar in Aberdeenshire bemoaned the breakdown of mutual respect between farmers and farm servants that had taken place over the previous half-century. Like many of his contemporaries, he blamed the 'roving disposition' of farm servants not only on the erosion of their prospects but also on the 'idleness and dissipation' encouraged by the biannual feeing fairs, when farmers went to market to hire strangers on the strength of outward appearance alone.[8]

At the same time, the profile of Highland migration changed significantly, as the protracted economic problems in many parts of that region vastly increased its dependence on migrant income. In the first place, migration expanded to incorporate virtually the whole crofting area. Secondly, it began to encompass many more people, from a much wider spectrum of Highland society, as heads of household were forced to join their children on the southward trek in order to earn enough money to pay the rent. Thirdly, the distinction between temporary and permanent relocation became increasingly blurred, as migrants postponed their return for months or even years, impelled not only by acute need at home but also by enhanced employment opportunities in the Lowlands that allowed them to dovetail different types of seasonal work. Permanent migration developed more readily among southern and eastern Highlanders, whose associations with the Lowlands went back to the eighteenth century, than among crofters from the north and west, who tended to regard it as a short-term expedient. Established patterns of movement were reinforced, as Edinburgh recruited migrants from the central and north-east Highlands, Dundee and Perth recruited from Highland Perthshire, Aberdeen drew on the eastern parts of Ross, Cromarty and Inverness-shire, and the western Lowlands continued to pull in large numbers from Argyll, Bute and parts of the Hebrides. In 1851 11.33 per cent of Greenock's population was Highland-born, and the chain migration which saw that town forge strong links with particular parishes in Skye, or Edinburgh receive large numbers from the eastern seaboard of Sutherland, was to be replicated time and again in patterns of emigration. Highland migrants found work in domestic and farm service, the east coast and Clyde herring fishery, industrial enterprises and construction, but military service, which had been so important between 1760 and 1815, became much less significant after the end of the Napoleonic Wars.

For both Highlanders and rural Lowlanders, the burgeoning industrial towns provided the main stimulus to migrate, thanks to higher wages and the perception of better conditions than in farming or crofting. By 1851 Scotland was the second most urbanized country in Europe, surpassed only by England and Wales. By the end of the century a third of the Scottish population lived in one of the four main cities of Glasgow, Edinburgh, Dundee and Aberdeen, with the spotlight falling primarily on the geologically rich area of the west-central belt. This was where the textile industries of the early nineteenth century gave place first to coal and iron extraction, and subsequently to the related industries of heavy engineering, steel and shipbuilding. The workforce for these enterprises came largely from Scottish migrants and Irish immigrants. By 1901 the western Lowlands contained 44 per cent of Scotland's population, some counties doubled, trebled or quadrupled their numbers between 1831 and 1911, and Lanarkshire increased its population by a massive 356 per cent. In 1851 Glasgow held 329,097 people, 35 per cent of whom had come from other parts of Scotland. By the end of the nineteenth century nearly 2 million of Scotland's 4.5 million people lived in and around that city, a trend which was further reinforced after 1900.

The road to England

The scattering of Scots across the length and breadth of England is so ubiquitous as to be taken almost totally for granted, and there is remarkably little scholarly or popular commentary on this most obvious and persistent form of migration. Even in the nineteenth century, when demographic upheaval becomes more measurable, the southward trek of Scots to England is more difficult to quantify than internal migration, since the county of birth of Scottish immigrants was not stated in the English census until 1911. Anecdotal evidence indicates, however, that there was a long-established tradition of cross-border mobility, dating back to medieval times, and until 1800 England was probably the major recipient of Scottish emigrants. In the mid-fifteenth century there were up to 11,000 Scots in England, coming mainly from eastern Scotland and settling primarily in Northumberland if they were unskilled and London if they were skilled tradesmen or professional men. In 1705, just before the parliamentary union, there were allegedly between 500 and 1,000 Scottish hawkers in England.[9] The flow increased significantly after 1707, and by the mid-eighteenth century the main concentrations of Scots were found in the border counties, Lancashire, East Anglia and London. The formation of the Norwich Scots Society in 1775, to relieve indigent Scots, was a reflection of the significance of itinerant harvesters in Norfolk, at the same time as permanent Scottish settlement was taking place in the English coalfields, and around 10,000 Scottish craftsmen were making their way annually to London. Several contributors to the *Statistical Account of Scotland* mentioned that London in particular had become a magnet for many enterprising young Scots, sometimes as a first destination, sometimes as the ultimate move in step-migration, and sometimes as a staging post on a route that eventually took them overseas. Whereas those who went south to 'Edinburgh, Glasgow, Paisley or London' from the parish of Dyke and Moy in Morayshire seldom returned, the opposite was true of those who went to England from Kilfinichen and Kilviceuen in the Western Isles and from Kells in Kirkcudbrightshire. In the former it was 'common practice' to migrate in April – to England as well as the Lowlands – and return in November, while young men from the south-west tended to ply their trade as pedlars in England for up to twelve years, after which those who were 'sober and industrious, commonly return … with L. 800 or L. 900, or L. 1000.'[10] John Harrower from Shetland was less fortunate. When his business failed and he left Lerwick in 1773 with a supply of stockings to sell, it was his intention to make his way to Holland, where he would repair his fortunes and subsequently return home. Instead, after being forced to sell his wares at a loss in Newcastle and Sunderland, he landed in London, where, reduced to utter penury and unable to find work, he was obliged in February 1774 to take out an indenture 'to go to Virginia for four years as a schoolmaster'. Once across the Atlantic, his prospects improved, but his hopes of bringing his wife and children to join him in 'the woods of America' were dashed by his death in 1777.[11]

As Harrower's experience shows, Scots did not always have an easy time in England. Anti-Scottish prejudice was rife even before Dr Johnson turned the invective into a fine art. Penniless pedlars who allegedly jostled the English on the Great North Road, selling 'cheap trinkets and trivial household devices' as they made their way south, were lampooned in abusive doggerel in the windows of inns along the route. Until 1834 Scots vagrants were able to exploit the more

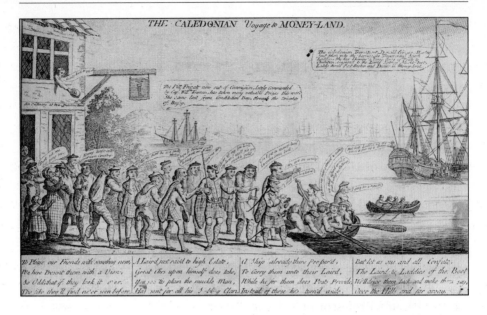

1. Cartoon of 'The Caledonian Voyage to the Money-Land', early nineteenth century.

liberal administration of the poor laws in England, although they were much less prominent than the Irish as supplicants for poor relief. Meanwhile Scots who went to London to follow their professions often found that they could achieve credibility only by anglicizing their names and disguising their accents.[12] English antagonism was rooted in the belief that avaricious Scots were taking the best jobs and consuming the wealth of their southern neighbours, particularly during the highly unpopular rule of Lord Bute, the first Scottish prime minister, in the 1760s. But not only were Scots caricatured as 'a set of hungry adventurers'; they were disliked on account of their allegedly disproportionate success in business, allied to a mixture of clannishness, drunkenness and moralistic, judgemental Presbyterianism. And in his tongue-in-cheek diatribe *The Unspeakable Scot*, T. W. H. Crosland described England in 1902 as 'a Scot-ridden country' which had a 'rooted dislike' for the 'bumptiousness and uncouthness' of its immigrants from the north. 'The Scot,' he asserted, 'never soars above mediocrity; he never has an inspiration or a happy thought; he cannot rise to occasions, and while he is most punctual in his attention to duty and most assiduous and steadfast as a labourer, his work is never perfectly done, and too frequently it is scamped and carried on without regard to finish or excellence.'[13]

Sporadic hostility was no deterrent, and during the eighteenth century Scots became prominent in English administration, medicine, journalism, publishing, engineering, banking and architecture. In London, where the Adam brothers made a significant impact, St Martin-in-the-Fields, Somerset House, Blackfriars Bridge and Greenwich Hospital were also designed by Scots, while engineers like Thomas Telford, John Rennie and John Macadam transformed road communication across Britain. Throughout London, according to Charles Knight, 'they swarm in counting-houses and engineer shops', while at government level the patronage of Henry Dundas won them clerkships in the India Office as well as cadetships in the East India Company's service.[14] Doctors such as the neurologist Charles Bell, the obstetrician William Smellie and Sir John Pringle, King's Physician and President of the Royal Society, paved the way for their nineteenth-century successors, many of whom also 'swarmed to the highest heights' of their profession.[15] Thomas Graham of Glasgow held the Chair of Chemistry at University College London from 1837 to 1855, while his former pupil Joseph Lister became Professor of Clinical Surgery at King's College, as well as the pioneer of antiseptic procedure. St Bartholomew's Medical School was established by two Scots, David Pitcairn and John Abernethy, while the medical schools and infirmaries in Liverpool, Manchester, Birmingham and Sheffield were all founded by Scots. Most of these doctors had been trained at Edinburgh or Glasgow, but the first eye hospital in London – Moorfields – was founded by an Aberdeen graduate of the city's Marischal College, John Farre. A survey of the careers of Aberdeen University students after the fusion of the city's two universities in 1860 reveals that of 1,115 Scots-born medical graduates sampled between 1860 and 1882, 298 spent the whole or part of their careers in England. The largest numbers were to be found in London, Yorkshire and Lancashire, but Scots-born doctors made their way to almost every English county, and in virtually every year examined England was the first destination of Aberdeen's medical graduates. They included Aberdonian John Baker, who became Medical Superintendent at Broadmoor State Mental Hospital, and Home Office Medical Adviser on the Criminally Insane, Peterhead-born epidemiologist Charles Creighton, who went to Cambridge, and Ellon-born James Reid, who became Royal Physician to Queen Victoria and her two successors. A rather less orthodox career was followed by another Aberdeenshire man, William Stables, who successfully combined the careers of naval surgeon and novelist.[16]

In the sphere of the arts, the *Pall Mall Gazette* was founded by George Smith from Morayshire, while Aberdonian James Perry became proprietor of London's *Morning Chronicle*. Smith was also responsible for co-publishing the

poems of Robert Browning and John Ruskin and the novels of Charlotte Brontë
and William Makepeace Thackeray, as well as commissioning Thomas Hardy to
write *Far from the Madding Crowd* for the *Cornhill Magazine*, a journal which he
helped to revitalize. Other notable Scottish publishers in London included
Daniel Macmillan, John Murray and Adam Black. By the late nineteenth
century, however, Scots publishers and journalists in England had acquired a
rather tarnished reputation on both sides of the border. The Scottish journalist
in London was allegedly worthy but stodgy, 'punctual, dogged, unoriginal and
a born galley-slave ... a plagiarist of ideas'.[17] Novelists and publishers, meanwhile, were seen as not only defecting to England but also selling their literary
souls to the English market. The once vibrant *Edinburgh Review* and its Tory
rival *Blackwood's Edinburgh Magazine* steadily lost subscribers as they became
indistinguishable from their English counterparts, just as *Chambers' Edinburgh
Journal*, which had enjoyed enormous popularity when it first appeared in 1832,
suffered a similar fate after editorial control shifted to London and it began to
cater for an English readership which demanded stereotypical Scottish anecdotes. But the critics' greatest wrath was reserved for the three novelists of the
kailyard school and their mentor, William Robertson Nicoll, an Aberdeenshire
minister who moved to London to become editor of the nonconformist evangelical magazine *The British Weekly*. S. R. Crockett, J. M. Barrie and Ian
Maclaren all came to novel writing via journalism, and the books they produced
in the decade after 1888 were – on Nicoll's instruction and in response to the
demands of an English readership – characterized by a sentimental, Eden-like
rural domesticity that was very far removed from the nasty, dirty, unhealthy and
poverty-ridden reality of life for a growing number of urban Scots.

There was less equivocation about the impact of Scottish businessmen and
industrialists on England's economic development. In the eighteenth century
the Lancashire cotton industry attracted several Scottish entrepreneurs, including the McConnels, Kennedys and Murrays of Kirkcudbrightshire, all of whom
came to Manchester in the 1780s as apprentice spinners to fellow Scots William
Cannan and James Smith. By 1816 Adam and George Murray employed 1,125
workers in their own Manchester factory, while McConnel and Kennedy, who
had joined forces in the 1790s, employed 1,020, including several Scots, in what
was to become the largest cotton-spinning firm in Britain. The exploitation of
shared origins was also evident in the case of the Grants from Speyside, a father
and son who, after the famine of 1782 in Scotland, gave up their precarious
living as cattle drovers and came to Lancashire, where, having failed to secure

work in Manchester despite a letter of introduction to Richard Arkwright, they were employed by another Scot, one Mr Dinwiddie, in his printworks at Bury. Further anecdotal evidence suggests that 'vast numbers of Scotch artisans' were employed 'in every factory in England', with William Cobden being criticized for employing too many Scots in his establishment at Chorley and Scots achieving publicity as both strikers and strikebreakers in an incident at Bridgewater Foundry in 1836.[18] While many Scots established their own firms in England, others invested in chemicals, shipping and heavy-industrial enterprises, and both raw materials and processed goods crossed the border in an interdependent, two-way flow. At the same time the Scottish banks – the first of which opened a branch in London in 1864 – were also an important source of investment funds, not least in Cumberland, where they bolstered the commercial connections between that county and the west of Scotland iron industry.

By 1851 there were 130,087 Scots resident in England and Wales and between 1830 and 1914 600,000 trekked south. Some, like Samuel Chalmers of Aberdeen, stayed only briefly, spending part of 1854 working as a druggist's assistant before enlisting in the service of the East India Company. Although he immediately capitalized on the widespread network of Scots in the capital and attributed his employment to the fact that 'the Scotchman is preferred here to any other', he also attempted, somewhat incongruously, 'to forget our Scoticisms as fast as possible'.[19] Nor did he find the streets of London to be paved with gold, for on 12 March he wrote to his father, 'Please send me £1, as I am almost bankrupt and very hungry.' Not all transient or seasonal travellers made for London. Every year thousands of Scottish herring fishermen and women gutters followed the fishing to Great Yarmouth and Lowestoft in an industry which remained buoyant on the whole until the First World War. Other transients came to work in construction or in the extractive industries, such as coal mining or the Westmorland and Welsh slate quarries. The vast majority, however, settled permanently, attracted by higher wages and better opportunities in trades and professions. 'A distinct people they undeniably remain,' observed Charles Knight of London's Scottish community,[20] yet on the whole – and T. W. H. Crosland's acerbic observations notwithstanding – Scots who settled south of the border in the nineteenth century generally became an integral part of English society through a seamless, largely unnoticed and steady migration.

The continental and Irish traditions

The distinctiveness of the emigrant Scot was much more noticeable in an overseas setting. Between the fifteenth and seventeenth centuries many made their
mark as mercenary soldiers, notably in Scandinavia, but also in France, Prussia,
Spain, Poland and Russia. The kings of Denmark and Sweden recruited heavily
in Scotland, particularly during the Thirty Years War (1618–48), when up to
25,000 Scots signed what for many amounted to their own death warrant, and
over 3,500 Scottish officers have been identified among British forces in Scandinavia and the Baltic states.[21] Others who had gone to the Netherlands, initially
to fight against Spain, were re-formed into the Scots Brigade during the Thirty
Years War, and many survivors later settled down in the Netherlands. The Low
Countries also attracted Scots of a more peaceful persuasion, including scholars
who studied medicine and law at the universities of Utrecht and Leyden,
Calvinist churchmen fleeing the religious intolerance that blighted seventeenth-
century Scotland and merchants who traded their coal, wool and fish at ports
like Veere. Bruges had established a Scottish altar in a Carmelite church as early
as the fourteenth century, Danzig in the fifteenth century, and other European
trading centres such as Copenhagen, Elsinore, Dieppe, Bergen-op-Zoom and
Regensburg in the early sixteenth century. By 1700 there were 1,000 communicants in the Scots Kirk at Rotterdam. To ensure maximum attendance at the
biannual Communion season, the Rotterdam congregation altered the dates of
the sacrament to avoid both midwinter, when Scottish merchants were away in
the Mediterranean, and midsummer, when they were absent in the Arctic.

Scottish merchant-pedlars had frequented the Low Countries – as well as
Scandinavia, France and Prussia – since the 1500s, but the country which drew
them out in greatest numbers was Poland. Scots citizens were present in Cracow
as early as 1509, but the biggest concentrations were found in the Baltic ports of
Danzig and Konigsberg, where Scottish shipowners liaised with their fellow
countrymen in other parts of Poland to buy up flax and hemp to take back to
Scotland. All Polish commerce was left to foreigners, and Scots from many
walks of life flocked to Poland to take advantage of this opportunity, pushing
their fortunes as craftsmen and itinerant pedlars, particularly in the century after
1560. By the 1620s, when the movement peaked, the Polish ambassador in
London estimated that there were 30,000 Scots in Poland, most of whom settled
there permanently and assimilated.[22]

Russia was another significant destination for eastward-bound Scots. Many
of them, like their countrymen in western and northern Europe, were merce-

naries. Scottish soldiers had probably gone to Russia since the fourteenth century, but began to form a significant nucleus in the 1550s, when a number of Scottish mercenaries in the service of Sweden were captured by Ivan the Terrible and brought to Moscow. Eighty years later Alexander Leslie, after fighting for both Poland and Sweden, was sent to Moscow by the Swedish king and recruited 5,000 foreign mercenaries – including Scots – for the unsuccessful siege of Smolensk against the Poles. But arguably the most famous Scottish soldier in Muscovy was Patrick Gordon of Aberdeenshire, who in 1661 was enticed by the prospect of better pay and conditions to move on from Swedish and Polish service and begin a thirty-eight-year career as a Russian mercenary. Scots also held key positions in the Russian army and navy in the first half of the eighteenth century, at the same time as the country was penetrated by engineers, architects, travellers and scholars. Scots doctors too had a significant role in Russia in the century after 1750. Sir Alexander Crichton and his nephew, Sir William Crichton, both served the Russian imperial family in the early nineteenth century, while Sir James Wylie was chief medical inspector of the Russian army between 1806 and his death in 1854. And Russia's economic development was aided by men like the unscrupulous Charles Gasgoigne, managing director of the Carron Company at Falkirk, which exported armaments to the Russian navy from the early 1770s. Gasgoigne himself settled in Russia in 1786, leaving behind considerable debts but establishing cannon factories, iron foundries and a textile mill, to which he introduced western technology and Scottish and English workmen. Several of his enterprises were taken over by fellow Scots, including his former interpreter Alexander Wilson (who became engineer-general) and Charles Baird, who had come over from Carron with Gasgoigne and later developed his own industrial empire in St Petersburg. In a very different capacity, Scottish missionaries were active – if fairly unsuccessful – in the Caucasus from 1802 to 1833 and in Siberia from 1819 to 1840 under the auspices of, respectively, the Edinburgh Missionary Society (later renamed the Scottish Missionary Society) and the London Missionary Society.

In the course of the seventeenth century, however, Scots began to look west rather than east, initially to Ireland, but increasingly to America. Although Scottish mercenaries – galloglas – had played a part in Ireland's struggles against the English from the thirteenth to the sixteenth centuries, significant settlement began only in the early 1600s. That was when James VI and I instituted the Ulster Plantation, whereby Scottish undertakers, mainly small tenant farmers from the overpopulated south-west of Scotland, with a smattering of

lairds from Lothian and Fife, were settled in the six forfeited counties of Ulster.
Highlanders – with the exception of some Argyllshire emigrants to Antrim –
were deliberately excluded from the Plantation, for fear they would ally with
the native Irish, but up to 30,000 Lowlanders may have moved to Ulster by 1641,
probably from the home areas of the 'undertakers'. Statistics are scanty thereafter, but a further 60,000–100,000 Scots could have crossed to Ireland by the
end of the seventeenth century. The Irish economy improved as the Scottish
economy deteriorated, particularly in the 1690s, when large numbers of Scots
were driven out of their homeland by harvest failure and famine.

America beckons

Until the late seventeenth century relatively few Scots looked across the
Atlantic, unlike their English neighbours. The exceptions were mainly criminals
and political prisoners who were given no choice in the matter, including almost
2,000 Cromwellian prisoners in the 1650s and a smaller number of Covenanters
in the 1670s and 1680s. Many of these unwilling exiles were taken to Virginia as
indentured servants. Religious persecution was the driving force behind two
other emigrations in the 1680s, the attempt to found a Scottish Presbyterian
colony in South Carolina in 1684 and the settlement of Scottish Quakers in East
New Jersey three years later, while America also became a bolthole for out-of-
favour Episcopalians after 1689. In the vanguard of a steady flow of Episcopalian clergy was James Blair, a graduate of Marischal College, Aberdeen, and
subsequently minister of Cranstoun, near Edinburgh. In 1685 he went to Virginia, where in 1689 he became the Bishop of London's commissary and in 1693
the first president of William and Mary College, where he seems to have modelled the curriculum and teaching methods on his own alma mater. As Virginia's
most influential Scot in the early eighteenth century, Blair (who died in 1743)
was to act as a conduit for fellow Episcopalians from north-east Scotland to
secure positions as colonial clergymen, tutors and schoolmasters. His blatant
manipulation of patronage sometimes infuriated the colony's governors, as he
imprinted a Scottish influence on the Virginian Church that was clearly disproportionate to the number of Scottish communicants in that colony.[23]

Political prisoners and religious refugees were not necessarily averse to
serving in colonial militias or engaging in commercial ventures. The Reverend
William Dunlop, factor of the short-lived and largely forgotten Carolina
Company, held the rank of major in the local militia at Port Royal, South Car-

olina, and immigrant indentured servants often formed the rank and file of local militias. The Carolina Company's subscribers were mainly Covenanters from south-west Scotland, but the venture involved extensive commercial networking on the west coast. The aim was to form a joint-stock company which would trade with local Spanish and Indian people, exchanging precious metals and skins for Scottish manufactures such as cotton and linen cloth, shoes, hats and scissors. The expedition of around a hundred colonists and thirty-five prisoners sailed under Lord Cardross, but when the infant settlement at Port Royal was destroyed by Spain, the experiment was abandoned. Some subscribers returned home, but others, including Lord Neill Campbell (whose brother, the Earl of Argyll, was beheaded in 1685), invested in an alternative venture in East New Jersey. That settlement was sponsored by twenty-four proprietors, half of whom were Scots. It was initially promoted by George Scot of Pitlochie, who died, along with his wife, while accompanying a shipload of prisoners and indentured servants to the colony in 1685, and the leading Scottish Quaker, Robert Barclay of Urie. Yet while less transient than the South Carolina colony, the East New Jersey venture was not sustained beyond the Revolution of 1689–90, despite Barclay's careful planning and assurances of good trading prospects.

A number of Scottish entrepreneurs, many of them with good connections at court, therefore defied the English Navigation Acts to pursue commercial ventures throughout the American colonies. The most famous – or infamous – of these ventures was the Darien Scheme. In 1695 an act of the Scottish Parliament created the Company of Scotland trading to Africa and the Indies, by which the Scots hoped to set up, on the humid and swampy isthmus of Panama, a colony that would trade simultaneously with the Atlantic and the Pacific. The result was an unmitigated disaster, attributable to poor planning and market research, the choice of a location that (like Port Royal) was claimed by Spain, the devastating impact of tropical disease on the settlers, and the determination of the English East India Company and the English government to undermine a scheme that threatened, respectively, its commercial monopoly and its delicate relationship with Spain at a time of joint action against France. The first contingent of 1,500 emigrants in five ships left Leith in July 1698, but within six months of arrival half the colonists had died and the survivors had fled to Jamaica in the face of a threatened Spanish attack. Two months after a second contingent of 1,300 colonists arrived at the deserted Darien settlement in December 1699 they were attacked by Spain from land and sea, and in March they surrendered, abandoned the colony and prepared to sail back to Scotland via Jamaica. Very few ever arrived, since all three ships were wrecked in August 1700, and the whole Darien venture collapsed spectacularly with the loss of almost 2,000 lives and most of the investment capital that had been subscribed by a wide spectrum of Scottish society. The country was virtually bankrupted.

Within seven years of the Darien disaster, the Scots' interest in transatlantic emigration and investment was legitimized by the union of the parliaments, which gave Scotland unfettered commercial access to England's colonial empire. That constitutional change heralded a steadily growing Scottish partic-ipation in transatlantic trade and settlement alike, so that by the end of the eigh-teenth century Scots had a significant, and sometimes dominant, influence in many of the American colonies. Contrary to popular perception, until the 1760s the majority came from the Lowlands, driven by a combination of ambition and frustration. They included artisans and tradesmen responding to advertisements for better wages and living conditions, or impelled by periodic trade recessions; farmers banding together in land companies; tobacco merchants pursuing their fortunes in the Chesapeake; fur traders recruited by the Hudson's Bay Company; doctors and scholars, who made a distinct impact on American med-icine, philosophy and education; and, further south, an influential network of Caribbean planters.

Some ambitious Scots, finding their route to office and status blocked at home, sought public positions in the colonies, manipulating their access to patronage for all they were worth. While India remained a rich source of patronage, a significant number of Scots secured public offices in the American colonies, some of them at a very high level. The best known are Cadwallader Colden, the lieutenant and acting governor of New York, Alexander Spotswood and Robert Dinwiddie, governors of Virginia, James Glen, governor of South Carolina, Gabriel Johnston and Thomas Pollock, both governors of North Car-olina, and John Murray, governor of New York and Virginia. In all, there were thirty Scottish governors and lieutenant governors in the American colonies in the seven decades before the Revolution. These men in turn used their positions to promote the interests of their fellow countrymen through appointments and land grants, an activity which undoubtedly generated much of the anti-Scottish resentment that was evident in colonies like Georgia by the 1770s.

Others sought to achieve their ambition through commerce. After serving a three-year mercantile apprenticeship in London in the early 1730s, James Murray of Roxburghshire became a successful merchant-planter and member of the governor's council in North Carolina, bolstered by the patronage of the colony's new Scottish governor, Gabriel Johnston. Roderick Gordon of Carnousie, a doctor, ship's surgeon and slave owner, fits the image of a Scot on the make. In 1734, six years after he settled in Virginia and began to try his hand as a trader, he wrote home:

> My situation in this Colony is tolerable and we live in the most plentifull country in the world, for all necessaries of life; for our estates consist cheifly in land and nigros; which nigros make grain in plenty to raise all necessary provisions within ourselves, as also a great deal for export; which returns us rum, sugar & molasses from the Caribee Islands & wines from other islands; and the tobacco, made att the same time by these slaves, returns us from England all necessary appearrel for ourselves & slaves ... I beg pardon for this tedious description of our country, but did thousands in Scotland know it they would desire banishment never to return.[24]

The tobacco trade to which Gordon referred was probably the most visible manifestation of Scottish entrepreneurial expertise in the American colonies. The Scottish merchants, who congregated mainly around Chesapeake Bay in Virginia and Maryland, stole a march on their English counterparts by operating a store, as opposed to a consignment, system. After purchasing tobacco directly from the planters, the resident factors exported it to Glasgow on ships which, on their return voyage, brought in consumer goods for sale to the planters. Influential men like Robert Dinwiddie, whose brother was twice provost of Glasgow, used their positions to help Glasgow merchants become dominant in the colonial trade, to such an extent that by the 1770s there were well over sixty retail stores in Virginia belonging to two dozen Glasgow firms, most of the 2,000 factors who managed the trade in the colony were Scots and the rise of Glasgow as the second city of the Empire was based on its role as a tobacco entrepôt.

Many of the tobacco factors were indentured to their trade. But indenture, which originated in Virginia in the seventeenth century, was of much wider significance, being of key importance in the settlement of the eastern seaboard of what in 1783 became the United States, as well as parts of the Caribbean. By the 1700s it was no longer primarily a device for transporting criminals and political prisoners, but a profitable enterprise for merchants and ships' captains, who advertised extensively in the Scottish press, recruiting America-bound passengers to fill the holds which they had just emptied of tobacco or cotton. Indenture also benefited colonial employers, since the indentured servants were cheaper than slaves, while the employees too found that, as the colonies developed, skilled tradesmen could command high wages, as well as a free passage and accommodation in return for up to seven years of servitude. Although it was obviously a device particularly suited to emigrants who could not afford to finance their own removal, the recruits were not necessarily impoverished, except perhaps during the recession of the early 1770s, when a higher proportion of families, as opposed to single men, took up indentures.

But not all emigrants needed or wanted to tie themselves down to an indenture. Lowland farmers who objected to increased rents and new agricultural practices sought better prospects overseas by forming themselves into self-financing emigration companies, complete with written constitutions. The best known of these enterprises was probably the Scots America Company of Farmers, formed at Inchinnan in Renfrewshire in 1773 and commonly known as the Inchinnan Company. It had 138 members, mainly farmers, but also included forty tradesmen, ten servants and a few merchants. Two representatives sent to America in 1773 to explore likely locations eventually purchased a tract of land at Ryegate (now in Vermont). They had been steered to that area by Dr John Witherspoon, a land speculator and president of the College of New Jersey, who had emigrated from Paisley in 1768 and later achieved fame as a delegate to the Continental Congress and a signatory of the Declaration of Independence.

By the 1770s, however, the spotlight had moved from the Lowlands to the Highlands, and from individual to extended-family, or group, emigration. Between 1773 and 1776 a remarkable 18 per cent of all British emigrants came from the Highlands and Islands, many of them leaving in large parties on specially chartered ships. Some eighteenth-century Highland emigrants were given no choice about leaving. Around 600 Jacobite prisoners – including many Highlanders – were exiled after each of the two major risings, in 1715 and 1745–6, mainly to the Cape Fear River area of North Carolina. But, contrary to popular perception, most other eighteenth-century Highland emigrants were not expelled by poverty or landlord compulsion, the vast majority paying their own way across the Atlantic against the wishes of landlords, who feared a shortage of labour on their estates. While harvest failure, cattle disease and fluctuating seasonal employment opportunities undoubtedly boosted emigration figures in certain years, the main irritant for the emigrants was the social dislocation that resulted from the complete reorganization of Highland estate management.

Clanship was destroyed as much by commercial landlordism as by government legislation. As traditional townships were broken up, as competitive bidding for conditional leases became the norm, as rents rose inexorably and as multiple-tenant farms gave way to single-tenant enterprises for cattle ranching and commercial sheep farming, erstwhile clansmen were 'cleared' to newly created crofting communities. There they were expected to pay their ever-increasing rents by combining subsistence agriculture with a variety of ancillary employments – kelp manufacturing, fishing, illicit whisky distilling, quarrying and seasonal employment in the Lowlands. Emigration was for most a reaction against these radical changes, an attempt to preserve or re-create a way of life that was being destroyed, particularly from the late 1760s, when the pace of change was stepped up in response to buoyant southern markets for Highland produce.

Highland emigrants were not only driven away by economic, social and demographic dislocation. They were also lured across the Atlantic by the offer of abundant freehold land, readily available, affordable passages, and the assurances of earlier emigrants and agents that conditions and prospects in North America were the opposite of those that were creating hardship, disgruntlement and apprehension at home. Chain migration and the liberal land policies of Governor Gabriel Johnston made North Carolina a focus of interest for almost half a century before the American Revolution, particularly among emigrants from Argyllshire and Skye, including the renowned Flora Macdonald and her husband. Similar links were forged with Georgia and New York, and information and aid flowed back to Scotland in a swelling transatlantic stream of letters, press reports and travellers' accounts. Most emigrant Highlanders were middle-ranking tenants who were able to finance their removal by realizing livestock and household goods, and they were well served by ships which often came to quite remote west-coast locations to pick them up. Much of the organization was in the hands of tacksmen. Formerly linchpins in the military structure of the clan whose nominal rent had borne no relation to the value of their land, they were increasingly perceived by their superiors as expendable middlemen once military service had become obsolete. Tacks were now rarely hereditary, but were given to the highest bidder, and since leases were granted to a much wider class, the tacksmen were no longer able to pass on their rent increases to sub-tenants. Their interest in emigration was sharpened not only by their loss of social and economic status but also by the particular opportunity that some of them had to acquire land in America. After 1746, when Highland militarism was harnessed to British imperial ends, many tacksmen had crossed the Atlantic as officers in Highland regiments, serving in the wars of 1756–63 and 1776–83. When the British government rewarded veterans with colonial land grants, the tacksmen became prominent colonizers, dispensing information about overseas opportunities and often recruiting fellow clansmen in order to establish prefabricated Highland communities on their American land grants. This was particularly evident after 1783, when proprietary soldier settlement was more explicitly encouraged in strategic parts of Britain's remaining American territories. Dispossessed loyalist Highlanders also flocked north, many of them joining their countrymen who had been attracted to Prince Edward Island and Nova Scotia since the early 1770s by the organizing abilities of Scottish land speculators as well as tacksmen.

By the 1790s emigration had therefore clearly become a familiar part of life throughout Scotland. It was the subject of frequent comment in the *Statistical Account of Scotland*, and the ministers' observations corroborate many of the trends already highlighted. In Lowland parishes it was associated mainly with ambitious artisans 'in quest of better encouragement', usually in North America, but also in the West and East Indies.[25] Emigrants from Orkney and Shetland invariably went into the service of the Hudson's Bay Company, usually with an eye to returning home eventually, while those from the Hebrides and mainland Highlands were driven overseas permanently by explicit opposition to the commercialization of agriculture, particularly the raising of rents and the consolidation of farms into sheepwalks. 'Flattering accounts' from those already settled in America were also crucial in persuading friends and relatives that they could live in 'ease and opulence' on the other side of the Atlantic.[26]

Lowland opinion differed over whether emigration should be commended or condemned. The minister of Torthorwald in Dumfries-shire referred to a number of young emigrants who, by their success overseas, 'have done honour to the place of their nativity'. Kirkcudbright too had dispatched large numbers of young people abroad, many of whom had, 'by their industry and application', not only retained their integrity but also acquired 'ample fortunes'. Still in the south-west, very different sentiments were voiced by the minister of Cummertrees, who told the cautionary tale of fifty local emigrants, several of whom had returned home 'miserably deceived and disappointed', after being enticed to America by fraudulent speculators in the early 1770s. More vitriolic – if less specific – in his criticism was the minister of Whithorn, in his description of the fate of a handful of people who had emigrated from the parish in 1774: 'They left their native country, their relatives, and abounding means of enjoyment, to

settle in woods, among savages and wild beasts. Many of these deluded creatures were rich, and left very profitable leases, to bemoan their folly in unculti-
vated deserts.' Meanwhile, on the other side of the country, the minister of
Cushnie in Aberdeenshire spoke of emigration in the same breath as murders,
suicides and banishments from the parish. And in the Morayshire parish of
Duffus, the return of some disillusioned emigrants from America, 'bringing bad
tidings of the country', had resulted in a shift of focus from overseas to home
migration.[27]

Highland commentators were more consistently critical of the transatlantic
haemorrhage that had hit their region especially hard since the end of the American War of Independence. Emigration was unequivocally an evil to be
opposed, and particular opprobrium was heaped on proprietors whose acquisi-
tive attitudes had effectively banished their tenants by depriving them of land
and a living. But the minister of Callander in Perthshire was the only contributor explicitly to expose the nub of the problem. Emigrants, he asserted, were
people of 'spirit and wealth' who paid their passages and 'carried away their
riches', while dispossessed tenants 'of less spirit, the dregs of the people, have
remained at home, and have found an asylum in villages ... [which] are filled
with those naked and starving crowds of people, who are pouring down every
term, for shelter and for bread'. [28]

The ethics of emigration: antagonists and advocates

The concerns of the Callander minister may not have been typical of comments
in the *Statistical Account*, but they certainly reflected the major preoccupation of
opponents of emigration in the eighteenth century. Until at least 1800 there was
almost universal public and political antagonism to the outflow, particularly
from the Scottish Highlands, where the loss of muscle, money and cannon
fodder was perceived to be most serious for the nation's health and security.
Government, landlords, employers, travellers and the establishment in general
all lined up to deplore emigration as detrimental to the economic health and stability of the region, and some investigations – notably those of John Knox in the
1760s and Thomas Telford around 1800 – deliberately tried to stem the flow
through investment in fisheries or infrastructure. Touring the Highlands in
1773, the lexicographer and scourge of Scottish Romanticism Samuel Johnson
admitted that individuals might well benefit themselves by going to America,
but deplored the effect on the nation of the Highlanders' 'epidemick disease of

wandering'. Taking the same tack as the Callander minister twenty years later, he asserted that the country was losing the flower of its population: 'Once none went away but the useless and poor; in some parts there is now reason to fear, that none will stay but those who are too poor to remove themselves, and too useless to be removed at the cost of others.'[29] His concerns were fuelled by evidence that substantial amounts of specie were being taken away by Highland emigrants, and some tenants clearly used the threat of emigration as a bargaining counter to improve their tenancy agreements at home. Johnson's remarks also came at a time when relations with the American colonies were deteriorating and transatlantic emigration was posing a threat to national security, even more than to economic prosperity. In August 1775 the Lord Justice Clerk in Scotland, Thomas Miller, voiced publicly his fear that the emigrants, whatever their loyalties when they left home, might take up arms against the king once they arrived in America, and in September the Lord Advocate imposed a legislative ban on emigration to America for the duration of hostilities.

After its defeat in the war the British government – recognizing the vulnerability of the redefined American frontier – began to see some virtue in populating its remaining territories with loyal settlers, particularly ex-soldiers. The Highland landlords, however, with undimmed confidence in the viability of their estate development plans, remained implacably and solidly opposed to emigration until the end of the century, particularly those on kelping estates. Only with the backing of a large tenantry, they argued, could their estates be turned into profitable commercial entities, and it was with this in mind that the landlord lobby, in the guise of the Highland Society, in 1803 steered on to the statute book the ill-conceived Passenger Vessels Act. Masquerading as a piece of humanitarian legislation while its real aim was to make emigration prohibitively expensive, it was provoked by the activities of emigration agents in the Highlands and inflated, panic-stricken calculations of the numbers likely to leave at their behest. The resumption of hostilities with France meant that the act was passed without debate, but although it certainly curtailed emigration, it did not eradicate it entirely.

By 1815, when peace finally broke out, widespread public and political aversion to emigration had been transformed into swelling enthusiasm for a device which many now regarded as a safety valve rather than a threat. Pressure of population, aggravated by a tide of demobilized soldiers, brought the spectre of massive unemployment, pauperism and social conflict. In the Lowlands, distress was probably most evident among handloom weavers, who continued to flock to an oversupplied and increasingly archaic trade, while in the Highlands severe economic dislocation came about as the boom prices paid for commodities like kelp and cattle during the wars gave way to slump and collapsed markets. The government responded to the crisis by giving limited and short-term assistance to impoverished Scots and Irish to settle in Canada and the Cape between 1815 and 1823, but its priority was to avoid positive intervention, so the repeated pleas of 22,000 destitute weavers from the west-central Lowlands for state-aided emigration generally fell on deaf ears. Meanwhile, in the Highlands, land-lords responded to the increasing congestion, poverty and land hunger on their estates by encouraging and even subsidizing emigration, in a complete reversal of their earlier stance. The safety-valve argument, which persisted in the High-lands throughout the famine years of the mid-nineteenth century, then re-emerged in a national context during the depression of the 1870s, in strident assertions that the twin problems of overpopulation in Britain and a colonial labour deficit could be solved by state-funded emigration. Yet despite the rec-ommendations of a succession of official investigations throughout the century, state-aided emigration remained firmly off the agenda until the Empire Settle-ment Act of 1922 demonstrated the government's rearguard attempt to cement the crumbling fabric of the British Empire in an uncertain post-war world.

Although particular migration policies were dominant at different times, they were never unanimously endorsed. The ethics of emigration remained a subject of hot, and recurring, debate, revolving around whether the exodus rep-resented a threat or an opportunity to both donor and destination countries, as well as different perceptions about the calibre of the emigrants. In the eigh-teenth century, mercantilist opposition to emigration, particularly among High-land landlords, was fuelled by the activities of emigration agents like the Earl of Selkirk and Hugh Dunoon, who sought to recruit Highland colonists for their Canadian land grants, as well as by the British government's reluctance to condemn imperial colonization wholeheartedly after 1783. But the Malthusian safety-valve policies that emerged in times of domestic recession were also crit-icized in the press and Parliament either as expensive and ineffective or as uneth-ical. While overseas commentators alleged that their countries were being used as dustbins for Britain's surplus or disaffected population, in Scotland there developed an enduring and powerful mythology of enforced but ineffective expatriation, particularly in a Highland context. At the same time – and despite overseas complaints of disparities between demand and supply – many nine-teenth-century commentators echoed the earlier concern of Dr Johnson and the minister of Callander at the high quality of Scottish emigrants. Edward Gibbon Wakefield, who orchestrated schemes of systematic colonization and positive Empire settlement in the middle years of the nineteenth century, was criticized for promoting an exclusive policy which took away the best and left the most needy, while attention was also repeatedly drawn to the vast numbers of provident unassisted emigrants, who invested their savings in land or employment abroad. Policy-makers always walked a difficult tightrope. Not only did they struggle to promote imperial colonization while discouraging foreign emigration, particularly to the United States; they were also bombarded with contradictory accusations from opposing vested interests that they were stripping Britain of the bone and sinew of its population yet simultaneously populating the Empire with paupers, social misfits and political agitators.

The ethics of emigration *per se*, along with the pros and cons of different destinations, were hotly debated not only by policy-makers and political pundits. Authors of guidebooks and editors of newspapers tried to influence their readers and steer them in particular directions, although most claimed that they simply offered 'facts rather than … opinions' to those who had already made up their minds to leave.[30] Emigrants themselves often sat on the fence in terms of giving advice, for fear they might be blamed for subsequent disappointments. 'There is much to induce you to emigrate, and much on the other hand to plead for your remaining in your own native land' was the rather unhelpful observation of one Scottish settler in Illinois, a sentiment that was echoed from the other side of the world by a correspondent who, after three months in Australia, was equally noncommittal. 'To come, or not to come, that is the question; but this I cannot resolve for you.'[31]

As a rule, however, correspondents and commentators did offer some kind of qualitative assessment, even if it was of a fairly general nature. There was unanimous agreement about the need for hard work, self-denial and perseverance on the part of the emigrant and widespread discouragement of overspecialized craftsmen, those of sedentary occupations and anyone who expected to make a quick fortune. 'There is nothing in the soil or climate of America which can impart wisdom to the fool, energy to the imbecile, activity to the slothful, or determination to the irresolute,' wrote Patrick Shirreff in 1835, a sentiment that was reiterated in respect of many other destinations.[32] Emigrants were warned against believing everything they read, and some editors, notably William and Robert Chambers, made a particular point of stressing their impartiality. The Chambers brothers, who admitted in 1834 that emigration was 'a favourite subject with us', included articles on a variety of destinations in their cheap, popular periodical *Chambers' Edinburgh Journal*, and in the 1840s and 1850s devoted specific attention to the United States in, respectively, *Information for the People* and the twenty-part series, *Things as they are in America*.[33] But despite their alleged impartiality, the brothers' sympathies lay in North America and in 1848 they were taken to task by the St Andrew's Society of Adelaide for a hostility to Australia that had 'sealed the fate of emigration to this land among the labouring masses' who read their 'extensively-circulated Journal'. Sixteen years earlier they had condemned the moral and physical climate of New South Wales in no uncertain terms, claiming that no country had been 'so shamefully overpraised' in books that had been 'written to decoy settlers', and that the emigrant who settled there 'generally bids adieu to comfort and peace of mind'.[34]

The Chambers brothers were not the only commentators to condemn Australia, although their attitude – at least towards New South Wales – underwent a distinct change in the late 1830s, as assisted passages were extended to Scots and the colony became more popular with emigrants, at the same time as a political crisis in the Canadas stemmed the flow across the Atlantic. In 1838 too the immensely popular *Counsel for Emigrants*, published in Aberdeen by the bookseller John Mathison, included Australia – which had previously been ignored – in its third and final edition. A few letters also began to appear in the press promoting Australia over Canada and attempting to dispel fears about the long voyage and the prospect of settling in a distant, dangerous country. But emigrants continued to receive very mixed messages concerning Australia throughout the century, and the British press as a whole frequently tried to dampen what it felt was the misguided enthusiasm of many that they could easily make a quick fortune there. The stigma of transportation was also difficult to erase and in 1845 a correspondent of the *Aberdeen Herald*, writing from Van Diemen's Land, warned readers that 'robbery, violence, and indolence' continued to 'stalk through the land'.[35] South Australia, which had been established as a British colony in 1834, was untainted by convict settlement but its promoters were heavily criticized for painting a fraudulent picture of a temperate land where emigrants could earn high wages and readily establish themselves as farmers. According to *Tait's Edinburgh Magazine* and a number of newspaper correspondents, these promises bore little resemblance to the realities of unbearable heat, a high incidence of disease, rampant land speculation and the concentration of disappointed settlers in the 'miserable village of Adelaide'. The discovery of gold in Victoria and New South Wales in the 1850s invoked further warnings from critics about the violent conduct of many gold diggers and the lawless, uncivilized nature of their settlements.[36]

The negative side effects of New Zealand's gold rush in the 1860s provoked less criticism and on the whole New Zealand was more highly regarded than Australia by emigrants and commentators. This was thanks largely to the successful colonization of Otago and Canterbury according to Wakefield's principles of systematic colonization. Earlier, however, the New Zealand Company had been criticized for making misleadingly optimistic allegations in its efforts to attract settlers, and three decades later, in the 1870s, when New Zealand's economy was in difficulties, emigrants were repeatedly warned about an overstocked labour market, low wages, high living costs and poor farming prospects. Some correspondents at that time claimed that the Vogel government had deliberately and deceptively offered 'enticing representations' to emigrants in the hope of easing the colony's financial problems, one dissatisfied settler publicly expressed his regret that he had believed the 'lying handbooks of New Zealand' and editorials in the *Shetland Times* repeatedly warned readers to treat with a pinch of salt the promises of agents who were making particularly assiduous efforts to recruit settlers from the Northern Isles.[37]

An overenthusiastic agent also caused problems in South Africa in 1881, when the Shetland-based recruiter, John Walker, was hauled over the coals by his employers at the Cape for misleadingly assuring emigrants that they would be settled in 'the fairest land to be found in any country'.[38] Throughout the century South Africa was only occasionally recommended as a destination, and encouragement was often qualified by reservations about limited openings and the high cost of living. Andrew Murray, who served as minister in the Dutch Church at Graaff-Reinet for forty-five years, advised his sons in 1842 that while there might be openings at the Cape in theology, medicine or commerce, 'I should never wish you to think of the law, as our Bench and Bar and Notories are of such principles and morals that I should tremble for any contact with them.' He was equally scathing about farming opportunities, claiming that 'to study the improved modes of agriculture practised in Scotland and come to South Africa where in all the inland districts nothing will grow without irrigation, and on an extensive and expensive farm there is often only water for a garden or sowing two or three buckets of wheat would be perfectly ridiculous'.[39] Ten years later a rather different picture was painted by James Arbuthnot, who, having emigrated from Peterhead to Ilovo in Natal, claimed in an open letter to his former local newspaper that a working farmer with £300 capital could, in the course of only a few weeks, become 'more comfortable, and more independent of the world, than ever he can expect to be by farming in Buchan'.[40]

Mixed messages about opportunities for emigrants were not confined to literature on new destinations in the southern hemisphere. The United States had a long history of settlement but an equally long tradition of disputed claims about its desirability. The competing claims often reflected different political viewpoints and although most of the reservations were voiced in respect of the high cost of living, the lack of employment or the unsuitability of the land or climate, at the root of all these warnings was a basic distrust of American society. Hostility waxed and waned in tandem with the strength of political antagonism. It was strongest in the early nineteenth century, when several Tory commentators, fearing that the United States intended to indulge in a policy of territorial aggrandizement at the expense of British America, advocated emigration to Canada for purely strategic reasons rather than for its own sake. Others preferred to steer emigrants in the direction of Australia, fearing that 'the half of those who reach it [Canada] may find their way to more genial climes' to the south. Even after the military threat had abated, some editors continued to criticize the United States for poaching British emigrants who had originally settled in Canada, and warned those who favoured the Republic that they were likely to be cold-shouldered and treated as aliens.[41]

Whether emigrants regarded the prospect of a republican, egalitarian society as a threat or an opportunity depended on their position in society and their attitude to their circumstances at home. Letters quoted in *Counsel for Emigrants* reflected a range of viewpoints. 'If you *do* come to this country I will answer for your happiness, or I am much deceived,' wrote a settler in Michigan to his friends in Aberdeenshire in 1834. Others, however, emphasized deficiencies in the American lifestyle, warning that the 'religious morals' of many people were 'far from what we would wish to expose our young families to imitate'. Children were allegedly encouraged to resist parental control and English and Scottish settlers often had to endure criticism of their homeland and ignorance of their customs. As one Scottish settler in Buffalo declared:

I like this country very much but am by no means particular to some of the Yankie habits. Mechanics are here nearly as busy on Sunday as any other day, and many of those who are not employed go to the woods with the rifle. Few of them have any religion whatever, and many of them are never baptized. If a man contrive to cheat his neighbour, he is said to be 'quite a smart man,' and instead of being despised, is by many more respected for so doing.[42]

The guidance given to farmers thinking of emigrating to the United States was also more equivocal and less convincing than the almost universal recommendation of British North America. Encouragement was frequently tempered by warnings to exercise caution when buying American land, and in particular to ensure that the bargain was concluded in writing. The Homestead Act of 1862 did not usher in equitable land distribution, partly because the system remained open to abuse by speculators, and emigrants were repeatedly warned about fraudulent land schemes, particularly in Texas. Even the advice to tradesmen, which was generally more extensive and sympathetic, was not unambiguously positive. Earnings might be lucrative and employment opportunities more varied than in Canada or the Antipodes, but the United States did not enjoy unbroken economic health. Heavy taxes and living costs eroded wages, emigrants were warned that employment was by no means assured in a labour market that was periodically glutted and occasionally characterized by 'panic, ruin and bankruptcy', and press evidence suggests that there may have been a higher rate of disillusioned return from the United States than from other emigrant destinations.[43]

Although settlement in the United States rather than in Canada was sometimes advised, most commentators favoured the opposite course of action, and Canada was more consistently recommended than any other destination by emigrants and editors, at least to those who intended to farm. Even so, there were still warnings, not least about the exaggerated claims made by land companies. The Reverend Patrick Bell, who emigrated from Scotland to Upper Canada in 1833, was particularly critical of the Canada Company:

They held out great prospects to Emigrants at home and coaxed and flattered every one that thought of coming to this Country through their hired Agents the Editors and Proprietors of several British Newspapers until their ranks were filled to overflowing – when their troops arrived in this Country they too often found that they had swallowed the bait and it was not such an easy matter to get out of the Canada Companies fetters. They had their money and what could they do? After taking possession of their lots they found that the promised well made roads were nothing better than ill formed tracts through the woods – the promised mills and bridges were in many cases never finished … the price of produce dwindled to one half of what was held out while the necessaries of life that they required to purchase were double what they expected. The settlers on the large Huron tract were last winter literally starving and in a state of open rebellion against their cruel seducers.[44]

Four decades later, similar warnings came from the pen of Shetlander Michael Tait, who had emigrated to Illinois in 1838, but subsequently spent three years in Canada before returning to his farm at Joliet. In his opinion, too many Scots trod the well-worn trail to Canada unthinkingly, simply on the urging of relatives, and invested capital unwisely, only to find that 'when it is gone they resemble a prisoner on a small island; there they are, and there they must remain'.[45]

Conclusion

As global wanderers the Scots have a long and impressive pedigree. The destinations may have changed, but the twin driving forces of adventure and exile have remained consistent, in their varied manifestations, as have the recurring concerns of sponsors and opponents about the ethics of an extremely complex movement. The story of the Scots overseas can be told chronologically, geographically, biographically or thematically. The thematic option has been chosen here in order to demonstrate continuities and changes in an era when the long-standing and well-attested restlessness of her people became a relentless tide that swept Scotland almost to the forefront of Europe's emigrant exporters.

EXPELLING THE UNWANTED

'… their miseries are increasing, and their only hope is emigration …'[1]

Emigration could be either an escape route for the poor and persecuted or an avenue of advancement for the ambitious and adventurous. Often it was both. Push and pull influences were rarely mutually exclusive, and in all but a few cases emigrants evaluated the discouragements of their existing circumstances against the attractions of life overseas. This complex fusion of pros and cons varied according to time, location, occupation and individual, but it was a complexity that was often ignored by emigrants themselves, as well as by observers and sending agencies, who tended to depict the exodus either as exile or adventure. The Scottish debate, as we have seen, was characterized by this simplistic, polarized approach, particularly in the nineteenth century, when the trauma of Highland clearance and Lowland recession could be set against alluring agricultural and investment opportunities in a range of overseas locations. While a detached analysis of Scottish emigration would probably highlight overseas incentives over domestic ills, the public perception of the nineteenth-century exodus frequently emphasized the expulsion of the unwanted. This negative image was fostered by a variety of commentators, including those who enthusiastically advocated emigration as a safety valve, emigrants and policy-makers who reluctantly accepted overseas relocation as a last resort, and polemicists who deplored any attempt to 'shovel out the paupers'. Emigration as expulsion in a Scottish context has traditionally focused heavily on cleared and destitute Highlanders, but it also incorporates unemployed weavers from the central belt, Lowland agriculturists whose status and prospects had been eroded by modernization and commercial fishermen who could not weather the financial storms of the 1880s. But economic imperative was not the only catalyst for exporting the unwanted; in addition, judicial decree and financial or moral scandal also played a part in ensuring that a small proportion of emigrants did not leave voluntarily.

Crime, punishment and self-exile

A minority of emigrants had no choice whatsoever in the decision to send them overseas. Throughout the seventeenth and eighteenth centuries, the sentence of banishment was imposed on men and women alike for misdemeanours ranging from theft and housebreaking to adultery, incest and murder. In addition to 1,200 exiled Jacobites, David Dobson has estimated that approximately 400 Scottish criminals were banished to the colonies between 1707 and 1763, their precise destinations depending on the whim of ships' captains, while the *Aberdeen Journal* in the fifty-three years from 1748 to 1800 reported on at least 135 verdicts of overseas banishment handed down by circuit courts at Inverness, Perth and Stonehaven, as well as Aberdeen itself.[2] At the other end of Scotland, the jail books of Dumfries, which exist from 1714 to 1839, include several references to convicts of both sexes who were sentenced to transportation or whose death sentences were commuted to transportation.[3]

If convicted felons were unwilling exiles, so too were those unfortunate individuals who fell victim to the kidnapping trade, in which Aberdeen gained a particular notoriety in the mid-eighteenth century. Whether or not it was provoked by the city magistrates' concern at an influx of vagrants from the rural hinterland during the famine years of 1739–42, it was deemed sufficiently significant by William Kennedy to merit a two-page discussion in his *Annals of Aberdeen*, the only reference to transatlantic links in that two-volume survey. In 1742 and 1743, according to Kennedy, there

> appears to have been carried on, by certain persons in Aberdeen, a very nefarious traffic with Virginia, being a species of the slave trade ... It would seem, that young boys of the country, who had occasion to repair to the town, and were without the protection of their friends, were enticed to enter into engagements with the traders to go to the plantations in America. Many of these unwary youths were, in this manner, decoyed, and transported to Virginia, where they were disposed of to the best account; and, being kept in a condition which never enabled them to redeem their freedom, they continued in bondage as long as their masters thought proper to detain them.[4]

The kidnapping trade, Kennedy continued, did not at the time 'seem to have much attracted the attention of the people, or to have occasioned much alarm in the town', perhaps because the citizens were unaware of the fate of the victims. That ignorance was to change as a result of the well-documented action of Peter Williamson, who in 1742, as a twelve-year-old boy sent from Aboyne to stay with an aunt in Aberdeen, had been apprehended at the docks, detained below decks for a month, and then shipped to Philadelphia. There, for the sum of £16, the captain sold him into seven years' indentured service with a Scottish farmer from the Forks of Delaware who had himself suffered the same fate in his youth, and who treated him well, sent him to school and left him a substantial legacy. Sixteen years later, after acquiring and losing both a farm and a wife to Indians, and suffering periods of captivity, ill-treatment and injury at Indian and French hands before and during the Seven Years War, Williamson was repatriated. Returning to Aberdeen in June 1758, he proceeded to sell copies of an autobiographical pamphlet describing his adventures since the time he had been kidnapped. His allegations were highly embarrassing to the city merchants and magistrates named and shamed, and at their behest an initially successful libel action was raised against Williamson, who was fined, imprisoned until he apologized and banished from the town, after seeing the controversial parts of his book torn out and burned at the market cross. But he was not silenced. Moving to Edinburgh, he sued the Aberdeen magistrates through the Court of Session, leading, in February 1762, to a unanimous judgement in his favour, and a substantial award of compensation and costs against the Provost, Dean of Guild and four baillies of the City of Aberdeen.[5]

After the loss of the American colonies put an end to transatlantic transportation, overcrowding in British jails forced the government to seek an alternative outlet for prisoners, and in May 1787 the first fleet of convict ships left England for Australia. Although 160,000 convicts were transported over the next eighty years, only 5 per cent (approximately 7,600 individuals) were tried in Scotland, perhaps reflecting a general trend away from banishment in the second half of the eighteenth century before transportation was stepped up after 1820. Best known, though numerically insignificant, were the political prisoners transported in the 1790s and 1820s. Thomas Muir and Thomas Palmer, campaigning for parliamentary reform in the wake of the French Revolution, were convicted of sedition and sentenced to fourteen and seven years' transportation respectively in 1793. Almost thirty years later, during the depression that followed the end of the Napoleonic Wars, similar agitation among the 'Bonnymuir weavers' led to twenty-one men being charged with treason for taking up arms against the government. Two were hanged and nineteen transported to Australia, while in the 1840s transportation was also employed as a weapon against striking miners, Chartists and food rioters.

Recent scholarship has questioned the traditional perception of Scottish convicts as the most degenerate. Most were single males in their teens and twenties who came from the Lowlands and belonged to the labouring classes. Up to three-quarters had previous convictions, usually for theft, and those from central and southern Scotland were held in Edinburgh's Calton jail before being sent to hulks in the Thames and then on to New South Wales or – more commonly – Van Diemen's Land. Female convicts tended to be slightly older, were more likely to be married and had generally been convicted of persistent petty crime and prostitution. Sentences were normally seven years, fourteen years or life, although well-behaved convicts, or skilled tradesmen, might be given some freedom through the grant of a 'ticket-of-leave'. Conditions in the penal settlements varied considerably. A few prisoners – notably the political prisoners – were allowed to acquire their own land, but most were employed at land-breaking for the government or individual masters, sometimes in chain gangs. Some returned to Scotland when their sentences expired, but others were joined by their families. One Colonial Office register of 1,323 applications for passage made by convicts' families between 1848 and 1871 includes sixty-seven Scottish applicants, most of whom were from the Glasgow area, although almost every part of Scotland was represented, including the islands of Shetland, Skye and Lewis.[6]

While convicts were exiled at the behest of the authorities, some emigrants chose self-exile rather than face the consequences of financial or moral indiscretions. In 1832 Thomas Milne had his goods impounded for the recovery of debts after he had allegedly 'absconded' to America without fully paying the rent of his shoemaker's shop in Fraserburgh.[7] In 1833 a committee was appointed in Aberdeen to tackle the problem of debtors resorting to emigration in order to escape their creditors, and in 1834 both leading Aberdeen newspapers reported on the persistence of this 'cowardly and worse than thievish practice'. Later that year a petition signed by the city's 'Merchants, Manufacturers and Inhabitants' was sent to the local MP, Alexander Bannerman, for presentation to Parliament, 'complaining of the practice of Clandestine Emigration to the United States of America, and praying for an enactment to protect the public against the same'.[8] Similar practices were castigated by the minister of the

Dumfries-shire parish of Hutton and Corrie in his entry in the *New Statistical Account*.

> Much loss and mischief are occasioned by dishonest emigrants to America. It is
> well-known, that the United States and the North American British Colonies are
> the quarters to which the eyes of thousands, who find they cannot thrive in their
> own country, are anxiously directed. And of these a considerable proportion are
> guilty of dishonest practices. During the ministry of the present incumbent, not
> much short of a score have left this parish under charges of various kinds; some
> to avoid supporting illegitimate children, – some, after swindling practices and
> committing forgery, – and some after committing frauds of all sorts, with a view
> to emigrate with their ill-gotten gains. The state of our North American
> colonies is such, that it may be said to hold out a premium to the practice of
> villany in the mother country.[9]

Kirk session records also document the disappearance overseas of men
arraigned for fornication, while some of the illegitimate children admitted to
Quarrier's Homes had been left destitute by a disgraced parent who had fled
abroad, and of seventeen boys admitted to the Aberdeen Industrial School
between 1867 and 1877 because a parent had emigrated, six had come into care
because their father or mother had abandoned the family when they went
abroad.[10]

Post-war dislocation and assisted artisan emigration

Throughout the nineteenth century most of those who left Scotland reluctantly
were driven out by the threat or reality of economic hardship rather than crime
or scandal. But economic coercion was not a characteristic just of nineteenth-
century emigrants. Among the negative reasons for the notable haemorrhage in
the early 1770s were a crisis in the Lowland textile industry and, in the Highlands, the combined effects of cattle disease, low stock prices, successive poor
harvests and rising rents. Many of these problems were documented explicitly
for the first time in the *Register of Emigrants*, which contains almost twice as
many negative as positive statements by departing emigrants. 'For poverty and
to get bread' was the collective reason for emigration given by the 212 passengers aboard the *Commerce*, which in February 1774 left Greenock for New York.
Of these, 178 were from Paisley, where large numbers of weavers had been

thrown out of work as a result of the collapse of the four-year-old Ayr Bank in 1773. 'Want of employment' was the complaint of all sixty-two Borders emi-grants aboard the *Gale* of Whitehaven and some of the thirty-one passengers from the same region aboard the *Adventure* of Liverpool, both of which sailed for New York in May 1774. A handful of the 147 emigrants who left Stranraer on the *Gale* in June 1774 were also unemployed or hoped to do better, while the Lowland farmers and tradesmen aboard the *Glasgow Packet* and the *Christy*, both of which left Greenock in April 1775, complained of 'racking rents' and unemployment.[11]

Economic dislocation in the aftermath of the Napoleonic Wars stimulated a much more significant outpouring of the unemployed and destitute. Demobi-lized soldiers returned to an already overstocked labour market, compounding the effects of agricultural and industrial depression, at the same time as a rapid growth in population and rising Irish immigration combined to put unprece-dented pressure on the inadequate poor laws of both Scotland and England. In Ireland, landlords, unable to collect their rents, were consolidating their minutely subdivided farms and dispossessing redundant tenants, many of whom flocked to central Scotland, where they generated huge discontent among the native population. Their persistent determination to swell the ranks of handloom weavers simply exacerbated existing, deep-seated problems in that industry. Although the market was chronically oversupplied and the develop-ment of power looms had clearly sounded the deathknell of handloom weaving, aspiring weavers continued to be drawn into a dying trade until the 1840s, attracted by its cottage-based working conditions and the ease with which it could be learned. 'The situation of the country becomes more and more deplorable,' lamented the *Scots Magazine* in 1816, and by 1819 unemployed weavers had divided into two camps, espousing either radical reform or assisted emigration.[12]

There was already some precedent for assisted emigration. Soldier-settlers had been eligible for land grants since the 1760s, but in 1815 the British govern-ment – concerned at the vulnerability of the Canadian frontier after the attempted American invasion of 1812 – extended the offer to civilians who could provide certificates of character along with a returnable deposit of £16 per male emigrant and £2 for his wife. Under this venture approximately 700 Scots were enticed to the new Ottawa Valley townships of Bathurst, Drum-mond and Beckwith by free transport, 100-acre grants, free rations and cheap implements. By autumn 1816 the early settlements in Lanark County had grown to approximately 1,500 civilians and ex-soldiers, but the policy was abandoned on grounds of cost and lingering disquiet about the merits of assisted emigration. Two years later it was replaced by a scaled-down scheme to grant land in Upper Canada and the Cape of Good Hope to individuals who promised to recruit settlers and deposit £10 for each person so recruited. Over 300 Scots from the Breadalbane district, as well as 172 from Ireland and fifty from England, took advantage of the Canadian offer, although it is unlikely that the Breadalbane farmers who settled in Beckwith Township funded themselves. Allegedly 'reduced to such a state of extreme poverty as to be able to procure but one scanty meal per day', these families, who had been pushed out by consolidation of their farms, were also unable to supply the shipboard provisions required by the new Passenger Act of 1817.[13]

Until 1819 the government's primary concern in subsidizing emigration had been one of imperial defence, and it argued that it was simply redirecting emigrants who would otherwise have settled in the United States. But as economic conditions worsened it began to see emigration as a form of poor relief, a change of perspective brought about by lobbying from both the ruling élite and the unemployed in the affected areas, where by the winter of 1819–20 up to 15,000 individuals were dependent on charity. Emigration societies sprouted across the west of Scotland, particularly in Lanarkshire and Renfrewshire, where there were soon thirty-five associations, representing over 13,000 handloom weavers. From April 1820 their activities were supervised and coordinated by the Glasgow Committee on Emigration, led by Lord Archibald Hamilton, Whig MP for Lanarkshire, and the Tory MP, cotton manufacturer and former Lord Provost of Glasgow, Kirkman Finlay. These opposing politicians had been brought together by a shared fear of radical insurrection after the failure of public works programmes to relieve distress, and in May 1820 they successfully brought the case for assisted emigration before the House of Commons.

> Many persons in that country [Glasgow] were in such an absolute state of destitution, that they looked on their existence as a burthen which they could scarcely support. They could neither maintain themselves nor their families; and the period was fast approaching, when without food and without raiment, they must either perish, or prolong their existence by the plunder of their neighbours ... He [Lord Hamilton] must say, that, from the spirit and temper of ministers, they seemed to have greatly under-rated the distress which at present existed in the northern part of the kingdom. They had ascribed a larger proportion of the dis-

turbance to disaffection than to distress, and had applied force to quell disturbances which would have been more effectually suppressed by furnishing the
means of subsistence. The right hon. Gentlemen opposite were more willing to
facilitate emigration to the Cape of Good Hope than to any other quarter of the
world; and the reasons for this preference he could not perceive, especially as
most of those who were inclined to emigrate from Scotland had powerful
reasons to induce them to go to our settlements in America, rather than to Africa
… He concluded by observing, that any delay in the application of a remedy to
the evils which he had pointed out would not only be disastrous in itself, but
would render more difficult the attainment of that intimate object which ought
to be kept in view – the suppression of the present disturbances in Scotland.[14]

In responding positively to these pleas, the government was also influenced
by a barrage of petitions from the weavers themselves. Drawing on the example
of the Breadalbane emigrants and adapting the long-standing support structure
of the trade guilds, in 1819 distressed weavers began to bombard both the
Lanarkshire County Meeting and the Colonial Department with petitions for
assisted emigration. Unable to save themselves from 'starvation or becoming a
burden on the parish', the people of Lesmahagow in January 1819 asked the
County Meeting to respond to the 'stagnation of trade' by devising 'some
means (either by applications to government or otherwise) of conveying us out
to the Colony of Upper Canada and supporting us ther[e] until such time as we
could provide ourselves with the necessary means of subsistence'. Three
months later Charles Baillie wrote to Lord Archibald Hamilton on behalf of 'a
few of the inhabitants of Hamilton', asking him to relieve their 'wretchedness
and misery' by using his influence to have them transported, free of charge, to a
British settlement overseas.[15]

On the basis of these petitions, the Lanarkshire heritors appealed to the
Treasury to subsidize emigration, appeals which were ignored until the emigration societies began to bombard the Colonial Department directly and sys-
tematically, coordinating their efforts in response to the political debate and
playing on the government's terror of insurrection in the way they framed
their petitions. 'If Upper Canada be overstocked at all it is with trees,' retorted
the chairman of the Anderston and Rutherglen Society to the Chancellor of
the Exchequer's statement that weavers should not go to Canada, since it was
also experiencing economic depression.[16] 'We have used every lawful means in
order to obtain our Desired object but without effect,' complained Robert

Beath, secretary of the Kirkfieldbank Emigration Society in 1821, in response to the very limited government subsidy given to the first batch of weaver-emigrants the previous year.[17] The implicit threat of resort to unlawful means was heightened by Beath's earlier arrest for radical activity in 1812, although most radicals deplored emigration as a response to poverty, and the bulk of the many thousand petitions submitted by up to thirty-six emigration societies by 1821 simply emphasized the sufferings of the unemployed weavers and their longing for independence through the possession of colonial land. Many, including the following plea from Rutherglen, made directly to the Colonial Secretary, also stressed the petitioners' loyalty to the government:

> That Your Lordship's petitioners, being heads of families, have for a considerable time been desirous of emegrating to His Majesty's province of Canada to avail themselves of the encouragement granted to settlers by His Majesty's Government; but by reason of their poverty they are unable to procure a passage thence and do therefore pray your Lordship to transport them with thier families to that setlement and Your Lordship's petitioners will oblige themselves in any manner Your Lordship may think fit in order to the re-embursement of the expences incurred as soon as thier cercomstances will admit. The Muslin weaving being the occupation Your Lordship's petitioners usually follow, is at present so bad and wages so low and the prices of provisions so high that it is with the greatest difficulty they can procure a subsistance for themselves and famelies, and are intirely incapable of providing for sickness or other emergencies and there being no poor rates in this part of the kingdom renders them liable to the greatest hardships and deprivations.
>
> Your Lordship's petitioners have all born arms in defence of thier King and country. If therefor thier loyalty to thier King and service to thier country can have any influence with His Majesty's Ministers they would fondly cherish the hope of your Lordship assistance which should they obtain will forever bind them under the strongest ties of gratitude to Your Lordship and to His Majestys Government in whose defence they are bound and determined in whatever place or in whatever circumstances they may be to render all the services that may be in their power.[18]

In July 1819 the weavers of the newly formed Bridgeton Transatlantic Society also implored the Colonial Secretary directly to fund their relocation in Canada – but not the Cape of Good Hope – 'as the only place where their labours shall meet with due reward and where they and their families shall be put out of the fear of want'. In the current distress the stark alternatives, they claimed, were starvation or parish relief, 'and the last alternative is nearly as galling to the feelings of your memorialists as the first would be, because they have always supported themselves by honest industry and have been taught by the precept and examples of their fathers to look upon independence as their chief pride'.[19]

How did the government respond to all this lobbying? In May 1820 it authorized a loan of £11,000 to assist 1,100 members of the emigration societies to go to Upper Canada, offering free transport from Quebec to their destination, a 100-acre grant to each family, seed corn and implements, and staggered loans of £10 per head, to be repaid within ten years. Since the emigrants had to fund their transatlantic passage, supplementary funds were sought from private charity on the basis that 'by assisting a few hundred persons in this way, the condition of those who remain will be rendered more comfortable'. Robert Lamond, secretary of the Glasgow committee established to organize the venture, not only assured donors of the integrity and political conservatism of the emigrants but also repudiated concerns that they might 'carry away with them the science and intelligence of old Scotia'. Appealing for donations of Bibles and other books, so that they might 'cultivate the best of fields, the human mind', he predicted that before long, 'by the aid of a generous public', a 'little Glasgow may be built in that quarter of the world'.[20] By June and July 1820 enough money had been raised in Glasgow, Edinburgh and London to embark 1,200 emigrants on the Clyde in three ships, but the flood of petitions continued, and in 1821 a further 1,883 people from the counties of Lanark, Renfrew, Dunbarton, Stirling, Clackmannan and Linlithgow sailed on four ships, to seek, in the words of the *Scots Magazine*, 'subsistence on the other side of the Atlantic'.[21] Since there were many more applicants than places, lots were drawn in both years, although in 1821 preference was given to relatives of those who had come out in the first contingent.

Although these emigrants represented only a fraction of the members of the societies, by 1821 conditions had begun to improve, leading the Glasgow Emigration Committee to observe that 'many of the persons who have lately embarked, have been induced to do so, from other considerations, rather than the want of employment at home'.[22] The focus therefore shifted from Scotland to Ireland, and in 1821, 1823 and 1825 the government allocated a total of £113,000 to assist emigration from the south of Ireland to Canada and the Cape. In 1826, however, renewed unemployment not only spawned a further flood of petitions from all parts of the British Isles; it also led to the appointment of a parliamentary select committee to investigate the pros and cons of systematic state-aided emigration. A familiar refrain echoed through the Scottish weavers' petitions and evidence, namely, a request for assistance to join friends and relatives who had been helped to emigrate earlier in the decade and who were allegedly doing well in Canada. Joseph Foster and James Little, members of the Glasgow Emigration Committee who appeared before the select committee on behalf of 140 families, testified both to a revitalization of the emigration societies and to 'all the horrors of despair' that would seize their members if they were unable to emigrate. William Spencer Northhouse, of the *London Free Press*, speaking on behalf of an estimated 11,864 people in thirty-two emigration societies in Lanarkshire and Renfrewshire, alleged that a threefold increase in the cost of emigration – a result of recent shipping legislation – had prevented many would-be emigrants from responding to the encouraging correspondence of their countrymen already in Canada. And two MPs, Thomas Kennedy and Henry Home Drummond, representing Ayrshire and Stirlingshire respectively, spoke of deep distress among handloom weavers, the inability of local gentry to ameliorate conditions and the problem of Irish labourers displacing native Scots.[23]

The select committee, having identified widespread distress and unemployment, particularly in Ireland, recommended the assisted colonization of vacant colonial lands, provided that the colonists left voluntarily and the assistance was ultimately repaid. At least one witness, Henry Bliss of New Brunswick, was particularly keen to receive Scottish settlers, who, he claimed, 'never fail; they are industrious, thrifty, sober, and obedient to the laws'.[24] The select committee was concerned, however, to prevent central Scotland and northern England from being overrun by Irish labourers, whom it blamed for many of the problems in these manufacturing districts, and it suggested that £50,000 should be allocated to assist emigration from all parts of the British Isles. But the government, concerned at the cost of its earlier experiments, and anticipating an economic upturn, refused to dip into the public purse again, so it was left to the emigration societies to make renewed appeals to private charity. By 1828 the Paisley Emigration Society had raised enough funds locally to send a shipload of 117 weavers and their families to Quebec. Further contingents followed over the next two years, after the government offered fifty-acre land grants to members of some emigration societies, provided the societies covered the cost of transportation and provisions from renewed appeals to private charity.[25]

For a decade the government had flirted intermittently with state-aided emigration, partially sponsoring almost 7,000 people to go to Canada, and a further 3,569 – the latter primarily English emigrants – to the Cape. Although only a minority of the emigrants were impecunious handloom weavers and only a fraction of the artisans who wished to leave were able to do so, the Scottish exodus of the early 1820s was identified largely with that occupational group and emigration societies became part of the fabric of the western Lowland exodus to a much greater extent than elsewhere in the British Isles, retaining their influence long after government interest had waned. Petitions continued to be sent – unsuccessfully – to the Colonial Office year after year, and the societies re-emerged strongly during subsequent recessions. In 1841 600 emigration society members went to Canada, mainly with the aid of private donations. They were followed by 1,000 in 1842 and 900 in 1843, but, as before, those enabled to emigrate represented only a fraction of the societies' membership of approximately 4,500. Paisley, the textile centre that had shown symptoms of distress among weavers as early as 1773, continued to experience the greatest hardship as handloom weaving collapsed completely. By the early 1840s it had become the most depressed town in Britain, the subject of special investigations and a key catalyst in the decision to reform the Scottish poor law. Paisley's weavers, it was agreed, were now too destitute and numerous for emigration to have a beneficial effect, individually or communally. Although the Royal Commission into the Condition of Unemployed Handloom Weavers in the United Kingdom (1841) endorsed emigration as 'the most immediate cure or palliative of a redundant population', both the assistant commissioners who visited Scotland agreed that it was 'not one of the means by which the condition of the hand-loom weavers as a body is likely to be materially improved'. Not only did they allegedly lack the skills, stamina and 'capacity for active muscular exertion' required of pioneer farmers; the weavers themselves did not believe that they could emigrate in sufficient numbers to benefit those who remained.[26] Two years later an investigation into the plight of Paisley's population found that although numerous applications had been made to two relief funds set up specifically to aid emigration, only sixteen people had been able to go to Port Phillip and a few more to New Zealand and Canada, the majority of applicants having insufficient funds to assemble the necessary outfit.[27] And in 1844 Archibald Alison, Sheriff Depute of Lanarkshire, contrasted the optimism of weavers in Glasgow, where between thirty and forty societies continued to apply to him annually for assistance to emigrate, with the pessimism of their counterparts in Paisley:

I suspect that the persons who, in Glasgow, join these societies, are not reduced to the lowest state of destitution, and therefore, have spirit enough to bear the idea of a transatlantic voyage. But in Paisley they are in such a state of destitution and depression, that the very idea of removing is horrible. I have seen cases in which people, who, when beginning to be in distress, would willingly have emigrated, but who, when they had tasted the full measure of wretchedness, would not.[28]

Highland hardships: coercion and emigration

Lowland weavers were not the only distressed and discontented Scots to petition the government for assistance to emigrate. Equally vociferous were Highland petitioners, who argued that they were being marginalized and pauperized by the socio-economic transformation of the Highlands. Although they were less successful than the weavers in their pleas for government intervention, they were subsequently to emigrate in far greater numbers, over a much more prolonged period and with much greater controversy than the weavers. Indeed, as we have seen, images of destitute Highlanders dominated public perceptions of Scottish emigration throughout and beyond the nineteenth century, setting the context for a long-running and passionate debate on the ethics of expelling the unwanted.

Like their Lowland counterparts, nineteenth-century Highland emigrants could look back to an earlier tradition of unwilling exile. For some, like a party from Barra in 1770, the sole catalyst was poverty, which had driven them from an island where 'it is cold, the land is thin, and there are too many of us'.[29] According to the *Register of Emigrants*, however, most were pushed out by a combination of economic and social dislocation, arising from rising rents, crop failures and the widespread restructuring of estate management. They included 106 passengers from Stornoway to Philadelphia in May 1774, all of whom emigrated 'in order to procure a Living abroad, as they were quite destitute of Bread at home', and another fifty-nine emigrants to New York in November, who left 'on Account of their being greatly reduced in their Circumstances'. A contingent from Strathspey that left aboard the *George* of Greenock was driven out by 'High Rents and Deerness of Provisions', while those who went to Wilmington, North Carolina, in August 1774 spoke primarily of 'high rents and oppression', complaints that were echoed by a shipload of Breadalbane emigrants, sailing from Greenock to New York in June 1775. The repercussions of commercial sheep farming were cited by a group of reluctant Argyllshire emigrants to Wilmington in September 1775:

> The Farmers and Labourers who are taking their Passage in this Ship unanimously declare that they never would have thought of leaving their native Country, could they have supplied their Families in it. But such of them as were Farmers were obliged to quit their Lands either on account of the advanced Rent or to make room for Shepherds. Those in particular from Alpine [Appin] say that out of one hundred Mark Land that formerly was occupied by Tennants who made their Rents by rearing Cattle and raising Grain, Thirty three Mark Land of it is now turned into Sheep Walks and they seem to think in a few years more, Two thirds of that Country, at least will be in the same State so of course the greatest part of the Inhabitants will be obliged to leave it. The Labourers Declare they could not support their families on the Wages they earned and that it is not from any other motive but the dread of want & that they quit a Country which above all others they would wish to live in.[30]

The complaints of eighteenth-century Highland emigrants pale into insignificance when compared with the bitter experiences of their mid-nineteenth-century successors. As the Highland economy went into severe retreat in the aftermath of the Napoleonic Wars, landlord optimism about wholesale estate reconstruction evaporated and emigration – which they had earlier opposed tooth and nail – came to be regarded as the main remedy for overpopulation and increasing poverty. The collapse of the kelp, cattle and distilling industries severed the tenants' major income sources and forced them into even greater dependence on the potato, while their landlords responded to the prospect of falling rentals by allocating more and more land to commercial sheep farming, the only sector of the economy that was still buoyant. Even by the 1810s, the 'dread of want' that had characterized emigrants in the 1770s was being replaced by the urgent realities of destitution and widespread eviction. Faced with deteriorating conditions, Highlanders who had previously left on their own initiative in order to escape rising rents and unacceptable tenurial arrangements were increasingly pushed off the land, often to be replaced by sheep. For some the euphemistically entitled assisted passage became the only alternative to starvation at home, and any concept of emigration as a negotiated movement was replaced by potent and indelible images of enforced exile.

The Highlanders' distress was documented in a number of petitions made to the Colonial Office on their behalf. Donald Sinclair of Dunbeath, Caithness, who had previously recruited emigrants on behalf of Lord Selkirk and later sent them out on his own account, asked the government in November 1818 to assist the emigration of 'several thousand families in the North of Scotland' who, having been 'removed and their possessions turned into sheep walks', were 'quite destitute and ... very desirous of going to North America'.[31] In the same month Donald Logan of Rogart in Sutherland, a timber merchant who had also supervised the emigration of fellow Highlanders, urged the government to provide sufficient funds for him to continue that work:

> I am originally a native of this county (Sutherlandshire) and emigrated to Nova Scotia in 1803 and having in 1807 understood that by reason of various new arrangements many of my friends and acquaintances were put out of their lands and otherwise rendered uncomfortable – I returned to my native county and got about one hundred and twenty of them removed this season to North America. But many were unable to pay the half of their passage and some not able to pay almost anything at all after settling their debts in the country. Under these circumstances several hundred of the minor tenants who understood no other line of business than farming and whose farms the proprietors have considered more lucrative to lay under sheep are removed to either waste ground or other allotments so exceedingly unsuitable as to render it alike the interest and the desire of those unhappy people to seek shelter in some more propitious quarter of the world.

Like the weavers whose petitions were simultaneously flooding into the Colonial Department, the Highlanders were allegedly 'dutiful and loyal subjects', whose 'peaceable dutiful disposition', 'moral and exemplary habits' and 'unremitting indefatigable industry' made them ideal candidates for colonizing British North America. But Logan feared they were more likely to be overlooked than the weavers, since 'the distance of the residences of these people from Edinburgh and there being no local agent so far North, put it out of their power to avail themselves hitherto of the protection lent by Government to poor persons in like indigent and critical circumstances in Scotland'.[32]

The Highlanders' plight was also reflected in some of the petitions presented to the select committee on emigration in 1826–7. From Fort Augustus came a request for information on passage regulations made on behalf of 337 people who 'are desirous of going to Canada, but are utterly unable to pay for their passage'. From Duirinish in Skye came a petition for assisted passages to America from forty-four small farmers and labourers who, 'from the depressed state of agriculture and the cessation of public works, have been reduced to poverty and deprived of their farms, which have been converted into sheep walks'. Their complaint was echoed by fifty-one petitioners from Glengarry whose 'wretched condition' afforded them no means of paying their own way to Upper Canada. And from Moidart and North Morar came pleas for assistance made on behalf of a total of 528 individuals who 'have been reduced to the lowest state of poverty by the minute subdivision of land, and by the failure of the herring fishery'. Some of the North Morar petitioners claimed that if the government helped them to cross the Atlantic, they could then call on the assistance of 'numerous friends in Canada and Nova Scotia', a reference to earlier emigration that was reinforced in several other submissions.[33] Some petitioners promised to repay any advances made to them, and one army veteran from Dornie in Kintail also assured the government of the Highlanders' loyalty:

> Applicant states, that he not only applies on behalf of himself and family, but that of a number of families of his neighbours (in the Western Highlands,) who are most anxious to emigrate to British America; that these families are without the means of subsistence, as they cannot even get a bit of ground to plant potatoes, nor any employment; that it would be a great blessing, if Government assisted them to emigrate to Canada, and that they would cheerfully pay back any money that might be advanced for that purpose in a few years; that they would not desert to any foreign state, but on the contrary serve their King and country. States that, for his own part, he is in the same situation with the other poor families who wish to emigrate, and although he served many years in the army, he did not claim a pension, as his friends were comfortably situated; but reverse of fortune obliges him now to apply for a free passage to Canada, which he will repay with interest; that necessity compels this application on the part of himself and others.[34]

Landlords and factors too lobbied the government to subsidize emigration from their estates in the 1820s, but on their own conditions. 'If the Proprietors are not allowed to exercise very considerable influence in selecting the Emigrants,' warned Duncan Shaw, factor of the Clanranald estates in 1827, 'assistance will be given where it is not required, the most wealthy and industrious of our population will emigrate, and we will be left with the dregs.'[35] Shaw's proposal that proprietors, factors and clergy should select emigrants whose relocation in Canada would then be funded by the government fell, not surprisingly, on deaf ears, as did most similar requests. Having tried unsuccessfully in 1823 to obtain state funding to remove tenants from one of his Inner Hebridean islands, Rum, Maclean of Coll dipped into his own pocket three years later when, cancelling all their arrears, he bankrolled the removal of 300 of the 350 islanders to Cape Breton at a cost of £5 14s per adult and then leased Rum to a single sheep farmer. According to Alexander Hunter, who superintended the emigration, some were willing to go, but others 'did not like to leave the land of their ancestors', and the episode falls into the growing category of forced clearance rather than voluntary relocation. The landlord's motive was profit, not philanthropy, for the new tenant paid nearly three times as much annual rental as those who had been evicted. Maclean's subsequent approach to the government for assistance in removing 1,500 redundant tenants from his estates was unsuccessful, and as landlords came to realize that state assistance was a vain hope, increasing numbers began to fund their own emigration schemes.[36]

The rising tide of support for Highland emigration among policy-makers is evident in subsequent public commentary about the region's crumbling economy. In a prophetic statement made in June 1837, shortly before a combination of bad harvests and potato famine created a major subsistence crisis in the west Highlands, Robert Graham warned the House of Commons that state-aided emigration was the 'most effectual' remedy for the region's recurring problems:

> To whatever extent in other ways employment can be found, emigration, in one shape or another, must continue to take place. Probably it would, in the long run, be the most expedient, the most efficient and the most economical expenditure of the public money if His Majesty's Government were to assist in establishing a system of emigration on a great scale. To give effectual relief, it must be done generally, and on a great scale; if it is done partially, and to a small extent, the relief will not be recognized … if the Government is to embark in this, the sooner it is begun the easier it will be effected. The time is favourable for doing it; and if done, it were well to do it before the undertaking becomes too gigantic.[37]

Four years later, Graham's views were echoed by a select committee appointed specifically to investigate Highland distress and 'the practicability of affording the people relief by means of emigration'. Reflecting the unanimous views of witnesses, it reported that there were between 45,000 and 60,000 people too many living on the western seaboard. Extensive state-aided emigration, the committee concluded, was the only way to ease the burden of overpopulation on landlords, as well as an essential preliminary to effective long-term recovery for the region.[38]

Three years on, in 1844, the Scottish Poor Law Commissioners' report referred to a steady haemorrhage of impoverished Highlanders, particularly from Skye and the Outer Hebrides. Witnesses such as the Reverend Dr Norman McLeod of Glasgow and John Bowie, manager of several west Highland estates, both of whom had given evidence to the 1841 select committee, remained steadfast in their support for emigration as a preliminary form of poor relief. McLeod knew of 'no other way in which the Highlands of Scotland can be put on a footing with the other districts of the country' and cured of their long-term economic 'evils', while Bowie claimed that since 1839 he had over-seen the emigration of 3,250 islanders, all of whom had been 'successfully and comfortably removed, without pressure or force'.[39] And in 1851, while the Highlands and Islands were still in the grip of the devastating potato famine that beset the region for virtually a decade after 1846 – an event which has been described as 'one of the greatest economic and social disasters in Highland history'[40] – Sir John McNeill, chairman of the Poor Law's Board of Supervision, toured twenty-seven of the worst-affected parishes with a view to ascertaining the most effective means of relief. His report, as well as the evidence of several witnesses in the Hebrides and western mainland, discredited charitable relief and unequivocally endorsed assisted emigration. Charles McQuarrie, a merchant in Bunessan, Mull, declared:

> I see no prospect of relief for the population, without emigration. Many who declined to emigrate, would now desire to go if they could find the means. I am of opinion that if a thousand persons were to emigrate from the Duke's property, it would not be too much, and that there is no way in which the proprietor could more advantageously employ funds, than in aiding emigration.

Further north, in Skye, McQuarrie's views were echoed by Thomas Fraser, Sheriff Substitute of the island, who was 'reluctantly driven to the conclusion, that a considerable emigration is indispensable to restore the people of Skye to the condition of a self-supporting population, and that it would not be safe to trust to any system of amelioration, unaided by the alleviation of the burden which emigration would afford'. Angus MacDonald, ground officer on Lord MacDonald's Sleat estate, agreed that there was 'no possible means of extricating' the destitute population of Skye 'unless they can be enabled to emigrate', a view that was echoed by – among others – the parochial boards of Lochcarron and Gairloch on the Wester Ross mainland.[41]

To what extent were these recommendations put into practice, and with what repercussions for the emigrants themselves? The government, ideologically committed to laissez-faire economics, remained reluctant to subsidize Highland emigration throughout the traumatic 1830s and 1840s. Relief for victims of the first potato famine came, not only in the form of provisions from destitution relief committees, but also by the extension to Scotland of a scheme which used money from Australian land sales to assist the passages of eligible emigrants – that is, those under thirty-five with character references and farming skills. Most of the 5,200 Scots who left under this bounty programme between 1837 and 1840 were Highlanders, many of whom allegedly begged to be sent to New South Wales, where there was a pressing demand for agricultural labour. While the selecting agents' emphasis on élite recruitment provoked some conflict with destitution relief committees, which accused them of selecting the cream of Highland society, the scheme was administered flexibly, and regulations were often relaxed to permit elderly or unemployed relatives to accompany eligible emigrants on specially chartered ships. The *Inverness Courier* was in no doubt that the Highlanders wanted to emigrate, at least from Lochaber, where in May 1838 over 1,200 signed up to leave:

> After some months of expectation and anxiety, Dr Boyter, the Government emigration agent for Australia, arrived at Fort William. The news of his arrival, like the fiery cross of old, soon spread through every glen in the district, and at an early hour on the Monday, thousands of enterprising Gaels might be seen ranked around the Caledonian Hotel, anxious to quit the land of their forefathers and to go and possess the unbounded pastures of Australia. While we regret that so many active men should feel it necessary to leave their own Country, the Highlands will be considerably relieved of its overplus population.[42]

Australia again became the focus of emigrant attention in the wake of the Great Highland Famine. Between 1852 and 1858 the Highland and Island Emigration Society expedited the removal to the Antipodes of almost 5,000 'surplus' Highlanders from ten impoverished western estates. The Society was initially conceived by Sheriff Substitute Thomas Fraser of Skye as a small-scale charitable venture to enable more islanders to emigrate under the auspices of the Colonial Land and Emigration Commission after the cessation of the ineffective government-funded famine relief and improvement schemes. It quickly evolved, however, into what T. M. Devine has aptly described as 'a government project in all but name'.[43] At the helm were two implacable opponents of charitable relief, Sir John McNeill and, more significantly, Sir Charles Trevelyan, Assistant Secretary to the Treasury and until 1850 the civil servant primarily responsible for Irish famine relief. Their aim was to develop a tripartite scheme involving landlords, the Emigration Commission and the Society, by means of which entire families would be sent to Australia in the confident expectation that they would readily adapt to pastoral occupations and replace the labour which had deserted to the gold fields. Responsibilities were clearly demarcated, with landlords paying a third of the cost of removal (approximately £1 per head), the Emigration Commission waiving some of its regulations on eligibility, and the Society defraying the cost of outfit, conveyance to the embarkation port and the passage of eligible emigrants. Emigrants were expected to repay the Society's expenses in due course, while landlords could reduce their expenditure by taking advantage of the government's only legislative concession to the famine, the Emigration Advances Act of 1851, which allowed them to borrow money at favourable interest rates to assist the emigration of tenants.

Highland emigration to the Antipodes was sporadic rather than steady, the product of specific, short-lived schemes. Much larger numbers went to Canada, increasingly financed by landlords who were becoming convinced both that it was the only alternative to tenant starvation and proprietorial bankruptcy, and that the government was unlikely to relieve them of their responsibility through systematic or long-term state aid. The *Scotsman* of 25 August 1849 estimated that the previous decade had seen 20,000 Highlanders emigrate to Canada, while in that season alone almost 4,000 had left Glenelg and South Uist. The tally increased in the early 1850s, as Outer Hebridean proprietors in particular responded to persistent famine and the facilities of the Emigration Advances Act with intensified emigration programmes. Of 14,000 emigrants estimated to have been assisted by Highland landlords between 1815 and 1856, almost 11,000 left in the decade 1846–56, with Sir James Matheson of Lewis, John Gordon of Cluny, proprietor of South Uist and Barra, and the Duke of Argyll among the

2. A Coronach in the Backwoods, *oil painting by George W. Simson, 1859. The
emigrant is playing a lament (*coronach*) beside his weeping wife after receiving
news from home. He is shown with the axe he has used to clear the forest. In the
background stands the log cabin he has built.*

most active participants in that era. Gordon dispatched 3,200 tenants to Canada, 2,337 were sent out from Lewis and one-third of the entire population left the Duke of Argyll's island of Tiree.[44]

But did the tenants really wish to emigrate? Were they encouraged or coerced? The *Inverness Courier*, as we have seen, was in no doubt in 1838 that the surplus population of the Highlands was happy to emigrate to Australia under the auspices of the Colonial Land Fund. Official agencies reinforced their pro-emigration rhetoric by emphasizing the Highlanders' 'great disposition' to go overseas, attracted by prospects of 'a comfortable independence after the lapse of a year or two'.[45] 'Their prejudices against emigration are entirely gone,' declared Norman McLeod to the Poor Law Commissioners in 1844, while Lord MacDonald's Skye and North Uist tenants had displayed, according to John Bowie's evidence to the same inquiry, 'an anxious desire to emigrate'.[46] Sir John McNeill noted that James Ewan Baillie, the Bristol merchant and banker who was proprietor of Glenelg and Lochalsh, and John Gordon had received petitions from tenants wishing to emigrate. On Gordon's Hebridean estates 'men of all classes and denominations' agreed that the people's plight 'would have been more wretched than it is had not the proprietor enabled a considerable number to emigrate', while Hector McRae, a crofter at Inverinite in Kintail, told McNeill, 'There are many persons who would desire to emigrate if they could find the means of carrying themselves and their families to one of the colonies.'[47]

But such apparent enthusiasm should be taken with a pinch of salt. Even in the 1820s the 'desire' to emigrate was generated by poverty, and the reluctance of some of the Rum emigrants did not go unnoticed at the time. Although bounty emigration in the late 1830s was partly a response to agency propaganda and should not be equated with landlord-instigated clearances, the catalysts for most emigrants were famine and high rents. In the 1840s and 1850s the correlation of clearance and emigration became much more distinct, and in both Canada and Australia they came to be seen as 'two sides of the same coin'.[48] It was in this period that the negative concept of enforced exile became firmly embedded in the psyche of emigrants and commentators alike, and even the reports of those who promoted emigration contain clues that many Highlanders did not share their views. Thomas Knox, chamberlain of Lewis, and a supporter of the replacement of people by sheep, told the 1841 Select Committee that seventy emigrants, whose passage three years earlier had been paid by the land-lord, Stewart Mackenzie of Seaforth, 'did not wish to go, but farms were cleared to make sheep walks'. And Duncan Shaw, factor for Harris and North Uist, described to the same inquiry the way in which troops had been used in an abortive attempt to orchestrate eviction and emigration from the farm of Borve in Harris in order to lease it to a single sheepmaster:

> Three years were allowed them to prepare. At Martinmas 1838, they were told they must remove at Whitsuntide 1839. Such of them as from age or other infirmities were unfit subjects for emigration, were offered better lands elsewhere in Harris; those able to emigrate were informed their whole arrears would be passed from, that they and their families would be landed free of expense, with the proceeds of their crop and stock of cattle in their pockets, either at Cape Breton, where their friends and countrymen were already settled, or in Canada, at their choice; these offers were then considered generous, and no objection was made to them. In the meantime, however, occurrences of an unpleasant nature had taken place in the neighbouring island of Skye. Some people on the estate of Macleod fearing a removal, wrote threatening letters to MacLeod, of Macleod, and his factor. Inflammatory proclamations of the same description were posted on the church doors, and some sheep belonging to a sheep grazier were houghed and killed ... Exaggerated accounts of these occurrences soon reached Harris, and joined with bad advices from those who ought to have known better, wrought an immediate change on the tempers of the people ... they defied and severely maltreated the officers of the law.[49]

The evidence of three clerics to the Poor Law Commissioners painted a picture of reluctance rather than of enthusiasm. John McKinnon of Strath in Skye reported that the islanders were 'not disposed to emigrate if they can live comfortably at home', while Colin McDonald of Portree believed that unenthusiastic reports from earlier emigrants had made people 'not so much inclined' to follow their example. More emphatic was the statement of the minister of the Small Isles, who was 'persuaded that nothing but absolute distress in the parish' would induce his parishioners to emigrate, since 'they are so much attached to their native parish.'[50] Similar evidence was presented to Sir John McNeill. The people of Kilfinichen in Mull, especially the poorest, were generally 'not inclined to emigrate', while witnesses in Kishorn and Torridon had 'no reason to believe' that crofters had any desire to go overseas. McNeill also referred to opposition to emigration in Lewis and Harris, where proprietorial offers to cancel arrears, supply provisions and fund passages had been cold-shouldered by the population. It was clearly a sensitive subject. Not only did McNeill observe that 'several persons' who acknowledged their support for emigration in conversation were unwilling to confirm their views in written evidence, 'fearing that such an assertion of their opinion might give umbrage to persons whom they desired not to offend'. In Glenelg, James Ewan Baillie's fear of being accused of enforced clearance led him to make his offer of cancelled arrears and free passages conditional on the emigrants pulling down their houses before departure and funding their way to the Clyde ports. Not surprisingly, his offer attracted only one applicant, although twenty-five years earlier the tenants of Glenelg had petitioned the government for assistance 'to emigrate to a country [Upper Canada] where their nearest and dearest relatives are already settled and form no inconsiderable colony'.[51]

Even the landlord-supporting, pro-emigration *Scotsman* was concerned about the ethics of large-scale evictions from Lord MacDonald's Skye estates. After removal notices had been served on 600 families in summer 1849, it anticipated with some trepidation the eviction of 3,000 people from the island:

> Means of emigration to Canada, we believe, will be provided, but the case is an extremely painful one, and it will probably lead to an inquiry, suggested by the *Scotsman*, whether the ordinary law of landlord and tenant is suited to districts like those in parts of Ireland and the Hebrides! The extraordinary power possessed by one individual in such circumstances is certainly anomalous, and ought to be exercised with great moderation and humanity. The condition of these remote Highland properties is a subject surrounded with unusual difficulties and responsibility ... When the lands are heavily mortgaged, the obvious, though harsh resource, is dispossessing the smaller tenants, to make room for a better class able to pay rent, and this task generally devolves on south-country managers or trustees, who look only to money returns, and cannot sympathise with the peculiar situation and feelings of the Highland population.[52]

If emigration to Canada presented a painful case, so too did the exodus to Australia, according to a correspondent of the *Inverness Advertiser*, who witnessed the traumatic embarkation of a group of Locheil and Ardgour emigrants in September 1849:

> He states that it was heart piercing to hear them wailing – the Highland wailing – and when the bagpipes struck up 'Lochaber no more', the passionate outburst

of their grief broke through all restraints. It was at midnight this scene took place, and by the aid of the steamer's lights alone they were able to take their last look at the hills of Lochaber, from the great bosom of which they were thus wrenched ... The distress of many of the emigrants was greatly aggravated, owing to their being compelled to leave members of their families behind, from inability to pay the passage money.[53]

Advocates of Highland emigration – particularly landlord-sponsored movement – had good grounds for caution. They were attacked on a range of fronts at home and abroad. Canada's chief immigration agent, Alexander Buchanan, was scathing in his condemnation of the deliberately inadequate provision made by some proprietors, who, having chosen Canada for its proximity and cheap access, exported their problem by shipping maximum numbers of emigrants at minimum cost, expecting his department to foot the bill for onward travel from the port of landing. In 1848 Lachlan Chisholm sent out 134 emigrants from South Uist, most of whom could not speak English. All were 'in very poor circumstances, and required assistance from the department for their removal from Quebec to their places of destination'.[54] A year later Buchanan reported the arrival of 1,625 Highlanders in the month of August alone, all from the Hebrides, and sent out by the Duke of Argyll, Lachlan Chisholm and John Gordon:

They are respectable orderly people, but many of them very poor. The passengers by the 'Charlotte and Barlow,' were all forwarded to Montreal by the ship, those by the remaining vessels landed here, under the impression (from the information they received, and the promises made to them before leaving home) that they were to be forwarded to their destination by this department. But few of them could speak English; and, after investigating their cases as strictly as circumstances would permit, I was under the necessity of forwarding upwards of two-thirds of their number at the Government expense.[55]

By the autumn Buchanan was still reporting grimly on an influx of destitute Highlanders. October saw the arrival of a shipload from North Uist, sent out by Lord MacDonald as far as Montreal. 'They were all extremely poor, and at that port became chargeable on this department for their food and transport to Hamilton, their destination being the London and Huron Districts. On arrival at Hamilton, they were sent into the interior at the expense of the Hamilton and

Toronto St. Andrew Societies.'[56] The year 1850 saw little improvement, with the arrival in Montreal in August of a shipload of eighty-two emigrants from Oban, bound for Glengarry. 'Owing to the number of women and children,' noted Buchanan, 'it was found necessary to provide them, at the expense of this department, with a free passage to Lancaster.'[57]

Particular opprobrium was reserved for John Gordon of Cluny, who in 1851 shipped out 1,681 emigrants from Barra, South Uist and Benbecula to the port of Quebec but failed to pay for their onward transport to Upper Canada. In September Buchanan wrote to the Provincial Secretary, asking that Gordon should reimburse his department 'for the expenses incurred ... on account of his people'. Writing to Gordon's factor two months later, Buchanan was unequivocal in his condemnation of the estate's policy, which he compared with the 'wholly different circumstances' under which Sir James Matheson had financed the transfer of 986 tenants from Lewis all the way to their final destination in the Eastern Townships:

> Quebec is practically the only seaport of Canada; and being situated in a country already fully supplied with a population speaking a different language, this city and neighbourhood afford no opening of any extent for the employment of the destitute emigrants who arrive in large numbers and at a particular season of the year ... The mere transfer to this port of an indigent tenantry, without an alteration in any respect in their condition, gives no reasonable ground for expecting their subsequent successful progress. The numerous inconveniences which attend emigration are sufficiently trying to every class, and, with the addition of distress and privation, must always induce unfavourable representations by the emigrants to their friends who remain at home.[58]

John Gordon, one of the most infamous evictors, was further vilified in the Canadian press for the brutal recruitment techniques allegedly used in rounding up emigrants, as well as the lack of concern for their subsequent fate. An account in the *Quebec Times* casts doubt on Sir John McNeill's assertion that Gordon's tenants had petitioned him for assistance to emigrate:

> Many of our readers may not be aware that there lives such a personage as Colonel Gordon, proprietor of large estates, South Uist and Barra, in the Highlands of Scotland; we are sorry to be obliged to introduce him to their notice,

under circumstances which will not give them a very favourable opinion of his character and heart.

It appears that tenants on the above mentioned estates were on the verge of starvation, and had probably become an eyesore to the gallant Colonel! He decided on shipping them to America. What they were to do there, was a question he never put to his conscience. Once landed in Canada, he had no further concern about them. Up to last week, 1,100 souls from his estates had landed in Quebec, and begged their way to Upper Canada; when in the summer season, having only a morsel of food to procure, they probably escaped the extreme misery which seems to be the lot of those who followed them.

On their arrival here, they voluntarily made and signed the following statement:- 'We the undersigned passengers per Admiral from Stornaway [sic], in the Highlands of Scotland, do solemnly depose to the following facts:- That Colonel Gordon is the proprietor of the estates of South Uist and Barra; that among many hundreds of tenants and cotters whom he has sent this season from his estates to Canada, he gave directions to his factor, Mr. Fleming of Cluny Castle, Aberdeenshire, to ship on board of the above named vessel a number of nearly 450 of said tenants and cotters from the estate in Barra – that accordingly, a great majority of these people, among whom were the undersigned, proceeded voluntarily to embark on board the Admiral, at Loch Boysdale, on or about the 11th August 1851; but that several of the people who were intended to be shipped for this port, Quebec, refused to proceed on board, and in fact, absconded from their homes to avoid the embarkation. Whereupon Mr. Fleming gave orders to a policeman, who was accompanied by the ground officer of the estate of Barra, and some constables, to pursue the people who had ran [sic] away among the mountains; which they did, and succeeded in capturing about twenty from the mountains and islands in the neighbourhood; but only came with the officers on an attempt being made to handcuff them; and that some who ran away were not brought back, in consequence of which four families, at least, have been divided, some having come in the ships to Quebec, while other members of the same families were left in the Highlands.

The undersigned further declare, that those who voluntarily embarked did so under promise to the effect, that Colonel Gordon would defray their passage to Quebec; that the Government Emigration Agent there would send the whole party free to Upper Canada, where, on arrival the Government Agents would give them work, and furthermore, grant them land on certain conditions.

The undersigned finally declare, that they are now landed in Quebec so destitute, that if immediate relief be not afforded them and continued until they are settled in employment, the whole will be liable to perish with want.'[59]

This Canadian criticism was given wider circulation through the publication in Toronto in 1857 of the third edition of Donald McLeod's anti-clearance polemic, *Gloomy Memories in the Highlands of Scotland*, in which he also drew on an eyewitness account of the Barra evictions:

The unfeeling and deceitful conduct of those acting for Colonel Gordon ... cannot be too strongly censured. The duplicity and art which was used by them in order to entrap the unwary natives is worthy of the craft and cunning of an old slave-trader. Many of the poor people were told in my hearing, that Sir John McNeill would be in Canada before them, where he would have every thing necessary for their comfort prepared for them. Some of the officials signed a document binding themselves to emigrate in order to induce the poor people to give their names; but in spite of all these stratagems many of the people saw through them and refused out and out to go. When the transports anchored in Loch Boysdale the tyrants threw off their mask, and the work of devastation and cruelty commenced. The poor people were commanded to attend a public meeting at Loch Boysdale where the transports lay, and according to the intimation, any one absenting himself from the meeting was to be fined in Two Pounds. At this meeting some of the natives were seized and in spite of their entreaties were sent on board the transports. One stout Highlander, named Angus Johnstone, resisted with such pith that they had to hand-cuff him before he could be mastered; but in consequence of the priest's interference his manacles were taken off and marched between four officers on board the emigrant vessel. One morning, during the transporting season, we were suddenly awakened by the screams of a young female who had been recaptured in an adjoining house; having escaped after her first apprehension. We all rushed to the door and saw the broken-hearted creature with dishevelled hair and swollen face, dragged away by two constables and a ground officer. Were you to see the racing and chasing of policemen, constables, and ground officers, pursuing the outlawed natives you would think, only for their colour, that you had been by some miracle transported to the banks of the Gambia on the slave-coast of Africa.[60]

By the 1850s the major waves of clearance and emigration were over, but the memory of the Highlanders' unwilling expatriation was vividly revived within thirty years by a sudden flowering of literary and political interest in the 'Highland problem' in the early 1880s. It was spearheaded by Alexander Mackenzie's immensely popular *History of the Highland Clearances*, which articulated the crofters' grievances during the previous century as a justification for their current attempts to regain their lost lands by means of rent strikes and forcible reoccupation. Enforced emigration was a recurring focus of Mackenzie's vituperation, as he catalogued a series of incidents across the Highlands and Islands in which he claimed reluctant emigrants had been tricked or forced into relocating overseas. As many of 5,390 inhabitants of Strathglass and the surrounding area were, we read, 'driven out of these Highland glens' and shipped to Pictou, Nova Scotia, between 1801 and 1803, while, in an echo of Donald McLeod's images of slavery, Mackenzie described how in 1847 many of the famine-stricken tenants of Knoydart had been 'packed off like so many African slaves'.[61]

The theme of enforced emigration espoused by Mackenzie and other protagonists of the Gaelic literary revival was reinforced when the government, alarmed at the escalating land war, appointed a Royal Commission in 1883 to enquire into the condition of crofters and cottars. Grasping the unprecedented opportunity of the Napier Commission to voice their grievances, assisted by radical land reformers like Alexander Mackenzie, and emboldened by the support of the Gaelic literary movement, crofter-witnesses drew heavily on oral tradition to construct a picture of landlord betrayal, eviction and enforced exile over a century and more. John Mackay of Kilpheder in South Uist recalled the well-publicized evictions of 1851, when he had seen 'a policeman chasing a man down the machair towards Askernish to catch him in order to send him on board an emigrant ship lying in Loch Boysdale', while John Morrison of North Uist remembered that 'many were compelled to emigrate' from Sollas. Only 17 per cent of those selected for emigration by Sir James Matheson in 1851 had been willing to leave Lewis, although over 2,000 were eventually shipped out, with 1,180 summonses of removal being issued between 1849 and 1851. As the Reverend Angus Maciver told the Napier Commission, 'Some say it was voluntary. But there was a great deal of forcing and these people were sent away very much against their will. That is very well known and people present know that perfectly well. Of course, they were not taken in hand by the policemen and all that, but they were in arrears, and had to go, and remonstrated against going.'[62] These images were reinforced by the Reverend Alexander Mackintosh of Daliburgh, South Uist, who claimed that 'of the crofters removed many were, against their wishes ...

forcibly put on board emigrant vessels and transported to North America'. In his
opinion, forced emigration was responsible for much of the current unrest and
land hunger in the Highlands, and he was one of several witnesses who urged the
commissioners to tackle the region's ongoing demographic problems by redis-
tributing land rather than expelling people.[63] The commissioners, however, were
swayed by the estate managements' claims of continuing overpopulation, and in
1884 accordingly recommended a measure of 'properly conducted' state-aided
emigration as an 'indispensable remedy' for the region's problems. For once the
government, which throughout the century had been so loath to respond to pleas
for state-aided emigration, was spurred into action out of concern at continuing
social and economic tension in the Hebrides, and in 1888 it allocated £10,000
towards the settlement of 100 crofting families from Lewis, Harris and North
Uist on prairie homesteads at Killarney in Manitoba and Saltcoats in the North
West Territories. The various interested parties were represented by an emigration board which administered the scheme and tried, unsuccessfully, to collect the
settlers' repayments over an eight-year period from 1892.[64]

Agricultural adversity: abandoning the rural lowlands

Much emigration from the north and west Highlands was provoked by unsuccessful attempts to reorientate the economy, particularly in response to acute
subsistence crises in the 1830s and 1840s. But dramatic images of evicted Highlanders dragged aboard emigrant ships have tended to obscure a persistent
exodus from the rural Lowlands that also stemmed in part from the dislocating
effects of agricultural restructuring. Since the eighteenth century the commercialization of farming had on the one hand improved yields and profits, but on
the other eroded the expectations of farm servants and small tenants throughout
much of Lowland Scotland. Changes included a greater variety of crops,
farmed in scientific rotation on land which was efficiently drained, artificially
fertilized and worked with new, labour-saving implements. While East Lothian
became Scotland's girnel, selective stock-breeding schemes, made possible by
systematic enclosure policies, improved feeding regimes and better communications, saw the emergence of the north-east as a beef cattle centre and the south-
west as a dairying region. High prices until the 1860s made it worthwhile for
farmers to invest in improvements, and the amount of land under cultivation
was extended by constant reclamation, with consolidation of farms as bigger
units were created in a bid to maximize efficiency.

Such changes demanded significant adjustments in rural communities, reshaping the social as well as the physical structure of the Lowlands and producing both winners and losers. Yet there was no single template and regional variations created a complex tenurial tapestry in which rural populations were both anchored and uprooted. In the dairying districts of Ayrshire, Renfrewshire and Lanarkshire, where tenancies were reconfigured rather than transformed, small family farms were retained and the population remained stable, while in the north-east the need for land reclamation produced fragmentation of holdings and created an army of crofters. The hill country of the Borders, however, experienced levels of depopulation comparable to the Highland experience and the rich grain-farming lands of the Lothians, along with areas like Fife and Kinross, saw a clear shift towards consolidation.

Those who stood to benefit most from the new economic order were the proprietors and the developing élite of capitalist tenant farmers, men who had the resources necessary for profitable investment in expensive development of their land. Other farmers were less sanguine about the benefits of nineteen-year leases, which, while granting them some security of tenure, offered none of the independence and status they craved. Central to their sense of insecurity was the fear of eviction. A tenant's fortunes depended on the whim of his landlord, exercised through his right to terminate tenure without explanation. A capricious landlord might evict tenants who held political or religious opinions with which he disagreed. In the 1840s Free Church tenants allegedly suffered disproportionately from consolidation of farms, and in 1872 the Liberal Unitarian George Hope lost the lease of his farm of Fenton Barns in East Lothian after he had stood against his landlord in a local election.[65] But even if landlords were fair and just in their dealings with tenants, agricultural developments in themselves were a cause of concern. Not only were the terms of leases made more exacting, as well as being more strictly enforced; the increased rent of a renewed lease, perhaps for a consolidated farm, might be beyond the means of sitting tenants, as many landlords abandoned patriarchial attitudes in favour of economic criteria. The traditional nineteen-year lease was reckoned to give a tenant insufficient time to recover his capital and interest, let alone reap any personal profit for his labour, before a new lease was imposed at a higher rent, sometimes with very little warning.

Discontent was not confined to tenant farmers. Although a tight labour market offered ready employment at good wages to farm labourers and servants, their status and prospects were threatened by consolidation, which deprived them of the treasured opportunity to graduate from wage labour to tenancy. Particularly in north-east Scotland, most farmers recruited their servants from the families of local smallholders, but very few of these men regarded farm service as a permanent career. Most aspired either to take over the family holding or to lease a croft of their own, a realistic ambition in the days when farmers were anxious to reclaim waste land through granting peripheral crofts on 'improving' leases, but a pipedream by the 1840s, when increasing pressure of population was curtailing their access to land and promoting mobility. In that era landlords were impelled not only by farming considerations but also by the fear that a new poor law would require them to support paupers on their estates. Their reaction was both to reduce the number of smallholdings whose tenants they regarded as potential paupers and to refuse cottage accommodation to married farm workers, who were required to board their dependants in a nearby town, while they themselves were housed communally on the farm, in a steading or bothy.

Demographic pressure, the curtailment of opportunities and the threat and reality of landlessness in a context of impartible inheritance inevitably strained relationships between farmers and servants. As the big farmers grew richer, their expectations and experiences became ever more divorced from the smaller farmers and labourers with whom they had been closely associated in the earlier stages of improvement. As tenants and sub-tenants sank to the position of landless labourers, a social as well as an economic wedge was driven between them and the more successful farmers. A ploughman who could in earlier days look forward to the prospect of working his own holding allegedly had, by 1851, 'nothing before him but a life of drudgery and an old age of poverty' and consequently lost all pride in himself and his work.[66] He, and others, were also much more likely to move regularly from job to job and area to area. Such mobility was exacerbated both by the harnessing of accommodation to employment and by the biannual feeing markets, when farmers, instead of re-engaging their existing workforce privately, went to market to hire strangers on the strength of mere outward appearance.

Such discontented restlessness was easily converted into emigration. Many emigrants referred in their letters to the disillusionment they had felt as their prospects of independence were eroded and their expectations of equal treatment were overturned. Surveys such as the censuses of 1831 and 1841, the *New Statistical Account* of the late 1830s and early 1840s and the 1844 *Report on the Scottish Poor Laws* all agreed that the depopulation of the rural Lowlands was attributable mainly to the consolidation of farms and the eradication of small-holdings. In the southern uplands, where the encroachment of commercial sheep farming had since the eighteenth century reduced arable cultivation and displaced the local population in a manner reminiscent of the Highlands, emigration seems to have been a common response to economic and social dislocation. In 1818 Alex Gordon, the Steward Depute of Kirkcudbrightshire, petitioned the Colonial Department to grant an assisted passage to Canada to a former tenant, William Bell, and his family, who had fallen on hard times after moving to an estate which had come under the management of rack-renting trustees. Further east, Samuel Porteous, of Whitton, near Jedburgh, implored the Colonial Secretary to assist the emigration of three families who, as a result of 'this distressing crisis', were likely to come on to the poor rates and who were pained that 'instead of being usefull to ourselves we should in the prime of our lives be a burden to our country'. And from the Dumfries-shire parish of Hutton and Corrie, according to the *New Statistical Account*, emigration had taken place because of 'pecuniary distress' arising from low farm wages and profits, although there is also contemporary evidence that 'unwanted radical sentiment was exported to Upper Canada', at least in the 1820s.[67]

While the Duke of Buccleuch's factor was happy to see the departure of 'discontented radicals', his view was not shared by James Hogg, the Ettrick Shepherd, who deplored the loss of 'brave and intelligent Borderers [who] rush from their native country, all with symptoms of reckless despair'.[68] In the north-east too there was widespread criticism of the way in which rack-renting, engrossment of farms and the loss of independence were driving the most enterprising tenants and farm servants overseas. A tract of 1837 placed the blame firmly at the landlords' door. After describing the plight of tenants, 'torn an' rackit in body an' mind, squeezing oot o't tither enormous rent, an' hardly makin' a sober livin' efter an a'', it went on to predict an increase in the number of emigrants who were already leaving 'in awfu' droves':

> This state o' things canna gae on unco lang as it's deein, or I'se be boon for't, them 'at his still a twa three notes tae the fore 'ill e'en try an' better their sitivation, by emigratin' tae the Canadas or some ither quarter ... The spunky, interprisin', an' industrious bleds o' oor kwintry, will they sit, do their lordships think, an' be crushed tae the earth, year after year, scrapin' thegither the tither terrible rent, fan they can live in comfort, an' be lairds themsels, on the ither side o' the Attalantic?[69]

Similar sentiments were expressed, albeit in rather different style, by the editor of the *Aberdeen Herald*. Commenting in 1852 on recent correspondence about the causes of vagrancy in rural communities, he claimed that consolidation of farms was destroying the backbone of rural society by driving farm servants off the land:

> They were honest, plain, industrious men, who looked forward to the day when they or their sons would be able to get larger and larger farms as their honest savings increased. These men, in many cases, have been obliged, along with their families, to take refuge in our towns, or have emigrated to countries where their skill and industry will be more highly appreciated. And a farm servant, who may have saved fifty or sixty pounds, can get no small farm upon which he might lay out his little capital. His only refuge is a foreign land; and thus it is that our very best agricultural labourers are driven from the country by the folly of a 'penny wise and pound foolish' landocracy.[70]

Some time later the editor of the same newspaper blamed emigration on the appalling living conditions endured by farm servants:

> It is clear that the cold and damp bothy – without a fire till the men light it … with the single dish unwashed from term to term – with stepping stones to walk over pools of water and mud to bed – and with the everlasting meal and milk from Whitsunday to Martinmas, and from Martinmas to Whitsunday, will not induce our young ploughmen to remain at home and give up their chance of comfort, if not wealth, in America or Australia.[71]

Shifting the surplus population: depression and emigration, 1880–1914

Disgruntled Lowland agriculturists, even those who were evicted, were clearly in a different category from starving Highlanders. Their emigration was influenced more by overseas opportunities than by domestic hardships and provoked concern, not relief, among contemporaries. Towards the end of the century, however, a widespread farming depression shifted the perspective in a more negative direction. As foreign competition in the form of cheap cereals from the American Midwest flooded the British market, prices fell dramatically, at least in the wheat-growing Lothians. Unjust game laws and a series of bad seasons compounded the farmers' problems, and many farmers and farm servants, discouraged by 'high rents and wet seasons', cut their losses by emigrating.[72] Once again, however, there was considerable regional and sectoral variation. Overall the Scottish agricultural community, with its emphasis on mixed farming, was much more resilient than its English counterpart, and in many areas emigration was still a consequence of rising expectations rather than redundancy. Far from reducing expenditure by economizing on labour, farmers often had to raise wages in an attempt to retain a workforce that was haemorrhaging from the land, convinced that higher status, better opportunities and a more comfortable lifestyle could be enjoyed in the towns or overseas. The trend was acknowledged by a Board of Agriculture report in 1906 on the reasons for the decline in Britain's farming population, which, alongside mechanization, poor accommodation and the attractions of urban life, cited, particularly in Scotland, 'the absence of an incentive to remain on the land and of any reasonable prospect of advancement in life'.[73] When A. D. Hall toured the agricultural areas of Britain on behalf of *The Times* in 1912, he confirmed that 'the great emigration to Canada' that was still taking place from Aberdeenshire in particular was due primarily to the onerous and unrewarding nature of smallholding in the region, as well as the inferior accommodation available for farm workers, who, as in earlier decades, often emigrated when they married rather than face the problem of finding a cottage at home.[74]

Depression was not confined to the agricultural sector. Since the 1820s the Scottish herring fishery had grown steadily in scale and profitability, with buoyant markets and prices. In 1884, however, it experienced a major reversal which lasted until the end of the decade and resulted in significant emigration from a community which until then had shown no interest in going overseas. The change of heart was clearly provoked by financial hardship, as curers went bankrupt, fishermen and ancillary workers such as coopers lost their livelihood, and the whole fishing enterprise slowed down considerably. In fishing centres such as Peterhead and Fraserburgh, where the health of the herring was an index of the general health of the town, poor law records during the 1880s and 1890s contain several applications for relief from the dependants of fishermen and coopers who had emigrated in an unsuccessful attempt to keep themselves and their families above the breadline.

The press record too confirms not only that emigration, sometimes temporary, was taking place from fishing communities but also that it was often controversial and regarded very much as a last resort. In remarking on the 'extraordinary rush' of emigrants from the country in 1888, the *Aberdeen Journal* mentioned, for the first time, that fishermen were participating in the movement, predicting that before the end of the summer over 150 fishing families would have emigrated. Throughout the spring it went on to document departures from a number of fishing centres, as fishermen, curers, coopers and also tradesmen whose businesses were suffering as a result of the crisis decided to cut their losses. A number of Banffshire fishermen, including fifty families and young men in Findochty and a large number of tradesmen from Buckie, had sold their houses and gear in readiness to emigrate, mainly to British Columbia, where Alexander Begg, a native of Caithness, was trying to establish a colony of Scottish fishermen. Begg's original scheme to transfer 1,250 Hebridean crofter families to Vancouver Island was rejected by the provincial government, which feared the arrival of hordes of destitute Highlanders, unable to repay their advances and likely to become a public charge on the province. The attempt to extend the experiment to east coast fishermen was, however, opposed by the British government, which would not countenance subsidizing emigration beyond the only part of Scotland that it recognized as a distressed area.[75] There was also considerable press hostility to fishermen's emigration, as well as some deliberate misinformation about overseas conditions. While the *Fraserburgh Herald* did not object to the departure of redundant coopers and curers, it denied that there was any need for fishermen to emigrate. It urged them to be patient, in the expectation that 'by and bye the business will assume its former flourishing condition', and warned those contemplating going to British Columbia 'to look before they leap', since 'by leaving home, fishermen may find when it is too late that they have sown the wind only to reap the whirlwind'.[76]

An economic upturn in 1889 and 1890 brought further confirmation that fishermen emigrated out of desperation rather than desire. 'Emigration from the district fell off considerably during the year,' commented the *Aberdeen Journal* with reference to Fraserburgh in 1889, adding that 'this fact ... guarantees that the wave of depression has commenced to roll back'.[77] A year later it claimed even more explicitly that Fraserburgh's emigrants were expelled by adverse circumstances: 'Another proof of better times is the marked falling away of emigration. For two or three years back there was a continual stream going from the town and district to America and other parts of the world, but within the last twelve months comparatively few people have considered it necessary to leave the old home.'[78] On the whole, the period from the early 1890s until 1914 was one of prosperity and growth in Scottish fishing, and there is little evidence of emigration, although ancillary tradesmen sometimes emigrated if they could not attract sufficient business. Isabella Milne, a cooper's wife, applied to Fraserburgh Parish Council for assistance in 1909 after 'her husband left for America 2 months ago because he could not get work in Fraserburgh'.[79] In January 1911 the *Aberdeen Journal* predicted that around 300 emigrants, mainly coopers and their families, would leave Fraserburgh that season for Canada, particularly for British Columbia, as a result of the competition created by barrel factories in the town, and in December it confirmed that an exodus of 350 had indeed taken place.[80] Again in May 1912 the same newspaper reported the departure of several hundred people from Fraserburgh that spring, mostly the families of coopers who had already settled abroad. But it went on to indicate a more serious problem in the east coast fishing community. Whereas in 1890 110 boats had fished out of Stonehaven, fifty miles to the south, by 1911 this number had fallen to fifty-two, and competition from German trawlers had greatly reduced the value of the catch. Once again, emigration seemed to many to be the only remedy.

> Even little Stonehaven with its 4577 people has arranged for a special train to be run from its station to Glasgow this month to take 200 men, women and children from the neighbourhood for whom Scotland is so hopeless that they are leaving her for ever. Sturdy fishing folk these whose forbears came over with the Danes. But what can their little 15-ton cutters and yawls do against the thirty German steam trawlers that are constantly flooding the market of Aberdeen with shots of 700 tons of cod caught on a three weeks' voyage to Iceland?[81]

A government committee in 1914 reported that the major problem facing Scotland's commercial fishermen was their inability to afford the huge cost of converting to steam drifters or steam trawlers. Witnesses in a number of fishing centres claimed that financial hardship was the main reason for renewed emigration from these communities; indeed, perhaps more fishermen were emigrating now than during the earlier crisis, for in the 1880s many more had had their capital tied up in boats and had been unable to emigrate. By 1914, however, far fewer fishermen could afford to take up a share in a steam drifter or a steam trawler, and those who faced the prospect of simply becoming deckhands on a vessel in which they had no personal interest might well resort to emigration. John May and James Sim, fishermen in Inverallochy and Fraserburgh respectively, told the committee that fishermen and their families were taking the unusual step of emigrating to Canada, simply because they could not accumulate enough capital to buy a share in a boat or nets. According to May:

> There are thirteen emigrants leaving St. Combs because of the hard living. If the Government could advance money at reasonable rates, I know that we could save £100 annually, which would mean a very large sum out of a fisherman's earnings ... I have never seen a fisherman emigrating from my locality in my life before. These are the first of our fishermen that I have ever seen emigrating.[82]

On the Moray coast, Alexander Cowie, a fish salesman in Lossiemouth, confirmed that about six young men had emigrated from there to Canada within the previous two years, prepared to take 'anything that turned up'. They too had been discouraged by the difficulty of raising enough money to participate in fishing on a shareholding basis.[83] And James Slater, a fisherman in Buckie, alleged that the capital needed to acquire and maintain a steam drifter was often not offset by the vessel's subsequent earnings; he claimed to know of at least one skipper and mate who were emigrating because they could not afford the high operating costs of this new, highly capitalized fishing.[84] R. W. Crowly, an engineer and journalist in London, recommended that the government should advance loans to fishermen to equip their boats with motors, for unless some such incentive were offered the current 'constant emigration' would continue and increase. John Buchan, a retired Peterhead fisherman, supported Crowly's forlorn hope that state loans should be advanced to young fishermen in order to prevent further emigration, for several such emigrants had already left his district for Canada, forced out by financial hardship.[85]

Conclusion

In highlighting some of the ways in which emigration was employed as a response to destitution and disgruntlement among a range of occupational groups across Scotland, the spotlight has inevitably fallen most sharply on the Highlands. But although it was there that famine and clearance wreaked particular havoc and attracted greatest opprobrium, as well as producing the most dramatic and concentrated examples of unwilling emigration in probably the entire history of the Scottish diaspora, economic hardship and negative sentiments were not the exclusive preserve of Highland emigrants. At the same time, neither Highlanders nor Lowlanders were one-dimensional pessimists. Despite the demonization of Highland emigration by polemicists who have depicted it as an uninterrupted tragedy of savage clearance perpetrated by capricious landlords on an unwilling tenantry, the emigrants were characterized by variety rather than uniformity of background, motives and experiences. They responded to opportunities as well as threats, and disillusionment and destitution were frequently eclipsed by the anticipation of betterment.

ATTRACTING THE ADVENTUROUS

'This is a country of hope, *and the other of* fear *for the future.'*[1]

For most emigrants, hope and adventure were far stronger sentiments than despair and resignation. Whatever the time period and location, and however distressing the circumstances that had unsettled them, bitterness was rarely unmixed with an element of ambition, even among cleared Highlanders and unemployed artisans. At the very least, they anticipated an improvement on conditions and prospects at home, often for the sake of the next generation as much as for themselves. Very few were so paralysed by poverty or persecution that they did not seek betterment, albeit emigration might be regarded as a last, desperate and unwilling resort. But by no means all emigrants were destitute, disillusioned or hounded out. Many had cash in their pockets as well as hope in their hearts, and carried with them a clear plan for the future as well as the means to implement their ideas. They were not reluctant refugees from a backward rural economy, but voluntary exiles from a vibrant, industrializing and increasingly urban society which offered good employment opportunities and a rising standard of living. Shiploads of emigrant Scots were, according to contemporary commentators, 'furnished with funds'[2] and opponents of emigration frequently expressed concern at the loss of the flower of the population, those who were rich in skills and enterprise as well as in capital.

Why, then, against a background of expanding domestic opportunities, did so many Scots emigrate? Primarily because overseas alternatives, particularly in underpopulated countries which were rich in resources, were more attractive to Scots with marketable skills than openings in Scotland's low-wage economy. While some emigrants made an explicit comparison between domestic discouragements and overseas opportunities, others, without any particular axe to grind, simply saw the potential for profitable investment of their labour, talents or capital in the vast virgin territories or burgeoning cities of the New World or the Antipodes. Nor were there any major psychological barriers to surmount, since by 1800 Scotland had such a well-established culture of mobility, in terms of both internal relocation and entrepreneurial emigration overseas. In the course of the eighteenth century the focus of Scotland's overseas enterprise clearly shifted from Europe to America. By 1774–5, when the *Register of Emigrants* offered a fleeting statistical insight into the extent of transatlantic movement, North America and the Caribbean had become the major destinations for Scottish emigrants, bolstered, no doubt, by the vital and durable connections that had also developed in the military, political, administrative, commercial and intellectual arenas. By no means all the statements captured in the *Register* reflected poverty, unemployment or distress. Most of the twenty-four passengers on the *Magdalene*, which sailed from Greenock to Philadelphia in August 1774, went for reasons of health or business, while at least some of the emigrants on two subsequent ships to the same port went to follow their business, to see friends or family or to 'better their fortune'.[3] All eleven passengers aboard the *Jamaica Packet*, which left Kirkcaldy for Antigua in October 1774, 'Emigrate in hopes of earning their Bread in a more easy Manner than in their Native Country', while several of the eighty-one emigrants aboard the *Jackie*, sailing from Stranraer to New York in June 1775, anticipated 'good employment', 'making rich' and 'a better way of doing' as well as family reunions.[4]

Even in the eighteenth century Scottish emigration was therefore clearly associated with positive precedent, family connections and economic ambition, characteristics that became even more evident as time went on. Just as there was an industry of anti-emigration propaganda and literature that equated all emigration with destitution and despair, so there was an even bigger industry of guidebooks, pamphlets, newspapers and letters that skilfully targeted and fed the unfulfilled ambitions of a restless nation throughout and beyond the nineteenth century. Continuities and changes in these mechanisms themselves, as well as in the nature of the encouragement they offered and the destinations they recommended, indicate something of how, why and whither the ambitious and adventurous, as well as the destitute and disgruntled, were persuaded to emigrate and guided in their preparations. Since the clearest continuity, throughout the entire nineteenth century, lay in the unremitting stream of positive propaganda that was given to farming opportunities, particularly in Canada, the focus rests primarily on different dimensions of the lure of the land.

Communal colonization schemes

'This is a country in which the farmer may make rich and the poor man live,' wrote an emigrant in Boston to his father in Galloway in 1772.[5] That many others shared his view is evident both in the frequency with which agricultural opportunities were discussed in correspondence and in the popularity of American land speculation among Scots in the late eighteenth century. Relatively prosperous tenant farmers reacted to rising rents and falling prospects by forming themselves into emigration companies with written constitutions and share subscriptions, publicizing their activities in pamphlets and sometimes dispatching representatives to evaluate American lands and make purchases if appropriate. The Scots American Company of Farmers, constituted at Inchinnan in Renfrewshire in 1773 'for purchasing and improving of lands' in North America, had 138 members, who quickly raised £1,000 by selling shares at £2 10s each.[6] After two delegates, sent to America in March 1773, had spent seven months exploring various options, a 23,000-acre tract was purchased at Ryegate in New York on the advice of the theologian and politician Dr John Witherspoon, who was speculating in land at Ryegate along with the Pagans, a family of Glasgow merchants and shipowners.[7] A year later another Scottish emigration society, the United Company of Farmers for the Shires of Perth and Stirling, purchased a 7,000-acre tract at Barnet, near Ryegate, after £500 had been subscribed and two of the 100 subscribers sent out to reconnoitre a site had made contact with Witherspoon and the Inchinnan pioneers.

Within a few years, however, the American Revolution brought these enterprises to a premature end and put paid to further land speculation in the United States for some time. The focus of emigrant attention therefore shifted elsewhere and for a brief period in the late 1810s fell on the Cape of Good Hope, Britain's possession of which was confirmed at the Congress of Vienna. First to draw attention to the Cape's potential was Benjamin Moodie, who in 1817 responded to a downturn in the fortunes of the family estate in Orkney by selling up and recruiting 200 Scottish mechanics and labourers, mainly from around Edinburgh, whom he took to South Africa under eighteen-month or three-year indentures. Such was the demand for their labour that he was able to recoup his expenses by selling the indentures – sometimes to the recruits themselves – for more than double the amount he had spent on their passages. Two younger brothers followed him to South Africa, where Donald subsequently became one of the founders of Natal and John sojourned for ten years before returning to Britain, marrying the authoress Susanna Strickland and settling with her in Canada in 1832. Although all three brothers obtained government land grants at the Cape in 1820, Benjamin Moodie was dissatisfied with the outcome of his venture, claiming that colonial government officials had failed to support him as promised, while many of his recruits were hired, without his permission, by employers who failed to pay him anything for the indentures they had purchased. Unsuccessful attempts to prosecute these defaulters plunged him into debt, as did his efforts to take action against shippers who assisted some of his recruits to leave the colony illegally. The heads of the recruits were allegedly so turned by the monetary rewards offered by competing employers that many of them broke their engagements and reneged on their debts to Moodie, who commented ruefully that 'the change that took place in their conduct would have been scarcely credible to any one who knew the same men in Scotland'.[8]

While Moodie felt he had been cheated, the success of many of his recruits helped to persuade the British government to launch the short-lived 1820 Settlers' Scheme. Funded by a £50,000 parliamentary grant, it attracted 9,000 applicants, 4,000 of whom were chosen to colonize the district of Albany in the Eastern Cape under leaders who were required to pay a deposit on each recruit. Free passages were provided and 100-acre grants allotted to each male adult, title deeds being granted after three years to those who had remained on their land. Scots, who comprised about 10 per cent of the colonists, included a contingent of Highlanders and a party of twenty-four from Berwickshire who settled near Cradock under Thomas Pringle, a journalist, poet and the colony's first librarian.

Financial constraints, combined with problems in securing enough colonists with practical skills, soon snuffed out the flickering candle of official and public interest in settlement at the Cape. By the time the Albany scheme was under way, the concepts of both emigration society and land company had re-emerged in Canada, where in the 1820s and 1830s they were to have a particularly Scottish focus. Although the weavers' emigration societies examined in the previous chapter were composed of largely urban artisans, it was in order to take up land that they emigrated. The tone of their correspondence suggests that the transition was generally successful and may well have induced chain migration:

> I have got my land and money, and everything as was said. I am just going off
> on Monday to build my house ... I am very sorry, father, that I did not take you
> out with me, and if you had come you would have got the same as I, for if you

do not get into some society, as I got, the expense will be great to take you from Quebec as they impose upon strangers so much, but, coming under government grant, we were well assisted.

Let my brother Robert, James and Andrew know, that I wish they would come here, if they can, as I think this is the country to live in. I will write you as soon as I can, to tell you what to do… I never thought such a country was here, and I wish that I had been some years sooner. You may tell all my friends that they need not come here but for farming; no tradesman is wanted hardly at all …[9]

So wrote William Miller, a member of the Anderston and Rutherglen Society, to his father. His encouragement was echoed by Andrew Boag, of the same emigration society, in a letter to his sister in Scotland. Even though the land where Boag had settled with his wife and father was subsequently described as 'worthless' in an inspection in 1834, he declared, 'I was never so happy in my life. We have no desire to return to Glasgow, for we would have to pay a heavy rent and here we have none. I had to labour 16 or 18 hours a day and could only earn about 16 or 18 shillings a week; here, I can, by labouring about half that time, earn more than I need.'[10] Further endorsement of farming opportunities, as well as of openings in domestic service, was provided by William Gourlay of Greenock, a member of the Muslin Street Emigration Society, who, like Boag, came to Canada aboard the *Brock* in 1820, accompanied by his wife and two children:

We are getting over the winter easier than we expected; we have not that fretful anxiety of mind how to get through, as we had in the old country. We have no landlords nor tax-gatherers here. I am very uneasy to know how all the poor people with you have got through the winter. I wish that many of them were here, for they would be able to make themselves comfortable in a short time. Come out yourselves, also, if it be possible, bring Janet and Mary, for they could get service quite fast; servants are very much wanted and get from three to five dollars a month.[11]

William Davie was equally emphatic in recommending Canada to his children and insisting that no inducement would lure him back to Glasgow:

Were I to get a gift of a free house and shop in Parkhead, and one hundred pounds beside, I would not exchange. I value my present situation more than that. I can see men here, who have not been more than two or three years on their land, who have now three head of cattle, and forty fowls about their doors, and living in the greatest plenty. Now only compare this scene with that of the weavers at home, and you will be able to judge for yourselves. We would all be pleased exceedingly, were every one of you to come to this place; should you do so, I will do every thing in my power to make you comfortable.

Andrew Angus, writing to his parents two months later, also liked the country 'very well', thought anyone willing to work hard for two years 'may look forward to something like independence' and observed that large families were a particular asset. 'If trade is no better in Glasgow, you could not do better than come out,' he concluded. By 1826 James Dobbie and his family were 'still taking well with this country'; the difficulties they had encountered 'are nothing in comparison to your wants in Glasgow; we have always had plenty to eat and drink, and have always had a little to spare'. Urging other relatives to join him, he reported in a subsequent letter, 'All this settlement is striving to do well; were you here, and seeing the improvements that are going on amongst us, you would not believe that we were once Glasgow weavers.'[12]

At the same time as these letters were stimulating continuing Scottish interest in the Ottawa Valley, the Canada Company and the British American Land Company were making strenuous efforts to attract Scots and others to their lands in, respectively, Upper Canada's Huron Tract and Quebec's Eastern Townships. The Canada Company, founded in 1824 by the Scottish novelist John Galt and chartered in 1826, secured a bargain of over 1 million acres of government land, on condition that it improved and populated its huge grant in the area bordering Lakes Huron and Ontario. Within ten years it succeeded in selling half these territories, before the flow of settlers dried up in the wake of the Canadian Rebellion of 1837. Particular inducements were offered to the settler with capital, who was told that he could 'look forward to the enjoyment of comfort and independence as a proprietor of land'.[13] Scots, according to a Company pamphlet, made the most successful settlers, and the Company's wares were heavily touted by shipping agents and newspaper editors.

The Canada Company's efforts in Upper Canada were matched in the Lower Province by the British American Land Company, formed in 1833–4 by a group of Montreal and London businessmen and modelled on the Canada Company. Having purchased nearly 1 million acres of Crown land in Quebec's

Eastern Townships, south of the St Lawrence River, bordering the American states of Vermont and New Hampshire, it attracted large numbers of Outer Hebrideans, initially to the townships of Bury and Lingwick. The first Scots arrived in 1838, when the Earl of Seaforth, proprietor of Lewis, negotiated with the Company to send sixteen families from the island to Bury and Lingwick, as part of a larger Company-sponsored emigration of sixty Highland families. Three years later these pioneers were joined by a further contingent of 223 Lewis crofters and, in subsequent years, by small groups and individual families from the Hebrides and other parts of the Highlands who spread out into the adjacent townships of Winslow, Whitton, Hampden and Marston. 'Oh! young men of Ness, I want you to come here, and be not afraid,' wrote Donald Campbell of Lingwick in 1851, while Donald McLean, writing from the same township, assured his correspondent that 'labourers in this country get bed and board as good as the common gentleman in your country'.[14] By 1881 there were around 4,000 Scots in Compton County,[15] and although many had undoubtedly emigrated unwillingly from a background of poverty, famine and eviction, some were attracted to the expanding Gaelic-speaking community which, according to one Gaelic guidebook, offered abundant water, timber and grazing, as well as a fertile soil, proximity to American markets and a range of social amenities.[16] With the promise of landownership ringing in their ears, it was not surprising that impoverished Highlanders saw emigration to the Eastern Townships as a means to 'better their chance for their families' in a familiar social environment.[17]

'Comfort and independence': attracting the farming emigrant

Canada-bound emigrants did not have to acquire their land from large colonization companies. Crown land could be obtained by free grant before 1827 and by purchase at auction thereafter. A land act in 1841, at the time of the Union of the Canadas, set prices which were meant to be low enough to attract genuine farmers but high enough to deter speculators, who were to be further discouraged by stricter supervision of settlement duties. Free fifty-acre grants, increased in 1853 to 100 acres, were also offered to able-bodied settlers on certain colonization roads, while after Confederation the Dominion Lands Act of 1872 regulated the allocation of land in the new prairie territories. Free quarter-sections (160 acres) were offered to heads of families, or to anyone over twenty-one, on payment of a $10 (approximately £1.80) registration fee. Full legal title was given after three years' actual occupancy and on proof of a certain amount of cultivation; and adjoining quarter-sections could be pre-empted at a price fixed by the government. Homestead grants of 100 or 200 acres of bush land were available in the older provinces, and 'improved' farms could be purchased at prices of £4–£10 per acre. Land could also be acquired from private vendors, many of whom were moving on to new frontiers after clearing and cultivating wild land, from speculators such as Adam Fergusson and James Webster, who sought to establish 'a thriving community of Scottish emigrants' on the 7,367-acre tract they purchased in Southern Ontario,[18] and, by the end of the century, from the Canadian Pacific Railway which desperately needed to generate freight income by populating its vast grant of prairie land.

By no means all the petitions submitted to the Colonial Department in the 1810s came from impoverished weavers and tenant farmers. A significant proportion came from would-be investors, as well as retired army and navy officers on half-pay. They included thirty-five-year-old bachelor Robert Weir of New Kilpatrick, Stirlingshire, who took £300 sterling to Canada when he emigrated in 1817 in response to a newspaper advertisement for government land grants, and Francis Hall from Clackmannan, a married man with a family, who had capital of £500. 'If it be necessary for me to state my reasons for leaving the country,' he wrote, 'they are as follows – being bread [sic] to agricultural pursuits in my younger days I afterwards learned the trade of weaving, but I still prefer agricultural pursuits as most congenial to my health, and think there is no place where I could follow that pursuit with so much advantage as in British America.' The government's Scottish agent, John Campbell, specifically recommended that encouragement be given to Robert Scott, a saddler, 'in hopes of diverting his mind from the United States. For having lived so much abroad he is more indifferent where he settles provided he gets an opportunity of promoting the advantage of his family and improving the capital of which he is possessed.' Another petitioner, James Whyte from Fife, had previously lived in both the United States and the West Indies, but by 1818 wished to devote his energies – and his considerable but unspecified capital – to Upper Canada, where he hoped to farm in partnership with his brother. 'With ample means of carrying his intentions into effect, and being a man ardently devoted to the interests of his king and country [and] already well acquainted with the affairs of America', he petitioned the Colonial Department for a 1,000-acre grant. When John Haldane of Edinburgh promised to invest £2,000 sterling, possibly more, in clearing and cultivating land in Upper Canada, he too requested a large tract of unappropriated Crown territory for himself and his sons, a pledge which the government refused to give in advance of his emigration.[19]

The benefits of Canadian landownership were ceaselessly touted in the Scottish press. The contrast with Scottish farming prospects was a favourite topic of the *Quarterly Journal of Agriculture*, which was the initial forum for the dissemination of Adam Fergusson's *Practical Notes*, but it also frequently reproduced letters from satisfied emigrants to illustrate its case.

> I have not the slightest hesitation in declaring, that it appears to me as plain as the sun at noonday, that a farmer in Scotland, occupying a farm that does not pay him, distressed as he must be, perplexed and degraded, toiling from morning to night, with a degree of mental anxiety and anguish pressing upon his mind ... and yet, after all, quite unable to support his family or better their circumstances in any degree; I say, that a farmer in such circumstances, and continuing so, while so much land lies in Canada to occupy, acts the part of an insane person.[20]

So wrote James Somerville, an emigrant from Edinburgh to the Whitby area, to a friend at home. The 1830s was a time of rapidly rising land prices in Canada, and Somerville's advice to emigrants not to delay was reiterated by a number of other contemporary commentators. 'In a short time, there will be no cheap land to be procured about these parts,' wrote a clergyman, settled near Guelph, to his brother in Scotland in 1832, in a letter quoted in John Mathison's popular pamphlet *Counsel for Emigrants*.[21] Also quoted in this compilation was a letter written in 1833 by a recent emigrant who had just bought 200 acres in Clarence Township, on the banks of the Ottawa River, in which he urged his mother and brothers to join him as soon as possible: 'You can have no idea of the comfort and independence which characterise the circumstances of Upper Canada squires ... The best way for my brothers to lay out their money here is in buying land, which is every year rising in value.'[22] The importance of acting quickly was further emphasized a year later by a correspondent of the cheap and widely read *Chambers' Edinburgh Journal*, who predicted that 'a year or two will make a serious difference in the purchase money'.[23]

Chambers' Edinburgh Journal consistently sang the praises of Canadian farming. Shortly after it first appeared in 1832, it published a glowing review of Martin Doyle's guidebook, *Hints on Emigration to Upper Canada*:

Just fancy yourselves possessed of *real property*, on such terms – no yearly ten-
antcy [*sic*] – no terminable leases to breed *interminable* jealousies at the change
of occupants, but pure fee simple – no rent to pay – after labouring here for a
shilling, or tenpence, or eightpence, or sixpence, a day. What a happy change
would this be, and how irresistible the temptation to make the experiment! And
only think of the advantage of working a rich, maiden soil, that will yield abun-
dantly, instead of ploughing or digging a worn-out one at home, without
manure to *mend* it, and which, without abundance of it, will not yield a crop sufficient to pay its labour.[24]

Forty years later, it was still promoting Canadian land settlement, when it
reminded readers that 'the inducements to immigrate to Canada are not
simply good wages and good living among kindred people, under the same
flag, in a naturally rich country, possessing a pleasant and healthy climate, but
the confident prospect that the poorest may have of becoming a possessor of
the soil, earning competence for himself, and comfortably settling his children'.[25] The promise of independence and modest prosperity through landownership was also regularly aired in the editorial, correspondence and
advertising columns of Scottish newspapers, and in the 1880s in the Napier
Commission Report's publication of the formulaic and somewhat disingenuous promotional letters of Benbecula crofters who in 1883 had been sent by
Lady Emily Cathcart to establish a prairie colony near Wapella. One
Hebridean wrote home:

> Dear brother, I am very sorry indeed that you have not all come out with me. If
> you, and Donald, and Morag had come, we would have got three homesteads,
> and by taking one pre-emption we would have a whole section to ourselves; we
> would be settled together, and would be as happy as the day is long … Dear
> brother, it makes my heart sore to think of the way you two are working at
> home, and having so little thanks or comfort for it, when we might have been
> here very well and happy if you had come.[26]

So wrote William McPherson in June 1883. His sentiments were echoed by
Lachlan McPherson, who claimed that 'everything bad that we were hearing
before we left was all lies'. After observing that 'the moskittes was pretty bad last
month, but not much worse than the mitches when they are bad at home', he
went on to predict that the settlement would be full within a year and hoped that

his brothers would join him, since 'they would do better here in one year than three at home'.[27]

While Canada clearly led the field in the volume and diversity of encouragement offered to agricultural emigrants from Scotland, it did not have a monopoly on such inducements. The attractions of farming in the United States, which absorbed more Scots than any other destination in the nineteenth century, were advertised in many guidebooks and newspapers, and in 1837 a correspondent of *Chambers' Edinburgh Journal* reminded readers that American land, particularly in Michigan, was now cheaper and more easily obtainable than that in Canada.[28] As the frontier moved steadily westwards, emigrants in the years before the Civil War were encouraged to penetrate further into the country, beyond Pennsylvania and Ohio, to Indiana, Illinois, Wisconsin and Iowa, as well as Michigan, often to specific tracts of land which were offered for sale. After 1862, when the Homestead Act allowed any family head who had taken out American citizenship to claim 160 acres of surveyed public land free on condition that he paid a registration fee and lived on his grant continuously for five years, the spotlight of encouragement fell increasingly on the Midwestern prairie states of Oklahoma, Kansas, Nebraska and the Dakotas, along with Texas and the Pacific North-West. Editors engaged the attention of Scottish readers not only by publishing straightforward advertisements but also by drawing attention to the correspondence of successful emigrant farmers. *Counsel for Emigrants,* for instance, which gave impartial coverage to both Canada and the United States, quoted from the letter of a settler in Illinois who declared in 1834 that a family man would be delighted at the prospects for his children in a country where they could easily become owners of the soil they cultivated, and where they could enjoy the 'certain prospect of wealth and respectability, if they were industrious and economical'.[29]

Encouragement to farmers to emigrate to Australia was more sporadic and qualified by warnings of heat, drought, disease, widespread speculation and overblown land prices. Yet the prospectus of the Australian Company of Edinburgh and Leith, founded in 1822, claimed that 'the fertility of the soil' and 'the salubrity of the climate', along with the abundance of mineral resources and navigable waterways, 'make Australia the most suitable of all our Colonies for the reception of British settlers'. Emigrants who wished to take advantage of these facilities during the Company's ten-year existence had to be men of means, for the cost of passage from Leith ranged from twenty-four guineas steerage to fifty guineas cabin, although limited assistance was provided to

3. The Caledonian Gathering, Melbourne, 1 February 1892, from Illustrated Australian News

artisans.[30] During this period those with over £500 capital were encouraged to emigrate to Van Diemen's Land 'on account of its fertility and its general respectability'; it was, according to the *Quarterly Journal of Agriculture*, a place where 'the man who can muster a few hundreds, and who is fond of agricultural pursuits and rural pleasures' could be enabled, within a few years, 'to transmit to his family an estate sufficient for the subsistence of many generations'.[31] Those of more modest means might have to wait until the bounty schemes of the late 1830s brought the cost of passage within their reach, although even in that period the unassisted movement from Scotland was proportionately greater than that from England or Ireland. As we have seen, it was through assisted passages that large numbers of impoverished Highlanders were brought to Australia in the 1830s and 1850s. Some subsequently contrasted Scottish poverty and Australian prosperity in a way which the Highland and Island Emigration Society used to justify its policy, and which may also have encouraged further emigration. 'It is no profit to me to tell you lies,' wrote one satisfied emigrant. 'I heard at home good accounts of Australia; but I never believed it till I saw it with my own eyes ... They do not care about a sovereign here more than you of a penny at home.'[32]

Would-be emigrants could also seek advice from a growing library of guidebooks, including those produced by the prolific pen of Dr John Dunmore Lang, the pugnacious Greenock-born cleric who, between his own emigration in 1823 and his death in 1878, encouraged hundreds of Scots to follow his example and used the colonial bounty scheme to introduce settlers to his brother Andrew's extensive property in the Hunter Valley. New Zealand too was well promoted in guidebooks, newspapers and journals after it became a British colony in 1840. 'Almost every man who has been here eight months has a piece of land in the town that costs £30 or £40,' wrote Paisley emigrant James McDonald from Wellington in 1842.[33] 'A very healthy country ... the soil is splendid,' reported Robert Donald, a gardener from Aberdeen, also of Wellington, in 1851,[34] and although by the 1860s and 1870s early enthusiasm was giving way to warnings of high living costs and poor prospects in a country where 'farming is carried on in a very careless manner',[35] some correspondents remained unequivocal in their encouragement:

Father could get land cheap, and it costs nothing to keep the cattle. Here there are no byres, and the beasts are out all winter. There are stables for the working-horses; the rest are out all winter. Wood is cheap, and father could build very

nice wooden houses. What splendid potatoes there are here, and peas and cab-
bages grow with no trouble, and very little manure. I am surprised at the easy
way the men work. The food they get is also something very superior to what
they have, for the most part, been accustomed to at home.[36]

'A farm of one's own' : the lure of the land

This varied catalogue of commendation did not fall on deaf ears, particularly
when the encouragement was contained in a private letter or verbal encouragement. In the 1830s and 1840s the neighbouring counties of Ashland, Richland
and Huron in Ohio saw an influx of land-seeking Scots significant enough to
have a 'powerful influence' on the area's development. Most were 'relatives,
friends and neighbours' from a cluster of adjacent parishes in west Aberdeenshire, several of whom emigrated in 1836 and 1837 aboard the timber ship *Arkwright* from Aberdeen to New York. They included George Beattie, who
arrived from Insch in 1837 with his wife, seven children and a £50 loan from
Joseph Beattie, presumably his brother, 'to enable him to purchase land in
America'. Alexander Thom, an estate foreman who also came from Insch in
1837, having borrowed money to finance his family's passage, took up share
farming in Huron County, where he was joined several years later by his
brother. The Scottish connections were perpetuated through intermarriage, but
also extended geographically when a number of the Ohio settlers and their offspring moved west to Cedar and Poweshiek Counties, Iowa, generally to take
up larger farms.[37] On the other side of the world, the Galbraith family was in
1881 attracted out from Glasgow to the Bay of Plenty in New Zealand's North
Island by the well-advertised settlement scheme of the Irish emigrant and speculator, George Vesey Stewart. They settled in Te Puke, where John Cameron
Galbraith established and ran the Pioneer Store for many years, before settling
on a dairy farm at Papamoa. As the area steadily filled up, he developed a thriving business with the neighbouring farmers, holding monthly cattle auctions as
well as supplying his customers with hardware, groceries and clothing. He
wrote regularly to his adoptive father, praising the climate, business opportunities and deferred-payment system for the acquisition of land, and before the
year was out had succeeded in persuading him that the rest of the family should
also emigrate:

The climate of New Zealand is something superb. I would not go home supposing anyone was to offer me £500 a year. The air is so nice and you appear to be so free, not caring for anyone and have not the same appearance to keep up. No, I don't think anything would tempt me to change home ... [Mother] longs till you and the rest come out and I think you should come out as soon as possible ... You must push out here to get on and if you do so, and don't liquor, you are bound to succeed.[38]

Among the many examples of Scottish emigrants who purchased Crown land in Canada, the experience of the Fletcher and Farquharson families from Aberdeenshire demonstrates the close correlation between opportunities at home and abroad, as well as the relative affluence of the emigrants and, as in Ohio and Iowa, the importance of chain migration. In 1836 John Fletcher exchanged his life as a schoolteacher in Glengairn and Brechin for that of a frontier farmer in Tilbury East, Ontario, where in 1840 he purchased a bush farm. By his death in 1873 he had increased his holding to almost 1,000 acres, specializing in horse-rearing, although he continued to teach, and also served as township clerk. On two occasions he made further investments in wild land, on behalf of his son, James, and brother-in-law, Charles Farquharson, remaining convinced that such land offered the best bargain to the hard-working emigrant. In 1842 he was joined from Scotland by his brother William, who also bought land in Tilbury East, where he lived as a farmer and 'bushman' until 1847. For the next five years he too worked as a schoolmaster, after which he entered the Presbyterian ministry, holding charges in Ontario and Manitoba. His nephew John from Tilbury East joined him in 1870 in Manitoba, where both men took up homesteads. William Fletcher, however, had been investigating farming opportunities across the border, in Iowa and Nebraska, and in 1872 he settled in the latter state, where he died sixteen years later. In 1879 he was joined there by another nephew, George, son of his brother David, who had emigrated to Tilbury East in 1866 to buy his brother William's original bush farm.

When David Fletcher emigrated to Ontario in 1866, he did so as part of a contingent of twenty-six from the parish of Logie Coldstone in Aberdeenshire. He and his brother-in-law, Charles Farquharson, are the prime examples, among the members of the two emigrant families, whose decision to go to Canada was precipitated by difficulties in farming at home. Throughout the 1840s and 1850s David Fletcher maintained a correspondence with his brothers, and several times sought their advice on the propriety of emigrating. In April 1845, with two years of his lease still to run, and the prospect of a rent increase thereafter, he expressed doubts about Canada on the grounds 'that money is scarce, and the dealing mostly in barter', but expected that William would in due time 'tell us how we should do'.[39] Four years later local prices for cattle and grain were depressed, with little hope of improvement. David wrote to his brother John how times were not good for farmers at home, 'for what we have to sell is very cheap, and what we buy is dear, and servants fees is very high'. He asked his advice on purchasing land in Canada, and predicted that other emigrants would follow their example, given the current economic crisis:

> If times be with you as I expect they are, I expect to go out with the St. Lawrence Ship in the Spring. I expect to get some pleasing accounts from you before that time. I would like to know [for] what I might buy a farm about 30 or 40 acres clear for the plough, as you have had experience of that … Our parents no doubt will be unwilling to let us go, but we can see little prospects at home.[40]

David had recently married Rebecca McCombie, also of Logie Coldstone, and she too was eager to emigrate. His wife's sister Margaret had likewise expressed interest in accompanying them if John and William Fletcher gave a good account of prospects in Canada. David Fletcher's plan to emigrate in 1850 was thwarted, but his intentions were not altered. Charles Farquharson wrote to his brother-in-law in January 1851, 'David is determined to go out to you, as he is free from any ingagement here.' He continued in a postscript, 'write as soon as you receive this, as David is now very ancious about going. Your father is not willin for David to go to America if he would be content to stop at home; but as he cannot be satisfied here, I think it is best for him to go.'[41] James Fletcher senior recognized the limited prospects in Scotland and wrote frequently to John and William about the hard times in farming at home; and although in 1846 he took a new lease of his farm of Balgrennie, the terms were unfavourable.

Charles Farquharson himself had more qualms about emigrating. His life as a tenant farmer at Parks of Coldstone was blighted by high-handed estate management and the fear of increased rentals, with no compensation for the improvements made by tenants. John Fletcher, aware of these difficulties, repeatedly highlighted the favourable openings for farming in Canada, and in 1861 purchased a bush farm in Tilbury East as an investment for Charles, in case he should decide to emigrate. 'We can live easy here and are healthy generally but do not make much money,' he wrote at that time.[42] Writing again in March 1865 as the expiry date of Charles's lease drew near, he repeated his view that 'this is a superior country for every man that has to work for his living as all of you have'. But at the same time he tempered enthusiasm with caution. 'What I have always studied to prevent is that no one should have too high an opinion as it causes disappointment,' he added, explaining again in his next letter in July that he had deliberately not given unequivocal encouragement to emigrate because it 'would not be to your advantage to have too high hopes of the country'. By then, however, he was convinced that it would clearly be to Charles's and David's advantage to come to Canada. Many people who had come out with nothing had prospered, 'so if you have enough to pay your passage fear nothing. If spared I can help you the first year; afterwards if your family are in health you can do well enough – This is a poor man's country.'[43] Having still received no word from the indecisive Charles, he wrote again in December, urging him to make known his plans, so that if he were to come out a house and some ground could be prepared in readiness for his arrival.

As his lease neared its end, Charles Farquharson was under growing pressure. The part of the Invercauld estate in which his farm was located had recently been sold at a high valuation to an English lawyer, and on 17 April 1865 Farquharson wrote to John Fletcher:

> The present here is a time of great anxiety. We have got a new Laird. Invercald [sic] has sold all his land in Cromar, so that we have new folks to deal with. The land is sold very dear, and our farms are all valued very high. Mine is valued at 150 pounds, a rise on the present rent of about 20 pounds in the year; and I am determined not to give that at any rate, and I do not expect to get it cheaper, so that I may say we have almost made up our minds for Canada, although I have not said so as yet. But the next letter I send you, which I expect will be in the course of three or four months, I think I will be able to say determinedly whether or no.

According to his son Donald, the idea of settling on their Canadian investment, 'free from rent and expiring leases',[44] was an attractive one; yet, when his father wrote to Fletcher again on 3 July, he still had not quite made up his mind – the new laird was not going to visit his estate until August and he expected to reach his decision then. He was, however, moving more clearly in the direction of emigration, for, as he told John, 'I have been reading over your letters and William's, and I am quite satisfied that the chances of comfortable and independent livelihood is better with you than with us.'

We learn from Donald Farquharson's later memoir the probable cause of his father's equivocation, which had to do more with domestic circumstances than his brother-in-law's reservations:

> Mother was very unwilling to cut herself off from touch with her sole surviving sister and the scenes and surroundings of her youth, and father therefore did his best to find another farm in the county that would suit. One such appeared to be the farm of 'The Knock' … The owner of this farm was the Prince of Wales, the future Edward the Seventh. Dr Robertson, the Prince's Factor, would fain have favoured my father, whom he well knew, but a wealthy competitor had offered a higher rent than had my father, which, when both were submitted to the Prince, was by him naturally accepted…
>
> At that time, land hunger in Scotland was exceedingly acute, and the acquirement of a suitable farm extremely difficult, and generally called for a lengthened period of waiting, such as none of us was disposed to put in exercise. So, at once arrangements were made for a displenish sale of goods and chattels, and our passages were booked for the Port of Quebec and the town of Chatham in Upper Canada.[45]

The Farquharsons sailed from Glasgow on 6 June 1866, on the SS *St Andrew*, assisted and accompanied by William Fletcher, who kept the promise he had made to Charles in a letter six years earlier:

> I have always liked Canada and have never wished to be back in Scotland to live, but would enjoy a short visit very much; and although I am much pleased to hear of you all doing well in Scotland, I would welcome you all to Canada; and if you resolve to come, send me word and I will go home to help you pack your baggage, tell you what to bring, and accompany you across the ocean, and introduce you to many kind friends here.[46]

The striking connection between Upper Deeside and Tilbury East, which reached its climax in 1866 but was evident for many years before and after that date, was attributable not only to the way in which the difficulties of tenant farming in Scotland were set against the opportunities for landownership in Canada but also to the assurance that these opportunities could be enjoyed in a familiar and welcoming environment. John Fletcher himself had been drawn to Tilbury East by the proximity of the Coutts family, earlier emigrants from

Deeside, and the steady creation of a 'colony' of Deesiders in that vicinity encouraged even the hesitant and fearful that emigration was not a step into the utterly unknown.

The Scottish communities in the Eastern Townships and at Tilbury East were created through land company activities and the purchase of Crown land respectively. Similar colonies were established when land was purchased from speculators like Adam Fergusson, who had a specific interest in Scottish settlers. Following his exploratory tour of Canada and the United States in 1831, Fergusson emigrated with his family and business partner, lawyer James Webster, in 1833, founding the town of Fergus in Nichol Township, and using his guidebook to encourage Scottish settlement in the area. A number of wealthy Scottish emigrants did invest, most of them coming from Perthshire and the southern Lowlands. But Fergusson's second wife belonged to Aberdeen, a connection which may have helped to bring about the establishment of an explicitly Aberdonian settlement in the vicinity of Fergus in the 1830s. First to arrive, in 1834, were four friends who, with their families, made up a party of fourteen on the Aberdeen timber ship the *Sir William Wallace* and duly bought 100- and 200-acre plots in Fergus at $4 (88p) per acre. One of their number, George Skene from Fyvie, whose main reason for emigrating had been his desire to purchase, rather than simply rent, land, was particularly impressed with the 'independent spirit' of the pioneer settlers in Nichol Township, and wrote approvingly in a letter home that 'Whitsunday and Martinmas are words that are not in use here'.[47]

Meanwhile, back in Aberdeen, Adam Fergusson's writings, along with the publication of favourable correspondence and articles about emigration in the press, had attracted the attention of a group of friends who for some time had been meeting together to debate the pros and cons of emigration.

> They were well educated, intelligent, respectable people, with sufficient means to enable them to emigrate comfortably and to purchase land. They were led to think by the glowing accounts sent home by those whose interest it was to sell land that if they once owned a few hundred acres of land in Canada they must needs be independent, and they finally resolved to send one of their number to see, judge and purchase a block of land, one direction being that there must be church and school within reasonable distance.[48]

George Elmslie, a merchant in Aberdeen, was chosen as the pioneer who would seek a suitable location for the establishment of an 'Aberdeenshire colony'. He left Scotland on 30 June 1834, with instructions to make the purchase from Adam Fergusson if the land matched up to his glowing accounts of it. In Toronto he joined forces with an old friend from home, Alexander Watt, and the two men travelled to Fergus in search of land.

By autumn 1834, however, Fergusson's canvassing had worked so well that there was not a large enough block left for Elmslie and Watt to purchase. But, liking the location, they managed to find suitable land about two miles further down the Irvine River, at Elora. Elmslie recorded his impressions in his diary:

> I was now satisfied. We had found a block suitable in all respects for our pro-
> jected colony. The quality of the soil, as indicated by the trees and their size, was
> equal to any we had seen; watered in such a manner as we had nowhere seen; the
> streams living, clear, rapid, and the chief of them on a limestone bed, and there-
> fore healthy; the society was superior to what we could have anticipated – the
> newer settlers almost entirely Scotch, the older, around and in the neighbour-
> hood of Elora, respectable, intelligent Englishmen.[49]

Elmslie and Watt returned to Toronto, where Elmslie negotiated with the vendor for the purchase of 1,200 acres at Elora. Watt was inclined to favour the township of Whitby, where settlement was further advanced and where several of his old acquaintances were located, but he was persuaded by his recently arrived sisters and brother-in-law to follow Elmslie's lead, and he duly purchased 800 acres at Elora.

Having completed the negotiations, Elmslie moved to Nichol, sent home word of his purchase and began to clear the sites of his own home and those of his friends who were to join him later. In one of his five letters which appeared in the third edition of *Counsel for Emigrants*, he referred to the proximity of 'a knot of Scotch, many of them from Aberdeenshire', including George Wilson, formerly an advocate in Aberdeen, and the Fyvie emigrants, George Skene and James Duguid.[50] Just as planned, in spring 1835 a party of around twenty emigrants came out from Aberdeen to take up the holdings which Elmslie had bought on their behalf, in a settlement which was named 'Bon Accord', after the motto on the coat of arms of their native city. They included Robert Melvine (who was to die of tuberculosis within six months), his wife, child and two servants; Peter Brown, his wife, six children and maid; and John Davidson, a carpenter, whose subsequent articles about Canadian bush life were published in the Aberdeen press. Two further contingents followed in the same year, including two of Elmslie's sisters, as well as Alexander Dingwall-Fordyce, a wealthy Aberdeen businessman and acquaintance of Adam Fergusson, who took up a 600-acre farm in the township, and David Chalmers of Aberdeen, who purchased 1,000 acres.

The exodus continued unabated throughout the 1830s, with most of the emigrants sailing on timber ships from Aberdeen to Quebec. Other north-east Scots made their way to Nichol Township after initially stopping elsewhere in Upper Canada. George Barron, for instance, had emigrated from New Deer some years before he arrived in Bon Accord. He had saved his fare out of his wages as a farm worker, taking the precaution of saving enough extra money to take him back to Scotland if he did not like Canada. He had then gained valuable experience of Canadian farming techniques in the older settlements around Whitby before moving to the still-uncleared territory at Bon Accord in 1835. William Tytler from Kincardine O'Neil, who emigrated in 1835, had a look around various settlements before deciding to locate in Bon Accord. Having made that decision, he then advised all his friends and relatives to follow his example, which they did, for among the 1836 arrivals were his two brothers, sister and brother-in-law. Travelling on the same ship as Tytler was the Hay family from Slains, who briefly took up farming in Seymour township, Northumberland County, before Tytler persuaded them to move to Bon Accord, where they had several acquaintances. There they were joined in 1836 by their former neighbours from Slains, Robert Cromar, his father and sister, who, like the Hays, lodged temporarily with the widow of Robert Melvine, to whom they were related.

Although Bon Accord's pioneer settlers came from a variety of occupations at home, most intended to take up farming, even if they combined it with a trade or profession – George Elmslie, for instance, like John Fletcher, was both a farmer and a schoolteacher. Many brought large families with them, and their emigration was clearly provoked not only by their own desire for land but also by a determination to secure a better future for their children. Surviving letters to the pioneers from relatives who had remained in Scotland show that they too were concerned about the deleterious effects of agricultural changes at home, and the pros and cons of farming in Canada. In June 1836 William Beattie of Broomhill, Strathdon, wrote to his brother George at Nichol, complaining about rising rents and asking him to look out for a partially cleared farm in his neighbourhood. A year later, after a bad harvest and late spring, William Beattie junior wrote to his uncle, remarking on the 'streams of emigrants going to America this year', while his brother John, writing four months later, reiterated the complaints about crop failures and problems with his father's lease:

> We are losing greatly every year, and we have sent this letter to you to let you know how things are going on, and as soon as you receive it you will be as good as write us immediately by post, to let us know your fair and candid opinion whether you think it best for us to go to you or stop where we are. I have told you what way we are here and you know yourself what sort of prospects there is for us with you ... My Father wants to know what a farm of 100 acres with 6 or 7 acres clear could be bought at in Nichol, & he also wants to know the value of wild land all together without any clearance upon it.[51]

It was presumably on the basis of George Beattie's positive advice that William and Elizabeth Beattie and their two sons emigrated to Nichol in 1839.

Money and connections

Most of those who settled at Bon Accord and Tilbury East viewed emigration as a positive investment of their capital and talents. None was impoverished, and several were men of some means who could afford not only to pay their own passages but also to purchase farms on arrival, with no need to seek preliminary wage labour. Some, like George Elmslie, Alexander Watt and Alexander Dingwall-Fordyce, employed contractors to clear sections of their substantial properties, while others came to take up lands which their parents had purchased on their behalf. Confirmation that much emigration was not a flight of the poor is found in guidebooks, press correspondence and advertisements, which often took it for granted that readers had the wherewithal to invest in land. 'For the matter of a few hundreds of pounds', the Chambers brothers reported in 1834, farmers could obtain fertile lands in Britain's colonies or in the United States 'which, in a short time, by active exertion, will repay all that is expended upon them, and remain a permanent and valuable freehold for their family'. Even £100, invested by parents on behalf of their sons in North America, 'would make them proprietors of farms, and stock them sufficiently with all that is necessary for thriving and becoming healthy'.[52] Readers were regularly reminded that a sum equivalent to a year's rent at home could buy an improved property in Canada, while the lamentations of those who claimed that Scotland was losing its most enterprising farmers and farm servants suggests that the problem was not lack of savings in the rural community but an inability to invest those savings profitably at home.

Further corroborative evidence of the relative prosperity of many Scottish settlers is found in reports of the departure and arrival of shiploads of emigrants, particularly in Alexander Buchanan's reports of emigrant vessels arriving at Quebec. 'They are all in good circumstances, and are amply provided with means to proceed to their destination,' he observed of two shiploads from Aberdeen and Hull in July 1840, while two vessels from Glasgow, which arrived in August 1856, brought 'respectable farmers and agriculturists, generally in comfortable circumstances', all of whom emigrated 'to join friends'. His reports frequently bracketed English and Scots emigrants together as settlers of a 'superior class', 'intelligent' and 'respectable in appearance', who were 'in comfortable circumstances, and intend to enter at once upon the occupation of land'.[53]

Buchanan's comments on the frequency with which emigrants came out to join friends and family, often with the aid of remittances or prepaid tickets, also remind us of another crucial catalyst in chain emigration, the provision of practical, pecuniary assistance from pioneer emigrants to those who had initially remained at home. The significance of this phenomenon was reinforced by a report in the *Illustrated London News* in April 1857 which, after commenting on the spring sailing from north-east Scotland to Canada of about 1,500 emigrants, mainly young, newly married agricultural labourers, observed that 'large sums of money continue to be received from settlers in Upper Canada, who had previously gone out' and predicted that 'before many years, few agricultural labourers will be left at home'.[54] Eight months earlier, James Thompson, who had emigrated from Aboyne in 1844 and worked at his trade as a baker in Canada and the United States until he had earned enough money to buy a 150-acre farm in Ontario, funded the passages of his elderly father, his sister and two children of a deceased sister. Until then he had been maintaining them in Scotland, a responsibility which increased in 1855 when his father lost his job as bridgekeeper to the Marquis of Huntly following his employer's bankruptcy. Long aware of his family's precarious finances, James had first suggested in 1849 that his father and his brother Sandy might emigrate. In 1851 he noted that Sandy's wage as a ploughman was insufficient to maintain a family and during a visit home in 1852 he gave him some money towards his passage to Canada, promising also that 'if he decides on coming here I shall see that he has a house to go in to on arrival'.[55] Sandy, however, did not take good care of money. By

May 1854 he had spent up to £20 of the remittance, and although his father banked subsequent sums sent by James, Sandy was not included in the family party that joined James Thompson and his wife at Edwardsburgh in 1856.

Some Highlanders too seem to have possessed funds, foresight and the support of friends. The 200 Long Island emigrants whose departure from Tobermory in 1835 was witnessed by Lord Teignmouth had, he claimed, 'received no assistance in the prosecution of their undertaking from any quarter; were in high spirits, and much encouraged by the accounts which they had received from their friends who had preceded them'. Highland emigrants, he continued, 'generally carry out sufficient capital to enable them to settle; are located on their arrival, whether in Canada or in the United States, usually among their own kindred or former neighbours, who have paved the way for them; or enjoy the benefit of arrangements framed for their accommodation by government or by societies'.[56] Even during the famine, the picture was not entirely negative, as middling crofters, particularly from Argyllshire, continued to finance their relocation through the sale of cattle and other assets. Over 300 well-clothed and provisioned emigrants from Islay and Kintyre who sailed from Glasgow to Quebec in July 1847 had, according to the *North British Daily Mail*, 'paid for their passage money', while evidence to the Napier Commission thirty-six years later suggested that a total of 1,200 unassisted emigrants had left Islay for North America and Australia between 1841 and 1851.[57] In 1848 the *Scotsman* reported that of the 5,165 steerage and 277 cabin passengers – mainly west Highlanders – who had left Glasgow and Greenock in the first six months of that year, 'a good number ... were in possession of considerable sums of money and were well supplied with clothes and provisions for the voyage', while a shipload of Highlanders who sailed from Ardrossan around the same time had taken 'a good quantity of property'.[58] More than three decades later newly arrived settlers at Wapella reminded their correspondents in the Hebrides that emigrants to the prairies should have £100 on arrival 'for their farm implements and house furniture'.[59]

Opportunities for investment

Most Scottish emigrants were people of modest ambitions and modest achievements. A significant minority, however, saw in the vast open spaces of the Antipodes or the Americas major investment opportunities which, although often connected with land, went far beyond the limited horizons of a family farm. In 1825, the year before Britain granted recognition to the Republic of Argentina, John and William Parish Robertson, two brothers from Kelso, signed a colonization contract with the Argentine government under which they promised to introduce at least 200 European families to land which the government would grant in perpetuity. By May 1825 they had recruited 220 Border Scots, who within three years established a thriving agricultural and cattle-raising colony at Monte Grande near Buenos Aires before the settlement fell victim to the unstable economic and political environment of the new republic. A generation later, in New Zealand's South Island, Scots were disproportionately represented among the runholders, particularly in Otago, but also in Canterbury and Hawkes Bay. Holdings ranged from over 315,000 acres to a few hundred acres, and Scots were generally employed as shepherds and station managers. While some of these investors had come straight from Scotland, others had cut their sheep-farming teeth in Australia, where, as Eric Richards has noted, 'corporate enterprise from Scotland in pastoral pioneering was a phenomenon of the middle years of the century'.[60]

Prominent among landed entrepreneurs in Australia were three of the 'surplus younger sons' of William Leslie, laird of the estate of Warthill in the parish of Old Rayne in Aberdeenshire. Their sheep-farming investments not only lined their own pockets but also brought about the emigration of several of their father's tenants, who were attracted overseas by the prospect of lucrative employment with employers who were already known to them. The Leslies' interest in Australia began in 1805 when their uncle, Walter Davidson, went from Aberdeenshire to take up a 2,000-acre land grant in New South Wales. Although he did not remain permanently in the colony, he developed extensive business interests there, and when he required an overseer for his pastoral estates, he offered the job to his nephew. Thus it was that in 1834 nineteen-year-old Patrick Leslie was sent out to New South Wales. His objective, in the words of his uncle, was 'to form a Nucleus for a grand Leslie family property' on which he would subsequently be joined by his brothers Walter and George. 'I do predict,' wrote the optimistic Davidson to the Leslies' father, William, 'that the Warthill property, good and solid as it is, will be nothing to your family's Australian property twenty years hence if these 3 dear Youths' lives be but mercifully spared.'[61]

Until such time as his younger brothers could be sent out, Patrick was instructed to assess the viability of Davidson's proposal. He was first taught the art of sheep management by settlers from Devon, the Macarthurs of Vineyard,

near Sydney, before being sent in 1836 to manage Davidson's property at Collaroi on the Krui River. Patrick warned his parents against encouraging casual
acquaintances to come to Australia on his recommendation but he shared his
uncle's optimism about the colony's prospects and suggested that his youngest
brother, Tom, should also be 'broken in' for emigration:

> He must push his fortune some way in the world and as well he does here when
> he will have his three brothers and also much better scope & many more advan-
> tages than in any other part of the world that I know of. By the time he is old
> enough to come out I will be an *Old hand* in the Colony and can take him well
> under my wing.[62]

Tom Leslie did not in fact go to New South Wales, but Walter and George
arrived in March 1839. They were less impressed than Patrick with the drought-
ridden colony's prospects, George describing New South Wales to his parents
within four months of landing as 'a very nice agreeable country for a person to
stay a few years in but to *settle* ultimately in it *would never enter my head*'.[63]
George never subsequently disguised his intention to make money in Australia
in order to spend it in Britain, a sentiment that was shared by Walter, who told
his sister that he 'should not like to remain in this country after having made
myself independent for whatever people say there is neither society nor amusement like what there is at home'.[64]

Perhaps the younger brothers' reservations were attributable partly to a
bitter quarrel that had broken out between Patrick and his uncle as a result of
Patrick's allegedly inefficient accounting and general mismanagement of the
estate. Resigning his position at Collaroi in the very month that his brothers
arrived in Australia, Patrick began to look for a property where they could farm
independently. In a long letter to his father two months later, he complained of
Davidson's shabby treatment of him and justified his own conduct, before out-
lining the brothers' future plans:

> We mean to be proprietors of cattle and horses only connected with agriculture
> and not to have sheep for I am convinced that sheep will not pay now as they
> used to do for we have to hire all our men & sheep farming requires such a very
> great number of hands besides cattle & horses. We mean to form our stations to
> the northward on a large river shed which will bring us near Sydney by means of
> water carriage ... We will not have to purchase our Land there for a length of

time very likely but I may find it advisable to purchase one section on which to build & commence farming operations. Now we are to go into partnership in this way I find one half the Stock of Cattle & of mares & pay one half the Expenses of everything connected with the concern. W. & G. find the other half of the stock & pay the other half of the expenses between them & of course one half the profit is mine & the other half between W. & G. We were obliged to do it in this way as W. & G. could not afford to get each the same quality of stock I have. If they could have done so it would have made the Expenses fall lighter on me however it was impossible unless they borrowed money which I would not do on any account. We have got between 30 and 40 breeding mares and I mean to maintain about 50 or 60 if we can – If we find the country where we go is fit for sheep or so open as to allow of keeping a very large number of sheep in a flock so as to diminish the number of shepherds we might get some sheep also but that must be determined when we see what sort the country is. I intend to rent a farm somewhere in this part of the country and I will keep one horse stock and 40–50 of the best of our cows there to breed bulls for the herd.[65]

The Leslies were to be accompanied on their expedition by Ernest Elphinstone Dalrymple, whose father's estate of Logie bordered the Leslie estate in Aberdeenshire. According to Patrick, Ernest, who had come to Australia with George and Walter, 'tells me his funds & I will put him in the way of investing them best'. While Ernest was 'a very nice companion' who was likely to make a good settler, Patrick Leslie was less complimentary about Ernest's inexperienced and domineering brother Alastair, who had also come to Australia, but who he hoped would settle some distance away, 'for I am determined my Brothers & him should not be associated'.

Patrick's letter consisted largely of detailed instructions regarding the shipment of workers and, to a lesser extent, stock from home. The unsupervised nature of work on the vast cattle and sheep farms rendered it imperative that a proprietor employ servants on whom he could rely, but the Leslies and their acquaintances were dissatisfied with the existing channels of supply, not so much convicts as bounty emigrants, whom Patrick condemned as 'the sweepings of the Parishes they come from'.[66] Perhaps he was also prompted by the example of Hugh Gordon, another emigrant acquaintance whose family estate of Manar also bordered Warthill, who had already acquired some Scottish emigrants as his servants. At any rate, rather than engage in the lottery of acquiring labourers under the bounty schemes, Patrick asked his father to send out six handpicked men from his own estate – a carpenter, a blacksmith, two stockmen and 'two complete servants' who were particularly skilled with horses – promising to pay them the colony's going rates of £18 to £25 a year. While he would prefer the carpenter and blacksmith to be single, the stockmen and horsemen should be married, especially if their wives could work as dairymaids and harvesters. 'If they were newly married & no children so much the better but on no account would I take more than one child to each couple & if they have none so much the better,' he added. Patrick even had potential recruits in mind:

> W. & G. talked of Adam Singer's second son as wishing to come out. Perhaps he would make one of the farm servants if he is old enough. You may also remember a lad Willie Lyon who was once hind at Warthill and a capital worker. W. & G. say he was at Middleton of Blackford when they left. If he were to get married he might be one of the farm servants. I daresay he could soon find a wife & they then if married for the occasion would not have any children when they arrived – however you my dear Father are a better judge of who are the best men to come out & if you will do so we will be very much obliged but I certainly would like people from Warthill as they should be attached to us very likely. Now I think I have said all I remember about the men & you can tell them if they choose to come out to me I will hire them & they will only have to let me know through you when I am to expect them. If Wm. Lyon is not married I would just as soon have him.[67]

Correspondence from Scotland clearly reflects the way in which the Leslie brothers stimulated emigration from their home area to New South Wales, through informal networks and word-of-mouth encouragement in which their parents played an integral part. In August 1840 William Leslie responded to his son's request by shipping out an Aberdeenshire bull and two cows under the charge of James Fletcher of Culsalmond, a 'steady active young fellow' who had first visited the Warthill estate four months earlier 'to ask the best mode for getting out to New South Wales'. Although the bull died while crossing the Bay of Biscay, Fletcher, who was 'well recommended as a good servant', was retained by the Leslies when he arrived in Australia.[68] Meanwhile, a former Warthill ploughman, Sandy Wright, was by August 1840 earning £40 a year as overseer on Patrick's rented farm at Dunheved near Penrith, after Jane Leslie had taken him under her wing. Having told her sons that Wright looked to them 'for advice and protection till some situation can be found for him', she wrote again in 1839, in a letter to Walter carried out by Wright himself. He had, she explained, used up all his cash to fit himself out and was therefore in need of work, but expected that all his difficulties would be over once he met the Leslie brothers, and was confident of earning a good deal more money in Australia than at home. Jane urged her sons to do their utmost to assist Wright, who

> may not be *full* of good manners but having good upright intentions will improve after he has seen a little, & how others do, for as yet he never has been out of his Father's house and is what may be termed rather a *green Horn* and I wish he was *safe* and *sound* in New South Wales. I have heard a *love* match made him determine on this step, as his Parents were against the Marriage and would not give him any part or portion of the farm – so some say the match is given up, and others say they will meet in Abdn and be married and go together.[69]

She also mentioned the imminent departure of another local emigrant, James Durno, who wished to invest his capital in New South Wales. He was of good character and well brought up, and was relying on the Leslies' experience to guide him in the wise investment of his savings. He left Leith on the *North Briton* in December 1839, bearing with him a part of Jane Leslie's journal, a letter from William Leslie to his sons and a packet for the Dalrymple brothers from their family.

It is unclear if the Leslies subsequently employed Durno, but by September 1840 at least one other Aberdeenshire Scot was working at the Leslies' newly established sheep station at Canning Downs. Patrick wrote to his parents with the details:

> We have another Aberdeenshire man with us he has been with me 2 years he is up with Watty – one of the most valuable fellows I ever met with a most invaluable man to us he is ... This man's name is *James Hay* he comes from *Tarland* his father is a carpenter there and he is also a carpenter by trade indeed he is everything & is Watty's factotum & from knowing all about us he is much attached to us – he knows Warthill well & knows you my dear Father by sight very well he has an uncle residing near Foudland estate hills – & I know some of your Tenants are near relations of his ... If you should be any chance ever be near *Tarland* it would be very gratifying to Hays father to know he is 'wi kent folk' and doing so well.[70]

William Leslie was in no doubt about the value of having acquaintances from home in a strange land. In a letter to his son George in 1841 he mentioned by name the various employees who had been sent out and, like Patrick, stressed what an advantage it was to 'have kent folk near in a wilderness'.[71]

In 1840 Patrick Leslie had led an expedition to the Darling Downs, discovered in 1837 by the Scottish botanist and explorer Allan Cunningham – an acquaintance of the Leslies – but thirteen years later still north of the limit of settlement. He chose the area that was to become Canning Downs for his first sheep station, leaving Walter in temporary charge until he moved there in 1842, along with his brother George, Ernest Dalrymple, Sandy Wright, James Fletcher and another Scottish emigrant, Archibald Farquharson. Throughout the 1840s the Leslies were the leading pioneer settlers in the area, and their activities continued to attract attention back home. In 1845 their father received yet another appeal from a neighbour whose son wanted advice and the promise of employment:

> My son James has taken it into his head to go to istralia and if he is determined I shall not seek to hinder him … I am shure that ther is non that can give a more true account of it than you can do. I am hapy to say that he is a very stu[r]dy young man and of sober habits he is a great youse to me but if it wer for his good I should be willing to part with him – was flattering myself that you having so many of your sons ther that he might have a chance of getting a situation from som of them but you will wreat me soon what incoragment ther is in going to that coutry.[72]

After a brief trip home in 1844, Patrick returned to Australia, first to Brisbane, where he built a house. In 1847 he sold this property and bought another station on the Darling Downs, Goomburra, where he remained until he returned to Britain in the mid-1850s. George Leslie, who took over the running of Canning Downs in 1847 but managed it at a distance after he too returned to Britain, used the Scottish press and the government nomination scheme to recruit employees until he sold the property in 1854.

Investors as well as employees from the neighbourhood of Warthill continued to be attracted to Australia. Not only the Dalrymple brothers but also, among others, Charles, James and Norman Leith Hay, three of the sons of Colonel Sir Alexander Leith Hay of Rannes and Leith Hall, began sheep farming on the Darling Downs in the 1830s, before selling out to Patrick Leslie in 1853 and moving inland in search of a larger holding. Alexander Anderson Seton, of Mounie, another local laird and cousin of the Leslies, had clearly read some of Patrick's enthusiastic letters when visiting Warthill, and as early as 1837 gave his nephew David a letter of introduction to his distant relative in New South Wales. The concentration of influential Scottish interest led in turn to the investment of a considerable amount of Scottish capital in the development of the Australian pastoral industry in the 1840s, primarily through the formation of two Aberdeen-based investment companies. The North British Australasian Company (founded in 1839) and the Scottish Australian Company (founded in 1840) subsequently provided much of the capital which financed the opening up of a chain of sheep stations in New South Wales and northern Queensland in the late 1840s and 1850s.

The Leslie family's interest in overseas investment was not confined to Australia. William Leslie, the eldest son, was the first to fly the family nest. In 1833 he went to Canton to work for his uncle, Walter Davidson, who had business interests there as well as in Australia. In 1844, returning to the East from a visit home, he stopped in Ceylon, where in a move provoked partly by the instability created in China as a result of the Opium Wars, he bought land for development as a coffee plantation. On the advice of a friend, he wrote to his father, 'I offered for and presume shall have got a tract of land for a Coffee Estate which my friends Jas and Geo Smith shall commence upon and attend to until one of my Brothers can come out and undertake the management of it.' He anticipated that each successive season would reveal more and more the 'immense resources' of the coffee industry, and continued:

> I calculate that allowing £300 p. annum to whoever may come and take it in hand, all my Outlay and Expenses will be repaid in 5 years and in under 5 years the property of 300 acres of coffee will give us back equal shares of fully £500 p. annum each as Income and this allows for every probable contingency. I should like George to come up at first as he is most systematic and likely to commence the thing right; in 3 years the Estate would be all planted and most of it bearing when all that would have to be done would be to keep it as it is.[73]

Although William was to be disappointed in his expectation that his younger brothers, who at that time were still in dispute with Walter Davidson, would be eager to leave New South Wales and join in his new enterprise, his estate was not short of Scottish neighbours. Most arrived in Ceylon during the 1830s and

1840s, when the coffee mania was at its height, and a disproportionate number came from Aberdeen and its hinterland, some via earlier employment in the East India Company. They included Robert Boyd Tytler, born in Peterhead and brought up in Inverurie, who in 1834, aged fifteen, had been sent to Jamaica to work on the sugar plantation of a family friend. Two brothers were already in the service of the East India Company, and in 1837 he moved to Ceylon, on the invitation of a relative who was a partner in the business of Ackland, Boyd and Company. That firm was in the process of establishing several coffee estates in Ceylon, and Tytler was initially employed as a manager before acquiring land of his own. In due course he became one of the island's biggest estate owners, as well as a member of the Legislative Council. Two of his sons followed in his footsteps, as did his brother-in-law, and these men formed part of a large community of expatriate north-east Scots who had a huge influence on Ceylon's economic development, for while it was claimed that 95 per cent of the overseers on Ceylon's coffee plantations were Scots, 50 per cent of that number were said to be Aberdonians.[74]

Thus in Ceylon as in Australia the Scottish connection extended beyond the big investors to the workforce required to man the plantations, a workforce that was recruited through private networking rather than public advertising. William Leslie, like his brother in New South Wales, asked his father to select and send out a reliable overseer, at a starting salary of £50 or £60 per year, to be raised to £100 once he had proved his competence. And like Patrick, he too thought one of the Singer family might be a suitable candidate:

> I shall want a good honest well brought up and educated young Scot for a Superintendant [*sic*] on my Estate and I wish that my dear Father would have an eye to any Lad of the above description ... not very stout, as the heat might disagree with him. A man who understood something of surveying and road making and all that kind of work would be preferable – but I should like one from near home whose honesty and general character would be known to you. One of Robert Singers Boys if grown up would be just the very person I want.[75]

There was also substantial Scottish investment in North America during the nineteenth century, an era when, thanks largely to the surplus capital generated by the textile and shipbuilding industries, 'Scotland was changed from one of the poorest to one of the most prosperous countries in Europe.'[76] In the late 1830s a number of Aberdeen-based companies invested in the Great Lakes area,

encouraged by George Smith, an emigrant from Old Deer who, having specu-
lated successfully in land, spearheaded the Illinois Investment Company in 1837
and in 1839 founded the first bank in Chicago. Later in the century, Scots
invested an estimated £6.5 million in the American West alone,[77] and although
the interest of many went no further than their shareholdings, the sheep and
cattle industries in particular generated a significant amount of emigration.
Some Scottish herdsmen rose from small beginnings to establish empires of
thousands of acres and huge flocks of sheep, dominating the industry in states
such as Wyoming and Idaho. Particularly successful were Archie, Peter and
John McGregor, whose parents had moved from Mull to Canada in the 1850s
and who began raising sheep in Washington State in 1882. To the east, Andrew
Little, who emigrated from Moffatt in 1894 as a wage labourer for a fellow Scot,
ultimately became known as 'the sheep king of Idaho', the most famous of
many Scots in a state that by 1918 was the world's second largest sheep centre.
Seven of Little's eight brothers eventually joined him in the Boise Valley and his
fame was such that on one occasion he allegedly received a letter from Scotland
addressed simply to 'Andy Little, USA'.[78] Like the Leslie brothers, many of the
successful entrepreneurs – including Little's first employer, Bob Aikman –
assisted several of their fellow countrymen to come and work for them as sheep
herders, and many of these employees later became independent flockmasters.

In the 1870s and 1880s Scottish investors, with companies based mainly in
Dundee and Edinburgh, also played a significant part in funding the development of the cattle industry of the western states, while some of those who emigrated as ranch managers became legends in their own lifetimes. John Clay, for
instance, successfully managed the Swan Land and Cattle Company in
Wyoming, while Murdo Mackenzie presided over the Matador Land and Cattle
Company Ltd and served as head of the American National Livestock Association. Both men were powerful and highly respected throughout the West, traits
which did not characterize some of the 'remittance men' who sojourned in the
West and were often more interested in the good life than in good husbandry of
land and resources.

By no means all overseas investment was in land. Scots also sank capital and
engineering expertise into mining ventures in South America as well as further
north. James Duncan (1859–1938), a stonemason from New Leeds in Aberdeenshire, went to Bolivia in 1882 along with a workmate whose uncle had extensive
silver and tin mining interests at Oruro. Branching out on his own account after
three years, he made a fortune out of tin, eventually returning to Scotland to

direct operations from the estate he bought, which itself became a notable centre for the breeding and fattening of livestock. Railway development was also popular with investors. Aberdeenshire emigrant Alexander Mitchell, a protégé of George Smith of the Chicago Bank and Wisconsin's richest citizen in the mid-nineteenth century, supplied much of the capital for expanding and equipping an efficient railway network throughout Wisconsin, Minnesota and Iowa, while Andrew Carnegie built his famous fortune not least on the manufacture of steel for railroad construction.[79] The Scottish cousins George Stephen from Dufftown and Donald Smith from Forres were the financial masterminds behind the construction of the Canadian Pacific Railway, while on both sides of the border much of the actual construction was undertaken by Scottish navvies.[80]

The industrial emigrant

As these examples demonstrate, Scottish involvement in American industry was not confined to investment. While most emigration propaganda was directed at farmers, Scotland in the nineteenth century was increasingly a land of towns and heavy industry, and this was reflected in the occupations and aspirations of many emigrants. Artisan emigration had a long and controversial history. It was the threat to emigrate made by unemployed Paisley weavers in 1773 that caused the Lord Chief Justice, Thomas Miller, to press for the investigation that subsequently led to the *Register of Emigrants* and to the reinforcement of a ban on artisan emigration that remained on the statute book until 1825. Miller clearly equated emigration with ambition rather than despair. After the conviction of seven of the Paisley weavers who had rioted, he declared that even transportation 'begins to lose every aspect of punishment' and expressed the hope that their 'ideas of migration to America may not become epidemical among the most useful of our people'.[81] During the nineteenth century, however, Scottish artisans, including many skilled craftsmen, were enticed to the United States by high wages and 'myriad jobs' in the rapidly expanding American economy.[82] They were particularly prominent in the textile industry of New England, bringing their skills to specialized gingham weaving and carpet making, as well as hosiery, thread and lace making and jute manufacture. Scottish looms, introduced into Rhode Island in 1817, soon spread throughout New England, and towns like Lowell and Waltham in Massachusetts, Thompsonville in Connecticut and New Ipswich in New Hampshire became virtual enclaves of Scots from the central belt. Paisley, whose weavers established the carpet industry in Lowell as early as 1829, also sent large numbers of emigrants to Newark (New Jersey), Pawtucket (Rhode Island) and Fall River (Massachusetts), where the Paisley firms of Clark, Coats and Kerr respectively established cotton and linen thread factories in the second half of the century. For thirty years Andover in Massachusetts became 'a second Brechin', after two emigrants from Angus established a linen factory there in the 1870s, while the entire American jute industry was for long dominated by a mill at Paterson, founded by a group of emigrants from Dundee in 1844. Women as well as men were attracted by the high wages, which at some factories were nearly double those paid in Scotland. Throughout the 1850s and 1860s agents actively recruited skilled Scots women, particularly from Glasgow. In 1869 the Amoskeag Mill in Manchester, New Hampshire, imported fifty Scots women gingham weavers, and up to 300 female weavers were brought to the Holyoke mills in Massachusetts six years later. Even when the Americans had trained up their own, cheaper, labour force by the end of the century, there was still a niche for the Scots, and it was by no means uncommon for Scottish artisans to rise through the ranks to become overseers, superintendents and even proprietors of textile factories throughout New England.[83]

The encouragement offered to textile workers was replicated in other branches of American industry. Opportunities were publicized through the usual public and private channels. Specific openings were advertised in newspapers, while periodicals gave background information and advice. An early issue of *Chambers' Edinburgh Journal* carried a series of articles directed at artisans as well as farmers. In 1840 it published a Scottish emigrant's essay on cotton manufacture in New England, and in 1842 it reviewed *A Tradesman's Travels in the United States and Canada*, a Stonehaven wool spinner's impressions of America gained during a three-year tour.[84] Artisan correspondence is harder to unearth, but several of the thirty-two letters that comprise the correspondence of the Kerr family of Dalry reflect a keen interest in American conditions and prospects, despite the recurring message of Hugh Kerr's letters that his sons John, a joiner in Illinois, and David, a carpet maker in New York, would do better if they returned to Scotland.[85]

As with farming opportunities, the encouragement did not fall on deaf ears. From papermaking and landscape gardening to steel and shipbuilding, Scots who were initially attracted by lucrative wages often moved into managerial positions after they had proved their worth and imparted their skills. The first

American census to report immigrant occupations, in 1870, indicated that 46 per cent of Scots were employed in manufacturing, mechanical and mining jobs, while port records suggest that building trades workers and miners were the two most prominent groups of skilled Scots.[86] The 1860s saw a significant influx of Scottish colliers, particularly to mines west of the Allegheny Mountains, lured across the Atlantic by high wages, quick, cheap steerage passages in the new steamships and the personal recommendations of Alexander McDonald, the Scottish miners' union leader, who paid three visits to the USA in order to investigate opportunities for his members. McDonald's two brothers were making good wages at mines in Ohio and Illinois, many acquaintances in the USA had also done well, and he claimed to keep his finger on the pulse of events across the Atlantic by taking thirty American newspapers a week. McDonald, who in the 1860s acted as an agent for at least one American mining company, in Virginia, publicized opportunities in the *Glasgow Sentinel* and encouraged colliers in the west of Scotland to form local district emigration committees, paying 6d per week to fund the emigration of members whose names would be pulled out of a hat. In 1865, when the scheme was at its height, parties of miners and their families left the Clyde in groups of about 100, and when McDonald visited pithead towns after the Civil War he found significant numbers of his fellow countrymen – 7,000 in Maryland, 3,000 in Pennsylvania, 2,000 in Illinois and 'large colonies' in Ohio.

A civilized society

While material gain was clearly the driving force for many emigrants, it does not fully explain the persistent tendency of Scots to seek out and settle alongside their fellow countrymen in Ontario, Otago and many places in between. The importance of family, friends and community has been woven into virtually every example used in this chapter – not surprisingly, for most emigrants needed to be reassured, not only of better working conditions, remuneration and prospects, but also that they would not be cutting themselves adrift from all the familiar and comforting associations of home. Such concern was evident in the 1770s, both among those emigrants whose motives, they told customs officers, included family reunions and the farmers who banded together in local associations like the Inchinnan Company. Half a century later, similar priorities were addressed in the colonization schemes that brought Lowland weavers and Highland crofters to the Ottawa Valley and the Eastern Townships respectively, emerging even more directly in the informal colonies of Aberdeenshire Scots established at Bon Accord and Tilbury East in Southern Ontario.

When George Elmslie was sent out on his reconnaissance mission, he was instructed not only to choose a fertile, well-watered tract of land but also to ensure that religious and educational facilities were available within a 'reasonable distance'. He took due account of his associates' wishes in his choice of settlement, for Bon Accord was adjacent to Fergus, where in 1834 Adam Fergusson's plans to establish a church and school were already well advanced. But surely the most striking feature of the Bon Accord community was the way in which the settlers 'came in parties, relatives and friends following each other at intervals, and all from Aberdeenshire'.[87] Many emigrant parties were made up of extended family groups, and the community was progressively augmented by secondary emigration on the part of people whose family, neighbours or business associates had preceded them to Nichol. Their favourable private reports of its social, as well as its economic, assets were reinforced by the *Aberdeen Herald*'s public endorsement of Nichol on the grounds of its 'pleasing and select' society, a recommendation based simply on the fact that so many of the settlers had been known to each other in Scotland; new arrivals could therefore feel confident that a bridgehead had been established and they were not coming to an entirely alien land.[88] The social cement provided by chain migration was equally evident at Tilbury East, and clearly helped to persuade Charles Farquharson to take the plunge. As he wrote to his brother-in-law a year before he emigrated:

> Some people say that you can not have the same comforts in Canada, being a new country, as with us. But I can not see why you would not, being in pretty well peopled place near railroads, near Church and School, and good communications everywhere ... And I am sure that I would have your experience and good advice as far as you could, for our comfort and well being, if you and we are all spared to meet.[89]

Across the border, the anticipation of familiar faces and an orderly society was as important to Scots emigrants to Ohio and Iowa as was the promise of land, while in the industrial arena, colliers, granite cutters and other artisans commonly banded together for mutual support, both in travelling and in their search for employment. Meanwhile, on the other side of the world, the Leslie brothers and their friends staffed their sheep-farming enterprises by offering not just economic incentives but also the prospect of something of a 'home from home', a policy that was beneficial to both employers and employees.

Propagandists were ever ready to exploit the familiarity factor, not least in Canada, where they could draw on a consistent tradition of Scottish settlement going back to the eighteenth century. The concerns of Gaelic-speaking Highlanders were addressed by a smattering of publications in their own language, notably Robert MacDougall's 1841 guidebook, *Ceann-Iuil an Fhir-Imrich do dh'America Mu-Thuath* (*The Emigrant's Guide to North America*) and the perodical *Cuairtear nan Gleann* (*Traveller/Sojourner of the Glens*). The latter was established and edited by the Reverend Norman McLeod, popularly known as 'Caraid nan Gaidheal' (Friend of the Gaels). Published monthly in Kingston, Ontario, between 1840 and 1843 and sold for 6d, *Cuairtear* aimed to make information on the British colonies available to Gaelic speakers, for many of whom the prospect of retaining their language and culture was a key ingredient in the decision to emigrate. '*Cha 'n eil teagamh nach bi Ghàilig ann an ùine ghoirid air a labhairt ann an America mu-thuath le barrachd dhaoine na th'ann an Gàidhealtachd na h-Alba*' (Doubtless Gaelic will soon be spoken by more people in North America than it will in the Highlands of Scotland), they were assured in an article in 1840 which stressed that Highland emigrants to Canada could effortlessly resume their old way of life among like-minded fellow countrymen.[90] *Cuairtear*, like many of the English-language periodicals and guidebooks, also repeatedly described North America as '*dùthaich an duine bhochd*' (country for the poor man), while New Zealand and Australia – with the exception of Van Diemen's Land – were equally recommended as places where Highland emigrants could make more money than their erstwhile landlords.

Although New Zealand attracted a significant number of Highlanders, not least to the 'Normanite' settlement at Waipu,[91] its appeal as a Utopian Scotland in the southern hemisphere was probably more influential in a Lowland context. It was the South Island province of Otago, centred on Dunedin (New Edinburgh) that was most explicitly recommended to Scots in these terms. Developed by the Free Church of Scotland as a Presbyterian colony in the 1840s, Otago enticed emigrants, particularly families, with promises of a well-ordered Christian society, good educational facilities and an unambiguously Scottish culture, in which old friendships could be renewed and new ones forged. Since 80 per cent of those arriving in the province between 1848 and 1860 were Scots-born, the promoters and pioneers clearly succeeded in laying the foundations of

4. Pewter communion token from Otago, New Zealand.

a distinctively Scottish colony, although one English commentator claimed this demonstrated an unattractive clannishness:

> This is the youngest province but one in the colony; the first settlement was planted in 1848 by an association of the members of the Free Kirk of Scotland. Scotch 'nationality' is as much cultivated, we fear, as some other products of the 'Land of Cakes,' and the emigrants from the northern portion of our island seem determined to maintain in New Zealand the same position relatively to their English fellow-colonists as in Great Britain. They have taken possession of one of the extremities, and that the coldest, of the country; and, unless they are greatly misrepresented, they manifest an unmistakeable desire to keep it entirely to themselves.[92]

Not every memory of home was a fond one to be re-created. Since taxes, tithes and the tugging of forelocks featured prominently among emigrants' grievances with life in Scotland, they were likely to be attracted to destinations where economic independence and familiar faces could be combined with social equality. 'You must know we are not here as in Scotland; we are respected as gentlemen, and styled Mr by the best gentlemen in the country, and invited to dinner with them at any time': so claimed a ploughman from Forgue in Aberdeenshire who in 1837 joined a party of twelve families going to the 'predominantly Scottish settlement' at Altamont in Jamaica. During 1836 and 1837 around 180 people emigrated from west Aberdeenshire to Altamont and Middlesex townships, in a chain movement that was facilitated by an enthusiastic agent, James Barclay of Auchterless, as well as the Jamaican Assembly's assisted passage and settlement scheme and the positive comments of emigrants, whose correspondence was quoted in the Scottish press.[93] Similar sentiments were expressed by a number of the Lewis emigrants in Quebec's Eastern Townships, including Donald McLean of Lingwick, who in 1851 assured his correspondent in Lewis that, as well as high wages on the railroad, 'labourers in this country get bed and board as good as the common gentleman in your country'.[94]

While colonial destinations like Canada were frequently commended for their classlessness, the United States was the most obvious choice on these grounds, at least for commentators who viewed egalitarianism as a blessing rather than a curse. In 1822 Highlanders were alerted to the attractions of Ohio in a Gaelic poster which assured them that 'the tenantry are the gentlemen of the country. They pay no rent and there is no restriction on hunting … they are not prevented from cutting wood or from fishing.'[95] A decade later, two Aberdeenshire farmers, whose letters were quoted in *Counsel for Emigrants*, recommended Michigan as a suitable destination for Scots who wished to 'throw aside a load of pride … and that eager desire to rise in the world' and come to a country where no one would despise them. One of the correspondents, who owned a productive farm in a growing settlement, was unequivocal in his preference for American democracy:

> To all lovers of gold and silver, of fine clothes, and high pretensions, who expect to make a fortune, and drive their carriage, have servants in waiting, and their neighbours to take off their hats to them, I say, once for all, keep away, far away, from America and the Americans. If you wish to enjoy equality, social and intelligent neighbours, with independence from all supercilious and browbeating superiors, independence from cares and poverty, I would say come here.[96]

Some commentators, including the Chambers brothers, were at pains to deny allegations that American society was unrefined and irreligious, pointing out that books, periodicals and newspapers were cheap and readily available, and

there was no lack of churches or preachers representing a wide range of denominations.[97]

Conclusion

Scots were lured overseas by a variety of economic, social and cultural inducements. Building on solid eighteenth-century foundations, the recurring promise
of independence through landownership was a powerful magnet, particularly to
those whose security and prospects had been eroded by the commercialization
of farming in Scotland. For a substantial minority with capital to spare, foreign
fields offered an attractive opportunity for the investment of both financial and
human resources, while the artisans produced by Scotland's increasingly urbanized, industrialized society sought higher wages and better working conditions
overseas, especially in the factories, mines and workshops of the United States.
For many, the anticipated neighbourliness, cooperation and familiarity of an
established Scottish settlement were incentives just as important as material gain
and the absence of domineering landlords, and clearly influenced their choice of
destination. Throughout the nineteenth century the bulk of the guidebooks,
periodicals and newspapers which poured forth an unremitting torrent of advice
and encouragement generally tried to steer emigrants in the direction of
Canada, although it is possible to chart changing policies and fashions in destinations through a study of emigration propaganda. But despite the prominence
and supportive influence of these sources of information, they were, as Charlotte Erickson has pointed out, 'much more noisy and conspicuous than effective
in prodding prospective immigrants to particular destinations'.[98] The most
effective encouragement undoubtedly came from the satisfied emigrant's
private letter home, particularly if it contained a remittance or a prepaid ticket
to galvanize an apathetic or indecisive correspondent. But for emigrants who
lacked overseas contacts, professional emigration agents might well be instrumental in the decision-making process, offering practical, on-the-spot but often
controversial advice in an increasingly competitive, confusing and cut-throat
market.

THE RECRUITMENT BUSINESS

'I encountered, while endeavouring to carry out the objects of my mission, the bitterest and most persistent hostility from landed proprietors, large farmers and generally employers of skilled and unskilled labour.'[1]

Emigration agents could provoke a variety of sentiments. Indeed, in the long-running, complex and often contentious saga of Scottish emigration, one of the most consistent, enigmatic and controversial characters has always been the emigration agent. Before, throughout and beyond the nineteenth century he – and occasionally she – appeared in a variety of guises and employed a range of strategies to stimulate, steer and sustain emigration to a host of destinations. In pursuit of these objectives, many of the agents made powerful enemies as well as grateful friends, for their activities often addressed the very core of the perennial debate on the ethics and expediency of emigration. Although personal persuasion was always the most influential stimulus to emigration, the integral role of agents in the recruitment and settlement process should not be underestimated, particularly with the evolution of a network of professional agencies in the second half of the nineteenth century.

Emigration agents can be defined in a general sense as all who spoke or wrote positively of overseas opportunities, privately as well as publicly, and offered their hearers encouragement – directly or indirectly – to take up these opportunities. A more meaningful and focused definition, however, is that they were individuals or institutions with a vested military, financial, commercial, philanthropic or political interest in encouraging large-scale emigration, as opposed to the relocation of specific individuals or families. Army officers, shippers, land speculators, employment agents, landlords, clergymen, charitable societies and governments all played a part in the recruitment business, not least in Scotland, where we have evidence of emigrants being enticed to America as early as the 1730s. While some of these agents did no more than dip an occasional toe into the waters of recruitment, others developed a sophisticated support structure which ensured that Scottish emigrants, wherever they were bound, and whatever their private support mechanisms, had access to a range of facilitators in planning and implementing their relocation.

From what sort of roots did the recruitment business evolve? What was the relationship between military and civilian recruitment, or between land speculation and agency activity? What part did shipping agents play in the upsurge of emigration from Scotland in the nineteenth century, and how did their role change as a result of technological advances and the centralization of embarkations? Were different recruitment strategies employed in Highland and Lowland, rural and urban constituencies? What part did British and overseas governments play in the recruitment process? What were the manifestations and effects of the increasing professionalization of agency recruitment? How did amateur – and sometimes maverick – agents coexist with professional recruiters? With what sort of problems and opposition did emigration agents have to contend? Why – and by whom – were they so frequently vilified?

Laying the foundations: eighteenth-century agents

Emigration agents in the eighteenth-century Lowlands were generally merchants, shipowners and captains, somewhat shadowy figures who operated a regular transatlantic trade in both merchandise and men. Vessels which imported Chesapeake tobacco or Caribbean sugar and rum frequently took passengers as well as freight on their return voyages to the colonies, most notably from Glasgow, but also from a variety of other Scottish ports. In north-east Scotland, for example, the advertising columns of the *Aberdeen Journal* reflect the large number of agents involved in overseas trade. Andrew Garioch and John Elphinston, both of whom were tarnished by the Peter Williamson abduction scandal,[2] sent several vessels to Antigua during the 1740s and early 1750s, and on at least one occasion Garioch toured the towns of west Aberdeenshire, 'so that he can be spoke with … by Servants who incline to indent.'[3] By 1751 Elphinston was acting in conjunction with Captain James Elphinston, presumably a relative, in operating the *Planter*, 'a fine new Vessel' with 'good Accommodation' between Aberdeen and Antigua, but by 1753 he had joined up with Garioch again to advertise the *Antigua Packet*, with good accommodation for fare-paying passengers as well as for tradesmen and 'servants of good character' who wished to indent. And a year later they collaborated in sending the *Planter* to Antigua and Jamaica, accompanied by Garioch, 'who is acquainted in those islands'. Indentures were offered at good wages to 'all men servants from 12 to 40 years old', but the agents promised to recruit 'no convicts, nor those addicted to thieving and drinking'.[4] At least seven other local merchants advertised transatlantic passages regularly in the Aberdeen press in the eighteenth century, while twenty-four advertised more sporadically. The vast majority were involved in Caribbean traffic, with Virginia the most regular destination among the mainland American colonies until the 1770s, when it was eclipsed by more northerly areas, including New York, Prince Edward Island and Nova Scotia. In 1773 Captain George Thomson of Old Aberdeen offered readers of the *Aberdeen Journal* the opportunity to buy 100 acres in Prince Edward Island, and in 1784 the *Mercury*, which was represented by agents in Montrose, Aberdeen and Inverness, offered £7 steerage passages to Halifax, where there was allegedly ample employment for 'Masons, House-Carpenters, Black-Smiths, Labourmen and Maid Servants'.[5]

Most agents offered general rather than specific encouragement to emigrants, although exceptions to these bland generalities might occur if the agent or master had business interests in the colonies. Some advertisers were themselves emigrating, or returning to the colonies after a spell at home, and wanted to recruit servants and tradesmen, either for themselves or for business associates. Fraserburgh merchant Alexander Low had a lengthy shopping list when he advertised in December 1751 for 'Bricklayers, Masons, Stone-cutters, Blacksmiths, Farriers, Cabinet-Makers, Joiners, Tanners, Shoemakers' to indent with him for employment in Antigua, where they were offered 'ten to twenty Pounds sterl. Yearly, beside Bed, Board, Washing and Cloathing, with other necessaries for space of four Years'.[6] While most recruiters were looking for single men, encouragement was sometimes held out to women, and occasionally to married men with families. Assurances about the salubrity of the climate were usually confined to advertisements for notorious plague spots, and when international conflict compounded the normal hazards of the voyage, agents armed their ships before sending them off in convoy.

Some shipping agents also dabbled in land speculation. In 1770 the Pagan brothers of Glasgow teamed up with Dr John Witherspoon, the clergyman who had emigrated from Paisley to New Jersey two years earlier to become president of the College of New Jersey and was later a signatory to the Declaration of

Independence. When the Renfrewshire-based Inchinnan Company sent two representatives to Philadelphia in 1773 to scout out suitable land they immediately made contact with Witherspoon, and ultimately purchased 23,000 acres from him in Ryegate Township, New York (later Vermont). But Witherspoon is better known as an agent in the settlement of Pictou, Nova Scotia, by Highlanders, also in 1773. Having taken over the ailing Philadelphia Company in partnership with the Pagans, he set about attracting Scottish settlers to this 200,000-acre wilderness, advertising cheap land and passage at £3 5s per adult. While a few emigrants were recruited at Greenock, the vast majority came from Ross-shire and Sutherland, thanks to the partnership's local agent, John Ross, a Dingwall merchant and manager of a linen station on Loch Broom for the Forfeited Estates Commissioners. Ross had collaborated with Witherspoon and the Pagans three years earlier in sending 200 Scots to Boston on the *Hector*, but when the same ship was sent to Pictou with almost 200 Highlanders, it became known as Canada's *Mayflower*, the harbinger of Nova Scotia's Highland identity.[7]

As a rule agents had a rather different role in the economically undeveloped and socially dislocated Highlands from their counterparts in the Lowlands. For much of the eighteenth century there was an ambiguous line between military and civilian recruitment. As early as 1735 Lieutenant Hugh Mackay and Captain George Dunbar were employed by the trustees of the recently established colony of Georgia to recruit a community of 'industrious, laborious and brave' Gaelic-speaking Highlanders to settle in the new colony, both to defend its frontiers against Spain and France and to make their twenty-acre land grants productive.[8] Encouraged by a personal grant of 500 acres in Georgia, and with the help of local clergymen, kinfolk and the Provost of Inverness, whose mercantile business provisioned the emigrants, Mackay launched a successful recruitment campaign in his home territory of Caithness and Sutherland. This success, he wrote to Georgia's trustees, had been achieved in the face of strong opposition, conducted in the 'vilest manner' by 'under hand Agents instilling terrible apprehensions in people's minds'.[9] George Dunbar, meanwhile, had concentrated on winning the ear of some of the leading gentry in Inverness-shire, and had recruited particularly successfully from Clan Chattan. In all, 177 colonists sailed from Inverness in October 1735 on a ship commanded by Dunbar, and three months later established the township of Darien on the Altamaha River, probably so called in defiance of the failed venture at Panama in the 1690s. The Highlanders soon won their military and agricultural spurs with the trustees. As a result a second contingent of forty-three was recruited in 1737 by one of the settlers, Archibald MacBean, who was sent back to Scotland for that purpose, and a third contingent of forty in 1741 by Hugh Mackay and military recruitment agent James Grey, again with the assistance of Provost Hossack of Inverness.

While the British government can be seen as an agent of Highland emigration through its sanctioning of military recruitment harnessed to colonization, the paradoxes and dilemmas of such a policy became increasingly acute as time went on. The deterioration of Anglo-American relations in the 1760s and 1770s on the one hand increased the government's prejudice against an empire of colonization, fostering an anti-emigration stance that endured until the 1810s. Yet on the other hand concerns of imperial security gave rise to sponsored, carefully directed military settlement, on the grounds that the ready availability of a large pool of officers and men would protect newly acquired territory and augment the regular garrison if necessary. At the end of the Seven Years War captains were allowed 3,000 acres, subalterns 2,000 acres and ordinary soldiers fifty acres, while at the end of the American Revolutionary War individual soldiers were allowed 100 acres, with a further fifty acres each for their wives and children. Military officers returned home to recruit settlers for their land grants, leading to the creation of concentrated clusters of Highland landownership in strategic parts of British North America.[10]

Once recruited, Highland emigrants had to be conveyed overseas. Shipping agents, whether tacksmen, military officers, landowners or merchants, were another vital piece in the recruitment jigsaw. Eighteenth-century Highland emigrants, including the first and second contingent of Georgia settlers in the 1730s, often left from Highland ports. Major Simon Fraser's ships ran so regularly from the 1790s and 1800s that he earned the nickname 'Nova Scotia'. In 1802, for example, he arranged for 128 Highlanders to sail from Fort William to Pictou. A year earlier the same two ports had witnessed the transfer of 569 Highlanders on two ships, the *Dove* and the *Sarah*, under the auspices of Hugh Dunoon of Killearnan in Easter Ross. As a landowner and merchant in Pictou, Dunoon was anxious to recruit emigrants to fill up his possessions, and although good reports were ultimately sent back by the settlers, his activities fell foul of the Highland Society, which was trying to restrict emigration on the grounds that it impeded economic development. Although a civilian agent, he was described by his opponents as a 'crimp', which was a derogatory – and largely disused – term for a military recruiter who secured his men by taking advantage of economic hardship in the recruits' place of origin. Indeed, it was the activities of men like Dunoon, Simon 'Nova Scotia' Fraser and a more famous agent, Thomas Douglas, the Fifth Earl of Selkirk, that gave rise to the Passenger Vessels Act of 1803, a disingenuous piece of legislation which, though ostensibly humanitarian in purpose, was in fact intended to put a stop to emigration by making it prohibitively expensive, as was demonstrated in Chapter 1.

The Earl of Selkirk: theorist and practitioner

Whereas Dunoon's agency seems to have been underpinned primarily by commercial motives, Lord Selkirk – who had rubbed shoulders with Sir Walter Scott at Edinburgh University – had a philosophical interest in overseas colonization. More practically, he also needed to adopt a 'cause' on which he could build a national reputation and thereby convince his contemporaries that he was a suitable candidate to be elected as a representative Scottish peer. The establishment of a colony in British North America seemed to be an appropriate public venture, although the controversy that raged round emigration clearly made it a high-risk strategy. Selkirk's involvement with colonization schemes began in 1801 when, at the age of thirty, two years after succeeding to his Galloway earldom, he tried to arrange a meeting with Bishop John Chisholm, probably to discuss the feasibility of collaborating in recruiting Catholic Highlanders (who were already emigrating in disproportionate numbers) for a colony in North America. Nothing happened, but the following year, in a change of focus, Selkirk petitioned the British government to pay the passages of a contingent of Irish Catholics whom he proposed to recruit and lead to Louisiana. The government, however, vetoed any interference with the 'intractable Irish', and redirected Selkirk's interest to Highland emigration, promising him an estate in Upper Canada, as well as cheap transport, free provisions and land on good terms for his colonists. By the end of November 1802 the Gaelic-speaking Selkirk and his agents had signed up over 100 Hebridean families for the venture, mainly from the Clanranald and MacDonald estates in Mull, Skye and the Uists. He also built up a substantial flock of sheep on the Baldoon estate, located near the present site of Sault Ste Marie, and advertised in the Lowlands for a few young men to 'cultivate an estate in Upper Canada'.[11]

But at the same time Selkirk was becoming embroiled in the bitter debate about the ethics of emigration. His claim that he was simply redirecting Highlanders who had already decided to emigrate to the United States convinced no

5. Memorial to the 800 Scottish settlers who came to Belfast, Prince Edward Island, in 1803 under the auspices of Thomas Douglas, Earl of Selkirk.

one, and landlord vituperation peaked late in 1802, with the publication of Alexander Irvine's *Inquiry into the Causes and Effects of Emigration*. Irvine, the Church of Scotland missionary at Rannoch in Perthshire, offered both a spirited defence of landlord policy and a vitriolic attack on those who 'go about recruiting for the plantations with the usual eloquence of crimps', although he did not mention Selkirk by name.[12] It is conceivable that that government's intention all along had been to rid itself of a thorn in the flesh by steering Selkirk into the spotlight of controversy and now, in the face of rising landlord and public anger, it withdrew its offer to provide him with land in Upper Canada. Faced with a commitment to transport hundreds of Highlanders across the Atlantic and provide them with land, Selkirk was forced to look elsewhere, and in March 1803 he managed to secure cheaply a number of lots in Prince Edward Island, a moribund settlement which desperately needed revitalizing and which could therefore be supported by the British government as a necessary rescue operation. At this stage, however, Selkirk fell foul of his recruits. Most of them had given up leases, paid their fares and deposited money to buy land in Upper Canada, and they resented the arbitrary change of destination to an island which, despite a tradition of Highland settlement, had acquired a bad reputation with emigrants. But just when it seemed likely that Selkirk's recruits would re-engage with other agents bound for other colonies, he was saved – unintention-ally – by Parliament, when the Passenger Vessels Act pushed virtually all other shippers out of the emigration business. Since only Selkirk could afford to meet the new regulations without raising fares, he secured not only his original recruits but also several other Highlanders who had sold up in the expectation of going to North America.

The upshot was that in June 1803 Selkirk accompanied 800 emigrants to Prince Edward Island in three ships, in what was to become the most successful of his three colonizing ventures. A year later, he launched his postponed Upper Canadian experiment, but the swampy Baldoon site was infested with malarial mosquitoes which devastated the 102-strong colony, the sheep farm was destroyed by invading Americans in 1812, and by 1817 fewer than ten of the original settlers were still there. Selkirk's final colonization scheme, at Red River on the site of present-day Winnipeg, fell victim to the warfare between the two rival fur-trading companies, the Hudson's Bay Company and the North West Company, and brought him to an early grave. In 1808 Selkirk invested heavily in Hudson's Bay Company stock and three years later he obtained a controlling interest with the help of his brother-in-law. At that time the Company granted him over 116,000 acres in return for a promise to recruit both Scottish employees for the Company and settlers for a colony at Red River.

The Red River venture was plagued with problems from the outset. Selkirk's recruiting activities in Stornoway were opposed by Simon MacGillivray of the North West Company, who alleged that misleading advertisements were luring Highlanders to an isolated wilderness that was infested with hostile Indians. At the same time one Captain Mackenzie, a military recruiter, obstructed the depar-ture of Selkirk's ships from Stornoway in June 1811, claiming that he was taking away deserters and other eligible fodder for the Napoleonic Wars. This first contingent, under the leadership of Knoydart-born Miles MacDonell, a veteran of the American Revolutionary War and an officer in the Canadian militia, whom Selkirk made governor of his new colony, sailed too late in the season to make the full trip to Red River that year, while the Irish and Scottish recruits who comprised the second party in 1812 fought each other on the way. When war broke out between Britain and the United States in 1812, Selkirk – in yet another manifestation of the dovetailing of military and civilian recruitment – approached the military authorities in London, offering to raise a 1,000-strong Highland regiment for service against the United States on condition that the soldiers and their dependants would be shipped from Scotland at public expense and ultimately settled at Red River. When in 1813 the people of Kildonan on the Sutherland estate offered independently to raise a regiment in return for a cessation of evictions, Selkirk seized an apparently golden opportunity to recruit the Kildonan men to his own colours, and relocate their families at Red River. In the firm belief that the government would commission Selkirk to raise such a regiment, the Kildonan tenants' spokesman, William MacDonald, recruited soldiers and settlers from the Sutherland estate, but when official funding failed to materialize, Selkirk was left with several hundred desperate would-be emigrants to whom he had to break the bad news that only a small number of single men could be taken to North America. In the event, several family groups were also funded by Selkirk and travelled in the ninety-four-strong party on the *Prince of Wales* from Stromness to Fort Churchill, enduring both a fever-ridden voyage and an overland trek to Red River, where they arrived in June 1814. Within a year most had abandoned the settlement, but some were persuaded to return and were reinforced in autumn 1815 by the arrival of a further contingent from Sutherland. But the North West Company employees, along with their Métis allies, were determined to sabotage the new settlement, which they saw as a threat to their economic security and identity. Things came to a head in a standoff at Seven Oaks in June 1816, when twenty of Selkirk's settlers were killed, and although he restored order in 1817 with the aid of a contingent of German and Swiss mercenaries, both Selkirk and his colony had been fatally weakened by the struggle, and he died in 1820, financially ruined and largely discredited.

Perhaps Selkirk's greatest legacy lay not in his transient colonies, but in his published articulation of theories of colonization, which undermined the solid wall of landlord hostility and marked a watershed in the whole debate on emigration. In 1805 he wrote *Observations on the Present State of the Highlands of Scotland*, the first major attempt to defend Highland emigration, in which he emphasized that while the Highlands needed to be modernized, the region's inhabitants had the right to emigrate in order to evade progress and protect their culture. This could best be done, he argued, through 'national settlements' in British North America, where the Highlanders would not only preserve their language, culture and customs in self-contained colonies but also prevent the British territories succumbing to the manners and morals of the United States. Three years later, in a pamphlet which advocated a universal system of military recruitment across the United Kingdom, Selkirk eroded the argument that Highland emigration should be discouraged on the grounds that Highlanders were uniquely important to the country's security.[13] Despite defensive and even hysterical reactions from some landlords and newspapers, Selkirk's writings were generally well received, and within a few years even the proprietors were forced to acknowledge the strength of his arguments, albeit tacitly. While his colonies perhaps served as a prototype for the systematic colonizers of the later nineteenth century, Selkirk, operating at a transitional period in the history of Scottish emigration, had through his pen created a less controversial climate in which his successors could practise their agency arts.

Shipping agents and the business of emigration

Nineteenth-century emigration agents therefore had a solid foundation of eighteenth-century precedent on which to build. This was evident not least in terms of shipping. Tobacco may have given way to timber as a transatlantic cargo, but the westward-bound timber ships continued to carry emigrants, just as the tobacco traders had done the previous century. By 1815 the Canadian timber trade had become a regular and often dominant business in a number of ports throughout the British Isles, and soon came to account for a third of all British tonnage to Canada. Having responded initially to wartime shortages of naval supplies, followed by Napoleon's Baltic embargo in 1807, the timber merchants soon expanded into emigrant transport, offsetting the damaging effects of the Passenger Vessels Act by offering competitively priced passages to the Maritime Provinces and the St Lawrence. But security as well as cheapness had to be emphasized by Stornoway merchant and shipowner John Mackenzie when in 1810–11 he negotiated with a timber shipper in Liverpool to pick up 150 Highlanders destined for Prince Edward Island. 'The *James* (350 tons) ... to sail from Stornoway to Prince Edward Island ... master well-armed now fitting out at Rodel in Harris' ran the advertisement in the *Inverness Journal* on 22 March 1811. As the timber trade expanded after the war, so these ad hoc arrangements gave way to a network of emigration agencies which advertised for passengers and arranged their passages on behalf of individual shipowners and firms. Major port cities such as Glasgow supported numerous agencies, but in the first half of the nineteenth century, when emigrant shipping to British North America remained decentralized, shipping agents could still be found in virtually all the ports that dispatched these human cargoes – including twenty-three Scottish ports in 1831 and 1832.[14] Sub-agents were also active in the hinterland of these ports; indeed, until the 1850s shipowners not only in Dumfries but also in the

Cumbrian ports of Workington, Whitehaven and Maryport found it worthwhile to employ agents at Annan, Langholm, Moffat and Hawick to recruit emigrants from the Borders.

While agencies in the big Lowland ports competed strenuously for business, Highland agents seem to have adhered to an unwritten gentlemen's agreement in determining mutually exclusive catchment areas. Moreover, whereas in the Lowlands the emigrant came to the agency, in the Highlands the agent generally sought out the emigrant. On 30 January 1829 the *Inverness Journal* reported the forthcoming emigration to Prince Edward Island of 'several hundred souls' from Skye. They had been recruited from Lord MacDonald's estates by two fellow islanders, 'men of substance and character', who had chartered 'one or more vessels' in an undertaking that was 'partly a trading speculation, and partly an act of philanthropy'. Like the tacksmen in an earlier generation, these agents were known to most of their recruits, but that was not always the case. In a region where emigration was often undertaken by large groups, frequently from a single estate, shipowners had to cope with fluctuating demand. They did this by employing agents as middlemen, to fill the erstwhile role of the tacksman-agent in terms of matching demand with supply. As well as relaying information about the volume and location of would-be emigrants to the shippers, they notified the scattered emigrants about embarkation times and places, and also sometimes helped to raise finance for the journey. Until the 1830s William Allan of Leith dominated the recruitment scene in Sutherland and Easter Ross. He enjoyed good relations with the Sutherland estate management and operated through a multiplicity of sub-agents – innkeepers, merchants, shoremasters, carpenters and postmasters – who sold the tickets and organized steamers to take emigrants to the main regional embarkation ports of Cromarty, Thurso and Lochinver. While many of Allan's sub-agents were located in Sutherland, they were also strung out along the Dornoch, Cromarty and Beauly firths, as well as south into Speyside. His counterpart on the west coast and in the Inner Hebrides was Archibald MacNiven of Tobermory, who claimed in 1841 that for the previous twenty years he had arranged ships for 16,000 Highlanders who had emigrated to British North America, over half of them to Cape Breton.[15]

By that time, however, Duncan MacLennan and John Sutherland were developing a monopoly of Highland emigration agencies, particularly in the area previously covered by William Allan, attracting custom through a huge network of sub-agents from the Orkneys down to Campbeltown, at the southern tip of the Mull of Kintyre. MacLennan, from Inverness, began operating in 1832, when he advertised in the *Inverness Journal* that he had 'entered into an arrangement with a major shipping establishment of Liverpool for the transport of passengers to Quebec, Pictou and New York'.[16] In 1840 he joined forces with Sutherland, who lost no opportunity to remind emigrants that he was both a Highlander and a Nova Scotian, having lived in the province for over twenty years. Both men were adept self-publicists, securing favourable press coverage of the departure and arrival of their vessels – nineteen of them by 1844. As well as emphasizing comfort and safety, the advertisements always gave detailed accounts of transatlantic farming and business opportunities, and, as agents for the two main land companies in the Canadas, MacLennan and Sutherland could offer a comprehensive service that included land as well as transport, just as Lord Selkirk had done to a previous generation of Highlanders. On 1 July 1842, for instance, readers of the *Inverness Journal* were told of the recent departure of the *Lady Emily* from Thurso and Loch Laxford, bound for Pictou and Quebec:

> Mr Sutherland, the emigration agent, who has been some time residing in Wick, accompanies the vessel to America, for the purpose of establishing a depot, and appointing agents in that country for facilitating the views of emigrants on their arrival. He also intends making arrangements for blocks of land, both in Nova Scotia and Canada, so that emigrants, proceeding by his vessels, may have the advantage of at once taking possession of farms or locations without losing their time and money in inquiries. The northern counties of Scotland are peculiarly indebted to Mr S. for laying on his vessels in this part of the country – for before he established himself, those desirous of emigrating had to bear the expense of removal to Greenock, which equalled, if not succeeded, the whole sum now charged for the passage to America. Nearly 2000 emigrants have been sent out by him within two years, in vessels of the first class. So far as we know, Mr Sutherland has left behind him a character for uprightness and integrity. His conduct to the poorer classes of emigrants has been very praiseworthy – he very frequently granting free passages to many members of a family where the head of it could not command sufficient means to carry them all out. Mr S. returns to this country in November next, when he intends carrying on the same agency, but on a much more extensive scale than hitherto.

When Sutherland sent the *Prince Albert* from Thurso to Quebec seven years later, the *John O'Groat Journal* intoned that the Thurso-based agent had 'every

6. Silver snuff box, inscribed to John Sutherland, a government emigration agent in the Highlands, 1849, made by Nathaniel Mills, Birmingham, 1846–7.

reason to be satisfied with the whole arrangements', and went on to paint a rosy parting picture:

> … there was wonderful order, both above and below, and the crew and emigrants seemed to be as little out of sorts as if they had been out at sea for a fortnight. Upon deck children were playing, young lads and lasses chatting, women knitting, men pumping, girls cooking, friends talking together for the last time, and the honest tars cracking their jokes at every body's expense.[17]

While Sutherland and MacLennan exercised a virtual monopoly in Sutherland and Caithness, the number of agents advertising vessels in the Aberdeenshire press was in some years almost as extensive as the number of ships on offer. Such competition not only helped to keep prices down but may also have contributed to a generally high standard of service, as agents who lost their reputations were well aware that customers could easily transfer their business elsewhere. Between 1830 and 1880, a total of fifty-nine agents advertised over 100 ships sailing from Aberdeen and other local ports with passengers to various destinations, primarily in Canada, although several dabbled in the Australian and American emigrant trade as well. Even in the less well-known embarkation ports, no single agent controlled the trade. Six agencies seem to have been active in Peterhead between 1832 and 1857. William Volum (1832 and 1842), John Skelton (1832) and George Skelton (1842) sent four shiploads of emigrants to Canada, A. & J. Clark and John Hutchison sent one vessel to the Australian gold fields in 1853, and in 1857 William Gammack advertised his services as agent for 'respectable houses' in the passenger trade to all parts of America and Australia. From nearby Fraserburgh two agents, John Wemyss and George Wallace, sent vessels to Quebec in 1843 and 1854, while from Banff in 1851 and 1852 emigrant ships were sent to Quebec and Melbourne by Thomas Adam and James Wood respectively.

Very few of these agents dealt exclusively in the passenger trade; most were importers of Canadian timber, while some, like the Duthie brothers and George Thompson of Aberdeen, were shipbuilders. Alexander Duthie, as well as being a timber merchant who dabbled in the emigrant business for eight seasons, also ran vessels in the guano trade and was the first Aberdeen shipowner to establish a regular mercantile business between London and Australia. His shipyard built a string of vessels used on the transatlantic emigrant run, including the extremely popular and commodious *Brilliant*, which was represented by his brother William for thirteen consecutive years. Another brother, Robert, advertised three Canadian timber ships at various times in the 1830s. George Thompson had many strings to his bow. Not only was he a prosperous shipowner who operated a fleet of vessels to Quebec, gradually buying out his associates and extending his shipping empire to the Baltic, the Mediterranean, South Africa, South America, Australia, New Zealand and the Far East; his Aberdeen Line and Thistle Line operated out of London and Liverpool respectively, and he also served as Aberdeen's Dean of Guild (1840), Lord Provost (1847–50) and MP (1852–7).

Of the fifty-nine agents who dispatched emigrant ships from the Aberdeen area, nineteen also represented the interests of individuals and companies in other ports. This type of depersonalized, long-distance agency became increasingly important in the second half of the century, when large shipping companies in Glasgow, London and particularly Liverpool came to monopolize the emigrant trade. Steamship lines such as the White Star, Dominion, Cunard, P&O, Anchor, Allan, Black Ball and Black Star employed an ever-changing network of agents throughout Scotland, not just in erstwhile embarkation ports but also in the rural hinterlands. Unlike the earlier generation of agents, many of these men had no previous connection with shipping, and no personal interest in the recruitment of emigrants other than the commission they could earn from the shipping companies by booking passages for emigrants on their vessels. They included shopkeepers, merchants and businessmen who simply sold tickets on a part-time basis, but before the end of the century they had been joined by firms such as MacKay Brothers and H. W. J. Paton, professional travel agencies which were to continue throughout the twentieth century. The booking agents were courted not only by steamship companies. Competing destinations relied on them to advertise, distribute literature and arrange meetings for their representatives, giving them commission on each 'eligible' emigrant they recruited. By the 1890s, for instance, booking agents who sent emigrants to Canada not only received the shipping company's commission of 6s per passenger and the railway company's commission of 5 per cent on rail fares; they were also entitled to a bonus of 7s from the Canadian government on each farm labourer and domestic servant sent to the prairies. In 1903 the system was extended to provinces east of Manitoba and in 1906 the bonus was raised to £1.

Even in the era of centralized embarkations, local shipping agents could have a vital role, not only in making the emigrants' travelling arrangements but also in actively encouraging them to take the plunge, through persuasive advertising, liaising with government agents to secure employment for their clients, and sometimes accompanying their recruits overseas. James Scott of Ayr was regarded as an 'A1 agent' who at the turn of the century brought Ayrshire to 'the forefront of the Scottish counties' in terms of Canadian recruitment. At the same time Alexander Longmuir, a booking agent in Stonehaven, regularly accompanied parties to Canada, where he himself had lived for sixteen years, using these summer visits to look up previous settlers and gather information about future employment opportunities for his winter recruitment campaign. In July 1907, for instance, having accompanied a party of 200 emigrants to Winnipeg and supervised their distribution to situations which he had secured for them in advance, he went on to Moose Jaw and Regina, where he visited friends and acquaintances from the north of Scotland, including a Stonehaven couple who had emigrated in 1906 and were running a temperance hotel, as well as farming their quarter section. This service was not offered only by individuals. MacKay Brothers, a booking agency with offices across Lowland Scotland, regularly chartered trains to bring recruits to Glasgow, accompanying them across the Atlantic and often giving them letters of introduction to employers, and similar facilities were offered by well-known firms such as Paton and R. & J. Davidson. Walter Easton of Jedburgh adopted a slightly different approach, using his position as manager of the *Jedburgh Gazette* to publicize his experiences during a tour of Canada, and subsequently publishing the collected articles in an illustrated guidebook. And Mary Farnon of Falkirk, one of the few female booking agents, was described as 'quite a hustler and very anxious for business', despite being handicapped by an inaccessible office and a poor advertising window.[18]

But shipping agents did not enjoy an unblemished reputation, and nineteenth-century operators were just as controversial as their eighteenth-century predecessors. James Robertson, a Scot living in Prince Edward Island, was criticized by the Duke of Atholl in 1808 for transporting 700 people to the island at a rate of £9 a head, 'to make a profit of £5 per head independent of profit on the sale of land'.[19] It was probably the same agent who was castigated in the *Inverness Journal* in 1810 as a 'philanthropic crimp' who enticed the unwary Highlander to Prince Edward Island with the promise of 'a lairdship and an air-built castle', demanding a 50 per cent advance on the passage money, with the balance to be paid on embarkation, defaulters forfeiting their deposit. The anonymous critic pulled no punches:

> A set of nefarious vagabonds are at the present moment traversing the Highland districts of Scotland, for the purpose of deluding the poor ignorant natives, and seducing them from their mountains. One of these *man-dealers* goes about from hut to hut using all the arts of presuasion [*sic*] on ignorant credulity, blending falsehood with truth, exaggerating all the evils of their situation and of human existence, and painting, in the most fascinating colours, the fabulous pleasures, wealth, and independence of a trans-Atlantic life ... The little croft is then dismantled, and every thing turned into money, to gratify the insatiable voracity of this human shark; and when an intended emigrant has a large family, he will often give every penny he is worth in the world to one of those unprincipled impostors, even to the amount of hundreds of pounds, for carrying him and his little ones from their native glens, to a distant barbarous region, where they shall be doomed, perhaps for the rest of their lives, to cheerless exile, and the most abject slavery and destitution.[20]

While William Allan enjoyed good relations with the Sutherland estate management, the same could not be said of Thomas Dudgeon, a local farmer who in

1819 formed the short-lived Sutherland and Transatlantic Friendly Association to raise money to encourage emigration from the estate to America. The estate's opposition to Dudgeon – who, it claimed, was motivated by a desire 'to satisfy an old grudge he has to the family' – ensured that the Association's fund-raising efforts were doomed to failure, and it collapsed within six months. Extracts from the letter book of estate factor and land agent, Francis Suther, reflect something of the hostility to the way in which Dudgeon was raising public awareness of the Sutherland clearances, coupled with a fear that his Association was simply a front for encouraging rebellion within the estate. His report to James Loch on 24 July 1819 implies something of a local conspiracy to defraud would-be emigrants:

> Dudgeon had another meeting on Saturday at which upwards of 1000 persons they say were present brought from all quarters [to Meikle Ferry] in expectation of their receiving money … from the most distant parts of Caithness. Dudgeon's business of that day was the reverse of giving them pecuniary aid. He got money off them to subscribe to a paper the purpose of which when returning home they did not know and for which subscription each person paid at least 6d to Mr Dudgeon or his buddy in the swindle Gibson of Tain academy a teacher, besides Thomson the third fiddle in the trio who keeps the public house of the Ferry.[21]

Criticism of Highland agents may have stemmed partly from the wider controversies that bedevilled emigration from that region, but Lowland shippers did not escape censure. In 1844 Mathew Somerville of Glasgow raised an unsuccessful action in the Court of Session against Samuel Hemmans, the government emigration officer at Greenock, at whose instigation Somerville had been imprisoned for three months for defrauding a Colonsay family by selling them tickets for an emigrant ship which had already sailed. Despite challenging the decision on fourteen legal technicalities, Somerville's conviction was upheld on the grounds that it had breached the Passenger Act of 1842 in several ways. As Hemmans pointed out in his submission:

> In the month of August 1843, a family of poor highlanders, of the name of McNeill, consisting of the father, two sons, and a daughter, arrived in Glasgow from the island of Colonsay, with the intention of emigrating to Prince Edward's Island in North America. The father was 65 years of age, and scarcely,

if at all, able to read English, and the others were unable to speak a word of the language. They arrived in Glasgow on the 2nd of August, and on that day John McNeill, the father, called on the suspender, at his office in Glasgow, for the purpose of making a bargain with him for a passage from Glasgow to Liverpool, and thence to Quebec. After considerable discussion, the suspender agreed to secure the passage of the McNeills from Liverpool, in a vessel called the 'Ayrshire,' and to carry them from Glasgow to Liverpool, for the sum of L.6 in all. McNeill accordingly paid the suspender a deposit of L.4, the balance of L.2 being, according to agreement, to be paid in Liverpool. The suspender made out a contract ticket ... and this ticket he read over to McNeill. In reading it, he stated the sum of L.6 as the whole passage-money, and L.2 to be paid in Liverpool, in terms of the bargain. He also stated to McNeill, that the 'Ayrshire' was to sail on the 5th of August, and that he and his family would arrive in Liverpool in time to take their passage by her; at the same time instructing him not to show the ticket to any one until he got to Liverpool. These instructions McNeill obeyed. He started from Glasgow for Liverpool, by steamer, on Thursday the 3rd of August, and arrived in Liverpool on Friday the 4th. He there found the Ayrshire had sailed on the morning of that day; and it turned out that, so far from having intended to sail on the 5th, she had been advertised to sail on the 18th, 20th, 26th, 29th and 31st July preceding – that she had cleared at the custom-house on the 1st of August, and had only been detained till the morning of the 4th by contrary winds. It was also found that the ticket did not bind any person connected with the ship, and that no provision had been made for a passage for McNeill and his family, on any terms, in any vessel. On applying at a party of the name of Sherlock, to whom the suspender had given a letter, McNeill was amused, for some days, with hopes of a passage in another vessel, but was ultimately put off; and on his case falling under the notice of the emigration agent in Liverpool, he discovered, for the first time, on hearing the ticket read by that officer that it bore not L.6, but L.11 as the passage-money, and that L.7 instead of L.2, was to be paid in Liverpool. The suspender had probably calculated on McNeill preferring to pay the extra sum to returning, and if McNeill had had the money, his anticipation might probably have been correct. But, unfortunately, the extra L.5, more than exhausted the poor highlander's stock. Accordingly, after living a week at his own expense in Liverpool, and after paying to Sherlock & Company 23s. for provisions for the voyage, which he never received, he spent the remainder of his money in returning to Glasgow with his family, and had to find his way with them back to Colonsay as he best could.[22]

Even in Aberdeen, whose shipping agents were rarely the focus of public complaint, shipowner and passage broker Alex Cooper was fined £10 in 1855 in respect of each passenger whom he had illegally detained by issuing fraudulently dated tickets.[23] Other fraudulent agents who refused to honour their agreements, sold worthless tickets, operated dangerous or overcrowded vessels, disembarked passengers at the wrong ports or generally flouted the passenger acts were periodically embarrassed in the press, as well as the courts, and in 1851 *Chambers' Edinburgh Journal* complained about the uncaring attitude of timber traders, who 'seem to export or take away emigrants pretty much as a kind of ballast'.[24] On 4 January 1884 a disillusioned emigrant to the Canadian prairies warned readers of the *Aberdeen Journal* 'not to put too much faith in the representations of land and steamship agents, whose only care is to reap the profit of passing emigrants through their hands'. And in 1907–8, R. B. Arthur of Aberdeen came under bitter and sustained fire from a contingent of labourers whom he had recruited for a six-month contract with a lumber company at Clarke City in Quebec.

While assiduous ticket agents could be a godsend to hard-pressed full-time recruitment officers, they could also be a thorn in the flesh. Longside tailor William Maitland was frequently hauled over the coals by the Canadian immigration authorities for carelessness in making passage arrangements and neglecting to submit his claims for bonus payments until several months after the emigrants had sailed. More seriously, in 1912 he was convicted in Aberdeen Sheriff Court of failing to supply contract tickets to two farm servants whom he had booked for Canada. William Walker and Peter Simpson, both of Echt in Aberdeenshire, had paid a deposit of £1 in return for assisted passages to Ontario and subsequent employment as farm labourers. When Maitland's failure to hand over contract tickets bearing the vessel's name and the appointed sailing date resulted in their missing the boat, the agent was fined £2 and told to improve his business practice. Two years later Maitland was described by G. G. Archibald, Canadian government agent for the north of Scotland, as 'a peripatetic sort of agent' who on the one hand generated a 'large business' but on the other hand also provoked 'many complaints … about his failure to implement his promises with regard to looking after the baggage etc., of settlers'. Much worse, however, was the complaint made by an unnamed Toronto newspaper about the 'damnable lies' allegedly spread by a Blairgowrie agent, Andrew Spalding, who was 'engaged in this mean and despicable method of making a fat living out of lean and poor people' and 'should not be left outside prison walls'.[25]

Some of the best-documented complaints against turn-of-the-century booking agents were made by overseas governments in respect of the calibre of their recruits. Too many emigrants, they claimed, were being indiscriminately selected and inadequately supervised by men who knew nothing of the destinations to which they sold tickets and whose only concern was to secure as much commission as possible. Although the Canadian government representative for the north of Scotland found MacKay Brothers were 'very active and energetic' in their work in Aberdeen in 1911, he sometimes found it necessary to restrain them, since 'in their anxiety to do business they are sometimes inclined to overstep the mark in advertising'.[26] But the ultimate sanction against overenthusiastic booking agents was revocation of the commission they had received on recruits who were deemed unsuitable by the receiving countries or who did not take up the stipulated occupations of farm work or domestic service. Many of these emigrants were young women. In 1913 the Canadian immigration authorities received a strongly worded letter from a solicitor in Napanee, Ontario, regarding two unsatisfactory domestic servants who had been sent out by MacKay Brothers of Aberdeen. Mary Rait had allegedly 'belonged to the criminal class before she left the Old Country and has since been deported. She was sent to Mrs. W. J. Dollar of Napanee and defrauded her out of her passage money and was absolutely useless as a servant and was of a very bad moral character.' Isabella Mitchell, who had been hired as a cook, 'did not profess to know anything about cooking, was absolutely filthy about her personal habits and no respectable housekeeper would want her about the premises'. It was not right, protested the solicitor, 'that people should be permitted to defraud Canadians out of passage money for useless so-called servants, as neither of these girls were fit to enter the premises of any respectable person'.[27] A year later MacKay Brothers were denied a bonus on a girl who had not only shown no serious intention of taking up domestic service but had also been arrested for vagrancy. According to the immigration authorities, this was 'only one of several cases which have lately come to our attention where girls booked by you to Canada have not made good'. In 1917 the spotlight of criticism fell on Paton's agency, which had sent to Toronto an unmanageable young woman, Rose McIntyre, who 'was not much use as a domestic, had no experience and was careless, indifferent and lazy. She does not want to stay in domestic service, but wants to play the piano in a moving picture show.' After surviving only one week with her first employer, the cigarette-smoking Rose stayed for a month in her second position, until bad timekeeping led to her downfall. In addition to keeping her employer's baby out for five hours longer than she should have done, 'on another occasion on her Sunday off she did not return until Wednesday'. After a six-week sojourn with a third employer, Rose worked briefly in a munitions factory, before eloping to the United States, leaving her mother in Scotland to settle her debts.[28]

Booking agents were criticized for apathy as well as avarice and careless recruitment. Of the 190 northern Scottish agents on the Canadian government's books in 1909, ninety did virtually no business, while only 20 per cent of the 241 booking agents in the Glasgow agency were active and enthusiastic. Some 50 per cent were 'fair' and 30 per cent 'quite indifferent or useless', and there was a great reluctance among them to shoulder any of the expenses – even the advertising expenses – of a lecture, although it was they who would reap the benefit in the shape of bonuses.[29] By the turn of the century the crumbling reputation of booking agents brought them under the scrutiny of the Dominions Royal Commission, with a view to tighter regulation of their activities. In 1917 the Commission recommended the licensing of passage brokers and their agents by a central emigration authority, with each agent paying an annual licence fee, as well as submitting detailed accounts and records of bookings, but nothing was done, and complaints continued sporadically throughout the 1920s.

The network expands: the birth and growth of professional agencies

An honest and active shipping agent could be a key player in the recruitment process. Some of these men, as we have seen, had business interests in the places to which they sent emigrants, or went to some lengths in promoting the welfare of their clients. But by the steamship era most of them were primarily administrative cogs – albeit important cogs – in the wheel of an increasingly professionalized recruitment network whose priorities were dictated by overseas governments and railway companies.

Full-time agents began to appear intermittently in the British Isles in the 1830s and by the 1870s had become a permanent fixture. In 1839 Dr Thomas Rolph, an English emigrant to Canada, appointed himself as an itinerant agent in Britain, stressing Canada's advantages over Australia, particularly for Highland emigrants. From late 1840 until December 1842 (when the Colonial Office discontinued his appointment) he was an official agent, and during this period he liaised with Dr Norman McLeod in the production of the Gaelic emigration-promoting magazine *Cuairtear nan Gleann*, as well as organizing the short-lived

British American Association for Emigration and Colonization, of which the Duke of Argyll was president.[30]

Recruitment for Australia in the late 1830s and 1840s was in the hands of agents representing the government and colonial bounty schemes. One of the most important operators, appointed by New South Wales in 1836, was ship's surgeon Dr David Boyter, with a roving commission and instructions to liaise with T. F. Elliot, the British government's Agent-General for bounty emigration, and his two sub-agents at Greenock and Leith. Although the indefatigable Boyter travelled the length and breadth of Scotland, he made a particular impact in the Highlands, where his campaign coincided with the repercussions of the first major potato famine. At times his selective recruitment aroused the antagonism of destitution relief committees, which accused him of taking the cream of the population and leaving behind the old, the ill and the otherwise ineligible. Boyter, naturally enough, defended himself on the grounds that he was employed to select useful colonists for New South Wales, not to provide an escape route for impoverished Highlanders, although that might well be a by-product of his work. His meetings certainly drew the crowds, and most of the 5,200 Scots recruited under the government bounty scheme between 1837 and 1840 were probably Highlanders. On 30 May 1838 the *Inverness Courier* reported that news of his arrival at Fort William, 'like the fiery cross of old, soon spread through every glen in the district, and at an early hour on Monday, thousands of enterprising Gaels might be seen ranked around the Caledonian Hotel, anxious to quit the land of their forefathers and to go and possess the unbounded pastures of Australia.' By February 1839 Boyter was based at Blairgowrie, and by August at Tobermory, from where he sent an encouraging advertisement to the *Inverness Courier*, published on 28 August:

> By recent official accounts I have received from New South Wales, the arrival of *all* the Emigrant Ships from the Highlands was mentioned (with the exception of the *Asia* which was not due.) It appears that the people were well received, and immediately employed at a high rate of wages. Some difficulty was felt by those who had large young families. In consequence of this gratifying information, I propose dispatching the last ship for the season from Cromarty, some time in the month of October, being found the best month in the year for a speedy passage. It is therefore requested that all those intending to take advantage of this opportunity, will send in their names by the 10th of September, that a ship of suitable size may be engaged for their conveyance.

Applicants were reminded to obtain testimonials, and not to make any arrangements until Boyter had issued them with a certificate of approval.

Boyter's work was matched by the efforts of Dr John Dunmore Lang to recruit Scottish settlers under the colonial bounty scheme for his brother Andrew's estate in the Hunter Valley, 100 miles north of Sydney. Lang, a native of Greenock and the colony's first Presbyterian minister, secured almost 4,000 impoverished Highlanders in 1837, continuing a long-standing tradition of clerical involvement in the encouragement of Scottish emigrants that had included Father James MacDonald's recruitment of 210 Catholic Highlanders for Prince Edward Island in 1772 and Norman McLeod's global odyssey, which saw him lead a shipload of 400 emigrants from Assynt to Cape Breton in 1817, on to Australia in 1849, and finally to Waipu in the North Island of New Zealand in 1851.[31]

It was the province of Otago, in New Zealand's South Island, that was to provide the most striking example of clerical agency in the nineteenth century. George Rennie's proposal in 1842 to found a Presbyterian colony in New Zealand was given added impetus by the formation of the Free Church of Scotland the following year, and by early 1844 over 200 people had registered their desire to emigrate and purchase land. By the time the pioneer expedition left in December 1847, the efforts of the Reverend Thomas Burns of Portobello had ensured the wholehearted commitment of the new Free Church to the scheme, and had opened the way for the establishment of Otago as a specifically Free Church colony. Burns toured Scotland, winning the support of fellow ministers, who often invited him to promote the scheme from their pulpits. But the reluctance of these same ministers to involve the Church in 'worldly' transactions led to the establishment in 1845 of the Lay Association of the Free Church, the body which was to be instrumental in negotiating with the New Zealand Company for the early settlement of Otago. John McGlashan, secretary of the Otago Association from 1847 until its dissolution in 1853, was another active propagandist. Not only did he edit and distribute many thousand copies of the *Otago Journal*, of which there were eight issues published between 1848 and 1852, he also advertised widely in provincial newspapers, and gave verbal as well as written encouragement, sometimes touring the country in company with Thomas Burns.

In a series of lectures delivered in Aberdeenshire in January 1850, McGlashan was at pains to alert disgruntled farmers to better prospects in New Zealand. Shortly afterwards, at a meeting of his Association's directors, he defended his decision to conduct a recruitment campaign in Aberdeenshire, rather than proceeding to Inverness in accordance with instructions. Although the change of plan was dictated partly by weather conditions, there was also a more positive reason:

After waiting upon Mr McCombie of Jellybrands, a member of the Association, understanding from him that there was a probability of much good being done by visiting various districts in the county, I at once resolved, with his advice, to hold meetings at the following places – Peterculter – Inverury – Kintore-Newhills – Woodside – Ellon – New Machar – Banchory-Devenick – Udney – Banchory-Ternan – Keig and Tough, and Aberdeen. The remainder of the week was devoted to preliminary visits to most of these places, to making arrangements for the proposed meetings, and to interviews and correspondence with individuals likely to advance the object.

A meeting was held at each of the above places; all of them were well-attended, and not by Free Churchmen alone, but by members of different Churches, particularly the Establishment; in several instances farmers were present from distances of 5 and 7 miles, and in many instances of 4, 3 & 2 miles from the place of meeting. The Clergy, Elders and Deacons of the Free Church, in every instance, gave their friendly co-operation in imparting an interest to the proceedings. The meetings were intimated on the preceding Sabbath from the Pulpits of the Free Churches, and sometimes of the Established Churches, and by Handbills distributed through the Parish and neighbouring Parishes; and many of the audience on each occasion manifested their interest in the statements made by asking questions and purchasing copies of the Otago Journal, of which and other papers a large number was sold and distributed gratis.

As to immediate fruits, I am able to report only two families; who purpose to proceed to the Settlement by the April or following Ship, and before sailing to purchase two Properties. I left with them Letters of Introduction to the Bankers. There is the strongest reason to believe, however, that much good will arise from what has been done. In Aberdeenshire, from all I could learn, small farms are being absorbed by union into large ones; and in Keig and Tough, on the property of Lord Forbes, many leases are out and I was told the tenants have received no intimation that they will be renewed. The conjecture was therefore most reasonable for directing attention to Otago; and the Clergymen and others in the several districts assured me that my Statements had excited great interest, would be discussed and pondered, and would produce a fermentation in the minds of many ending with the desired result. As a help to this, I succeeded in getting the address at Aberdeen reported in four of the Newspapers, of different politics, there published.[32]

One of the 247 pioneers who sailed from Greenock to Otago in December 1847, under the personal supervision of Thomas Burns, was James Adam, an Aberdeen shipwright. Ten years later, when the provincial government sent him back to Britain as an agent, several settlers offered to pay the passages of their friends if Adam could induce them to come to New Zealand, and during the following year he directly and indirectly encouraged 4,000 new colonists, 800 of whom were related to existing settlers. The influence of Burns and McGlashan in Adam's own decision to emigrate was made clear in his guidebook, *Twenty-Five Years of Emigrant Life in the South of New Zealand*, originally published in 1857 but reprinted on the occasion of Adam's second recruitment visit to Britain in 1873:

> On a dark night, nearly thirty years ago, I was passing through Belmont Street, Aberdeen, when I accidentally heard that two gentlemen from Edinburgh were to address a meeting in the Free South Church on the subject of emigration to the South of New Zealand. Having for some time entertained the thought of emigrating to America, I resolved to hear what could be said about the remote islands of New Zealand and its [sic] cannibal inhabitants ... The addresses of both gentlemen were very short, and the information of a very limited kind, for they were speaking of a country which they had never seen, and of a life to which they were utter strangers. I was, however, favourably impressed with what Mr Burns said ... I had sense enough to know that toil, and perhaps danger, were the concomitants of life in New Zealand; but the simple fact that Mr Burns had resigned his charge and cast in his lot with the emigrants, and would sail with the pioneers, gave confidence in the statements of the reverend gentleman.[33]

Adam was by no means the only Antipodean agent sent to Britain. As the various provinces of Australia and New Zealand began to attain self-government, so they began increasingly to appoint their own itinerant selecting agents. They included John Thorne of South Australia, H. S. Ranford of Western Australia and, most notably, Henry Jordan of Queensland. Having emigrated from Derby to Sydney and then Brisbane as a dentist and missionary in the early 1850s, Jordan returned to Britain in 1860 as an immigration agent for the new province of Queensland. Over the next five years he lectured and published widely, working closely with provincial newspapers to ensure widespread coverage of his work and with the Black Ball Line and its local agents to transfer his recruits on 5 per cent commission. His lectures were reinforced by press advertisements and handbills that emphasized the free land grants offered to full fare-paying passengers, as well as the assisted passages offered to poorer emigrants who could take up labouring jobs. In 1863 he undertook a lecture tour in the north of Scotland, and Queensland's sudden rise in popularity with Scottish emigrants in 1865 – when as many as 1,510 emigrants sailed from Glasgow – was undoubtedly attributable to Jordan's enthusiastic canvassing.[34]

Some of our evidence about the impact of Antipodean agents in the late nineteenth century comes from complaints made by their Canadian rivals. In 1874 the Canadian government agent in Glasgow noted that 'a very considerable number' of that year's potential recruits had been diverted from Canada to New Zealand as a result of the latter's offer of free passages. The same point was made more explicitly by Angus Nicholson, Canada's Special Immigration Agent in the Highlands:

> All the competing Emigration Agencies formerly reported on, are still at work as actively as ever. The New Zealand and Australian authorities are particularly alert, the streets of every town and village being always well ornamented with their bills and placards offering *free passages* and other inducements to emigrants. Not only so, but nearly all the newspapers being subsidized by means of their advertisements, are doing their full share in the same direction.[35]

In at least three annual reports to Ottawa – in 1881, 1882 and 1883 – the Canadian High Commissioner in London complained that the New Zealand government's offer of free passages to domestic servants, and the availability of £2 and £5 passages to New South Wales, were thwarting Canadian efforts to attract settlers, who had to pay their own fares. But more serious still were the activities of the Queensland government, which in the 1880s offered free passages to farm labourers and domestic servants, and assisted passages to selected tradesmen. Then, after being suspended during the early 1890s, Queensland reintroduced free passages by the end of the decade. As a result, in 1898 almost 400 Scots allegedly went to Queensland, as, according to the Carnoustie-based Canadian agent, Thomas Duncan, emigrants' attention was once more diverted from Canada by booking agents who were interested only in securing their commission along with the Queensland government's bonus of 10s 6d per adult. These complaints were reiterated eleven years later when an inspection of the Glasgow agency area revealed that, owing to better bonuses and more unambiguous encouragement, 'some of the booking agents have practically stopped working for Canada, and are now doing their best for Australia'.[36]

Surprisingly little reference was made by these Canadian officials to competition from American agents, although the United States attracted more Scottish emigrants than any other destination in the course of the nineteenth century. Following the largely unregulated and sometimes 'reckless' recruitment campaigns of Virginia, Tennessee, Georgia and particularly Texas in and before the 1840s, twenty-five of the thirty-eight states had developed official – and more circumspect – immigration programmes by 1870. Michigan led the way in 1845, while other northerly states such as Wisconsin and Minnesota followed suit, as state governments and railway companies sent their representatives to compete for emigrants from Britain and Europe.[37] In 1872 Angus Nicholson made mention of Nebraskan agents at work in the Highlands, in the same year as W. J. Patterson, after touring Britain and Europe at the behest of the Canadian government, identified a long list of competing agencies as well as the prospects for future Canadian recruitment. 'The immense emigration which takes place annually from Great Britain and the Continent to the United States', he noted, 'affords abundant evidence of the systematic activity of the various agencies set in motion to promote and increase it.'[38] Foremost among these agencies was the state of Minnesota, which had not only a highly salaried manager in London but also a Scottish representative, the Reverend Robert Kerr of Forres, who had recently returned from the state to promote a temperance colony in the Red River Valley, on land along the line of the Northern Pacific Railway.

Immigrants of all nationalities were recruited not only for rural America but increasingly to work in factories, mines and other industrial enterprises. This trend became particularly controversial towards the end of the century, as American labour grew increasingly resentful of the way in which employers used aliens to repress wages, break strikes and destroy attempts at union organization. When in 1885 the hostility took legislative form, agents had to tread warily to avoid falling foul of the Alien Contract Labour Law, which was designed to prevent the introduction into the United States of foreign contract workers to perform work that was the prerogative of native labour. George Berry was one agent who did not tread warily enough. In 1886 he came to Aberdeen promising at least eighteen months' work to up to 165 contract labourers who would accompany him to Texas to help construct the new State Capitol. Having failed to tell his recruits that they would be breaking a strike called by the American Granite Cutters' Union in protest at the use of cheap convict labour, he fell foul of the legislation, as did his boss, Gus Wilke, the main contractor, who in 1887 was fined $64,000 for violation of the Contract Labour Law, a penalty that was later reduced to $8,000 on appeal.

Equally controversial, though for different reasons, was an agricultural colonization scheme undertaken by the government of Cape Colony between 1877 and 1883. Encouragement to emigrate to the Cape had always been intermittent, low-key and heavily qualified, as economic and political problems, combined with continuous border unrest, made South Africa a less attractive proposition than North America or the Antipodes. The sudden demand for labour after the discovery of diamonds led to the appointment of a London-based emigration agent in 1873, and by the end of 1875 the sale of Crown lands had financed the importation of nearly 3,300 British emigrants for employment on farms and railway construction. Further legislation in 1877, by which Crown lands were set aside for immigrants, led to the introduction of several shiploads of Scottish and German agricultural labourers to the Eastern Cape, where it was hoped they would form a buffer against incursions by the Xhosa of the Transkei, and pacify farmers who had been complaining about the theft of stock and insufficient labour. During 1877 361 Scots from the counties of Aberdeen, Argyll, Ayr, Dumfries, Lanark and Perth were given free passages to East London and King William's Town, and settled in districts that were allegedly 'the finest in Cape Colony for farming', where 'for the industrious and persevering man of frugal and sober habits the chances of success are great'.[39]

Unfortunately, neither the new settlers nor the residents of East London saw things in the same light as the Cape immigration authorities. According to a correspondent of the *East London Daily Despatch*, one of the Scots immigrants told him that while 'he liked the place well enough ... the promises he had before he left Scotland, as regards the advantages he was to have in making himself a little better than he was at home, were a complete swindle'. The East Londoners, for their part, complained that many of the new arrivals were 'not the class the colony wants, or, I fear, the Govt fancies it is getting'. Far from being agriculturists, they 'have not the slightest knowledge of, or taste for, such a vocation ... [but] simply become loungers and hangers on about some public works learning lazy and dissipated habits, neither doing well for themselves, their families, or the country of their adoption'.[40]

A combination of border unrest and economic recession led to the tempo-rary suspension of immigration in 1878. Although the 105 Scots who followed in 1880 were mostly 'a respectable lot of people', they were equally unwilling to turn their hand to agriculture and incurred the wrath of immigration superin-tendent, J. B. Hellier, for making false statements about their treatment to the press and for seeking wage labour rather than taking up their land immediately. According to Hellier, misleading assertions by W. Burnet, the Cape govern-ment's agent in London, that farm labouring work was readily available, 'which is about as contrary to the fact as can possibly be', had encouraged too many men without means to come out to East London.[41]

In 1881 an even more controversial scheme was launched when Edinburgh-based John Walker, formerly an estate manager and magistrate in Shetland, was appointed as a temporary special agent, first to inspect vacant land in the East London district and then to recruit up to 300 agriculturists for a 'Scotch settle-ment'. Walker, who also had some Australian experience, was awarded a salary of £700 per annum, as well as travelling expenses, to recruit either tenant farmers under specific contracts or bona fide agricultural settlers with at least £50 capital. His appointment did not meet with the approval of the *East London Daily Despatch*. A strongly worded editorial on 12 October 1881 questioned his competence and expressed concern that public money was being wasted on a scheme that seemed likely to benefit only the landowners. Men such as Walker, it argued,

> when they come to the Colony, and assert themselves in this way and that, really ought to come before the public and present their credentials, and get themselves understood, before allowing the Government to broach their unknown names as guarantees for important undertakings … All that we want is to see them real settlers, and the parents of settlers, tillers of the soil, and the eventual backbone of the country. Nobody begrudges what is done for them, so long as this end can be assured. But we do not want them nominally occupying the soil, and secure of the tenure of it, but really earning a continuous living on the public works or in private establishments in town.

Two months later, similar views were expressed in a letter from a farmer who, while admitting the need for extensive immigration, argued that it was both cruel to the settler and detrimental to the development of the country for the government to 'lure people out by land or free passage and then leave them in the lurch' by failing to tell them of the drawbacks of distance from markets, the paucity of good land and the high start-up costs.[42]

Perhaps the Crown Lands Commissioner, J. X. Merriman, had these press criticisms in mind when on 17 December 1881 he chastised Walker for overzealous advertising:

> I cannot too strongly impress upon you that it would be misleading people were they to be induced to come out here under the idea that they will get 'first class' land. They will, in fact, get the leavings of the older colonists – good enough land, especially in Kaffraria, and land on which an industrious hard-working man may make a living … but it would be a misnomer to call it first-rate and the Govt is, before everything, anxious not to give a handle to those who may accuse it of misleading statements. The country is good enough, and the climate and the conditions of life are certainly easier than in Canada, for instance; but it is no Tom Tiddler's ground, where a fortune is to be picked up without working for it. In any future advertisements or circulars, I beg that the land may be described as 'fair' and not as 'first-class'.[43]

Undaunted, Walker continued to ignore orders not to exaggerate and repeatedly exceeded the authority granted him by the Cape government, browbeating Burnet in London and forcing him to secure passages for categories of settlers not included in Walker's original instructions. The result was considerable discontent among colonists who had erroneously expected grants of public money to establish them on their farms. To the disgust of Hellier and his colleagues, several either abandoned or never took up their holdings, refusing to sign leases which they claimed did not accord with promises made to them before they left and continuing to make 'unreasonable demands' for financial assistance and larger acreages. The location at Kei Mouth was a virtually roadless wilderness, remote from any markets, and with a preponderance of poor land where stock did not thrive. A correspondent of the *East London Daily Despatch* castigated the colonists for inciting native labourers to disobey orders to leave the farms where they were squatting, while the colonists berated 'a weak and imbecile government' for ineffective policing and claimed that they had been 'inveigled from home and comfort to mere abject poverty through the instrumentality of unscrupulous agents and untruthful pamphleteers'.[44] Amidst all these claims and counter-claims, the Kei Mouth settlement withered on the vine, a fiasco orchestrated by a fly-by-night agent whom the *East London Daily Despatch* denounced as 'an imposter or a fool'.[45]

The network matures: Canadian agents in Scotland

Available evidence indicates that the agents who made the most consistent and telling impact on Scotland were those who represented Canada after Confederation. But even before 1867, steps were being taken to promote and fund agency work. In 1852 the Province of Canada created a Bureau of Agriculture, with responsibility for promoting immigration, and two years later the legislature granted its first funds for that purpose. In 1859 a Canadian information office was opened in Liverpool, and itinerant agents appeared intermittently in Scotland and elsewhere, promoting particular provinces. One of those agents was James Brown, a native of Inverarity, Angus, who had emigrated to New Brunswick in 1810 and in 1830 was elected to the House of Assembly. While that province had received a steady stream of settlers in the first three decades of the nineteenth century, the economic downturn of the 1840s stemmed the flow. The appointment of Moses Perley as a London-based agent in the 1850s made little difference, and by 1860 the provincial authorities were uncomfortably aware that barely a tenth of emigrants from Europe who landed in New Brunswick actually settled there. After the Saint John Mechanics' Institute had run a prize essay competition on 'New Brunswick as a Home for Emigrants', the provincial authorities selected one of the three winners, James Brown, to tour Britain and Ireland, where he delivered sixty lectures in an eleven-month period in 1861 and 1862, and distributed large quantities of literature. The immediate catalyst for his appointment was the recent Glassville scandal, when William Glass, a Presbyterian minister and immigrant of twenty years' standing, had obtained a large plot of land near Woodstock and had returned to his native Aberdeen to recruit colonists. Concerned about bad publicity arising from poor conditions on the passage and the high price paid by the emigrants for infertile, uncleared land to which Glass had no rights, the provincial government recruited Brown to repair the damage and rehabilitate New Brunswick in the eyes of would-be emigrants. His diary, his published report at the end of his assignment and a substantial volume of correspondence together give us an insight into how he approached that task.

Brown sailed from Halifax to Liverpool, and almost immediately travelled north to Glasgow and Dundee, where he visited relatives as well as delivering twelve lectures in the county of Angus, and a further two in Glasgow and Ayr. His meetings in Glasgow and Arbroath drew audiences of 1,000 and 750 respectively, larger numbers than he was to encounter elsewhere, particularly in England, where at some venues the turnout was no more than fifty. After a tempestuous two-month sojourn in Ireland, he returned to Scotland, lecturing in Edinburgh, Fife, the Lothians, the north-east, Perthshire, Arran and the south-west before going south. Brown drew heavily on his own experiences as a farmer, emphasized the intellectual progress of New Brunswick and wherever possible tried to tailor his message to his audience by citing examples of local emigrants who had done well. But although the number of emigrants to New Brunswick rose briefly from 1861 to 1863, Brown's effectiveness was hampered by the lack of an 'advance man' to book venues, find a chairman and negotiate favourable publicity with local newspaper editors, and by competition from other destinations, notably Queensland, which at that time was being heavily canvassed by Henry Jordan. Brown was particularly handicapped by being forbidden to make any arrangements with shipping companies to subsidize passages to New Brunswick, or indeed to incur any liabilities on behalf of the provincial government. By no means all newspaper editors could be manipulated as he wished, and the organizational difficulties of an itinerant lecturer, without a base or administrative support, clearly militated against him. By the end of his tour he had wearied of the 'continual care, fear and anxiety ... with cost wholly beyond my expectation', but his most lasting regret was that the work he had begun did not lay the foundations for a longer-term strategy of professional promotion.[46]

Such a strategy was to be set in motion after Confederation, and by the end of the nineteenth century an army of professional Canadian agents had extended its tentacles into even the remotest corners of the British Isles, Europe and the United States. In 1867 the federal and provincial departments of agriculture were given concurrent responsibility for immigration, although in practice most of the promotional work was done by the federal department. In 1893 the headed notepaper changed, when responsibility was transferred to the department of the interior, but policy remained fairly consistent, irrespective of which office had its hand on the tiller. Resident agents were stationed in ports and other strategic towns throughout the British Isles to promote Canada as a destination and to inspect passengers as they embarked. The work was coordinated by a head office in London which after 1899 became both physically and functionally removed from the day-to-day control of the High Commissioner, with separate offices at Charing Cross (rather than Canada House in Trafalgar Square) and its focus on the world of business rather than diplomacy.

The ever-growing head of steam behind Canadian agency activity was partly the result of the concern of the federal government and the transcontinental railway companies to populate the vast prairie provinces for reasons of, respectively, national unity and economic viability. Between 1896 and 1906 an injection of C$4 million by the federal government gave the work an even higher profile, at the same time as an upsurge of imperialist sentiment in Britain fuelled enthusiasm for all things Canadian. Recruitment was targeted primarily on the farming community, not only because farmers were needed to fill up the west but also because the prolonged depression in British agriculture was likely to make them particularly susceptible to the promise of homestead land, and, as we have seen, booking agents could after 1893 claim a bonus on each farm worker recruited. When W. J. Patterson had investigated prospects for emigration from Britain and Europe in 1872 his report on Scotland was comprehensive and generally optimistic:

> Extensive inquiries in North Britain among mechanics, farmers, and gentlemen who know the condition of the people, convince me that a large emigration to Canada can be promoted – but in Scotland as in England, there is a remarkable lack of information as to the advantages offered to emigrants to the Dominion. There is a class of farm laborers (or hinds, as they are sometimes designated) in the Lothians, who, I am informed, would make good settlers. There are also the tenant-farmers in Kincardineshire, Aberdeenshire, and other north-eastern counties, among whom there is a growing desire to better their condition, while the disposition to emigrate is on the increase in most of the northern shires. The people of Shetland are very poor, and said to be unambitious, in consequence of their patient toil and endurance, but they might be stimulated to try to help themselves, if it were demonstrated that they could effectually do it by emigrating. The question of emigration is also not unknown in Orkney, and I am informed by a gentleman who has recently travelled there, that the Orcadians would make good settlers in any country where they had a fair chance to better their condition.[47]

The real linchpins of the network were the resident agents and their helpers. The number of agencies varied according to budgets and demand, but there were always offices in Liverpool, Glasgow and Bristol, and several special agents were appointed from year to year for temporary work in a wide range of locations. They were carefully chosen with reference to local needs and connections, so that virtually all the lecturers who visited the north of Scotland were Gaelic-speaking. They were generally either emigrants themselves, first-generation Canadians who had roots in the areas to which they were sent, or men such as H. M. Murray, the Glasgow agent, who had some specialist knowledge of emigration procedure, in Murray's case as a purser with one of the transatlantic shipping companies. These men were responsible both for generating interest themselves and for coordinating the activities of temporary helpers, visiting delegates and the mixed bag of ticket agents. They exploited every promotional tool available to them. Written advertising was the easiest method of blanket publicity and was reckoned to be the first step in alerting public interest, at least in the view of William Dixon, who in 1866 announced his appointment to the Liverpool office in 114 newspapers. His example was followed with great enthusiasm by counterparts all over the country, who, in addition to regular press advertising, also displayed colourful posters and handbills in libraries, post offices, railway stations, hotels and farmers' clubs. They also ensured that government-sponsored pamphlets were mailed to many of these institutions, as well as to individual farmers, clergymen and teachers. Essay competitions were organized for children and schools were given atlases, wall maps and other literature.

The written word was reinforced by a strong emphasis on visual and verbal promotion. Displays of Canadian produce were mounted at agricultural shows and markets, and also in the windows of the agents' offices, which were usually strategically located in city centres. During the summer, two travelling horse-drawn exhibition wagons toured the rural areas of Scotland and Ireland, and two motorcars were sent round England on the same mission. Lectures were generally illustrated by lantern slides, before the improvement of technology in the twentieth century gave rise to promotional movies. The agents set a particular premium on lecture tours, encompassing not only the urban hinterland but also the most remote parts of their districts, usually in the winter months. The resident agents themselves were assiduous lecturers, and they were frequently joined on the circuit by temporary assistants, provincial agents and railway company representatives. Delegations of journalists and tenant farmers were invited to tour Canada at government expense, in the hope that they would themselves promote settlement opportunities on their return home, while, reversing the process, successful settlers were also brought back at government expense to lecture on their experiences. Personal contact went beyond the formal lecture, for the agents spent a great deal of time interviewing interested parties individually, in their own offices, at regional booking agencies and on their frequent trips to agricultural fairs and markets. The personal touch was

7. Advertising for immigration to Canada by the federal authorities, 1905. A wagon pulled by horses, heavily laden with agricultural produce.

taken further by those who, like some of the more enthusiastic booking agents, also accompanied their recruits across the Atlantic, securing employment and helping them to settle in, at the same time as they collected fresh material for their winter campaigns.

What impact did these agents make on Scotland? From 1869 to 1907 the whole of Scotland, along with the north of England, was under the control of one agent, based in Glasgow. From time to time he was assisted by a variety of special lecturers, the first being Angus Nicholson, who was based in the Highlands from 1872 to 1875. In his first year he sent out 670 emigrants, and found the Hebrides his most promising area, as he indicated in his annual report:

> I made appointments and delivered addresses in Glasgow, Greenock, Rothesay, Perth and other towns. My meetings were generally well attended, and as I was able to address the people in their native tongue, the language many of them best understood, the enthusiasm created by, and the general interest taken in my work and the cause which I had to advocate, was all I could desire; but owing to the prosperous condition of those districts, which are principally occupied by large farmers and stock raisers, I was not able to do quite as much as I anticipated.

In the latter end of May I went to the Northern Hebrides and visited the islands of Skye, Lewis, Harris and Uist; I soon learned that more could be done there than in the Southern parts of the Highlands. On my arrival, I found the people in the height of an emigration excitement, not to Canada, however, but to New Zealand and Nebraska, and from the many agents representing these countries, I have met with considerable opposition; but I believe I have generally come out the victor, having sent most of those they had engaged at the time, to Canada, and I think, turned the current here for some time, if properly followed up.

As a field for emigration, the Highlands of Scotland is for various reasons, perhaps the most important district in Great Britain; there are many who need to benefit their condition by emigrating, many parts of the country being much over-peopled, owing to the large tracts cleared for sheep, deer and English pleasure grounds, and the inhabitants are generally admitted to be as desirable a class for the settlement of Canada as any we can get, but owing to the absence of any Canadian Emigration Agent there for many years back, and the false representations of parties interested in emigration to other countries, this field would have been lost to us, had it not been for the timely action of the Government in sending an agent there this year. Once the current of Highland emigration is started in any direction, it is hard to change it; hence the importance of keeping at least one agent permanently located in the North of Scotland.[48]

Nicholson's technique was to hold public meetings in the main centres of population, and to remain in the area for a short time so that people could consult him privately. He would then revisit the area at subsequent – well-advertised – intervals. He also made use of favourable letters from emigrants who had used his services, and in 1875 he had the help of the Reverend Lachlan Taylor, another Gaelic speaker, seconded from Devon, who encouraged better-off emigrants to go to Manitoba and the North West Territories. Nicholson was convinced that more generous subsidies would have paid dividends in the recruitment of poorer emigrants:

At some of the meetings large numbers of the people got up and offered to leave at once if we could provide the means to pay their passage, which they were unable to do themselves. These people, used to hardships and rough living at home, are well adapted to Canadian pioneer life, with its future prospects of independence. Those who had emigrated have not remained about the towns and cities, waiting for something to turn up, or complaining of the want of work. Two or three hundred people could be at once got to proceed from here to Manitoba if free passage could be granted, as is offered by New Zealand. Knowing the people and their characteristics so well, I could personally guarantee that nearly every one of them would stay in Canada, and prove a first-class settler.[49]

Although that suggestion fell on deaf ears, in 1879 the Canadian government recruited all but four of its first batch of fourteen farmer delegates from Scotland, and in 1892 appointed W. G. Stuart and Peter Fleming to assist the Glasgow agent by covering the north of Scotland and the Lowlands respectively. Stuart and Fleming delivered between them an average of 320 lectures per year during the 1890s, and both men emphasized the importance of this propaganda tool. In his report to Ottawa in 1896, Stuart wrote:

The people like to see, as well as hear, and in country districts, by far the most profitable field for emigration work, an illustrated lecture is a never failing attraction; and a crowded meeting means enthusiasm, rivetted attention, eager inquiry, and sometimes public discussion. After the lecture is over pamphlets are distributed which are carried home and read. People talk about Canada at their own firesides, and often write for further and fuller information. If at all practicable a personal visit is arranged and a decided impetus is given to emigration from that district, for the experience of the past four years has clearly demonstrated that it is only by earnest concentration of effort that a desirable class of emigrants can be secured. The Scotch are proverbially cautious; and they will not leave their homes nor change their mode of life until they have looked at the matter carefully in all its bearings, and come to the conscientious conviction that it is to their advantage to do so.[50]

Fleming confirmed the value of the personal approach. In an attempt to ensure interested agricultural audiences, he used the valuation rolls to write in advance to all farmers paying rents of less than £70 per annum, sending to each household a selection of Canadian literature, along with a handbill listing the places and times when he was to deliver lectures. Also writing in 1896, he described his approach to his employers:

I invariably adopt the conversational style of lecture, and at the outset invite my audience to put any question to me even during the course of my address, and in this way get facts driven home to them and give information and advice on points they are specially desirous of being enlightened upon, in a way which is not possible in a formal lecture with the usual paraphernalia of chairman and other accompaniments. The people are quite at their ease, feel quite at home, and judging from the intelligent questions which are put to me, they are as eager for information and as interested as if I were sitting vis a vis with each individual in my own office. At the conclusion of each meeting numbers of my audience invariably remain behind and an interesting and effective chat with them is the result. This method, after many years' experience in dealing with this class, I have found to be the most effective.[51]

Fleming was indeed a seasoned agent, having represented the Queensland government in Scotland in the 1880s, and having also worked as a travelling selecting agent for Western Australia at an earlier date. When his Antipodean employment ended with the cessation of assisted passages to Queensland in 1891, he turned his attention to Canada, familiarized himself with the country during a two-month tour in 1892 and then, armed with glowing testimonials from his previous employer, successfully offered his services to the immigration authorities. Stuart, based first in Nethy Bridge and later in Elgin, was an Inverness town councillor and a fluent Gaelic speaker who firmly believed that emigration was the only solution to continuing poverty in the Highlands. He had come to the Canadian government's notice during a six-month visit to the Dominion in winter 1891–2, as a result of which he was first appointed as a temporary agent at the Highland and Agricultural Society Show in summer 1892, and then as a supplementary agent for the north of Scotland in December.

By 1897 the Canadian government had located five agents north of the border, compared with three in Ireland, two in England and one in Wales. Chief agent, H. M. Murray, who had replaced Thomas Grahame in July 1897, was assisted not only by Stuart and Fleming, but also by John Grant of Dumfries, covering southern Scotland, and Thomas Duncan, a Scottish-born farmer and Member of the Provincial Parliament of Manitoba, who was based in Carnoustie but had a roving commission. When Fleming retired in 1898, Stuart extended his jurisdiction further south and east, with continuing help from Duncan and the use of a tent (supplied by the Glasgow office) which housed an exhibition of Canadian produce. After Stuart's death in April 1899, Duncan devoted most of his time to the north of Scotland until 1902, when he was transferred to London, and the withdrawal of Grant from agency activity in the same year meant that Canadian recruitment efforts became confined to the Glasgow office.

By that time, however, the intensified Canadian recruitment campaign, coupled with the extension of bonuses to the non-prairie provinces, was generating an unremitting stream of enquiries that the Glasgow office found it ever harder to cope with unaided. So in 1907, shortly after the Glasgow agent, J. Bruce Walker, had moved to London to become Assistant Superintendent of Emigration, he successfully argued the case for an additional permanent agent to be sent from Canada to cover the north of Scotland. While Malcolm McIntyre headed the Glasgow agency, lecturing and visiting booking agents in twenty-one counties, in places as far apart as Campbeltown and Crieff, Carnoustie and Castle Douglas, John MacLennan, a Gaelic-speaking Canadian of Highland descent, arrived in Aberdeen with his wife and two children on 4 February to open a new regional office at 26 Guild Street, adjacent to the docks and railway station. He followed the usual procedures of distributing literature to individuals and institutions, liaising with booking agents and lecturing and interviewing throughout his area. His surviving weekly reports to his superiors in Ottawa supplement his more general annual reports, giving a detailed insight into the range of his activities, and in particular revealing the daunting and unremitting workload that was imposed on him. Most of his office time was spent in initiating or answering correspondence, and in interviewing ticket agents or prospective emigrants. In his first annual report he noted that the office, which was open to the public from 8.15 a.m. to 9.30 or even 10.30 p.m., six days a week, had received an average of twenty-five to thirty visitors daily, but sometimes many more. During the first week of opening, he had conducted 258 interviews, 114 of them in one day, and during the following week he interviewed 345 visitors. He also received an average of 100 letters per week, though in winter 1909–10 his incoming mail increased dramatically, and during one week in January 1910 he received a record 1,299 letters. When he arrived in Aberdeen, he was faced with a backlog of mail to answer, and he continued to send out about 100 items of correspondence a week, including maps, atlases and parcels of promotional literature. During 1908 his office dispatched a total of 7,500 school atlases and 150 wall maps, as well as 45,000 pamphlets to booking agents, who clamoured for still more in order to keep up with public demand.

It was also part of MacLennan's duties to inspect all the booking agencies within his territory, as well as to receive their bonus claims and forward them to

Ottawa. By February 1909 he had visited – sometimes more than once – 149 of the 190 booking offices in his area, which sometimes involved making week-long trips to the Northern or Western Isles. He often took the opportunity, during visits to outlying areas, to interview individuals who were interested in emigrating but could not readily attend his office in Aberdeen; on one occasion in February 1911 he spent six hours one evening at John Sinclair's Elgin agency, interviewing twenty-three people, nearly all of whom he persuaded to book passages to Canada.

But probably more important than the formal interviews were the spontaneous discussions that arose in the course of MacLennan's attendance at markets, shows and hiring fairs all over his area. His weekly reports in May and November made frequent reference to feeing markets, and throughout the summer he was kept busy attending shows throughout the north. In July 1908 he was given the use of a motorcar (which was usually confined to England) to assist his summer campaign, and it duly appeared at seven agricultural shows, including one at Keith which was attended by over 20,000 people. In a four-week period in July and August 1909 MacLennan attended fourteen shows scattered throughout his enormous district, and he also made it his business to attend events as diverse as the weekly farmers' market in Aberdeen and the annual Highland gathering in Braemar. In addition, he undertook an extensive lecture campaign throughout his district, sometimes arranging his speaking engagements to coincide with visits to shows or hiring fairs. He was a popular speaker who often drew capacity audiences. In the season 1908–9, he delivered a total of eighteen lectures to over 6,000 people, while many others were allegedly disappointed in their efforts to hear him. On 28 January 1909 the *Aberdeen Journal* reported that – as in Huntly fifteen months earlier – hundreds had failed to gain admittance to a lecture in the fishing community of Fraserburgh; in the same month 400 turned out to hear him lecture in the small country town of Insch, while in March he was greeted by an audience of 1,800 in Elgin, the county town of Morayshire.[52]

MacLennan did not work entirely unaided. Probably his most successful assistant was Hugh McKerracher, a Gaelic-speaking Ontarion whose parents came from Glenlyon and Rannoch while his wife was from Aberdeenshire. He was appointed in May 1907 to take charge of the horse-drawn travelling exhibition wagon in the north of Scotland, as well as to assist MacLennan at agricultural shows with what the latter regarded as one of his department's most effective means of advertising. McKerracher's 'singularly fortunate' appointment and

'splendid work' were warmly commended by J. Bruce Walker, Assistant Superintendent of Emigration, while the *Aberdeen Journal* acknowledged his skill in
convincing his audience of Canada's attributes:

> Mr McKerracher has a frank, hail-fellow-well-met sort of manner, with a good
> gift of speech, and an unbounded enthusiasm for Canada. He has the knack of
> interesting those whom he meets by the glowing accounts he gives of the great
> field awaiting agriculturists in Canada. He shows how Scotsmen have developed
> the resources, and increased the land values of the country districts, and he has
> been adding his quota to the number of emigrants who have elected to make the
> Dominion their home.

Walker's successor, J. Obed Smith, reporting in 1909 on the work of the
Aberdeen office, confirmed that the choice of travelling agent had been vindi-
cated in that 'no better service could be accomplished' than that provided by
McKerracher, under MacLennan's guidance, and he went on to stress 'that to get
more of the class of people we require we must get away from the larger towns
into the smaller places, just as Mr McKerracher does among the Highlands of
Scotland'.[53]

A lengthy press account of McKerracher's visit to Carloway in Lewis in
April 1911 provides a clear snapshot of the practical application of Smith's principle:

> Behind and on either side of the waggon was emblazoned in golden letters the
> inspiring and much-favoured name 'Canada'. It was readily recognised as the
> Canadian Government waggon, and this happy discovery was sufficient to
> enkindle to the highest pitch the people's interest and enthusiasm, and secure for
> the gentleman in charge ... a warm, whole-hearted Highland welcome. The
> horses were pulled up in front of the Public School, and as the afternoon was
> one of bright sunshine and the occasion most opportune for exhibiting the
> young people's interest in Canada, all the senior classes were allowed outside,
> and with gladsome shout they soon arranged themselves around the waggon.
> Much interest was taken in the samples of seeds of different varieties that were
> displayed in glass cases effectively arranged on each side of the waggon in pleas-
> ing and characteristic manner. Mr MacKerrachar [*sic*], in his capacity as Domin-
> ion Government emigration agent, gave a short spirited address, and when he
> intimated that he would give a lecture in the evening on Canada, illustrated with

magic lantern views, the announcement was greeted with loud hurrahs for
Canada and the maple leaf for ever by the boys and girls as they rushed back to
resume work in school. It was felt that the evening meeting would soon be
widely advertised and the issue of bills for that purpose superfluous. Before
eight o'clock the accommodation of the school, large and commodious as it was,
was taxed to its utmost capacity, extra seats having had to be arranged along the
whole available floor space. When Mr Mackerracher [*sic*] appeared he found
himself face to face with a large and intelligent gathering … Mr Ranald Macdonald, J.P., headmaster, who presided, briefly introduced the lecturer, pro-
claiming his own partiality for Canada and his strong faith in its unlimited
possibilities and high destiny. His preference for Canada was enhanced, too, by
the fact that many of the choicest young men and young women who had passed
through his hands as pupils in the school were today scattered all over Canada,
and all doing well as was evidenced by their occasional ample remittances to
their parents at home. Mr Mackerracher [*sic*] spoke first in Gaelic and afterwards
in English. He undoubtedly had a good subject in Canada, and while he dealt
with it in all its aspects, forcefully and eloquently describing it as an unrivalled
field for emigration, a country of vast extent and inexhaustible resources and of
great potentialities for the future, it was felt, as view after view of scenes
throughout the Dominion appeared on the screen, that with all his praise of the
country in no instance did Mr Mackerracher [*sic*] exaggerate or overstate the
case for Canada.[54]

McKerracher continued to canvass the Highlands until the outbreak of the
First World War, when his horses were commandeered and he himself, being
too old for active service, returned to Canada in 1915. But his effectiveness was
such that, when the Canadian Immigration Department was looking to appoint
a travelling agent in the Highlands at the end of 1920, McKerracher was the
obvious choice. By that time, however, the Aberdeen agency to which he was
attached had undergone several changes of personnel. In April 1911 – at the time
of McKerracher's visit to Lewis – John MacLennan was moved to the Liverpool
office, being succeeded by W. B. Cumming, whose grandfather had emigrated
from Elgin to Canada around 1830. Both Cumming and his pre-war successors,
Frederick Campbell and G. G. Archibald, stepped up the winter lecturing campaign, particularly in rural areas; there were seventy-seven such lectures in
winter 1911–12, 103 the following year and 122 in 1913–14, delivered by the
agents themselves, the office clerk, James Murray, Hugh McKerracher and Mrs

H. Niblett of Winnipeg, with further talks by a number of farm delegates and unofficial lecturers, usually successful settlers who had come home to visit. Similar activity characterized Malcolm McIntyre's agency in the south of Scotland, where in January 1911 he addressed an audience of 3,000 in Glasgow City Hall, and in February 1912 anticipated a 'record year' on the grounds that agents and delegates were reporting a 'sustained interest' in Canada.[55]

'When I came back to Scotland Canada seemed to be the least mentioned and least thought about of the colonies, but a few months have changed all this': so claimed Thomas Duncan in 1897.[56] He was not the only agent to emphasize the effectiveness of his work. John MacLennan's weekly reports frequently mentioned the stir of interest in farming circles. In 1907 he reported that booking agents could not find enough accommodation on the ships to meet the demand from farm servants in his region, and in 1911 he claimed, 'Canada is the chief topic of conversation in the north of Scotland'.[57] Perhaps the opposition encountered by the agents was also a reflection of their impact on rural communities, as well as further evidence of the contentious nature of agency work. In 1908 – the season after the Clarke City dispute had been batted back and forth in the local press – John MacLennan complained on more than one occasion about how newspaper hostility was creating 'uphill work' in the recruitment of emigrants, with a noticeable slackening of business both at his own office and at the booking agencies:

> It is a difficult matter to create any enthusiasm this year for Canada. In spite of our statements that there are ample opportunities and abundance of work for the agriculturist and Railroad laborer, yet the Press has poisoned the public mind respecting the terrible suffering claimed to exist in Canada that our work this year is going to be greatly hampered and will show a big falling off. The same condition obtains everywhere through my district. Mr Bredin our delegate did not have a single caller in some of the offices visited.[58]

Conservative newspapers such as the *Aberdeen Journal* were also a mouthpiece for 'large farmers' who, according to MacLennan, opposed the depopulation of the farm servant community. By 1910 he was acutely aware of their antagonism:

> In meeting and speaking with the large farmers throughout the district, I find the feeling growing against our work. I am told everywhere that we are taking the best men and leaving only second and third class. I am confining my lectures

DOES

the present outlook for yourself and family satisfy your aspiration? If not, the Canadian Government guarantees placement of married couples and experienced and inexperienced men on farms without charge.

CANADA

is urgently calling for farmers and farm workers. The British and Canadian Governments assist to place desirable British families with some farm experience on Canadian farms and help and advise them until established.

Special reduced rates are available for settlers to whom these offers

APPEAL

Emigrate under direct auspices, of the Canadian Government, which guarantees employment and after-care and supervision.

For full information apply to Dept. 73
Canadian Government Emigration Agent,
107, Hope Street, GLASGOW.

8. Advertising for agricultural settlers by the Canadian government agent, Scottish Farmer, *29 January 1927. The format of advertisements changed little after the First World War.*

this year to the purely rural districts and trying as far as possible to meet the objections and opposition raised. It is indispensable to our success that we do not antagonise too much the large farmers, as they are still a powerful force in the community.[59]

But agents' comments on press attitudes convey a mixed message, encompassing apathy and enthusiasm, as well as overt hostility. Thirty-three years earlier, special agent James Ross had 'found the public press in both England and Scotland, with few exceptions, either lukewarm or utterly indifferent on the subject of emigration to Canada'.[60] By 1899, however, perhaps owing to the efforts of the agents themselves, chief Scottish agent H. M. Murray could claim that Canada held 'a good position' in the columns of the Scottish press, and he thanked the fifty newspapers in which he had advertised 'for the freedom with which they have granted us space for the insertion of many paragraphs and notices which might be of interest to the intending settler'.[61] And while the *Aberdeen Journal* was a constant thorn in the flesh of the agents by the early twentieth century, its Liberal rival the *Aberdeen Free Press* was regarded in a much more favourable light. In 1911 J. Obed Smith even recommended to his head office in Ottawa that its editor, John Bruce, should be given financial help with the publication of occasional illustrated supplements which advocated emigration. 'There is,' he wrote, 'no better friend to Canada than this newspaper, and it has an enormous circulation throughout not only the North, but extending to the Southern parts of Scotland'.[62]

Contention, contradiction and confusion were also evident from time to time in the relationship between federal agents and those who represented the provinces, the railway companies or simply themselves, as well as in arguments between agents and their recruits. Although federal agents were supposed to promote emigration to every part of the Dominion even-handedly, in the 1870s some of the older provinces felt that their interests were being sacrificed to the goal of filling up the prairies. For that very reason, the New Brunswick authorities in 1872 granted 50,000 acres in the heart of the province to William Brown, a captain with the transatlantic Anchor Line, in return for a promise that he would establish a 'Scotch Colony' on his land grant. Basing himself in his home town of Stonehaven, Brown enlisted the aid of his friend John Taylor, editor of the *Stonehaven Journal*, as well as Thomas Potts, the Canadian government's special emigration agent, and spent the autumn and winter on a lecturing campaign in the counties of Kincardine, Aberdeen and Banff. On 22 April 1873 he chartered a special train to take around 700 recruits to board the SS *Castalia* in Glasgow for the transatlantic voyage. After being piped ashore at Saint John by members of the local St Andrew's Society, they continued 168 miles upriver to New Kincardineshire, to find a mud-and-snow-encased shanty town that bore no resemblance to the picture painted by Brown. Although ninety houses had been promised, only forty had been started, of which two were finished, the logging road into the settlement had not been opened up, and, with snow still lying two feet deep on the higher ground and a similar depth of mud lower down, only a small area had been cleared to permit the movement of heavy sledges. Not surprisingly, the views of disillusioned settlers soon began to filter back to Scotland. One angry correspondent wrote to the *Montrose Review*:

> The place that they had planned out for us is very bad ... They said that there was about 40 trees on the acre; but 400 on the acre is like the thing. I never saw such a miserable looking place in my life. About half the colonists have left, and others are leaving every day ... We have been taken the advantage of too bad I think. I, for one, could take Brown the manager, and drown him. Drowning is

not bad enough for him. It makes my blood boil in my veins to think of it. The free men are not so very bad; but those who have a wife and family are very bad … Mostly all of them have left good places and come to this abominable place. Everything is very high in price, and not much work going on. If things do not change in a month or two, I will not stop here such a long winter and nothing to do. I could not think of stopping here. The land of the colony is awful bad; some places all gravel, others all large stones, and in some places about 2 ft. 6 in. of snow … There was no ground cleared and ready for cropping as was promised to be.[63]

William Brown was an amateur agent who acted largely on his own behalf and, although he was blamed for bringing out too many pioneers, harsher criticism was reserved for the New Brunswick government, which had not fulfilled its obligations to prepare the land for occupation and planting. Provinces which sent their own representatives to the British Isles often exasperated the federal agents. After a brief truce from 1874 to 1880, the in-fighting resumed when, led by Ontario, the older provinces began to reinstate separate offices overseas, leading, in J. Obed Smith's opinion, to public perceptions of 'an overdose of energy to induce people to emigrate to the Dominion'. John MacLennan also felt the effect of this conflict on northern Scotland when he complained in 1907 that the provincial agent for Ontario was determined to sabotage the work of the federal agents, finding 'general fault with everything we are doing [and going] among the agents discrediting the work of our Government in Ontario in matters of finding situations'.[64] He was also critical of some railway company agents who competed with each other and with the federal government for settlers. Others, like the Canadian Pacific Railway representative A. Moore of Calgary, were simply incompetent, for he had, claimed MacLennan, failed in his mission in Aberdeen because 'he is not a good speaker and has not a sufficient knowledge of general conditions to enable him to answer enquirers readily and satisfactorily'. The competence of some of the farm delegates also came under fire from MacLennan and not only because they were liable to promote their own area of settlement at the expense of the claims of Canada as a whole. He complained about two farm delegates from Manitoba who held meetings in his district in spring 1908. One of these men, A. R. Bredin, although 'very agreeable and approachable and thoroughly competent to answer questions', was 'not aggressive enough' and did not take the initiative with interviewees in terms of anticipating their questions and answering them 'without waiting'. And the demeanour of Donald Grant, who showed 'indifference to his apparel and personal appearance', militated against the success of his campaign.[65] Finally, relations within the ranks of the career civil servants who served as federal emigration agents were not always harmonious. In August 1912 W. B. Cumming resigned from the Aberdeen agency over a pay dispute, only a month after Malcolm McIntyre had been transferred from Glasgow to Birmingham because of an irreconcilable 'personal disagreement' with some officers of a Canadian steamship company operating out of the Clyde.[66]

Conclusion

From the earliest days of organized emigration, agents constituted a prominent and recurring thread in the complex fabric of movement from the British Isles. Nowhere was that thread more prominent than in Scotland, which was regarded as a particularly fruitful field of endeavour by agents whose priority was usually to secure competent agriculturists. While some agents may have played a part in igniting the initial spark of public interest, their real significance lay in the way in which they were able to translate a vague restlessness into the concrete decision to emigrate. At times this simply meant filling the otherwise empty head of the would-be emigrant with alluring images of the particular El Dorado that they represented, but on other occasions it involved the more difficult task of changing a mind that was already made up. Thus John MacLennan could congratulate himself when in 1910 he persuaded a wealthy farmer and his son to invest their savings of £2,400 in Calgary rather than New Zealand. In the same year Aberdeen engine driver Robert Rhynes took up a farm on the other side of Canada, after a chance encounter with an agent from Prince Edward Island. 'I was,' he recalled fourteen years later, 'intending to go West, but the agent representing the island was in Aberdeen, and I met him at the Kittybrewster [agricultural] Show. His story induced me to come here and look round, and I am not disappointed that I did not go West.'[67]

By marrying supply with demand, agents clearly filled a niche in the market, whether they were involved in the provision of vessels, land or employment, and their strategies became more complex as the century progressed and the volume of emigrants increased. Surviving evidence suggests that, despite some examples of sharp practice and disillusioned recruits – inevitable in such a diverse and long-term enterprise – most of the agents were honest brokers. Their clients were generally willing exiles, men and women of skill and initiative, who were inspired primarily by the quest for better conditions and prospects than they could secure in Scotland. The degree of opposition agents encountered from vested interests at home suggests that they were generally careful, rather than indiscriminate, recruiters, although at the same time as they were accused of draining Scotland of brain, sinew and capital, they had to field brickbats from overseas critics, whose perception of the calibre of the emigrants was very different. But whether they were regarded as a blessing or a curse, the ubiquitous agents played a key part in the scale and direction of emigration. By the end of the nineteenth century the thread of agency activity had been woven indelibly and indispensably into the fabric of Scottish emigration in an increasingly sophisticated, professional and multi-layered form.

HELPING THE HELPLESS

'Well-planned and wisely conducted child-emigration ... contains within its bosom the truest solution of some of the mother country's most perplexing problems, and the supply of our Colonies' most urgent needs.'[1]

'The majority of these children are the offal of the most depraved characters in the cities of the Old Country.'[2]

These contrasting sentiments represent the tip of an iceberg of controversy that raged around the emigration of disadvantaged children. For more than half a century after 1870 a barrage of bouquets and brickbats was bestowed on a complex movement that saw approximately 100,000 juveniles shipped overseas from British orphanages and rescue homes. Of all the debate generated by the emigration question, none has been more passionate and polarized than the debate surrounding child emigration. On the one hand, it was praised by its promoters as a means of repairing the economic and spiritual health of recruits, solving labour-supply problems at home and abroad, and bolstering the bonds of empire. On the other hand, it was demonized by its detractors, as either an unethical device for dumping destitute and degenerate juveniles on unenthusiastic colonies, a cynical strategy to delay state welfare provision at home, or a cruel disruption of the dynamic of the family unit, however dysfunctional that unit might be. In the middle of the debate stood the emigrants themselves, individuals who had little say in the matter or the manner of their relocation, and whose welfare hinged largely on a fortuitous placement with an understanding family. In recent years the subject has been revived by a flurry of books, articles and television programmes, some of which have sought to assess the emigrationists' aims, achievements and limitations in the context of their time, while others have favoured an overtly antagonistic approach, sometimes taking advantage of hindsight to sensationalize the movement.

What were the objectives, achievements, limitations and blind spots of those who promoted child emigration? What were the antecedents of a movement which grew from a trickle into a flood in the last quarter of the nineteenth century, and persisted until as late as 1968? Who were the Scottish philanthropists, and did their aims and activities conform to, or differ from, those of their better-known English counterparts? Where were the emigrants sent, for what purpose and with what effect? What can we learn about their experiences before, during and after their emigration, from their own recollections, as well as from the reports of their sponsors and the reactions of the host communities? In tackling these questions, we are fortunate in being able to draw on a wide range of contemporary as well as retrospective literature. Dependent on promotional pamphlets and attractive annual reports to stimulate public interest and donations, the voluntary agencies produced regular publications which contained both theoretical justifications and practical illustrations of their work, often incorporating letters from ostensibly satisfied emigrants. Some institutions also pioneered the modern social work practice of building up meticulous factual case files on all inmates, while extra endorsement of their programmes could be found in much of the British press and in hagiographies of their founders. Colonial newspaper editors and correspondents, on the other hand, were often less complimentary, as were the reports of occasional official investigations into malpractice, while Lucy Maud Montgomery immortalized the antipathy of Canadian society to home children in *Anne of Green Gables*. The jury is therefore not short of evidence on which to assess the merits and demerits of juvenile emigration.

Sponsored child emigration: theory and practice

Most child emigrants travelled and settled with their families, but by 1800 there was already a well-established tradition of sending batches of unaccompanied pauper children across the Atlantic, some as indentured servants, others as convicts. They generally remain shadowy figures, although there are a few well-documented exceptions, the most notable being Peter Williamson, who, as we saw earlier, was kidnapped with 'amazing effrontery' by a group of Aberdeen city merchants and magistrates and shipped to Philadelphia.[3]

By the end of the eighteenth century attitudes had begun to shift away from the simple punishment or indiscriminate export of delinquents and vagrants towards the rehabilitation of children through emigration. Yet the underlying philosophy remained contentious and contradictory, as emigrationists and commentators alike struggled to disentangle motives of reform from an ingrained desire to punish actual or potential criminals. In the 1820s and 1830s social reformers such as the Spitalfields Quaker Peter Bedford and the retired naval captain Edward Brenton sent destitute children from the streets of London to farms and households in Cape Colony. By the time that Brenton's Children's Friend Society was dissolved in 1840, amidst accusations that its recruits were treated like slaves or convicts, it had sent around 1,300 children to South Africa. The spotlight shifted to the Antipodes in the 1840s, when young delinquents were sent out from reformatories such as Parkhurst in the Isle of Wight and the Philanthropic Society's Redhill School in Surrey, while in the depths of the Irish Famine 4,175 workhouse orphans were controversially sent to New South Wales by the Irish Poor Law Commissioners. As President of the Ragged School Union, Lord Shaftesbury also advocated the removal of children to Australia until 1853, as did Thomas Guthrie, the Free Church cleric who opened three ragged schools in Edinburgh in 1847. When, in response to fears that they would be contaminated by immoral influences from the Australian gold diggings, ragged school recruits were redirected to North America, the foundation stones were laid for a movement that was soon to dominate the whole history of child migration from the British Isles.

In the second half of the nineteenth century, industrial schools and reformatories sprang up across Britain, the former catering for vagrant and uncontrollable children, along with those found in bad company or convicted of petty offences, and the latter dealing with those found guilty of more serious offences. Led by the Liverpool Education Authority, which by 1914 had sent out nearly 1,200 children to Canada, many of these schools played the emigration card, using agencies such as the Salvation Army, Dr Barnardo's, the Children's Aid Society and the Catholic Emigration Society to dispatch suitable children who had been given a basic education and training in a trade. To the surprise of a parliamentary committee which reported on Scottish reformatory and industrial schools in 1914, relatively few Scottish delinquents were sent overseas, perhaps because of inadequate public support.[4] Among those which did participate were Wellington Park Boys' School in Edinburgh, the Kibble Reformatory in Paisley, and in Glasgow the Girls' Industrial School and Reformatory and the Maryhill

Industrial School. In Aberdeen, site of the first industrial school in Britain, the governors worked hard during the 1860s to assist the emigration of former inmates. Between 1878 and 1915 thirty-three children in all emigrated from Aberdeen's four industrial schools, as well as twenty-four inmates of the city's two reformatories.

By the late nineteenth century, however, a growing army of philanthropists was more concerned that emigration should prevent, rather than cure, delinquency among juveniles. Charitable societies, both national and provincial, mushroomed in response to clamant social and economic problems, which were tackled from a range of motives and in a variety of ways. Assisted emigration was integral to many relief schemes, sometimes standing alone, sometimes incorporated into a home-based programme of reform. Charities did not concern themselves exclusively with juveniles; by the end of the century the Salvation Army claimed to be the world's largest emigration and employment agency for destitute or unemployed working-class people, while women's emigration had become increasingly linked with the Salvationists, as well as other specifically female sponsoring societies. But at the same time the sponsored emigration of children and adolescents had become a big and especially controversial business, associated partly with the Salvation Army, but primarily with the names of Thomas Barnardo and, in Scotland, William Quarrier, as well as a supporting cast of more obscure, but still significant, provincial philanthropists. As with assisted adult emigration, the focus of most of the children's schemes was Canada, the nearest and cheapest destination, and in 1889 the Canadian Department of Agriculture listed over fifty agencies involved in bringing juveniles from Britain to the Dominion.[5]

The main catalyst for the philanthropists was the practical argument that both the nation and empire would benefit from a policy of removing surplus citizens from Britain to thinly populated colonial locations. Not only would problems of overpopulation, pauperism and unemployment be solved, it was argued; incessant colonial demands for cheap farm and domestic labour would also be met. But philosophical considerations were of equal, if not greater, significance. Like Shaftesbury earlier in the century, many of the philanthropists were evangelical Christians, inspired by the biblical mandate to care for both body and soul, and they were convinced that the spiritual, as well as the economic, condition of their needy recruits would be improved if they were removed from depraved and deprived urban environments in Britain and sent to the morally unpolluted air of rural Canada. Those involved in child

care welcomed emigration as an ideal device to give destitute or abused children a fresh start in life by removing them from corrupting influences at home.
After 1900, when eugenic arguments about racial purity came into vogue and
the secular cause of imperialism replaced salvation as the main theoretical justification for assisted emigration, young emigrants were regarded as an even
greater asset, constituting 'the bricks with which the empire would be built'.[6]
In the eugenic context, rural Canada was commended more for its healthful
than for its moral qualities, as a land where the future of the empire could be
secured by transplanting young people from the overcrowded and debilitating
environments of Britain's city slums, before their constitutions had been
irreparably damaged.

Although the practice of child migration was to become associated primarily
with Dr Thomas Barnardo, the pioneers of the movement were two women,
Maria Rye and Annie Macpherson. In 1869 Miss Rye took her first party of
seventy-five girls (aged four to twelve) to Niagara-on-the-Lake, where, after
admitting them into her newly established receiving home in the former jail and
courthouse, she placed them out in the locality with farmers who promised to
treat them like their own children in return for the performance of light duties.
Five years later her work was subjected to scathing attack in an official report by
Andrew Doyle, an English Local Government Board inspector, who accused
her of bringing over larger parties than she could manage, providing inadequate
after-care facilities and lining her own pocket by charging English poor law
unions for the removal of paupers. As a result, restrictions were imposed on the
removal of pauper children for almost a decade, although the work of Rye's
contemporary, Annie Macpherson, largely escaped censure. Macpherson, a
social worker in the East End of London and the evangelical daughter of a Scottish Quaker, took her first party of 100 destitute children to Canada in 1870. Her
recruits were prepared for emigration in a British training home opened by Lord
Shaftesbury, where they were taught marketable skills while arrangements were
made for their supervised passage, reception and distribution. Macpherson
operated three distributing homes in Canada. The first, at Belleville, Ontario,
was managed for thirty years by her friend Ellen Bilborough, while her sisters,
Rachel Merry and Louisa Birt, were respectively involved both with initial
receiving centres in London and Liverpool and with distributing homes at Galt,
Ontario, and Knowlton, Quebec. Annie Macpherson's work was to provide
both the theoretical inspiration and the practical model for many later emigrationists.

Rye and Macpherson did not have the field to themselves for very long, although several evangelical children's societies which subsequently implemented assisted emigration programmes sent their young charges to Canada under Annie Macpherson's care. Barnardo used her receiving centres for ten years, until 1882, when he decided to develop his own system. He had been deterred until then by the restrictions imposed after the Maria Rye scandal, but by 1882 financial constraints on his work in Britain and the encouragement of influential supporters convinced him that emigration should form a more integral part of his rescue work. Following a donation from Liverpool MP and industrialist Samuel Smith, Barnardo sent his first party of fifty-one boys from Liverpool to Canada in August 1882. The success of that venture encouraged him to repeat the experiment the next year, when he also sent out a girls' party, and acquired his first Canadian distributing home, Hazelbrae, in Peterborough, Ontario. In 1887 he acquired an 8,000-acre training farm in Manitoba, where youths were tutored in the techniques of prairie agriculture with a view to taking up farm labour or applying for homestead grants, and his network of Canadian depots expanded steadily throughout the 1880s and 1890s. Very few children were sent to Australia because of Barnardo's concern about inadequate protective arrangements for a party of boys sent out in 1883, and his later idea of setting up children's homes in South Africa was abandoned on the grounds of cost and Dutch settler hostility to British immigration.

By Barnardo's death in 1905 33 per cent of his 60,000 children had been sent to Canada, and his homes rapidly became the biggest, best-known and most controversial of the growing number of juvenile emigration agencies, responsible for over one-third of all children sent from Britain to Canada between 1870 and 1930.[7] Barnardo was a contentious figure in Canada, particularly during the economic depression of the 1890s. The dregs of Britain's city slums, it was claimed, were filling Canadian jails, taking scarce jobs from unemployed Canadians and introducing defective children, such as George Green, a Barnardo boy with learning difficulties and bad eyesight whose employer was scandalously acquitted of a charge of manslaughter after George died following repeated beatings. Barnardo was also controversial in Britain, where critics claimed that he was depleting the ranks of female domestic servants and male farm workers, a claim which he firmly refuted by pointing out that the vast majority of his children were placed in situations at home.

Barnardo's rescue work was centred on the English city slums, particularly in London. Of a random sample of 5,655 emigrant boys taken from the

Barnardo archives for the years 1882–94 and 1910–12, only forty were Scottish. On the other hand, he did operate a receiving home in Edinburgh; the *Aberdeen Journal* of 19 January 1905 claimed that 'not a few' of the 60,000 children helped by Barnardo in the past three decades had come from the north of Scotland, and Scots were kept well informed about his work through regular fund-raising tours. Nor did Barnardo's limited involvement with destitute Scottish children mean that he did not know of the relief measures provided by others north of the border. As an integral part of the late Victorian network of evangelical philanthropy, he was well aware of the activities of contemporaries such as Lord and Lady Aberdeen, who opened their own orphanage on their Aberdeenshire estate in 1884. Barnardo and the Aberdeens alike were acquainted with William Quarrier, another Scottish evangelical and philanthropist whose name became synonymous with child rescue and emigration in a Scottish context, just as Barnardo's name was synonymous with such policies in England. Barnardo was present at the opening of Quarrier's Orphan Homes of Scotland at Bridge of Weir in 1878 and there were many similarities – as well as significant differences – in the emigration policies and practices of the two men.

The Scottish scenario: Quarrier's Orphan Homes

Of the 20,219 children received through the doors of Quarrier's Orphan Homes of Scotland between 1871 and 1933, 6,987 were sent overseas, almost all of them to Canada. By the 1860s William Quarrier had a prosperous boot and shoe business in Glasgow, but memories of his impoverished childhood, coupled with his lifelong Christian zeal, meant that he was already devoting much of his profit to the relief of needy children in that city. With moral encouragement from Annie Macpherson, and financial backing from Thomas Corbett, a wealthy Scottish businessman living in London, Quarrier established an orphanage in Renfrew Lane, Glasgow, at the end of 1871. By 1872 the premises were so crowded that two new sets of accommodation were added – in Govan Road and Renfield Street – and four years later Quarrier acquired the extensive rural property at Bridge of Weir, amid rolling hills and fields seventeen miles south of Glasgow, where in 1878 he opened his famous Orphan Homes of Scotland. Children qualified for admission if they were 'Orphan boys and girls deprived of both parents, children of widows or others with no relative able or willing to keep them, from 1 to 14 years of age, from any part of the country'.[8] In contrast to Barnardo and Maria Rye,

9. *Quarrier's Orphan Homes of Scotland and Mount Zion Church, Bridge of Weir, Renfrewshire.*

but following the example of Annie Macpherson, he did not advertise his financial needs publicly, but relied instead – and remarkably effectively – on freewill gifts to sustain both his domestic and his Canadian work. Most of the children were drawn from Glasgow and its hinterland. But there was by no means an exclusive concentration on the west-central belt. Children were referred to Quarrier's from virtually every corner of Scotland, as well as from a few English locations.

The emigration of suitable children was an integral part of Quarrier's rescue programme from the start. On 23 June 1872, he sent his first party of thirty-five Glasgow and Edinburgh children to Canada, having received sufficient donations to cover the transportation costs of £10 per child. In his first annual report he stated his faith in juvenile emigration, combined with domestic rescue work, on practical as well as moral grounds:

> By the emigration feature of the work we are enabled to place these children in Christian homes in Canada, where they will be kindly cared for and watched over by Miss Macpherson and her helpers. By this means we hope to be enabled yearly to rescue a fresh set of boys and girls, whilst, without this providential

outlet, we should be stocked up with the same set of children for four or five years, and unable to rescue more.

Countering criticism that he was damaging the national interest by depleting the labour supply, he continued, later in the same report:

And to those who object to emigration as withdrawing labour from this country, we would say, 'Come and see the children as we take them in, and you will perceive that not the labour market, but the crime market, is likely to be affected by our work of rescue.'[9]

The success of his first experiment encouraged Quarrier to make emigration a regular feature of his work, and within seven years 400 of the 700 children received into his orphanages had been sent to Ontario. In May 1878 he paid the first of several visits to Canada, accompanying a shipload of seventy-eight children, sixty-six of whom were from his orphanages. During his visit he met many of those he had sent out in the previous seven years, and came home resolved to dispatch even more, convinced 'that we can do nothing here for the class of children we help that will at all compare with what can be done in Canada'.[10] For fifteen years he used the facilities provided by Annie Macpherson and Ellen Bilborough in supervising and placing the children, but in 1887, faced with rising numbers of recruits each year, he decided to build his own reception and distribution centre. At Fairknowe Home in Brockville, Ontario – a location he claimed to have chosen because of its tradition of Scottish settlement – he employed a resident superintendent, matron and staff to find situations for the children and to supervise their after-care until they were twenty-one. In the months before an emigrant party arrived these staff advertised in the local press and in church circles for farmers who would either adopt a child or employ an older one under indenture, at the same time as a rigorous selection procedure was under way at home to ensure that only suitable recruits were chosen. In 1906, after more than thirty years' experience in sending children to Canada, Quarrier's annual report noted on 31 March:

Much of our time and thought have been taken up this month selecting and interviewing the lads whom we purpose sending to Canada shortly. Many things have to be considered in coming to a decision regarding each individual case. In the first place the boy himself must wish to go; then his character in the Home, in the school or the workshop must be of the best; physically and mentally he must be sound and must pass a rigid medical examination. After that relatives may have to be consulted, and therein often lies our greatest difficulty. However the day has passed when Canada was considered a place of exile and possible slavery and the thousands of our fellow countrymen who are now 'going west,' know that there work, which will provide an honest living, can be found by all who seek it.[11]

Why were the children taken into care in the first place, and what then determined whether they were shipped out to Canada? As might be expected, several were destitute orphans who had no one to look after them, and whose cases had been brought to Quarrier's notice by relatives who could not cope, concerned friends or employers, inspectors of the poor, local ministers or visiting 'Bible women' (colporteurs). In some cases a parent had become ill or disabled and could no longer support the family. Other children – many of them illegitimate – had been abandoned or neglected by one or both parents, cases which sometimes involved the intervention of the Society for the Prevention of Cruelty to Children. Occasionally a child was left destitute when a parent was committed to prison, in other cases the child had become uncontrollable and occasionally parents handed over their children because they wanted to give them a better chance in life than they could offer. Before admission into the Orphan Homes detailed enquiries were always made into an applicant's background and exhaustive efforts were made to find relatives who could take responsibility instead. Subsequent removal to Canada hinged on the child's age, health, adaptability and enthusiasm. Siblings were frequently separated by the selection process, which also sometimes brought Quarrier's into dispute with parents or guardians, who contested the decision to send their children overseas.

The most straightforward cases were the orphans. They included five brothers and sisters from Lossiemouth, aged between two and thirteen, who were sent to Quarrier's in 1888 at the behest of the local Baptist minister after their father and mother had each died of tuberculosis in August and October respectively. Although there were 'a good many relations', including an uncle in Assiniboia, 'none of them have taken any interest in or helped the family'. Not untypically, the children were sent abroad at different times, two girls and a boy in 1889, another girl – soon to die of TB – in 1890, and the final brother in 1896.[12] Even greater fragmentation occurred among an orphaned family of eight from Inverallochy after the death of their parents in 1892. Although the local parochial board had paid a aunt to keep them temporarily, no relatives were able to shoulder the responsibility permanently, so while three children remained in farm service and one was adopted locally, the rest went to Quarrier's, from where three of them were sent to Canada in 1894 and 1899 respectively.[13] Of a family of seven children from Botriphnie in Banffshire sent to Bridge of Weir in 1904, all but one girl (who died) later went to Canada in 1909, 1910, 1911 and 1920. After their father had died of TB in 1902 the parish had paid 10s a week to the family, but when the mother and another child succumbed to the same disease, her brother in Exeter requested that the family should be admitted to Quarrier's. Enquiries established that the mother's half-brother would have taken the eldest girl, but he agreed with the homes' recommendation that the family should be kept together, accompanied the children to Bridge of Weir, signed the emigration papers and continued to visit them periodically until they were sent to Canada. A paternal aunt in Buckie had also given permission for the children to be taken in by Quarrier's, even though she was a Roman Catholic and the homes were vehemently anti-Catholic.[14]

The death of the breadwinner – or the mother – in a family often caused such hardship that the children were admitted to Quarrier's even if the remaining parent was still alive. In 1884 John (eleven) from Stranraer was sent to the homes by his 'anxious' mother after the death of his father had rendered him 'unmanageable and very self willed'. He was eager to go to Canada, but although he got his wish four years later he was deported back to Scotland in 1891 after being convicted of theft.[15] Still in the south-west, two sisters from Wigtown were admitted in 1888 after their mother died of an ulcerated womb. Although the father was still alive, he was seventy years old and 'nearly done', and the emigration papers were signed by his son, the girls' half-brother.[16] Tuberculosis reared its ugly head again in the admission of three children from Udny in Aberdeenshire, brought to Quarrier's by an aunt in 1889, eight years after the death of their father, and in response to the worsening health of their mother, 'a very respectable person', who had signed the emigration consent form from her bed. She died four years later, followed by one of the children in 1894, while the two survivors were sent to Canada in 1894 and 1895.[17] In the same area, but somewhat disturbing, was the case of a boy from Woodside, Aberdeen, who was sent to Quarrier's in 1905 on the death of his father and with the consent of his pauper mother. When the mother requested his return four years later, her request was blocked by the local minister who had recommended the initial referral. He was supported by Quarrier's, which hastily sent the boy to Canada after the mother had made a second plea for his return.[18]

Disablement of one or both parents could also raise the spectre of destitution. In 1885 two sets of children from Aberdeen were admitted after their fathers had become disabled. In one case the father had been frostbitten while working on a whaling boat off Greenland and had lost the use of his hands and feet; his wife, according to the case file, was 'a very worthless low character' and the parish authorities seem to have sent the two boys to Quarrier's as much to remove them from the mother's influence as for financial reasons. The other case, in which two girls from a family of five were sent to Bridge of Weir, involved a fisherman who had lost an arm, and in each instance the children were sent to Canada within a year of being admitted to Quarrier's.[19] The following year saw the admission and subsequent emigration of two brothers from Cambuslang after the death of their mother left the poorhouse as the only alternative for their disabled and destitute father, as well as the children. And in 1892 Alexander, from Edinburgh, was sent to Quarrier's and on to Canada when neither his mother nor his invalid father could support their seven surviving children from an original family of fourteen.[20]

Several illegitimate children were admitted when they were left destitute by the death or desertion of their mothers. Four such children from Macduff, aged from six to twelve, were sent to Quarrier's on the recommendation of the local minister after their mother died in 1886. Since the father was unknown, the children were being maintained by the parochial board but were left in the charge of their maternal grandmother, who was 'old and deaf and quite unable to look after them'. Two of the boys were sent to Canada in 1887, another boy in 1888 and their sister in 1893.[21] John (seven), from Aberdeen, lost his mother in 1891. His father was unknown but his stepfather, who had four children already and could not take him in, agreed to hand him over to Quarrier's and he was sent to Canada a year later.[22] Jeannie (six) was sent from Elgin to Bridge of Weir in 1898 and on to Canada eight years later. In 1896 her mother, who had several other illegitimate children, had boarded her out with a woman in Elgin, promising to pay for her upkeep, but she had then disappeared and responsibility for maintaining the child had fallen on the parochial board.[23]

More controversially, children were removed from the jurisdiction of parents or guardians who were deemed unsuitable, neglectful, abusive or unable to control their charges. Like his fellow emigrationists, Quarrier was a firm believer in putting the Atlantic between his recruits and the corrupting backgrounds from which they had often been rescued. In December 1887 Miss Donaldson, a Bible woman in Inverness, secured the removal of two nine-year-old illegitimate children to Quarrier's. Bella was removed from the custody of a woman in the town who was allegedly keeping her for immoral purposes, while John was handed over after he had begged the Inverness police authorities to give him a chance in life by sending him away from home. Both children were sent to Canada in 1888, though John returned to Inverness in 1894.[24] In 1889 George (five), also illegitimate, was sent to Quarrier's at the behest of the minister in Kinellar, Aberdeenshire. Since his mother's marriage the child had been subjected to 'constant and cruel maltreatment at the hand of the stepfather', while the mother, who had just given birth to twins, could not cope with the elder child and willingly saw George sent to Canada in 1892.[25] Among children who had got beyond the control of their parents was Thomas (eleven), a pupil at Kelso Industrial School, who, having been 'keeping bad company', had been convicted of stealing a box of sweets and sentenced to a birching. He was admitted in 1885 at the behest of his mother, who was 'quite decided that Canada is the right place for him'.[26] Three years later David (thirteen), from Stirling, also had his emigration papers signed by his widowed mother, because 'he has been behaving very badly, neglecting school, leading his brother and other boys into mischief ... chews and smokes and ... needs to be where he will be forced to behave'.[27] Robert (fourteen) was removed from the care of his widowed mother in Dysart, Fife, in 1908 because he had 'got beyond control and would not attend school', and in 1909 another Robert (eleven) was removed from the care of his mother in Glenprosen, Angus, on the grounds that he had caused her 'a good deal of trouble recently, and she is totally unfit to manage him'. Both boys were sent to Canada, in 1911 and 1913 respectively.[28] And four children were removed from Aberdeen to Quarrier's in 1909 at the behest of a city missionary on the grounds of the mother's neglect, and the complaint of an aunt that 'the children have literally been in starvation, sometimes picking things off the street and eating them. They look very much neglected.' All four were subsequently sent to Canada between 1911 and 1916, and were forbidden to correspond with their mother because of her extremely bad influence.[29]

Parental alcoholism featured in a number of cases. 'Andrew has been times without number in Police Offices and from there sent to Poor Houses', read the report on an illegitimate boy from Castle Douglas whom the SPCC referred to Quarrier's in 1892. Two years later he was sent to Canada, in order to remove him from the influence of his mother, who 'earned a living by singing all over the country' and had become 'a wreck through drink and debauchery'.[30] In a somewhat similar case in Dundee, Richard (thirteen) and Jane (six) were taken to Bridge of Weir in 1894 after the courts had given a custody order to Quarrier. Their father, a collier, had died five years earlier and their mother, an alcoholic, had recently been convicted at Dundee for allowing the children to beg and sing on the streets. She had no fixed residence but was accustomed to travelling the country with the children. Although she had remarried, she had left her husband and was now living 'with some low character of a man in a common lodging-house and they are both living off proceeds of children's earnings'. Richard died two years after entering the homes but his sister was sent to Canada in 1897.[31] In 1902 two brothers from Elgin were admitted after their father had died of alcoholism and their mother, who was similarly addicted, had been in the poorhouse. The elder boy was sent to Canada in 1907 and the younger in 1909.[32] And the SPCC was involved in the case of John (nine) from Pitsligo, who in 1913 was removed from an unmarried mother who was 'much given to drink & immorality & lives in squalor & dirt', being sent on to Canada six years later.[33]

The SPCC was also involved in referring children who had suffered as a result of crimes perpetrated by their parents or guardians. Mary and Elizabeth Watts, half-sisters from Montrose, were brought to Quarrier's by their mother's landlady in Glasgow in 1890 while the mother was serving a prison sentence for harbouring prostitutes. They were subsequently sent to Canada after the mother, who had initially demanded them back, agreed that they should be taken into care.[34] Three years later James, Robert and David Smith were admitted after their father was sentenced to life imprisonment for murdering a fellow farm servant and wounding another at his workplace near Stonehaven. The mother, who handed over her sons but kept three other children, 'sees the desirability of removing them as far as possible from scene of father's crime', and the boys were sent to Canada in 1897 and 1907.[35] Frequently, however, the children were the direct victims of their parents' or guardians' crimes, many of which involved sexual abuse. In 1894, for example, Quarrier's admitted 'a very nice boy, with a very bad history'. This was the three-year-old product of an incestuous relationship between a domestic servant and her father. After the case came to light the father was imprisoned and the family scattered. The boy's removal to Quarrier's was recommended by a local minister, the admission papers were forwarded to the mother, who had emigrated to Boston, and the boy was sent to Canada in 1904.[36]

Most cases of cruelty and neglect were not discussed outside Quarrier's admission records, but a few attracted detailed press attention. In 1887 three brothers were taken from the Greenock Poorhouse to Quarrier's, and later sent to Canada, after their father had been convicted of a 'revolting case of assault' against the oldest boy, eleven-year-old Robert:

At Greenock Police Court this morning James Blackwood, joiner, was charged with assaulting his son Robert … In the course of his evidence, the little boy, who told his story in a very distinct manner, said that on Thursday night his father came home drunk after eleven o'clock, when he and his youngest brother William were in bed. Shortly after coming in his father vomited, and ordered him to get out of bed and lick it up. On his refusing to do so, he dragged him out of bed, forced him to do as he had ordered, thrashed him with a leather strap, and kicked him with his feet; and after ordering his other son James to lift the black coal from off the fire, he caught Robert by the body and thrust his head into the fire, singeing his hair and bruising his head. He again took up the strap and thrashed him, and compelled him to lick up some dirty water which was lying on the floor. Following up this, he ordered Robert and go and wash his hands, and, taking advantage of the chance thus given him, the boy opened the door, and getting out ran along Cowgate Street and Market Street, and up Ann Street, where he was found stark naked about three o'clock by a railway official who took him to a signal box at the Caledonian Railway Station in Regent Street, where he was kindly treated and wrapped in a heavy overcoat.[37]

Among the admissions to Quarrier's in 1910 were two illegitimate children whose stepfathers had both been charged with ill-treatment after Christmastime confrontations. Ernest McFarlane (eleven) of Edinburgh was beaten by a stepfather who had known nothing of his existence when he married his mother and who objected to paying 1s a week for his education in an industrial school:

it came to a climax on Christmas Eve. His mother was out, making purchases at the time. His step-father asked him to take off his clothes and lie down on the floor, while he went for the strap. The boy refused to lie down, although he had stripped, so the man took a hold of him, knocked him down, and commenced to beat him with the strap … The boy screamed with pain, but the man only put him into the bath and, as the boy said, tried to rub the marks off. His mother did not know of his injuries until the Monday, when she decided to send him to the Children's Shelter. Just as they were about to go the step-father came into the house, and on being challenged about his ill-treatment of the boy by a neighbour, he replied that he would kill him.[38]

The stepfather was imprisoned for twenty-one days and Ernest, after a spell at Quarrier's, was sent to Canada in 1911, a year ahead of Annie Harper (fourteen) from Gartly, Aberdeenshire, who had also been admitted to the Homes in 1910 as a result of parental cruelty. Regularly victimized in contrast to her four legitimate half-brothers, Annie had fled in desperation to a neighbour on Christmas Day, 1909. He immediately reported the case to the local police, setting in motion a chain of events that led to a court case, the conviction of her mother (but not her stepfather), Annie's admission to Quarrier's and her subsequent removal to Canada. In evidence at her parents' trial, Annie complained that:

> She did not get the same food, and had to take her meals at another table, and often had to take what the others left … She had to get out of bed at 5.30. when her step-father rose, and had to clean all the boots, and sweep and wash out the floor, carry water and provide firewood. Her bed was made in the floor among some bags, but the others had a bedstead to lie on … Her mother often beat her with her hand and sometimes with a stick. The boys had not to do any work, and were well treated. She hoped she had not to go back to her mother; she would rather go any where.

Annie's claims were corroborated by the procurator fiscal, who reported that:

> The girl had to lie on the bare floor, the only protection from the floor being two pieces of wet and filthy sacking. She had no under-clothing for months and months. She had to go about in the cold weather with boots which were quite worn down, and to such an extent that her feet got broken out in chilblains and then in open sores, and while she was so suffering her mother never gave her any treatment whatever. After a time a pair of new boots were got, and the girl was obliged to put these new boots upon the open sores. There were four other children in the family, and they were not ill-used.[39]

In the same area, four brothers from Cairnie, aged between one and eleven, were sent to Quarrier's in 1911 after their father was sentenced to ten years' imprisonment for the culpable homicide of his wife. At 2.30 a.m. on 20 December 1910 William Cumming (eleven) and his mother had come home after searching fruitlessly for the father, who had not returned from a trip to Huntly. On finding him in the house in a drunken state, a quarrel arose between the parents, and when William Cumming senior began to attack his wife, young William escaped with his brother George (nine), who had already suffered a head injury at the hands of his father. The boys ran to the police office in Huntly to get help, but by the time officers went to the household, it was too late:

> A shudder swept the Court when ... Sergeant Scott described his visit to the cottage. There on the floor lay the body of Mrs Cumming. Near at hand lay a pair of tongs, a ladle, and a poker – all bloodstained. On a bed, as soundly asleep as an innocent child, was William Cumming. Rousing the man they seized him, and soon the suspect was securely housed in the police station. Here his two little sons ... were soundly asleep before the fire. 'Cumming took no notice of them,' concluded the sergeant.

By the time the case came to court it had already been decided that the boys should be sent to Quarrier's, not least because the parish council thought it wise to remove them from the 'gruesome associations' of their father's crime. William and George were sent to Canada in 1913 and their younger brothers in 1921.[40]

William Quarrier, like his English counterparts, experienced some opposition. A man who liked to work independently and get his own way, he was impatient with committees and brooked no restrictions on the work which he believed had been entrusted to him by God. In 1882 that lack of accountability led to a court case and brought Quarrier into bad odour with both the Roman Catholic Church and the *Glasgow Herald*. The catalyst was the case of William Bradshaw, an orphan who had been admitted to the Orphan Homes at the request of his maternal grandmother, a Catholic. As a result of pressure from a daughter and the Roman Catholic clergy, the grandmother subsequently requested the child's return, whereupon Quarrier allegedly refused to relinquish the boy and physically assaulted a law agent employed to press his case. Although these allegations – made by Father Alexander Munro of Glasgow – were disproved and costs were awarded to Quarrier, his cause had been tarnished by the accusation that he misused public funds in order to entrap and convert Catholics, who were then sent to exclusively Protestant parts of Canada. More seriously, in the opinion of the *Glasgow Herald*, Quarrier's lack of accountability laid him wide open to any charge of misuse of funds and created legitimate grounds for public concern that 'Mr Quarrier himself is the Orphan Homes Institution'.[41] On another occasion, in the Court of Session, he engaged in unsuccessful litigation with Renfrew County Council over its demand that, after sixteen years' exemption, the homes should pay an annual rate.[42] At the same time, Quarrier's emigration practices were opposed on the two rather different arguments that 'you cannot do worse to a kingdom than to rob it of its people' and that Scotland's slums were allegedly being cleansed 'by the simple process of pouring their unpurified contents into our neighbour's premises across the water'.[43] In 1897 the Ontario authorities, heeding Canadian demands that the traffic in children should be more strictly regulated, and in specific response to scandal surrounding the death of a Barnardo boy, passed an act which subjected the Canadian receiving homes to much greater scrutiny. Although Quarrier's enterprise was singled out for praise rather than censure by the Ontario authorities, he still regarded the act as a personal insult and an unwarranted interference in charitable schemes which the province did not support financially. He therefore refused to send any more children to Canada, and it was only after his death, in 1903, that his family reactivated the practice, convinced that the legislation offered better protection for the children rather than being a hindrance to their removal.

The network expands: supplementary Scottish schemes

Although Quarrier's Homes undoubtedly dominated the Scottish scene as far as child emigration was concerned, they did not have a monopoly of the trade. Records survive for at least four smaller Scottish children's homes – in Edinburgh, Aberlour and Stirling – that dispatched around 650 recruits to Canada in the half-century after 1875, reflecting extensive cooperation among philanthropists in the practical arrangements for sending children across the Atlantic. One of the earliest, Mrs Blaikie's Orphan and Emigration Home in Edinburgh developed out of a chance meeting between the Blaikies and Annie Macpherson in Toronto in 1870. William Garden Blaikie, Free Church Professor and in 1892 Moderator of the General Assembly, was a well-known figure in Scotland, not least as a philanthropist. After meeting Macpherson, he and his wife returned to Edinburgh, 'with the conviction that here was a valuable outlet for the disposal of multitudes of children in our large cities who would otherwise be brought up in vice, misery, and degradation'. This led to the opening of a home which, like Macpherson's and Quarrier's, was funded by freewill donations, and which over a twenty-year period received an annual income of between £300 and £500. Of the 708 children taken under its roof, 301 were sent to Canada, and the alleged success rate of 95 per cent was identical to that claimed by Quarrier's. While some of the children were orphans, case notes indicate that many came from broken, drunken or violent homes, removal from which, it was argued, was their only route to safety. Typical is this account of the plight of two sisters, brought to Mrs Blaikie's notice by a city missionary:

> E. & H. – Mother dead. Father a drunkard. The children were found in a filthy room; no fire, no furniture, nothing in the room but a few bricks for a pillow; the father lying in the corner on a few straws with a coal sack over him. The children had a little bread and butter, and a jug of water on the dirty floor, and a piece of candle on the top of the loaf.[44]

The father's initial objections to his daughters' emigration were removed when he died from alcoholism, and the girls were included in the home's second batch of emigrants to Canada. There they were adopted and, when visited by the Blaikies in 1880, were about to embark on teaching and dressmaking careers respectively.

The closure of Mrs Blaikie's home after twenty years was attributed partly to the expiry of the lease on her premises, partly to the increasing difficulty in obtaining parental permission for the emigration of children, and partly to the perceived duplication of her work by the formation in Edinburgh in 1884 of a new shelter for the prevention of cruelty to children. That shelter was one of several linked enterprises initiated by Emma Stirling, who between 1886 and 1895 sent 200 children from Edinburgh to Nova Scotia. Raised in a gentry family in St Andrews, Emma Stirling's practical interest in philanthropy began after the death of her mother in 1874. Sustained by a substantial inheritance and an uncompromising Christian faith, she moved to Edinburgh, where in 1877 she opened the Stockbridge Day Nursery and Infant Home, the former for the benefit of working mothers, the latter for motherless children. Within a year she had appointed an advisory board of directors and renamed her enterprise the Edinburgh and Leith Children's Aid and Refuge Society (ELCARS). Her Shelter from Cruelty, opened at 150 High Street, represented an expansion of her work into the realm of abused children and soon eclipsed efforts by a group of Edinburgh citizens to establish a local SPCC. By 1886, when she launched the Canadian dimension of her work, she was operating – in addition to these institutions – two girls' homes, two boys' homes and a training farm, catering for 300, although illegitimate children were excluded except in cases of physical abuse. She had also recruited the Earl of Aberdeen as patron of her organization and had, on her own estimate, spent £8,000 of her personal fortune on the work, supplementing public donations and annual grants from Edinburgh Town Council.[45]

The extension of Emma Stirling's work to Canada was prompted by the need to find a cheap new outlet for the increasing number of children. As reported in the minutes of a meeting of the directors of ELCARS in November 1885:

> Miss Stirling gave a long and interesting account of her recent tour in America, and in particular of what she had seen of Nova Scotia and the Valley of Annapolis. Her tour had been undertaken partly with the view of ascertaining whether a favourable outlet existed in America for the young lads in the Homes who were rapidly growing up and for whom provision would soon require to be made with the view of setting them out in the world for themselves. After careful enquiries and consultations with various parties able to give advice in the matter ... she had come to be of opinion that it would be practicable for her to take a farm in America, to which a number of the lads might be transferred under suitable and responsible supervision, and these taught farming in a way which would enable them by & bye to hive off for themselves and be independent. She further showed that by means of the liberal grants which the government out there would give in and of such a scheme, it would not be so expensive as might be supposed, and at the same time she intimated that while she was anxious that the interest of the Directors should be engaged in this scheme, she could not expect them to regard it as within the limits of the work of the Institution. She therefore intended in the meantime at least to attempt it more as a private enterprise and for the purpose of carrying it out she intended to return to America in the ensuing Spring.[46]

With the initial blessing of her directors, Stirling accompanied her first party of twenty-five children across the Atlantic in May 1886, purchasing Hillfoot Farm at Aylesford in Nova Scotia's Annapolis Valley shortly after arriving. Another party of thirty-six arrived in September, after which Stirling returned temporarily to Scotland, going back to Nova Scotia with an even larger contingent of fifty-six in April 1887. By August 1887 she had decided to move permanently to Canada, informing the directors of her decision somewhat peremptorily:

After due consideration, I find the time has come to arrange my future position with the Society. I have now done what I wanted, and made a bridge between this and Scotland to give poor children a safe outlet, and fair chance here – on such terms that I can honestly advise sending them. In so far my object is accomplished, and those children for whom I care most are getting the benefit of it. If you carry out my request and send off the party of 20 or thereabouts you will clear off all boarded out children and also lighten the Homes. I now give warning that I will not be responsible for any expense connected with any of the Homes after the 11th of November ... This leaves me free to give all my attention to this place, where I shall be willing to receive such children as you send me and place them in homes, when I can be assured they are fairly worthy. But it must be understood the Society is to bear the expense of sending them. The work here prospers wonderfully and children are greatly in request. I have also a large house and means of receiving them comfortably. I think you should call a special Meeting of Directors and announce this conclusion at once in order that there may be no disappointment.[47]

Between autumn 1887 and the destruction of Hillfoot Farm by fire in April 1895, small parties of children continued to be sent out to Miss Stirling, not primarily by her former associates, but by another Scottish child rescue institution, Miss Croall's Home for Destitute Children in Stirling, or Whinwell Home. Following Emma Stirling's example, Annie Croall had opened a crèche for working mothers and a small orphanage in 1884, but in sending 100 children abroad over the next forty years she made more use of the infrastructure created by Barnardo and Macpherson than of Emma Stirling's limited facilities. Whinwell children, most of whom came from the central belt, found their way to the United States, South Africa and Australia as well as Canada, and also had an alleged success rate of 95 per cent. Annie Croall justified her emigration policy on the same grounds as her more famous contemporaries:

In all the different departments of child rescue work, no branch yields so much fruit as the Emigration. It is not only economical for the country but best for the children; they are cut off from the bad corrupting associations in which they have been brought up and to which many of them would go back again if not lifted right away, it assures for them a better future, there is far more scope for them abroad, and with few exceptions they become happy, contented and useful citizens in that great country. We are doing the colonists a great service. They want this young life – they have ample room for it – there is no limit to the demand. There boys and girls have every advantage on their side. We have trained them, drilled and tested them, they are strong and healthy and have no family responsibilities to handicap them.[48]

Meanwhile, further north, the Aberlour Orphanage in Banffshire had been founded in 1875 by Canon Charles Jupp as an Episcopalian institution with a nationwide catchment area. Abandoning his original intention that the orphanage should cater only for the children of practising Episcopalians, Jupp promised to admit any child in need, on condition that the parent or guardian agreed that the child be brought up as an Episcopalian. Most of the 3,000 children who passed through Aberlour's doors up to 1921 were placed in farm work, apprenticeships or domestic service in Scotland, but although only just over fifty were sent abroad – almost all to Canada – this institution too utilized Annie Macpherson's infrastructure, while its journals and case histories offer perhaps a clearer insight into emigrants' experiences than the sanitized literature of homes that were more unreservedly committed to emigration.

Just as Quarrier's work did not go uncriticized, very few of these smaller institutions escaped censure either. Mrs Blaikie closed her home largely because of 'some collision with parents and guardians' over her right to appropriate their children. Her rather high-handed approach is evident even in her husband's endorsement of her policy:

in no case was any pressure brought to bear on respectable parents to allow their children to go. It was only in cases of drunken and ill-doing parents that the benefits of emigration were strongly pressed, and I confess that even in their case we did not apply this pressure without a certain qualm that we were interfering with the law of nature. We could but fall back on the principle, that extreme evils require extreme remedies. For myself, I think I never spent a more uncomfortable half-hour than on one occasion on the platform of the Caledonian Railway. The parents and friends of the children had been invited to bid them good-bye. It was a great mistake, for they made quite a sensation, and created something like a furore by abusing the promoters of the emigration. One woman, very drunk, insisted on getting back her little girl, and almost dragged her from the railway carriage; and Mrs Blaikie was denounced for stealing the children of honest folk and selling them to foreigners. 'It's that woman wi' the

white shawl,' they said, 'that's at the bottom o' it a'. It oughn't tae be alloo'd.' I
went to remonstrate with the drunken woman, and a report was circulated that I
had bribed her to be quiet. I do not think the music of the railway guard's
whistle ever brought such relief as it did that afternoon.[49]

William Blaikie also recalled 'a more amusing scene' in which he had deliberately misled a mother who had demanded the return of her child the day before
she was due to leave for Canada:

> Both father and mother bore the worst character; they had no home, and were
> seldom sober. The day before the girl was to leave Edinburgh, the mother
> appeared at my door demanding her child. It did not seem that anything could
> be made of her by argument, so I resorted to a bit of diplomacy. 'Have you a
> home of your own?' 'No.' 'Where do you spend the night?' 'In a lodging-house
> when we have money, and on a stair when we haven't.' 'And where do you mean
> to keep your daughter if she stays in this country?' 'Oh, we will get her looked
> after!' 'Does your husband work?' 'He hasn't got any clothes.' 'Would he work
> if he had clothes?' 'Oh, yes.' 'Well, look here. Here's a shilling to pay for a
> night's lodging, and if you come here at ten o'clock tomorrow morning, I'll
> supply your husband with clothes…' the bait took. The woman went away to
> tell her husband; and by the following morning the child was on the way to Liv-
> erpool. The morning came, and so did the woman, and the whole wardrobe was
> punctually delivered — with what result it is hard to say. I was sorry for the
> woman, but who can doubt that in such a case we did the right thing?[50]

Both Mrs Blaikie and Emma Stirling were also vehemently anti-Catholic and
assumed that they had an unquestionable right to proselytize and convert
Catholic children. In Miss Stirling's case this led to costly litigation, particularly
in the case of the three Delaney children, who were sent to Canada against their
father's wishes. According to Stirling herself, Arthur Delaney, 'a man of notoriously bad character', had asked for his children to be taken into care and
brought up as Protestants, having 'tired of the neglect and tyranny of the
priests', but after four years had been encouraged by a priest to reclaim them.[51]
By that time they were in Canada, and when Delaney raised a lawsuit for their
return, Stirling was found in contempt of court for giving evasive answers as to
their whereabouts. But it was the directors of ELCARS in Edinburgh who were
made liable for her obduracy, a ruling which imposed further strain on the

already poor relations between Stirling and her advisory board. Irritated by her unexpected departure to Canada and subsequent refusal to cooperate, and financially embarrassed by the withdrawal of her subsidies, as well as a series of court cases over custody, the directors increasingly blocked Stirling's attempts to bring children to Nova Scotia. Nor was resentment confined to Scotland, for the fire that destroyed Hillfoot Farm in April 1895 was no accident. It broke out four days after its owner had laid charges against an Annapolis man who had allegedly impregnated one of her former pupils in his employment, as well as the doctor who had allegedly performed an abortion. The arson attack, coming four years after another suspicious fire which had destroyed her sawmill, was the last straw for Emma Stirling, who quickly sold Hillfoot and, disillusioned with the attitude of her Canadian neighbours, moved to the United States for the remaining twelve years of her life.

Perhaps the most puzzling conundrum in this study is the striking absence of evidence that Catholic orphanages in Scotland developed, or even discussed, emigration policies in the nineteenth century. We know that Catholic child emigration from England and Wales was orchestrated by the different dioceses, particularly the Liverpool diocese, and it has been estimated that approximately 1,760 children were sent to Canada by Catholic agencies between 1870 and 1903. After that date the work was coordinated by the Catholic Emigration Association, with most of the children being distributed by New Orpington Lodge in Hintonborough, Ontario, renamed St George's Home in 1904. Since the Church hierarchy sanctioned emigration, it seems likely that Scottish Catholics would have participated. Not only was there a fertile recruiting ground in the west-central belt, with its heavy Irish Catholic presence; the development of its own emigration facilities by the Scottish Catholic Church might have addressed the fear that its children would be poached by Protestant agencies, which were most active in areas which contained large numbers of poor – and therefore vulnerable – Catholics. But since the records of Catholic orphanages contain only passing, anecdotal references to emigration and the largest institution of all, the Smyllum Orphanage in Lanark, founded in 1864, is totally silent on the issue, the mystery remains unsolved.[52]

Emigrant experiences

How did home children make the transition from emigrants to immigrants? Quarrier himself frequently accompanied his charges on the transatlantic

voyage and his annual reports always mentioned the valedictory services held
for the separate boys' and girls' parties. E. J. Stobo, who in July 1872 accompanied the first contingent of sixty-four Quarrier boys who sailed on the *St David*
from Greenock to Quebec, kept a detailed diary of the voyage and onward
journey:

> To-morrow I mean to get the boys to pack our traps for our journey west. We
> expect to reach Quebec on Wednesday. We have just had to surrender our
> passage tickets, and a search has been made for stowaways. If we arrive on
> Wednesday we shall have been on our passage exactly 14 days. I have had
> service to-day on deck, and found, as it has been throughout, that many gath-
> ered to join us, esteeming it a blessed privilege. Our dear boys, the children of
> many prayers, have behaved remarkably well, considering the situation and the
> strong temptation there is on board ship to do out of the way things. Of course
> boys cannot be made girls, they will be boisterous and romping, and full of fun,
> and it's no use trying to coop them up in a corner to look [like] apes mumping
> nuts to kill time.[53]

After disembarking, they travelled on by train, first to Knowlton, Annie
Macpherson's receiving home in Quebec's Eastern Townships, and then to her
other centres at Belleville and Galt. The Marchmont Home in Belleville was,
wrote Stobo, 'a handsome plastered house, with good offices, trim grounds, and
pleasant surroundings' where, after an 'excellent breakfast', the children were
lectured 'on the value of good character, the reward of hard work, and the
grand future that was before them in Canada if they only behave'. Both there
and at the Blair Athole Home in Galt the children were made to sing to 'a good
many nice ladies' who came to view the new arrivals before they were distributed to households within a 200-mile radius. 'The demand for our children far
exceeded the supply,' observed Stobo, 'and it was quite softening to hear ladies
and gentlemen say, as they looked at our children, "Oh, what nice children –
how healthy and good-looking. May we not have one, Miss Billborough?" But
it could not be: they were bespoke.'[54]

   One of the main functions of the receiving homes was to vet applications for
children, some of whom were clearly regarded as commodities, or even fashion
accessories. One couple wrote to Quarrier's Fairknowe Home in 1888 with the
following specific request:

Hearing you have some children in your Orphan Home, Brockville, and as I am living beside a neighbour who got one three years ago, he being a very good little boy, I wish you would send us one of your girls of 10 to 12 years old. Please send us one with blue eyes, a good countenance, good disposition, and a healthy, active girl. We wish to take her as our own child, and if you send us such we will do well by her. I have 150 acres of land, and am near church and Sabbath school etc.[55]

The placement procedure involved formal, legal indentures which were designed to protect the children's interests. The exact terms varied according to age, but single placements were rare, especially for children who were sent to Canada while still very young. Although it was hoped that those under nine would be adopted, this rarely happened, and it was much more common for young children to be boarded out with foster parents who were paid by the homes for looking after them until they had reached the age of eleven or twelve. Once these payments ceased, many families could not afford to continue boarding the children, who were therefore sent to households which received no fee for keeping them, but where they were expected to perform light duties in return for their board, clothing and schooling. The payment of a wage came only at the next stage, when the children reached school-leaving age and were employed as full-time apprentices, a development which often required a further move, to masters or mistresses who could afford to pay the necessary wages.

Children and employers were not to be left entirely to their own devices once a placement had been negotiated. Every agency was committed – at least on paper – to a system of after-care, implemented by the receiving homes' staff through regular tours of inspection. Those who accompanied emigrant parties to Canada also used the opportunity to visit children sent out in previous years. E. J. Stobo was in no doubt that the Quarrier children settled around Knowlton were thriving:

They speak well of their treatment and of their food, and are quite delighted with the idea of being counted members of the family. In this country the servant sits at the table with the family, and what a table! – say, breakfast. – There, on the nice, neatly-spread white cloth, is laid out a large dish of *mush*, fried bacon, boiled green corn, potatoes, bread, stewed and raw raspberries or cherries, cucumbers, tomatoes, honey, dough nuts, brandy snaps, and I know not what. Such a change for our poor street children! Here the little ones, and there is no mistake about it, have a chance of life.[56]

When in 1880 Mrs Blaikie took the opportunity to visit several children who had been placed out on her behalf by Annie Macpherson's three receiving homes, she expressed unqualified satisfaction with their condition and prospects. They included Georgina, who 'was being trained by a very careful and particular mistress to be a good servant', Jeanie, who had been adopted by a doctor and his wife, and Minnie, who 'attends school regularly, but is not a very clever child'. Her only reservation was that one child, who had been adopted by a minister and his wife, 'should be spoiled by too much indulgence and liberty', a preoccupation with discipline that was also voiced by Robert Wallace of Quarrier's in 1866:

In the tours I have been able to make since returning I have seen a large number of this year's boys, and have been pleased to find them, on the whole, doing very well, settling down to their new life and work, and striving to adapt themselves to their new surroundings, thus by their willingness and industry winning golden opinions from their masters, and laying the foundation for a good character in the days to come ... If this is not the case I generally find the fault lies as much with the people as with the boy. In many instances too much liberty is given at first; they are encouraged to talk more than they ought for the sake of hearing the broad Scotch, which causes great amusement but tends to make the boy forward. Prompt obedience is not enforced, nor the general training, begun in the Homes, kept up, till they awake to the change that has taken place in the child. I am frequently told, with a shake of the head, Ah! Johnnie is not the boy he was when I got him. I reply by asking whose fault it is. Some seem to think they are so well trained and disciplined that they cannot possibly relapse, but like a clock wound up must go on and keep right without further trouble or attention.[57]

Children were strongly encouraged to keep in touch with both the Canadian receiving home and the sending institution in Scotland. Wherever they went, they were encouraged to regard the receiving home as their base, to which they could return if they were in need, and they were assured that problems of incompatibility would be resolved by immediate relocation. In practice, however, these promises were often rendered meaningless by distance, financial constraints and inadequate after-care provision.

What did the children themselves have to say about their experiences? Most of the boys seem to have followed the advised career of farming, at least initially, and several ultimately left Ontario to try their fortunes in the west. Girls were channelled largely into domestic service, although some became nurses and teachers, while a handful of boys also entered the professions. If we were to take at face value the glowing tributes of the correspondents quoted in the annual reports of the sending institutions, we would have to conclude that the movement was an unqualified success. These reports were liberally peppered with letters from contented children, all expressing gratitude for their fresh start in life. Typical is the following tribute by a girl sent out from Quarrier's in 1885:

My dear Mr and Mrs Quarrier, I am very sorry to say that I have not written to you sooner, but I know that you will forgive me for this time – you may be sure I won't do it again. Don't think it is because I am far from you, and that I have forgotten all about you. Oh, no! How could I forget my *best friend* next to my father and mother on earth? I have thought on you every day since I left you. Yes, every hour. Sometimes I would like to see you again; but I will never regret coming out the time I did, because I would not have got the home I have if I had stayed another year. I have got a good home and I am very contented in it. I am living with a Methodist minister; they have got three children, two boys and a girl; they are very good and obedient, they do for me just like they would for their mamma or papa.[58]

'I like Canada, and Canada likes me,' wrote one of Annie Croall's emigrants in 1906, while 'wee Harry', sent out from the same institution, wrote, slightly more expansively, that 'a Canadian farm is a fine place for a little boy to grow big and strong in'. Many of the letters published in the Whinwell Home reports bear a strong resemblance to Quarrier's correspondence, not least in the desire for the emigration of siblings expressed in this letter from an eleven-year-old emigrant in 1904:

I got a letter from my brother yesterday; he is getting on fine in Ontario and he likes it very well. I had a letter from my brother in Glasgow; he wants to come here too. I think he should apply to the Immigrants' Agent, and they would send him out at once. I have a good place for him near me, if I only had him out here. I am very thankful you sent me out. I should never be so well off as I am to-day if you had not sent me out.[59]

Two years later the Whinwell report carried an effusive letter from a girl whose family had been reunited in Canada:

> Montreal, June 1906. Dear, Dear Miss Croall. These few lines to let you know that our sister, Lizzie, arrived all safe in Canada. She sailed from Liverpool on 24th May. So we are all in Canada now, except our wee sister, Christina, thanks to you, as I suppose as a family of orphans (five in number) we would not be out here and so well done for, only for your kindness.[60]

On a number of occasions emigrants enclosed donations with their letters, often in order to bring out younger siblings, and some successful immigrants later applied for home children of their own. This former Quarrier boy had been in Canada for twelve years when he wrote to the homes with such a request:

> If I ever go back to the old country (Scotland) I will visit the Homes, as I would like to see them. I hope I will be able to give something to the Homes sometimes for the good it has done me. We had a very rough road since our mother died. We were very young too. I was in the Homes about two years, I guess, and came out here very small. I am twenty-two years old now. Are you sending out any boys to Canada now? Could you send me out one, or do you send them out in that way now? I am farming now, and I would like to get a good little Scotch boy, about ten years old.[61]

But we do not need to read many of these letters before we smell a very large rat. Their formulaic nature, with striking similarities of style and content, is hardly surprising, since annual reports were mailed to the children's Canadian addresses, and no doubt they modelled their letters on what others had written, on what their employers told them to say and on what they thought the sending institutions would wish to hear. Such correspondence clearly cannot be taken at face value. In the first place, unhappy or unsuccessful children were highly unlikely to express their grievances in letters at all. Furthermore, only the most positive letters were selected for publication by institutions obsessed with good publicity and the need to appeal to the hearts and pockets of a charitable public through carefully crafted annual reports.

Yet even in these positive reports there are sometimes hints of problems. From time to time staff at Quarrier's Fairknowe Home admitted that 'undesirable' placements had been made, that children had run away, or that they had been returned to the receiving home because of bad conduct or persistent bed-wetting (a recurring problem and a clear indication in itself that these children were unsettled). The constant shifting of residence was very disruptive, whether because placements were unsuitable or simply because a child had out-grown its placement. And from time to time there was a clear recognition – at least in private correspondence – that mistakes had been made. One such case was George, a Whinwell boy who, among other misdemeanours, 'got a March-mont girl into trouble', stole money from his employer and a gold chain from a visitor, and 'caused death of valuable heifer by sticking fork in it'.[62]

Loneliness was a huge problem for many children. If an employer did not come to the receiving home to collect them, or if a member of staff was not free to accompany them to a placement, newly arrived immigrants could well be dispatched alone on the train with a name tag around their neck, bound for an unknown destination and an unknown employer. One Quarrier immi-grant, writing in old age about his impressions as a newly arrived ten-year-old in 1894, recalled his mixed emotions during the early days in Canada, and in particular the lack-lustre way in which he had been greeted by his foster parents:

> We were 18 days reaching Halifax, and sat and slept on the slats in colonist cars to Brockville. A big boy looked after a small one. The menu was very plain. It took me three days to reach the farm in Monteagle Township, 175 miles from Brockville. I travelled by train to Ormsby the first day, then 16 miles to Bancroft on the old stage coach that carried the mail, and by wagon to the farm on the third day.
>
> It was nice meeting my sister, Sara, but still I had the feeling of meeting a stranger. James and Elizabeth Price, who were to be my foster parents for the next 12 years, were 40 years old at the time. There was no tender kiss on the cheek, no kindly handshake, no enthusiasm shown in meeting this small Scottish boy. It was just a matter-of-fact meeting.[63]

The problem of loneliness is perhaps brought out more explicitly in the annual journals of Aberlour Orphanage, particularly in the immigrants' corre-spondence published in them. There were certainly success stories – one boy in 1887 advised his former guardians to build their next orphanage in Ontario, where 'you can live so much cheaper';[64] other letters praised the abundant har-vests and the ease with which immigrants could make money. But that was only one side of the coin, and the Aberlour authorities, which saw emigration as a supplementary rather than integral part of their work, admitted that sending children to Canada was always something of a gamble:

> They left us with rather heavy hearts, poor boys, and we could not part with them without feeling. Life is such a lottery so to speak, we cannot tell what is before them. Trials and difficulties they and we know nothing of may await them; may they have strength to overcome all. We feel we have done our best to train and fit them for the trials of life, and can only pray that something they have been taught may be put into practice. They go out to some of our lads already there, so that we are comforted in this.[65]

Some of these fears were confirmed by the criticism voiced by children whose letters appeared in Aberlour's journals. Several openly admitted that they were lonely and often cried for home. One boy wrote wistfully in 1888:

> America is rightly called the 'New World' – everything is new here, and one seems to be in another planet altogether. But it is not all sunshine out here, the cold in winter is terrible, and the heat in summer overpowering. And it is not all who get on here, any more than in the old country, there are many failures, only none starve here, food is plentiful. The mind, somehow, will cross the Atlantic and wander among the dear old glens of home. I often seem to hear the roar of the old Spay [sic], as it dances among the stones and rocks. Tell the lads if they can live at home to do so, if not, they should come here. Let me hear all the news when you write.[66]

Others complained of onerous farm work and expressed bitter regret that they had come to Canada. One such correspondent wrote in 1891:

> If people patiently bore at home the hardships they have to bear here, and if they worked half as hard at home as they have to do now, they would be far better off than they are here. Clothing is very dear, and very poor stuff too. There is plenty of food, but it is very rough altogether. Everybody seems to be trying to save money, and they don't seem to care how they do it. But if I ever set my foot on the soil of the old country, I shall say no more Canada for me.[67]

Problems in adjusting to a different culture were evident in the letter of an outwardly successful Whinwell emigrant writing from New York, where he was about to enter medical school:

> Dear Miss Croall, I scarcely know how to write. Your 'Xmas card has made me feel a bit homesick. You may think I have forgotten you, but that can never be. Oh, no, Miss Croall, Whinwell shall never be erased from my memory, the days of my youth, tho' long gone can never be forgotten, and even yet are as dreams over which memory loves to linger, and as I sit here in the office, night after night when everything is quiet and still, I steal back on wing of memory and play in the old garden at Whinwell again ... and sometimes wish I was back in reality again and to spend even one Sabbath in the 'auld hoose at hame.' Here Sunday is like every other day, the same bustle and hurry, everyone seems to be bent on taking all they can out of this world never thinking of the next.[68]

In many ways the dice were loaded against the immigrant children. On the farmsteads they were often alienated by their employers' attitudes, for even if they were not physically maltreated, they were rarely integrated into family life. They were in an ambivalent position: because they were not members of the family, their status and rights had to be protected by means of legal agreements, but those indentures in themselves set them apart, and further eroded any illusions that they were like other members of the farm families. School could also be an uncomfortable place, for most children were not given the opportunity to attain anything like the level reached by the Whinwell correspondent. Employers whose primary requirement was a working pair of hands might well be reluctant to send the children to school, and non-fulfilment of educational obligations was a recurring complaint among the Quarrier immigrants. Even neutral or positive letters reflect these problems. 'I haven't started to go to school yet, as we are so busy cutting wood for the rest of the winter,' wrote one Quarrier child in January 1886, while later the same year another wrote, even more tellingly, 'I am not going to school till I learn to speak like the rest of the people.'[69] For the children, interrupted schooling often meant verbal and physical abuse, both from the teachers, because of their inevitable backwardness, and from the other pupils, because they were so demonstrably different in their background and experience of childhood, as well as their accents.

Many home children also felt themselves ostracized by the host society at large. Canadian attitudes to home children were somewhat ambivalent. On the one hand, they welcomed the availability of cheap labour, but on the other hand, they resented their country being used as a dumping ground for what they suspected were misfits and ne'er-do-wells who were not wanted in Britain. The very appellation 'home child' was a derogatory one, and sweeping generalizations about the overall character of juvenile immigrants were often drawn from the few well-publicized cases of children who had gone astray. They were stigmatized as the dregs of Britain's city slums, cheap – but potentially dangerous – commodities who were widely suspected of importing medical and moral pollution to rural Canada. Many employers expressed disappointment at the immigrants' sullenness, rough manners and failure to adapt readily to their new environments, and their complaints frequently 'rang with claims of promises betrayed'.[70] Yet many children had also been betrayed, and perhaps these employers expected too much, too quickly, from recruits whose traumatic experiences in their early years had often left them with deep psychological scars. In such an atmosphere mutual distrust and hostility could easily build up, which in turn sometimes led to physical abuse on the part of the employer, and on a few (well-publicized) occasions to the child's taking revenge by sabotaging the work of the farm or household. Even this self-consciously upbeat letter in Quarrier's 1912 annual report contained a veiled warning:

> I like the Canadian people and ways. They seem friendly and quick in their ways. Mistress says she thought she would have to attach an electric wire to me to make me smart. I guess if the Canadians were as slow as we Scotch they would freeze here in the winter. Tell all the girls who think of coming to Canada to get a hustle on them, for the girls who came out before me all tell that the Canadians think they are slow.[71]

In cases of ill-treatment, receiving homes were more inclined to believe the employer than the child. When ten-year-old George West was found wandering the streets of Ottawa after running away from his employer following a horse-whipping, he was sent back to his placement by Fairknowe Home at the insistence of the employer, despite a recommendation by the Canadian immigration authorities that William Graham was 'not a proper person to have charge of this boy and it is deemed advisable that you should at once remove him to some other home'. In its defence, Fairknowe claimed, rather complacently, that no complaints had previously been made against Graham, and, while condemning the use of the whip as an instrument of punishment, 'we do not think he beat the boy severely'.[72]

Conclusion

How should posterity judge the merits and demerits of a movement that over a sixty-year period sent 100,000 unaccompanied British children to Canada, most of them under the age of fourteen? Did this constitute a totally unacceptable face of emigration policy, or could such social engineering be justified in the context of the age? Philanthropists like Macpherson, Barnardo and Quarrier had not a shred of doubt about the ethics of sponsored emigration, although perhaps the most ringing endorsement and summary are found in the 1910 annual report of the less well-known Whinwell Home. As we have seen, Annie Croall claimed that 'no branch' of child rescue work was so successful as assisted emigration, asserting that those sent abroad had 'a better future ... far more scope ... [and] every advantage on their side' while their relocation was equally beneficial to the donor and receiver countries.

Others offered more qualified support. Although Mrs Blaikie's visit to Canada inspired her with 'greater confidence than ever in the good done by the emigration of little children', she did not dismiss the importance of parental responsibilities, and was also aware of the need to placate employers, who feared her policies would create a scarcity of labour at home.[73] The Aberlour Orphanage played the emigration card sparingly and with many reservations, but the most unequivocal contemporary criticism came from outside the ranks of the institutions, notably from the press. In 1883 a leading article in the *Glasgow Herald*, while acknowledging the 'benevolent' intentions of the emigrationists, expressed concern at the unregulated nature of a trade that saw children 'shipped off in large batches' by autocratic individuals who opposed any challenge to their authority as 'a deadly sin, to be regarded with uplifted hands, upturned eyes, and pious objurgations'. The editor continued to press his case in no uncertain terms:

Whatever may be the intentions of the promoters of this juvenile emigration – and we have never questioned the purity and goodness of their motives – there can be little doubt that their system of procedure is entirely wrong. We have said that they are practically irresponsible, and as such the children are made over to them for emigration. Considerable difficulty is often experienced in gaining the consent of the generally wretched parents of the children, and there is little wonder, because parental feeling, even in the poorest and most degraded, is not easily extinguished altogether, and the parents know that they will in all probability neither see nor hear from their children again. Once all control of the one has been signed away by the other, parent and offspring in too many cases become absolutely dead to each other. It will be maintained, of course, that in the cases referred to absolute separation between parents and children is the best thing that could happen, which may or may not be true; but it certainly ought not to be in the power of any irresponsible individual, male or female, to decide upon a matter of so much importance, and to act upon the decision, without the shadow of control.

Once a child was in Canada, the editorial continued, it became virtually impossible for outsiders to trace its progress, since the homes on both sides of the Atlantic 'allow no independent inquiries to be made, or take very good care that if they are made, no information will be forthcoming'. The carefully monitored correspondence of upbeat annual reports concealed all problems, and the article was highly critical of the apathy of the British government in tacitly condoning 'the irresponsible deportation of the unprotected'.[74]

Retrospective criticism has been even more vehement. After the First World War the policy came under political attack from socialists who claimed that it was a device designed to preserve the existing social structure and to divert attention from the need to introduce welfare provision in Britain. From a different perspective, child psychologists also began to stress the importance of maintaining the family unit and the damaging effects of uprooting children from their natural environment, particularly if their parents were still alive. They also pointed out that most of the children involved had no conception of what emigration involved. Many emigrants themselves later recalled that they had viewed the prospect of 'going to Canada' in the same way that they might regard an annual outing to the seaside, and they complained that their guardians had never made clear to them the irrevocable nature of the step they were taking. Added to this misunderstanding was the question of whether the movement was prompted by a desire of the authorities on both sides of the Atlantic to benefit the children, or whether the real motive was to secure cheap labour for Canadian farms. 'I really thought when I got off that boat that there'd be a bucket of gold, but all I ever got was a scrub bucket,' recalled a Quarrier girl who emigrated in 1911.[75] And it was certainly ironic that children who were too young to leave school in Britain were shipped to Canada primarily as cheap labour, with scant provision made for the completion of their formal education in a country which stigmatized them as social misfits.

More serious still, however, were the practical dangers involved in sending vulnerable children to unknown, isolated situations, where they could all too easily fall victim to physical, sexual and psychological abuse. Such problems have received extensive publicity in the media in recent years, and some home children have spoken bitterly of the misery of their early years in Canada, when they were at the mercy of brutal employers, but were either too young to articulate their grievances or too frightened to complain for fear of reprisals. Even those who were not ill-treated often longed to exchange the isolation of the Canadian farm for the cramped intimacy of the Scottish orphanage.

The receiving homes seem to have put too much faith in written indentures that employers could ignore at will with regard to treatment, schooling and wages, while some emigrationists, notably Emma Stirling, were more concerned with self-righteous image-building than with the practicalities of child care. Inspections of placements by most organizations were infrequent and cursory, with the result that employers could pull the wool over an inspector's eyes, and abused children, particularly in isolated communities which closed ranks against them, very often had no one in authority to whom they could complain. Only in 1924, a year after three home boys had committed suicide in Canada, was a British delegation sent out to investigate the whole system of juvenile emigration, which was subsequently restricted to the over-fourteens through new legislation in 1925.

No humane person would today advocate child emigration as a remedy for problems of homelessness and poverty, but we should beware of demonizing the Victorian philanthropists for failing to adopt modern child-care practices, at a time when the welfare structure to support such policies simply did not exist. William Quarrier and his contemporaries did what they thought was best in an age when neither society nor the state accepted adequate responsibility for the poor, and when, for many children, the only alternative to utter destitution seemed to be emigration, even if that meant separation from home and parents. In the context of their time, the emigrationists were confident that the policy was both philosophically sound and practically feasible; and if they were naïve in their early expectations, many of them soon proved themselves willing to amend their practices in the light of experience, for the better protection of their charges.

LEAVING AND ARRIVING

'Keep your mind easy on the voyage, and be always eating something.'[1]

'There is nothing more agreeable to picture and nothing more pathetic to behold,' wrote Robert Louis Stevenson, in a striking juxtaposition of image and reality in transatlantic travel. His sentiment could have been echoed by many emigrants throughout the nineteenth century. It was in 1879 that Stevenson crossed the Atlantic from Greenock to New York, and trekked on across the continent to California, in pursuit of his mistress, and future wife, Fanny Osborne. Stevenson's contrasting images also encompassed the attitude of the passengers, who were, by his account, 'a company of the rejected; the drunken, the incompetent, the weak, the prodigal'. Yet, incongruously, he continued, 'it must not be supposed that these people exhibited depression. The scene, on the contrary, was cheerful. Not a tear was shed on board the vessel. All were full of hope for the future, and showed an inclination to innocent gaiety.'[2] By the time that Stevenson went to America, steamships had totally eclipsed sailing vessels as emigrant carriers, and transatlantic travelling time had been slashed from between one and three months to less than a fortnight. Yet even so, a voyage in an emigrant ship was still no luxury cruise, as the ailing, eczema-ravaged Stevenson discovered to his cost. It was rather a test of endurance that did nothing to build up the passengers' strength for the challenges of the new life that lay ahead. Anaesthetized by the jet engine, which has for generations now shrunk the globe and made long-haul travel an everyday experience for millions of ordinary people, we find it difficult to appreciate the discomforts and dangers encountered by our nineteenth-century predecessors who chose to travel – or particularly to emigrate – overseas. But if steamship and rail travel were arduous, how much more hazardous, as well as incomprehensible to modern travellers, was the interminable voyage by sailing ship, often followed by a long overland journey, which was the lot of all emigrants until mid-century?

Our lack of comprehension is certainly not attributable to lack of evidence, for the actual process of emigration was always a subject of great human interest, lending itself particularly readily to eyewitness accounts. The travelling experiences of emigrants are therefore well documented, not only by themselves, but also by those who sought to advise them in advance, and by official inquiries which exposed fraudulent practices or picked over the pieces of shipping disasters in an attempt to learn lessons for the future. Commentary on the transatlantic passage and onward journey – much of it negative – is readily available in a Scottish context from the mid-eighteenth century, and increases in volume and variety after 1815, with accounts of the Antipodean experience beginning to appear, particularly from mid-century. From this plethora of material we learn how emigrants arranged their passages, how they coped on the journey to the embarkation port, as well as on the voyage itself, how they were received on disembarkation and how they made their way to their final destination. We also learn about the few pleasures and the many hazards of travel, as well as the spirit-crushing tedium of being cooped up in a floating village for weeks and often months on end. We learn about the differences between cabin and steerage passage, between transatlantic and Antipodean travel, between fraudulent and honest agents and captains, and between officious and helpful immigration officials. By the 1850s we can begin to detect the effects of technological development on both sea and land travel, and can compare the experiences of emigrating under sail and steam, or by bullock cart and railway carriage. And throughout the century we can set the travel diaries and autobiographical accounts alongside the protective mechanisms which were meant to safeguard the interests of emigrants. From this wealth of information we may also be able to assess the truth of Robert Louis Stevenson's emphasis on the contrast between image and reality as unrealistically optimistic shiploads of emigrants made the physical transition from the old world to the new.

Eighteenth-century emigrant travel: the *Hector* and the *Bachelor*

Accounts of the travelling experiences of emigrant Scots predated the nineteenth century. The major tourist attraction in Pictou, Nova Scotia, is a commemoration of the *Hector*, sometimes known as Canada's *Mayflower*, which in 1773 brought almost 200 Highlanders from Wester Ross to Nova Scotia and initiated large-scale Scottish settlement of the Canadian Maritimes. The waterfront complex, incorporating a museum and gift shop, and with a replica of the vessel itself as its centrepiece, focuses in particular on vibrant oral traditions concerning the trials and tribulations of the ten-week voyage from Lochbroom, during which there was an outbreak of smallpox and dysentery and eighteen children died. To make matters worse, provisions rotted and ran low, the drinking water grew a green mould and severe storms off Newfoundland added an extra fortnight to the voyage. The ship itself was old, slow and wet, and from the start the passengers allegedly occupied themselves by picking wood out of the rotting hull with their fingernails.

Others fared worse. In the same year the *Nancy*, sailing from Sutherland with 250 emigrants, lost eighty-one passengers, fifty of them children, before the ship docked in New York. Also in summer 1773, 280 would-be emigrants from Caithness and Sutherland who boarded the *Bachelor* in the expectation of settling in North Carolina got no further than the Northern Isles in an enterprise that quickly degenerated into farce. To begin with, the passengers gathered in Thurso in early July, on the instruction of their agent-organizer, tacksman James Hogg. The ship, however, did not arrive to pick them up until the end of August, having been delayed on its trip from America with a cargo of rice. The emigrants' food supplies, already depleted during this unexpected delay, decreased still further during the eighteen days it took to load the ship at Thurso. When the *Bachelor* eventually set sail, far too late in the season, it was caught by equinoctial gales in the notorious Pentland Firth and driven first into Stromness in Orkney and then into Walls in Shetland. Repairs were made, but when the ship was about to sail again, it was dashed against the rocks, suffering worse damage than before. By this time eleven passengers had died and most of the rest were destitute. Still denied access to the ship's supplies, they had used up their own provisions and were dependent on the limited charity of the Shetlanders. When the Leith-based shipowner James Inglis then ordered the captain to drop off the passengers at Thurso before bringing the partially repaired ship back to Leith for refitting, most of them refused, knowing that they were unlikely ever to see the *Bachelor* again or to have their passage money refunded. The result was that the ship limped back to Leith in April 1774 with all but twenty-eight of the surviving passengers on board. Protracted legal wrangles ensued, during which it became clear that the *Bachelor* was never going to be fit

for an Atlantic crossing. But by the time Inglis was found liable for the transportation costs of all the emigrants who had come down to Leith, most of them
had either booked passages on other ships, returned to the Highlands or settled
in the Lowlands, and there is no record of the shipowner ever discharging his
debt.

Advising the traveller

The fiasco of the *Bachelor*, the images of hardship associated with the voyage of
the *Hector* and ongoing evidence of inadequately provisioned, fever-ridden or
wrecked ships made emigrants very aware that crossing the threshold from the
old world to the new was no easy step, but a major leap of faith that required
careful planning, stamina and a strong stomach. Even in the eighteenth century
supporters of emigration began to offer advice on how to prepare for the
voyage, while those in the opposite camp sought to deter emigrants by warning
of the grave – perhaps mortal – dangers involved in crossing the Atlantic.
During the nineteenth century, as we have already seen, the giving of advice
developed into a sophisticated industry. It soon became virtually *de rigueur* that
wealthy travellers should publish their journals for the benefit of their contemporaries and posterity, while several emigrants also recorded and disseminated
their impressions and experiences. Booksellers' shelves groaned under the
weight of guidebooks offering hints on how to emigrate to an expanding range
of destinations, emigrants' letters contained detailed instructions to friends and
relatives who were following in their footsteps, and advertisements for passages
took up many column inches in national and provincial newspapers.

The voyage produced a reasonable – if implicit – consensus of opinion
among commentators that it was an ordeal to be endured, rather than a pleasure
to be enjoyed. Advice was frequently offered on when to leave, what sort of
passage to book, how to avoid being defrauded, what to take, how to avoid seasickness and other shipboard ailments, and how to proceed on disembarkation.
In 1803, offering advice to an unknown correspondent, John MacDonald of
Glenaladale recalled his experience of successfully escorting 210 Highlanders to
Prince Edward Island over thirty years earlier. Abundant water and preliminary
health care were of prime importance:

> If you go in Summer, that is in advance of May, you may reasonably lay your
> Account with a very long passage from the westerly winds, and the vessel being

constantly put out of trim by the people: the full allowance of water is rather more necessary than of the Provisions, and the distribution of the Water should be immediately put under regulation from the moment of going on board ... The health and cleanliness of the passengers should be looked after for as long a time as possible before embarking. It is a serious thing to bring any putrid disease on board, it being enough that they will be but too subject to the same at any rate from being crowded in too narrow a space, upon salt victuals, bad water and too rare ventilation ... The ship should not be overcrowded with numbers, and in all good weather they should be much on deck to ventilate below: if you do not look well to this the Highlanders will keep below until they rot.[3]

Until 1835 the official advice given to transatlantic passengers was to prepare for a twelve-week journey. Most commentators were therefore agreed that emigrants should leave early in the season, in order to be settled before the onset of winter. Those going to Canada were often advised, if they could afford it, to enter the country via New York and the Great Lakes, thus avoiding the hazardous St Lawrence Seaway, which was also ice-bound between October and May. The *Aberdeen Journal* on 6 December 1848 recommended emigrants going to New York City to embark as soon after mid-January as possible, so that they would be located and accustomed to their new homes before winter ended, as that marked the start of the business season and was therefore the best time for finding work. If they were going to the Midwest, however, frozen lakes and canals dictated a shorter travelling season, between April and September, as on the St Lawrence. For emigrants to the Antipodes, however, an August or September departure was recommended, at least by Jessie Campbell, a cabin passenger in the *Blenheim*, which left Greenock for New Zealand in August 1840.[4] And another New Zealand emigrant, steerage passenger Isabella Henderson, advised those of her friends who could afford it to take a cabin passage and 'to bring plenty of food suitable for children, sago, arrow-root, cornflour, rusks, etc.'[5]

Securing a passage was a notoriously hazardous business. A huge variety of vessels participated in the emigrant trade. Until the middle of the nineteenth century many of them were timber ships, which had built up a thriving business with the Canadian Maritimes and the St Lawrence ever since an embargo had been placed on the importation of Baltic timber during the Napoleonic Wars. The timber ships deposited their bulky but low-value freight at ports right round the British Isles and their agents and captains used the provincial press to advertise regularly for emigrants to make up a paying ballast on the return voyage, usually to Quebec or Montreal. Fares averaged £3–£4 in the steerage and £10–£12 in the cabin, and ships generally sailed in April and August. Some advertisers were at pains to reassure wavering passengers by emphasizing the particular facilities of their vessel or the good order that prevailed on board. The *Albion*, a long-serving timber ship based in Aberdeen, aimed to attract higher-paying cabin passengers to both Canada and the USA when it advertised in the local press in January 1835:

> The Cabin and Half Deck of this Vessel are commodiously fitted up for the accommodation of Passengers, to whose comfort every attention will be paid by Captain Leslie … The ALBION will afford a favourable opportunity to Passengers desirous of proceeding to the United States: there being regular conveyance thither from Halifax, and the distance only about two days sailing.[6]

In slightly different vein, the agents for the *Wacousta*, which sailed from Glasgow to Melbourne in 1852, gave assurances about the careful vetting of passengers:

> With a view to obviate, as far as possible, the many evils which experience has shown to arise from the indiscriminate association of all grades of character on ship board, and to give a comfortable assurance to Heads of Families and others purposing to emigrate, and generally to promote the well-being of all on board, it will be required that parties going by the above ship shall either be known or certified to be of good moral character, and this rule will be strictly adhered to.[7]

Some agents appended testimonials or letters from satisfied passengers to their advertisements. In 1855 a passenger on the Aberdeen-based *Aurora* advised emigrants who wished to sail to New York or Quebec to make their arrangements with John Muir of Aberdeen or one Mr Percival, who 'puts out the very fastest Passenger Ships that sail from Liverpool', while the following year the captain of another Aberdeen timber ship, the *Berbice*, was presented by his grateful passengers with 'a valuable Cameo Ring, set in Gold, and a set of Cameo Masonic Studs to match'.[8]

Obtaining reliable advice about ships and agents was particularly important for emigrants who had to make their travelling arrangements at a distance. Even when transatlantic emigrant shipping was fairly decentralized – organized more around the interests of merchants than the needs of emigrants – some passengers still travelled some distance to embark. Those bound for Australia, New Zealand and South Africa usually had little option but to take their passage from Liverpool, Glasgow, London, Plymouth or Southampton, and when steamships eclipsed sailing vessels embarkations to all destinations became even more firmly centred on the Clyde and the Mersey in particular. Britain was the first European country to introduce transatlantic steamships, when the Cunard Line was launched in 1840, although the facility was available for almost twenty years on the New York route before it was extended to the St Lawrence. It was the late 1870s before steamships became commonplace on the Australian run, replacing the legendary clippers and slower types of sailing ship. Steamship passages cost about a third more than those in sailing ships, but it was money well spent, for the ships were not dependent on the vagaries of wind and weather. Regular sailings became the rule instead of the exception, and the time spent at sea was slashed. Emigrant transportation came to be dominated by famous names like the White Star, Dominion, P&O, Allan and Anchor Lines, whose agents, scattered across the length and breadth of the British Isles, recruited the emigrants and sent them to distant ports by means of the ever-expanding railway network. When blacksmith William Shennan emigrated from Kirkcudbrightshire to Melbourne in 1870, he travelled by train to Plymouth and spent a week in lodgings and then in the emigration depot before embarking on the *Crusader*.[9]

Liverpool stood head and shoulders above all other ports as the main embarkation point for emigrants from the British Isles, but it could be a very frightening and dangerous place for the unprotected emigrant. It had an unenviable reputation as a place where naïve emigrants were highly likely to be defrauded and assaulted, particularly by the hundreds of 'runners' who frequented the railway stations and docks. These men received a commission for bringing emigrants to ship brokers, provision merchants and lodging-house keepers, and were not averse to seizing baggage, manhandling emigrants and changing their money into dubious dollars. If adverse weather conditions – or just sharp practice – prevented a sailing ship from leaving port at the appointed time, emigrants who had travelled from a distance were at the mercy of greedy hostel keepers, most of whom demanded exorbitant payments for their squalid, vermin-infested accommodation. But even if emigrants managed to avoid the runners and lodging-house keepers, they might find themselves left behind in the stampede of a last-minute embarkation. Since passengers were not usually allowed on board until the hold was loaded, there was often a frantic scramble to embark with their luggage before the wind and tide changed and the gangplank was lowered, with those who missed their chance making a last, dangerous attempt to leap on board as the ship began to move. When that happened, wrote a reporter for the *Illustrated London News*, 'their only chance is to wait until the ship reaches the dock-gate, when boxes, bales, barrels, and bundles are actually pitched into the ship, and men, women and children have to scramble up the rigging amid a screaming, a swearing and a shouting perfectly alarming to listen to'.[10] As soon as the voyage was under way, all passengers were summoned on deck while the crew searched the vessel for stowaways. The passengers were then subjected to a roll call, to ensure that all had paid their fares, and that parents had not tried to pass off adult or adolescent children as infants. Physically or mentally defective passengers were also pinpointed and returned to the shore by tug boat.

Many of the problems associated with the voyage did not go unnoticed by commentators. *Chambers' Edinburgh Journal* suggested that emigrants would avoid the problems of delayed departures and chaotic embarkation scenes by travelling on regular packets, rather than on chartered ships. The latter, they claimed, were interested only in the timber or general import trade, regarding the emigration business as 'only a secondary or incidental consideration'.[11] Alexander Buchanan, the Chief Canadian Immigration Agent, advised emigrants to secure a passage on a fast ship through a reputable owner, broker or captain, even if it was not the cheapest deal they could secure, to ensure that the ship was going to the port contracted for, and to avoid 'those crimps that are generally found about the docks and quays near where ships are taking in passengers'.[12] Most guidebooks also warned emigrants against fraudulent agents and captains, particularly on the transatlantic route. They often reprinted the official circulars issued by the Colonial Office and various immigration agents, and reminded emigrants of their statutory rights. Thomas Fowler, who published an account of his trip from Aberdeen to Quebec on a timber trader in 1831, stressed the importance of choosing a good ship and captain.[13] Three years later a correspondent of the Aberdeen bookseller and compiler of *Counsel for Emigrants*, John Mathison, warned against captains who landed their passengers at Quebec, although they had paid to be taken the extra 180 miles to Montreal. He urged emigrants to enter into written contracts in order to prevent misunderstanding.[14] *Chambers' Edinburgh Journal* in 1839 urged emigrants to Australia to elicit, before payment of passage money, a written agreement from the charterer, endorsed by the captain, setting out the facilities to which they would have access on board ship during their long journey.[15]

Emigrants were also given extensive advice on what to take with them. Money was always a good idea, and emigrants were repeatedly advised to accumulate savings. On the other hand, they were regularly warned not to encumber themselves with household goods, bedding or furniture. One female emigrant from Aberdeen wrote from Zorra, Upper Canada, to a friend at home, advising her on the one hand to bring a sufficiently large hatbox to hold all her bonnets without crushing, but on the other to keep her berth as empty as possible. She continued:

> Do not distress yourself preparing great store of things, as if you could get nothing here. We can buy cotton prints, and cotton of all kinds, as cheap as at home ... You will have to supply your own bedding on board of ship. Bring some blankets, as they are scarce here; 2 tea kettles, brander, and crook. Be sure to pack your dishes well.[16]

Another Zorra emigrant offered practical advice about life at sea, advising emigrants against berths opposite the hatchway if they wanted to avoid getting soaked, to take tin jugs and bowls instead of crockery, to mark all tin dishes, and to fit locks to all boxes and barrels in case the sailors or fellow passengers took a fancy to their contents.

In 1841 Robert MacDougall published *Ceann-Iuil an Fhir-Imrich*, or *The Emigrant's Guide to North America*. Written in Gaelic five years after the author had himself emigrated from Perthshire to Goderich in Upper Canada, it was directed specifically at Highlanders, whom he wished to counsel in 'how to leave, how to arrive, and what to do after arriving'. In a section entitled 'Preparations', he encouraged them to bring protective clothing and bedclothes, which were almost twice the price in Canada. They should bring spades and nails, but not small carpentry tools or axes, since 'the emigrant will not get the time to trifle with carpentry in Canada'. He also gave advice on personal security and health:

> The emigrant ought to place everything that he is bringing with him neatly in square chests, not too large, or in barrels, and to be exceedingly careful with his possessions when boarding a ship, especially if he is sailing from a city; for the rabble usually gather around that sort of situation, and every one of them is angling for anything he can get his paws on to snatch away suddenly.
>
> A variety of food is exceedingly pleasant, and also necessary at sea; and

every man who goes forth into the Atlantic Ocean ought to make the utmost effort to bring a little of each type of provision he can gather up. I am not at all recommending this to emigrants to make gluttons of them. I am actually cautioning them about variety because I know it is requisite for their health, and because I am of the opinion that the harbour is a terribly incommodious place for emigrants on their journey. Men ought to be watchful of their provisions after going on board also; for 'the mischief is not all on Bute'; there will be a deceitful sheep in the flock, even after going to sea, nor is this at all surprising.[17]

Emigrants had to be just as vigilant when they disembarked. New York ranked along with Liverpool as a place where runners and other crooks abounded, and many guidebooks advised against lingering in the ports of debarkation, where emigrants might be defrauded by unscrupulous lodging-house keepers and land agents. John Mathison warned his Aberdeenshire readers:

On leaving the ship, remember that you come into immediate contact with many people who will take every advantage over you which they can, so look sharp in your bargains, and after your luggage. Keep a strict watch over these *picaroons* wherever the boats stop in your voyage up the river, or on the lakes; for, on these occasions, crowds of people assemble, and come on board ostensibly to assist you, but often to carry off any handy article. Even on leaving the ship at Quebec, be on your guard, and call a muster of your various articles, in case the sailors should take a fancy to any of them.[18]

Emigrants to Canada were warned against those who would try to divert them into the United States and were generally advised to leave Quebec as soon as possible, and head further west, where the cost of living was allegedly cheaper.[19]

Protecting the traveller

Throughout the nineteenth century emigrants were bombarded with changing types of advice about how to leave and arrive safely. The preoccupation of early writers with problems of unscrupulous captains, delayed departures, inordinately long passages and exhausted rations was replaced, after the advent of steamships and railways, by guidance on how to choose a reliable agent, encouragement to book a through ticket from home to final destination, and tips on transcontinental rail travel. But emigrants were not left entirely to the mercy of agents, captains and guidebooks. Between 1803 and 1855 a series of passenger acts tried to rectify some of the problems and protect emigrants against fraud and abuse. The first, and most severe, act of 1803 was in part a response to abuses revealed by the investigations of the Highland Society of Scotland, but its real aim, as was mentioned in Chapter 1, was to put a stop to emigration through its strict conditions. Even so, the outflow continued, with a gradual relaxation of the restrictions, until another severe law was passed in 1823 which was then attacked by the Commons Select Committee on Emigration in 1826–7. All legislation was repealed in 1827, in a climate that was no longer hostile to emigration, but this was followed by a catalogue of disasters the next season. More moderate and realistic regulations were introduced in 1828; in and after 1832 emigration agents were appointed in the major ports to oversee the operation of the act, while in smaller ports this responsibility fell to the customs officers. But the appointment of agents was largely cosmetic, at least in the Atlantic context. Their duties were badly defined, and they were severely overworked in their task of selecting assisted emigrants for Australia, as well as chartering and surveying the government ships in that branch of the trade. Some improvements were made after the appointment of the Colonial Land and Emigration Commission in 1840. The act of 1842, for instance, legislated on living space, victualling in the event of a delayed departure, lifeboats and medical attendance, as well as requiring passage brokers to be licensed. Henceforth there were to be no more than two tiers of berths, six inches above the deck, six feet long and eighteen inches wide. Yet although discipline was tightened up, and further consolidating statutes were introduced in 1849, 1852 and 1855 to plug loopholes as they appeared, shady operators could easily evade the law, and the officers were hamstrung by the need to keep costs low. Four people continued to be bundled into rickety berths six feet square, with little attempt to observe the 1848 requirement that single men and women be berthed separately. More effective legislation in 1852 isolated single men and women at opposite ends of the steerage, with families in between, but on the whole improved conditions in the 1850s were due less to legislation and more to the combined effects of a reduced volume of emigrants and the advent of the safer, quicker steamships.

Problems tackled by the passenger acts went beyond delayed departures, overcrowding and mixed sleeping arrangements. They also encompassed inadequate sanitation, lack of cooking facilities and poor medical attendance. Many ships had no water closets, or, if they did, their deckside location made them unusable or even subject to destruction in rough weather. Those who brought their own food had to compete to prepare it on a couple of ineffective brick-lined, wave-lashed stoves on deck, while unscrupulous ships' cooks could confiscate the passengers' food or charge them for cooking it. Water was an even bigger problem and very few ships managed to preserve an adequate, unconta-minated supply throughout the voyage. Some did not even try, taking their water supplies from the river where the ship began its journey. And many pas-sengers took their own medicaments rather than subject themselves to the atten-tions of ships' surgeons, who were often poorly qualified, uncaring and sometimes non-existent, at least on the Atlantic run until 1855. Surgeons on gov-ernment-chartered ships to the Antipodes tended to be of a higher calibre, however, since they were paid by the government and supervised by the Colo-nial Land and Emigration Commission, an arrangement which tended to ensure better conditions overall on the Antipodean run.

Those who emigrated under the aegis of special societies were usually subject to stricter supervision. The diary of Matthew Rowan, who sailed from Liverpool to New York in 1855, offers a glimpse into the procedure followed on Mormon ships:

> The evening previous to our embarking, all the Pastors and Presidents of Con-ferences were called to meet with F. D. Richards [a Mormon missionary] at his lodgings for the purpose of getting instructions as to how to conduct ourselves and those on shipboard during our passage. It was prophicied [sic] by F. D. Richards and Daniel Spencer that if we on board did right we would be pre-served, and not a soul of us would die; but if we did wrong it would be other-wise with us. On the 21st our arrangements were made, and the ship was divided into 7 wards and each ward had a President, I being appointed to preside over the 5th ward, in which chanced to be quite a number of my old Scotch acquain-tances. The Presidents of each ward had each 2 counsellors, and in each ward were appointed 2 Teachers, to visit and keep the Saints in good order etc. Strict discepline [sic] was observed, cleanliness rigidly so, and the order was to retire to berths by 9 P.M. and get up in the morning by 5 A.M.[20]

The voyage experience: pains, perils, pleasures and pastimes

'I can get no liberty to write for people jumping over my back, so you must excuse the shortness of this scrawl,' wrote John Ronaldson, a flax heckler from

Fife, to his wife, on the day in 1852 when he took ship from Greenock to New York.[21] Writing letters or, more particularly, keeping a diary helped travellers to cope with boredom during a long sea passage. Scots were no less prone to journalizing than any other emigrants, and it is from their diaries that we gain the most penetrating insights into the realities of a passage to North America or the Antipodes. They have to be used with some caution, however, for although nine out of ten passengers travelled steerage, most surviving diaries – not surprisingly – view the ocean passage through the cabin porthole. But, despite their limitations, what better way to describe the pains, perils, pleasures and pastimes of the voyage than through the pens of those who experienced them at first hand?

Pain, of varying types and degrees, was a recurring preoccupation of the diarists. The first pain experienced was the pain of parting. Jane Burns was only twelve years old when she sailed with one of the two pioneer parties of Scottish settlers to the Free Church colony of Otago in New Zealand in December 1847. Her father, the Reverend Thomas Burns, minister of Portobello and nephew of Scotland's National Bard, had previously promoted the venture enthusiastically at recruitment meetings all over Scotland, and was now to pastor the new colony single-handedly until 1854. He shipped his wife and children aboard the *Philip Laing* at Greenock in a party of 247 emigrants under Captain William Cargill. Jane later recalled the dismal, wet journey from Portobello to the docks, the incessant rain, the life-threatening illness of one of her siblings, and the solemnity of the relatives who came to bid them farewell:

> I can yet recall our arrival at the station, the rain, as I said, fell in torrents, and there was a long flight of steps from the train to the street. I can see yet, as I stood at the foot of the stair, our Mother at the top with the baby asleep in her arms. Our Father put his large blue cloak around them both, and he was guiding them down the steps. A lamp at the top lighted the glittering stair, and a more dreary scene could hardly be depicted.

The *Philip Laing* had arrived from Liverpool in ballast, which had to be unloaded before the emigrants' luggage could be stored, and the passengers eventually embarked on 26 November. A valedictory service was conducted by a number of Greenock clergymen, after which the final farewells were made, relatives disembarked, and the vessel cast off. Jane continued:

never while I have the power of memory shall I forget that sad dreary day. I
cannot describe the discomfort around us. The poor passengers looked so dis-
spirited [*sic*] and weary; women weeping and little children looking so home-
sick, there seemed no room for them on the deck. I heard some one say – I think
it was the mate – 'The one half of these poor people will never cross the line'. I
turned down into our cabin, in the stern of the ship, to be out of the way of so
much sadness and discomfort. But things did not seem much better there.
However, a little wholesale work did wonders. We set to work to subdue the
confusion round us, and the short November day closed in, and we went to sleep
in our strange new home.[22]

Thirty-four years later Agnes MacGregor, also bound for Otago, found it
'pleasant though rather melancholy' to recall the 'comforts of home' and the
final parting at Greenock railway station:

But the most affecting scene to call up is where we were in the train – a crowd of
relations standing round ... I knew, by the choking sound I heard, that Mary
was crying at the thought of parting. And I did not notice so much that Janet
was sobbing aloud, and Aunt Nina was trying to smile, in order to hide her tears.
Ah, I forgot what came after. When we were walking dismally along the station
at Greenock, who should we meet but Aunt Grace and Aunt Iya! They went
with us to the end of the station, and then we had to part. Oh, I'll never forget
the warmth of Aunt Grace's embrace, and I am sure Aunt Iya's felt as much
though less demonstrative. I could not keep back the tears that rose to my eyes
for a good while after, nor can I as I write.[23]

For the vast majority of passengers, the next pain experienced was the physical pain of seasickness. While it was no respecter of persons, it was doubtless
more tolerable in the privacy of the cabin than in the fetid, overcrowded steerage. It was an ordeal that loomed large in the memories – and writings – of most
commentators. John Mann of Kenmore in Perthshire, who sailed from the
Clyde to New Brunswick in 1816, mentioned what he alleged was a common
practice followed by ships' captains on vessels which supplied provisions of
feeding the passengers on the first day with porridge and molasses, in order to
make them sick, and therefore unlikely to demand their due rations thereafter.[24]
Thomas Fowler complained bitterly about the quality of the food supplied by
the captain on the three-week voyage from Aberdeen to Quebec in 1831. During

most of this period Fowler remained prostrate in his cabin, showing little sympathy for the similar sufferings of the steerage passengers, 'because we were frequently disturbed with the noise they made'.[25] Equally unsympathetic was Jessie Campbell, a cabin passenger on the *Blenheim* from Greenock to Wellington, New Zealand, in 1840, when the maid of one of her fellow passengers became sick in the Bay of Biscay. She recorded tersely, 'Their maid got sick in my cabin and vomited on the floor, very angry at her and sent her to the water-closet till she was able to go to the steerage.'[26] John Mackenzie, one of sixteen cabin passengers sailing from Greenock to Port Phillip aboard the *Robert Burns* in 1841, took a bath as a remedy for seasickness, after which '[I] tickled my throat until I emptied my stomach'. He made no mention of the sufferings of the 200 bounty emigrants in the steerage.[27] Even the improved conditions of a steamship passage did not give immunity from seasickness. When Peter Wallace and his two sons emigrated from Scotland to Manitoba in 1881, sailing from Greenock to Halifax on the SS *Prussia*, they soon found a need to use the 'vomiters' attached to the side of their bunks. And ten years later the Countess of Aberdeen, travelling from Liverpool to Quebec on the much-vaunted SS *Parisian*, was sick crossing the Irish Sea, blaming a heavy cargo of iron which caused the ship to roll excessively.[28]

The pain of seasickness was compounded by the peril of stormy weather, when the passengers were often in mortal terror. As Isabella Henderson – who advised those back in Scotland to stay there – recalled four days into her voyage to Dunedin:

> We have encountered foul winds and now I could tell you what it is to have death brought very near to you. It came on at ten in the evening and continued all night. We were all shut downstairs, the lights put out, tins and dishes rolling in all directions. Everyone put into the greatest excitement, vomiting, in every direction children, the vessel heaving mountains high, the ship to our side was two or three times under the water. I felt very composed yet at times I felt overwhelmed with fear at the very thought of being ushered into eternity in an unprepared state for all your sins come rushing before you.[29]

Shipwreck was a very real danger for those who sailed on emigrant ships, as was fire, particularly on wooden vessels with open braziers and unguarded oil lamps. While it is not surprising that such catastrophes rarely feature in passage diaries, official investigations and press accounts catalogue the many mishaps that befell nineteenth-century emigrants in transit. Lurid emigrant shipwreck was grist to the mill of many Victorian newspapers and journals. Between 1847 and 1851, forty-four ships were wrecked on the transatlantic crossing and 1,043 people were drowned, including 248 who died in 1847 when the *Exmouth* was driven ashore on the coast of Islay shortly after leaving Londonderry for Quebec. On 28 September 1853 the *Annie Jane*, sailing from Liverpool to Quebec with a French-Canadian crew, a cargo of iron and around 400 steerage passengers, including almost 100 Glasgow artisans, was wrecked in the southern Hebrides. The A1-registered ship, newly built in Quebec in May, had already returned to Liverpool once for repairs after being damaged in a gale when it was dismasted again by another equinoctial storm, this time foundering in the surf and rocks of Bagh Siar on Vatersay. The ship split into three pieces and about 350 people were drowned. As naked and mutilated bodies were washed ashore, they were buried in a common pit, the site of which is now commemorated by a granite memorial. By the end of the year an inquiry had blamed the tragedy on improper stowage of the cargo, too few crew and 'useless' Canadians. Two Glaswegian survivors, blacksmith Angus Mathieson and joiner Abraham Brooks, recalled the events leading up to the shipwreck as well as the disaster itself. Mathieson testified to the captain's intransigence when the ship was damaged shortly after setting out for the second time:

> That they again experienced tempestuous weather, and the ship had scarce reached the same point in the Irish Channel which she had formerly weathered, when she again lost her foretopmast, maintopmast and jibboom. That the weather at this time was very tempestuous and coarse, but the captain still stood on. That some days afterwards the ship was labouring very heavily, and the passengers apprehending serious danger had a meeting amongst themselves, at which it was resolved to petition the captain to make for a port. And a petition was accordingly drawn up and presented to him; but instead of reading or paying any attention to it, he pitched it overboard, observing that they (the passengers) had got him to put about upon a former occasion, but that he would have satisfaction out of them the second time. It was a person of the name of Ross, from Glasgow, a cabinet-maker, who drew up the petition and presented it in the name of the emigrants to the captain. He was drowned at the loss of the ship.

Brooks, in his evidence, highlighted the death throes of the *Annie Jane*:

The wind blew a perfect hurricane. We now sighted Barra Head light-house, and great efforts were made to clear a reef of rocks which lay to seaward, and we were successful, but the captain seeing it impossible to clear the light house put into Veternish Bay. This occurred on the 28th day of September. After running her into the bay the captain ordered the yards to be squared, which was accordingly done. Directly after this the ship grounded. This might be between twelve and one o'clock in the morning of the 29th of September, and having had my spell at the pumps before this, I went to the poop door, and holding on by it I saw that the fore part of the ship was rapidly giving way. My brother came behind me at this time and was desirous that we should get upon the poop deck; I remarked to him that it was almost impossible to stand upon the poop, the breakers were so high, but to come further aft as the ship was rapidly giving way forward. We accordingly proceeded aft till we were stopped by the bulkhead, which separates the second cabin from the cabin. We stood there for about ten minutes: by this time a number of the passengers between decks were drowned by the sea rushing in upon them before they could get upon deck. Likewise about a hundred joiners and others, who rushed to the poop deck and clung to the boats which were lying with their bottoms upwards, were all swept overboard by a heavy sea which broke over them, with the exception of one young man of the name of Charles Smith who clung to the mast. The passengers rushed aft to the poop. At this critical period the lamp which hung at the centre of the poop went out, and left them in complete darkness. At this time some one handed me an axe, and with the help of the ship's carpenter I succeeded in breaking away the bulkhead and getting through to the cabin. One of the passengers, named Thomas Galbraith, in endeavouring to make his way from the poop to the cabin was ordered back by the captain, and refusing he was throttled by him, but, nevertheless, made his way to the top of the poop. At this time my brother, another passenger, and myself made our way through the companion and clung to the poop, where we remained till about seven o'clock in the morning, at which time, it being ebb tide, we were enabled to wade ashore about breast deep. Of the whole passengers and crew there were one hundred and two persons saved.[30]

Other perils of the voyage were more unambiguously manmade. Emigrants who were brave enough to cross the Atlantic during the Napoleonic Wars were advised to travel in well-armoured ships, and as late as 1837 a clergyman sailing from Leith wrote of the danger of piracy on the high seas, perpetrated by 'a set of desperate men often I believe Scotch'. The main cabin of his vessel, the *North Briton*, was furnished with guns and cannon as a defence against these pirates, who, he claimed, were prevalent in tropical latitudes, attacking becalmed ships, murdering all on board, stealing the cargo and sinking the ship with the passengers shut in the hold.[31]

Disease was a much more serious and persistent problem than piracy. Epidemics could spread rapidly in the squalid, unventilated steerage, particularly among passengers whose resistance had been worn down by poverty, reduced further by unwholesome food and water and aggravated by unhygienic shipboard practices. Jessie Campbell spoke disparagingly of the Highlanders who made up a large part of the steerage passengers on the *Blenheim*:

> Capt Gray and the doctor complaining woefully of the filth of the Highland emigrants, they say they could not have believed it possible for human beings to be so dirty in their habits, only fancy using the dishes they have for their food for certain other purposes at night, the Dr. seems much afraid of fever breaking out among them, this would really be a judgment on us, poor as I am no consideration on earth would tempt me to trust my little family in a ship with Highland emigrants if I still had the voyage before me.[32]

To Jessie Campbell's horror, one steerage passenger on the *Blenheim* was diagnosed with smallpox three weeks into the voyage, although the infection did not spread to others and he subsequently recovered. John Anderson, a steerage passenger to Dunedin in 1862, described graphically – if somewhat ungrammatically – the outbreak of illness and the callous attitudes on board the *City of Dunedin*, where the floor of the hospital was three inches deep in water:

> one of the young married men beside us has been badly this week those in the hospital are not better their [*sic*] is trouble amongst us the docter [*sic*] does not know what it is nor nobody in the ship ever saw or heard any thing like it it affects the brain at once two of them in hospital is that way one of them is very bad he came out during the night and was raving to himself on the deck till the sailors put him in the door is not locked and the docter orders nobody to attend on them two of the young women besides us were quite well last night one of the[m] turned bad in the night and has been raving even on the other one felt sick after breakfast and tonight she is as bad as the other the docter gave her a powder which made her worse she was in awful agony with it the docter and

captain came down at 10 0 clock and spoke to them then went on deck again never asked if any one was going to attend them or anything that is the treatment you get on board if you live you live and if you die you die it is all one to them.[33]

Shetlander John Tulloch, who almost died of typhoid on the voyage to New Zealand in 1863, blamed an incompetent doctor and a drunken captain for some of the forty-four deaths aboard his ship, while Isabella Henderson, who travelled steerage to Dunedin, also in 1863, spent much of the voyage caring for her sick 'mess mates' on a ship where whooping cough was rife. Jane Findlayson, who sailed to New Zealand thirteen years later, recalled a fatal outbreak of measles among the children and an occasion when her delirious messmate tried to commit suicide.[34]

For some emigrants, particularly children, the voyage was an end rather than a beginning. For obvious reasons, the Grim Reaper was much more likely to be mentioned in narrative diaries and letters than in promotional guidebooks. Passengers who were not involved in these tragedies sometimes commented on them with considerable detachment, while ships' crews could be completely callous, particularly on the Atlantic run as opposed to the more tightly supervised Antipodean voyages. Robert Cromar of Slains in Aberdeenshire, who kept a diary of his voyage from Aberdeen to Quebec in 1840, mentioned a number of burials at sea:

Sunday 26th ... Child belonging to one of the passengers died in the afternoon, and rolled up in the fashion of the dead at sea ... Monday 27th ... The child put overboard at half past five in the morning, none on deck but the child's father, two of the passengers and the seamen. I was too late of getting up to see the funeral ceremony but one of the sailors told me that the corpse was merely laid on one of the hatches and turned overboard into the sea without any ceremony whatever than a hearty curse from the Captain to one of the sailors for not turning the hatch in the proper way. I thought he might have let the cursing alone until the corpse was out of sight at any rate. The child's mother appears to be very sorry about it but no word nor appearance of any kind among the passengers of such circumstance taking place.[35]

The deaths of two young girls on the *Helenslee* en route to New Zealand in 1863 were recorded with considerably more sympathy by Mrs D. Bonthrow.

The first child to die 'used to run about the liveliest and most merry of all the little ones and when the Bagpipes were played by the Highland Pipers on board she would jump and clap her little hands so gleefully'. The second child to die, a month later, had never recovered from the effects of measles and her funeral, unlike the fiasco witnessed by Robert Cromar, was 'a solemn thing', with the body laid on a flag-draped plank, and a large gathering of crew and passengers paying their respects with psalms and prayers.[36]

But the recollections were most poignant when the writer had experienced a personal tragedy. Alexander Robertson left Monymusk in Aberdeenshire for Canada in April 1846, taking passage from the port of Aberdeen with his wife and seven children. Fourteeen days into the voyage, Ann Robertson gave birth to a premature child, which survived for less than two days. On Sunday 3 May, Ann herself – weakened by dysentery, seasickness and childbirth – also died, and was buried at sea after her infant daughter. On 29 May the vessel docked at Quebec and, after clearing quarantine, the family proceeded by steamboat to Montreal, where they were met by relatives who had emigrated earlier. By late July the Robertsons had established themselves on a farm near Montreal, but within a year Alexander too had died, and the subsequent fate of the seven orphaned children is not known.

The tragic events of the voyage were described in a detailed and surprisingly articulate journal purportedly kept by thirteen-year-old Charles, the eldest of the Robertson children, and in two letters later sent by Charles and his father to relatives in Scotland.[37] These documents reflect some of the crushing desolation of bereavement experienced by both father and son, and also give us a child's-eye view of everyday life aboard an emigrant sailing ship, Charles's sentiments lurching between hope and despair in tandem with the lurching of the ship and his mother's fluctuating condition. Charles Robertson's diary began on the day the vessel left Aberdeen and ended on the day it docked at Grosse Ile quarantine station. It is worth quoting at some length:

T[uesday] 14th. Left Aberdeen past three. On deck ere out between the pier head. Put the children to bed. My mother sick … ship heaving a little tonight. W[ednesday] 15th. Drizzling rain with high wind. Past Peterhead by 6 o'clock a.m … about 4 o'clock a child fell down the hatchway and cut its head very severely. They were obliged to sew it up … In sight of John O'Groats Castle there came a pilot boat alongside and offered to take the ship through the firth for 15 shillings, so we bargained with them.

Thursday 16th. Got through the firth. Had a terrible night of lurching past Dunnet Head lighthouse. The pilot was of no use to us – the captain raged terribly at him. The ship you would have thought would have turned on her broadside. Every minute shows us groups of hills, some of them very perpendicular. We are passing some ships that passed us in the firth like fury. There are a good many sick. We have had a good breeze of wind today. The children are running about on deck as though they were quite at home.

Saturday 18th ... There are not so many people sick today. My mother I think will soon get better. She is on deck at present ... About four days have we been on the sea and I like her better than I expected at first.

Sunday 19th. Got out of bed about 7 o'clock. The ship is going about 7 knots an hour – a knot is about a mile. The most of the passengers are keeping below as they can hardly stand on deck. The spray of the sea is coming on deck of the ship like a shower of rain, but no matter, for all that we are getting on at a good rate. My mother is still sick but there was some of the passengers who have not got out of bed yet.

Tuesday 21st. Last night 7 o'clock I saw a shoal of whales, some of them spouting. Today we are going at the rate of 3 or 4 knots an hour. My mother is a good deal better. Two ships in view. The sea fully as calm as yesterday. Towards evening we were going 6 knots an hour. One of the ships kept before us all day but now we left her like fury.

Friday 24th. Going at the rate of 7 knots an hour. The ships that were before us yesterday are out of sight behind us now. My mother is still sick. Most of the people have got out of bed here now.

Monday 27th. Terrible morning of wind and rain, the sea raging terribly. The pishpots are tumbling everywhere – some of them are not raising a delightful smell. My mother very sick today ...

Tuesday 28th. One sail in view, but we can scarcely see her for the wavings of the sea ... My mother was delivered of a girl during the night. She was not able to nurse it, but a woman on the other side of the ship took it, but it hindered none of them long.

Thursday 30th. The sea is very calm now. The child was let overboard today and two stones attached to it to make it sink. We are not over clean here but we work away the best way we can.

Sunday 3rd. The day dawned, bringing along with it a day of sorrow which I shall ever remember. Tonight about nine o'clock my poor mother drew her last breath and on Monday she was moored to her watery [grave] at 12 o'clock ...

The children little know their want. As yet the 3 littlest know nothing about it.

Tuesday 5th. Sunday was very misty and by night it came terrible lightning accompanied by torrents of rain, as if the elements were rejoicing that her soul is harboured safely into the harbour of eternal life, where I hope she wears a crown of glory. They say we are on the banks of Newfoundland and the mist is a little cleared today, and a ship in view …

Monday 11th. The mist is worse than yesterday and we are sailing among a flock of icebergs. Some of them are squeezing the ship's bottom and making her timbers shake. Some of the passengers are sitting preserving themselves as if the last day were come …

Wednesday 20th. Yesterday we dropped anchor at 12 and drew at 7. We had the tide with us and a good breeze. By 4 o'clock this morning we were anchored at the quarantine station. It is stationed at Grouse [Grosse] Island. The doctor was not a quarter of an hour looking over us … We are anchored at Quebec now. She has a most romantic appearance. We are stationed among a wood of ships. There appears to be a great many ships here. The country is far prettier than I thought, far more than old Scotland. We are expecting to heave away for Montreal tonight. Oh, but one is left lying on the sands of Newfoundland. Lonely is her grave among the blue waves of the Atlantic. No-one will tread the grass that sprouts from the sod that covers her. Her bed is a sheet of water.

Two months later, in a letter to an uncle in Monymusk, Charles enlarged on the circumstances surrounding his mother's illness and death. He admitted that she had bitterly regretted the decision to emigrate and had complained that 'sea-sickness was the sorest sickness she ever had'. She had not been shown much sympathy by the captain or other passengers, but her own family had done everything possible for her under the circumstances, 'so we have no stain impressed on our minds'. By this time Alexander Robertson had sent home to his parents-in-law a heart-rending account of his wife's death, written during the final stage of the voyage up the St Lawrence, when 'I often lean on the side of the ship that my poor wife was last seen':

I take up my pen to acquaint you with the dreadful affliction that has befallen me in the death of my wife … She grew ill as we left the point of the pier with sickness and continued to grow worse as we went further on. Some days she was a little better and able to be on deck, and often did we flatter ourselves that she would soon be better, but the weather grew bad and she was taken with dysentery, which reduced her to great weakness, when one dreadful night she was taken with the pains of labour. There was two midwives on board and she was safely delivered of a female child … alive but very small … It lived the next day and through the next night or morning, when it died … My wife was still in a fair way on Sunday [but] that day she grew worse, ere about nine o'clock at night, when her soul took its flight to that pure land where there will be no more sorrow nor trouble and where I long to follow. Oft since then I have lain beside my poor children and looked back to the many happy nights we have spent together, never, never to be recalled. The children do not feel their want – it is me alone that does suffer, but their time will come. I often wish that we would be driven against some rock, that we might all have the same grave.

While conditions on the government-chartered Antipodean ships were generally better than on the more unregulated Atlantic run, passengers were cooped up for a much longer period, and the death toll during a three–four-month passage could be severe. There were twelve deaths, mostly of very young children, on the *Robert Burns*, en route from Greenock to Port Phillip in 1841, and diarist John Mackenzie recorded the results of a post-mortem carried out on one three-year-old. It showed, he wrote, 'the whole frame in a diseased state, the intestines all inflamed, one of the lobes of the lungs gone, and one of the kidneys quite unhealthy, the poor little thing wasted to a skeleton, dysentery carried it off'.[38] There were nine fatalities aboard Isabella Henderson's ship to Dunedin in 1863. Most were children, including sixteen-month-old Ewen McLachlan, a friend's son, who died of bronchitis. Isabella recalled that 'the sympathy of all on board was extended towards him, even the hardest heart seemed to melt … The Captain came down and assisted the sailmaker to sew him up in a canvas sheet with a bag of sand at the feet to sink him' (12 August). On another occasion Isabella had to struggle to the ship's hospital in the teeth of a severe storm to dress the corpse of a baby. She described the conditions vividly:

Fine fun this morning. With the rocking about we are all in bed nearly as we can do nothing. The seas that are coming in are frightful. About 6 o'clock the water came rushing down the hatch and such a scene. The place swimming with water and all the folk in a terrible plight. See them standing up on boxes all the way along with faces pale with fears. We were thinking our mess were all well off as we had a high bed and away from hatches and ventilator but about 9 o'clock a heavy sea broke on the poop and took the glass off the companions right into the cabin, and took the folks up to the waist. It came down like a thunderstorm into our bed and ere we could do anything our blankets and beds were wet through and through so that we were done out of our beds. But that was not the worst. One of the men at the wheel was washed away under it. His body was caught under the wheel. His leg was broken and the other had his arm sprained and the night being so rough they were not able to take him forward to his own bed. He was brought down our hatch the married people's side, and before his leg was put to rights word came down from the hospital that the baby was dead. The next thing was who was to dress the corpse. I was terrified to face up the stair, the wind was howling at such a rate and sea washing the decks every minute. But as I was out of bed and doing nothing they asked me to come and dress the corpse so I could not refuse them. Two of us went up and men with each of us. We got safely across and found them baling the water out of the hospital. I dressed the wee, wee corpse, just like a doll.[39]

Cabin passengers were not immune from such tragedy. Twenty-three years before Isabella Henderson's voyage, Jessie Campbell gave a blow-by-blow account of the decline of the youngest of her five children, one of twin girls, who became ill on 2 October 1840 and died on the 23rd:

9th October – My little darling worse, Dr. dreads congestion of the brain ... Poor little Tibbie's head shaven and blistered tonight.

14th October Isabella much the same, her pulse rather stronger, still continues to drink the arrowroot; her father deeply distressed, gentlemen very considerate in keeping the deck quiet above our cabin, Dr. prevented the piper playing in the evening. Capt. Gray told the Dr. that in case of my little darling recovering he would keep 8 or 9 fowls for her own use.
15th October Isabella rather better, her pulse a little stronger, still very little hope of her recovery, still drinking a good deal, gets thin chicken soup occasionally; for a change she did not sleep well last night but did not seem to have any pain. Dear little lamb she likes so much to have me beside her in bed, even during the day she gives me her little hand to hold or sometimes puts it across my neck; she does not vomit, altho she does not eat she takes a good deal of nourishment in drinks, nothing seems to put her bowels right, she still passes very green stuff but has not a stool oftener than twice in the 24 hours.

Thursday 22nd October Dear little Isabella alive and that is all; she was taken very ill last night with violent pain, we thought in her bowels, Capt. C put the Dr. up, he gave her an injection which gave her immediate relief, he said the pain was caused by flatulence, she slept soundly till near morning, her hands have a slight convulsive movement today, she is laying quite quiet seemingly in a state of torpor; twice I thought she knew me, her eyes certainly followed me, her breathing quite regular, she still swallows a teaspoonful of drink at a time.

23rd October My dear little lamb lingered in the same state all night, she expired this morning at 8 o'clock; she resigned her breath as quietly as if she were going to sleep without the slightest struggle. What would I give to be on shore with her dear little body, the idea of committing it to the deep distresses me very much, she has made a happy change from the cares and miseries of this world, it is hard to say what misfortune may await us from which she has escaped. The Doctors did not seem to understand what her complaint was, both agreed it was brought on by teething and that she would have had the same on shore.[40]

Although death was a great leveller, a comparison of voyage diaries reveals an enormous disparity between conditions in the cabin and the steerage. When little Isabella Campbell first fell ill, the doctor 'ordered her into a warm bath', while Jane Bannerman's family had a piano in their cabin for their entertainment.[41] Cabin passengers had their accommodation cleaned at their convenience, but steerage passengers were turfed out on deck irrespective of the weather and took turns at cleaning duties. Jessie Campbell contrasted the 'indolence and filthy habits' of the Highlanders aboard the *Blenheim* with the cleaner, more easily managed contingent of emigrants from Paisley. Captain Gray, she noted,

complains woefully of the indolence of the emigrants, he has such a work every day hunting them out of their beds and keeping them on deck, particularly towards evening that their berths may cool before they go down to sleep ... [he] takes a great deal of trouble in obliging the emigrants to keep their places in order, he drives them on deck in good weather with a small cane in his hand.[42]

The perspective of the steerage passengers was rather different. According to Isabella Henderson, they were 'treated more like slaves than any other thing – ordered out of our beds at 5 o'clock in the morning, and get as much impertinence in one hour as would serve you for one twelve months ... And then we are smoked out of our place with tar, and with no other shift than decks swimming with water.'[43]

There were big contrasts in food as well as in accommodation. Cabin passengers on the fast packets between Liverpool and New York enjoyed a full and varied menu, often with champagne, but transatlantic steerage passengers were either given their daily rations by the ship's cook or steward, from barrels which were brought on to the deck or into the steerage, or they struggled to cook their own supplies on inadequate stoves on the soaking deck. Sheep, pigs and poultry killed during the voyage were fed to the passengers, with those in the steerage being given the inferior cuts. Jessie Campbell summed up the contrast:

> We had for dinner today roast ducks, boiled fowls and curried fowl and pea soup and pickled pork, this is the first day we have been without beautiful cabbage for dinner since leaving Greenock, the potatoes are still very good, our having such a good cook adds much to our comfort; all the steerage passengers got flour, suet and raisins served out to them yesterday to make puddings for their dinners today, most of them did not know how to use the ingredients, they eat the raisins their children going about with them in handfuls, made scones of the flour. I do not know what they did with the suet, they likewise got pickled cabbage, a good many cannot be prevailed on to eat it and were caught throwing it overboard.[44]

Whenever a sheep was killed Campbell's Skye-born maid was employed to make haggis, although she noted that on one occasion Captain Gray became 'very angry' at her for refusing to prepare it on a Sunday.[45] Steerage passengers did sometimes win small victories, as on the *City of Dunedin* in 1862, when a delegation persuaded the captain to revert to serving water out of iron tanks rather than wooden barrels, as some of the 'cabin gentry' had demanded.[46]

For Robert Louis Stevenson in 1879, the main advantages afforded by a berth in the second cabin were 'air comparatively fit to breathe, food comparatively varied, and the satisfaction of being still privately a gentleman'. His main impression of the steerage was of its overpowering squalor and stench:

> If it was impossible to clean the steerage, it was no less impossible to clean the steerage passenger. All ablution below was rigorously forbidden. A man might give his hands a scour at the pump beside the galley, but that was exactly all. One fellow used to strip to his waist every morning and freshen his chest and shoulders; but I need not tell you he was no true steerage passenger. To wash outside

in the sharp sea air of the morning is a step entirely foreign to the frowsy, herding, overwarm traditions of the working class; and a human body must apparently have been nurtured in some luxury, before it courts these rude shocks and surprises of temperature in which many men find health and vigour. Thus, even if the majority of passengers came clean aboard at Greenock, long ere the ten days were out or the shores of America in sight, all were reduced to a common level, all, who here stewed together in their own exhalations, were uncompromisingly unclean ... To descend on an empty stomach into Steerage No. 1 was an adventure that required some nerve. The stench was atrocious; each respiration tasted in the throat like some horrible kind of cheese; and the squalid aspect of the place was aggravated by so many people worming themselves into their clothes in the twilight of the bunks.[47]

For the duration of the voyage, the ship became a temporary village, with ships' newspapers being a particularly common feature of the Antipodean passage. But all emigrant ships were communities, a microcosm on life on land. Births and marriages were celebrated, as well as deaths mourned, schools were organized for the children and Sunday – sometimes daily – worship was an integral part of the voyage. There were six steerage births aboard the *Robert Burns*, on which John Mackenzie sailed cabin from Greenock to Port Phillip in 1841, as well as a school for sixty children. Jessie Campbell's disparagement of the Skye emigrants on the *Blenheim* a year earlier extended to one of six women who gave birth in the steerage:

A woman delivered of a son last night, this makes the sixth child born on board and all very fine, thriving children; this woman with all her former confinements had long and difficult labours, yesterday evening she did not feel herself very well, the Dr. desired her to go into the hospital, she thought she would have plenty of time to remove after she was taken ill, however matters came so quick upon her that the child was born before she could be removed; Dr. C. was very angry at her and no wonder, think how unpleasant for him going about her before so many women and married men who sleep in the same place; to crown all not one stitch had she prepared for the child, it was rolled in an old petticoat of the mother's. She is a carpenter's wife from Skye. All the other women had their baby things so neat and tidy, particularly the low country women; they come up on Sundays so clean and dressed some of them with white frocks and nice little hoods. [48]

The preservation of Christian ordinances was the priority of William Hamilton and his six fellow ministers who were sent out to Hobart and Sydney by the Church of Scotland aboard the *North Briton* in 1837. Soon after embarking they distributed tracts and arranged thrice-weekly religious instruction classes among the crew, as well as morning worship with the twelve steerage passengers. Public worship was also a vital component of life for the Highlanders aboard the *Blenheim*. Jessie Campbell recorded that while the emigrants 'had prayers and portion of the Bible read to them in Gaelic, we had the same in English by a very respectable steerage passenger of the name of Sinclair from Stirling'.[49] Public worship was conducted twice daily aboard the *Philip Laing* en route to Otago in 1847, but sixteen years later Isabella Henderson bemoaned the 'mimicry of God's worship' on her voyage to Dunedin: 'The preacher plays cards and drinks brandy all the week through, and then takes the place of minister on the Sabbath.'[50] Jane Findlayson also complained initially about the lack of Sabbath observance aboard the *Oamaru* in 1876, although she sang the praises of the minister, William Bannerman. She later reported that over 300 attended public worship, excluding several Roman Catholic passengers: 'We are amused and astonished at their mode of prayers; they are on their knees for nearly an hour saying their rosary and counting their beads.'[51] Bannerman, a native of Fife, had been twenty-three years minister in Dunedin and was married to our diarist, Jane, daughter of the Otago pioneer Thomas Burns. Religious services were also conducted on transatlantic ships. Alexander Muir, one of two cabin passengers on the *Lord Seaton* from Aberdeen to Quebec in 1845, noted that all seventy-one passengers and crew attended divine worship, and he himself organized a Sunday school for the thirty-one children on board.[52]

At the end of his journal John Anderson, who went to Otago with his wife and baby daughter in 1862, wrote to its unnamed recipient: 'You wanted me to keep a diary I have given you every day as near as I could but I think you will soon tire of it as it is always the same thing every day but you can form an idea what like your passage was by it.' As Anderson implied, the predominant sentiment of most diarists was of an increasingly tedious routine, and the recurring characteristic of most diaries was a constant preoccupation with weather and sea conditions. But various strategies were adopted for passing the time and alleviating the boredom. Transatlantic passengers looked out for icebergs, Antipodean ones for colourful flying fish. On all routes there were daily sweepstakes or competitions to guess the latitude and longitude, many diarists recorded the mileage covered each day, dancing was a popular pastime, and letters were written to those at home for delivery – if possible – to homeward-bound ships. When the weather was good passengers gathered on deck to play dominoes, draughts or cards, rain water was collected to wash bodies and clothes, and occasional lectures were given on the ship's destination. The long passage to the southern hemisphere was enlivened by the traditional celebrations on crossing the Equator, except on the *North Briton* in 1837, where, according to the Reverend Tait, 'There were none of the usual barbarous ceremonies allowed on board, our Captain being too sober and steady to permit such fooleries.'[53] John Anderson, however, who had a relatively pleasant and uneventful passage, described the ceremony on crossing the line. 'Neptune and his wife' were pulled along the deck on a gun carriage, and several members of the crew were shaved, before being thrown into a sail filled with water. Celebrations continued well into the night:

after tea we went on deck again and had a regular spree there was a great deal of drinking going on in the foscel [*sic*] the sailors had full liberty and we had dancing and drinking and fiddling till all hours some or [*sic*] them were well on there legs the cabin passengers were all singing in the cabin I went below about half past ten and found a lot of the men holding a concert with the young women we sang down below till near twelve o clock when the mate came down and ordered the men up.[54]

Jane Findlayson's description of the ceremony was very similar, but discipline on the *Oamaru* seems to have been generally tighter than on Anderson's *City of Dunedin*:

We have plenty of good music, we have no communication with the young men so its only a female dance. They are in the fore part of the ship we in the after part and the married quarters between, its a married man who gets up beside us to play the fiddle. Agnes and I were thinking that we had often heard of young women getting acquainted with young men on board ship and afterwards getting married after landing but that sort of work is utterly impossible here, we only see them at a distance, and those who have brothers on board have to get permission from the Doctor to meet half way along the deck and have a chat, if we had had male friends on board we would have thought this rather hard but as it is we don't care although we don't see a single man.[55]

Discipline was also strict on the *Crusader*, which took William Shennan to Melbourne in 1870, with the single girls being debarred from the deck in the evening and forbidden to speak to the young men or even the married couples.[56]

As in any community, shipboard life was not always harmonious, and tensions and disputes were regularly reflected in passengers' diaries. The twenty-eight cabin passengers aboard the *North Briton* in 1837 were, according to William Hamilton, composed of 'clergymen of different classes and adventurers of different ranks and characters', some of whom 'seek amusement in disgusting ribaldry'. Hamilton, who enjoyed the voyage, criticized those who complained about the quality of the food or who frittered away the time in 'idle talk' rather than in 'reading and patient application to study'. Even his colleagues did not escape censure. One in particular, Mr Lillie, was too worldly for Hamilton's liking, while the wife of another, Mrs Clow, was adjudged by Hamilton to be 'less amiable' than her husband, and by fellow cabin passenger Mr Tait to be 'a coarse vulgar looking woman ... [whose] mind somewhat resembles her outward appearance. She talks too much and seems to love to rail.'[57] When John Sceales of Edinburgh and his wife travelled to Sydney in the steerage of the *North Briton* a year later, there were twenty-two cabin and eighteen steerage passengers, although one of the former fell overboard en route. Sceales complained about the proximity of the ship's pigs to their living quarters, about an abusive and imperious first mate who on one occasion ordered his mess to extinguish all lights at nine p.m., and about a demanding fellow passenger who expected Mrs Sceales to dance attendance on his wife and newborn child.[58] Aboard the *Blenheim* in 1840, Jessie Campbell quarrelled with the steward about allegedly inadequate water rations, with one of her maids for insolence, and with her fellow cabin passengers, who, she claimed, were idle, of 'disagreeable temper' or had indisciplined children. One of the two doctors, Dr Sutherland, was small and plain, a well-educated Caithness gentleman's son with two brothers in the East India Company's service, 'but not by any means I should think a clever youth'; his colleague, the obliging Dr Campbell, 'may be a good doctor but you would never think so from his manner, he speaks with such a Highland accent and expresses himself so ill you would think he had not spoken English till he was at least twenty'.[59] John Chalmers, who sailed to India in 1855, entertained a very low opinion of three Baptist missionaries on his ship. 'I pity the poor heathens they go to convert,' he wrote to his parents in Aberdeen, after the missionaries had refused to contribute to a whip-round for the crew following the crossing of the Equator and berated the captain for allowing such a 'sinful upholding of superstition and the worship of a heathen god'.[60]

Discipline was often exercised on crew and passengers alike. Jessie Campbell recorded one such incident early in the voyage of the *Blenheim*:

> One of the sailors was complained of for the 4th time to the Capt. for being lousy and eating the lice, Capt. put him in irons on the poop, the rascal struck the Capt. on the face, he still wears the mark, one of the emigrants impertinently interfered and wished to rescue the sailor. Capt. Gray was going to punish the emigrant likewise until he begged his pardon and acknowledged his error.[61]

Many years later, Jane Findlayson noted the summary justice meted out to a cabin boy who, having stolen some money from the second mate's room, 'was put up on the top mast for four hours, he was stiff with cold e'er he came down'.[62] When John Anderson sailed to Otago in 1863, he recorded two skirmishes involving passengers. One concerned two steerage travellers who came to blows over a female cabin passenger during a dance. The other concerned an intoxicated cabin passenger:

> one of the cabin passengers got himself drunk and fell headforemost down our stair the captain ordered him to his berth he refused to go and the boatswain was ordered to take him in they had a fine strugle [*sic*] before they got him in he called the captain a damned swindler the captain ordered irons to be brought and the boatswain sat in his berth with him all afternoon and night till he got sober.[63]

In 1862 Isabella Henderson – whose sense of propriety was offended by a prank involving the debagging of the doctor by some of the female steerage passengers – declared that there was 'not a more perfect School for Scandal than on board ship ... There is nothing but tittle tattle on board. Everyone dissatisfied with their next neighbour. There is one very black sheep in our vessel. She makes a deal of mischief throughout the whole community. We have a very mixed lot.'[64] William Shennan too complained that there was 'nothing but quarrelling and fighting from morning till night' aboard the Melbourne-bound *Crusader* in 1870, the worst offenders being a large contingent of Cornishmen. Occasionally there were tangible scandals, as when Shennan recorded the birth of a stillborn child to one of the single women.[65] In 1876 Jane Findlayson and her friend Agnes shared a mess with six other girls, two Scots, three Irish and one

English, 'all agreeable clean girls', she commented on 2 October at the beginning
of the voyage. On 7 December, however, she had a different tale to tell:

> I am ashamed to tell you that one of our girls was confined of a daughter last
> night at half past 9, the doctor sent us all off from where he was, our place is sort
> of two apartments with only a short stair between us so just fancy 28 girls put
> out of our place, some of them took their beds with them and lay on the floor,
> we did not do so but on a form, we spent most of the night telling stories and any
> little bits of fun to amuse ourselves, we got back to our beds about 6 in the
> morning and stayed till dinner time. This has caused a talk all over the ship,
> when any of us goes out the men will pass remarks such as 'Who is likely to be
> laid up among the single girls'. The girl is from Ireland, a farmers daughter and
> had she not come away her father would have shot her, it was unfeeling of them
> to banish her away amongst strangers. The doctor is very kind to her, she is
> pretty well considering, the baby tho' small is a plump little thing. God knows
> what will become of her when she is well and landed.

Two days later, however, the baby was found dead, seemingly accidentally
smothered by its mother. In Jane Findlayson's opinion, 'she is a young girl not
19 without much sense, she appeared to be in a sad state about it, poor thing, its
best away as it puts us off our sleep for an hour or two'.

A few passengers positively enjoyed the voyage. While still en route to Port
Phillip, John Mackenzie closed his account in philosophical vein, stressing the
varied experiences of the previous ten weeks:

> The month of November has closed over my head and with it my book. Now at
> seventy-one days, I think nothing of a week or two, it would be but a play to go
> to America and in fact its nothing to come to Australia … speaking of the
> passage those who are in good health during it, can't but enjoy it, there is an ever
> varying change of scene, the grandeur of the storm – the beauty of a calm – the
> bright and variegated sunset – the rainbow 'based in ocean span the sky' – the
> light and sublimity of the stars, the clear blue sky changed for a clouded thun-
> derstorm – torrents of rain, and the burning heat of a tropical sun. Various lat-
> itudes, climates and temperatures, various tribes of birds and fishes, shooting
> and fishing, smoking and drinking, walking and talking, reading and writing,
> eating and sleeping, suffering and laughing, is something of whats to be seen
> and done on a voyage to Australia.[66]

The immigrants arrive

Whether the voyage had been a pleasure or – more typically – an ordeal, most passengers were eager to reach journey's end. Excitement usually rose as the ship neared its destination, especially for Antipodean passengers, who, unless they had touched at the Cape of Good Hope, might have been out of sight of land since leaving Scotland. Dr Grahame Todd and Jessie Campbell, who came to the pioneer Wakefieldian settlement at Wellington, New Zealand, in 1840, were both disappointed that the best landing place had not been identified in advance, and that the appropriate surveys had not been made by the New Zealand Company. Todd, who arrived with 120 Scottish settlers on the *Bengal Merchant*, complained that those landed at Port Nicholson often had to wade ashore in waist-deep water, while Jessie Campbell bemoaned the high winds and 'wild appearance' of the country.[67] The first impression of the pioneers who went to Otago seven years later was of a sea of mud, and even in 1862 William Smith claimed that Stafford Street in Dunedin was 'the most miserable place for mud under the sun'.[68]

Some ships were detained in quarantine, to the passengers' frustration. In 1831 Canada built a quarantine hospital for emigrants on an island in the St Lawrence. For several years the ever-increasing volume of sick and destitute emigrants arriving at Quebec City had been imposing an intolerable strain on civic resources. Referring to the situation between 1826 and 1832, Lord Durham wrote:

I am almost at a loss for words to describe the state in which the emigrants frequently arrived; with a few exceptions, the state of the ships was quite abominable; so much so, that the harbour-master's boatmen had no difficulty, at the distance of gun-shot, either when the wind was favourable or in a dead calm, in distinguishing by the odour alone a crowded emigrant ship. I have known as many as from 30 to 40 deaths to have taken place, in the course of a voyage, from typhus fever, on board of a ship containing from 500 to 600 passengers; and within six weeks after the arrival of some vessels, and the landing of passengers at Quebec, the hospital has received upwards of 100 patients at one time in the Emigrant Hospital of Quebec, for whom there was no sufficient accommodation ...[69]

In 1831, however, as cholera began to sweep Britain, the colonial authorities decided to build a quarantine station at Grosse Ile on the St Lawrence River,

thirty miles below Quebec City. Henceforth, no emigrant ship was allowed to
proceed upriver until the vessel itself, its passengers, crew and all their bedding
and clothing had been scrubbed and approved by government inspectors. Any
who showed signs of disease were detained in the new hospital and a tax of 5s
per head was levied on each adult passenger, in order to create a fund for sick
and destitute emigrants. In 1832 and again in 1834 the hospital had to cope with
major outbreaks of cholera, before an even worse epidemic – this time of
typhus – occurred in 1847, most of the victims being impoverished emigrants
from famine-ravaged Ireland.

Even the most stringent precautions could not prevent the spread of these
dreaded diseases to Quebec and Montreal. When Susanna Strickland arrived
from Leith with her Orcadian husband, J. W. Dunbar Moodie, in 1832, cholera
was raging in Montreal, and the fear of infection hung heavily in the air:

> The sullen toll of the death-bell, the exposure of ready-made coffins in the
> undertakers' windows, and the oft-recurring notice placarded on the walls, of
> funerals furnished at such and such a place, at cheapest rates and shortest notice,
> painfully reminded us, at every turning of the street, that death was everywhere
> – perhaps lurking in our very path; we felt no desire to examine the beauties of
> the place.[70]

But most Scottish diarists made only passing mention of Grosse Ile, for, unlike
New York's depots, it was always just a quarantine station, not a general reception area. Ships certified to be medically clean – like Robert Cromar's *Hercules*
in 1836 and Alexander Muir's *Lord Seaton* in 1845, both out of Aberdeen – did
not have to land at the island but could proceed straight to Quebec.

In order to mitigate the nefarious activities of runners, the huge numbers
of emigrants arriving at the port of New York were from 1855 received at the
former fort and concert hall of Castle Garden on Manhattan Island. Run by
the Commissioners of Immigration, it operated a labour bureau and sold the
new arrivals food, as well as railroad and canal tickets at fair prices. It also
forced them to take a bath before they were dispatched on their onward
journey, usually within six hours. By the 1880s, however, the administration
of Castle Garden had been vitiated by corruption and in 1892 a new immigration depot was opened at Ellis Island, managed by federal government
officials and supported by federal funds. After the original wooden building
burned down in 1897, its stone replacement became the gateway to America

10. Scottish immigrants arriving at Quebec, c. 1911.

for over 12 million immigrants of all nationalities until it finally closed its doors in 1954.

On the other side of the world, the quarantine station for passengers to Otago was an offshore island. When John Anderson's vessel was quarantined there for fourteen days in 1862, he enjoyed the discomfiture of the 'cabin gentry', who not only had to mingle with the steerage passengers whom they had formerly kept at arm's length but also 'had to cook and do everything for themselves'.[71] Jane Findlayson too enjoyed the freedom of the island, where married couples were accommodated at one end, single women at the other, and single men at a safe distance on an adjacent island. Most major debarkation centres also had emigration depots, or barracks, for the temporary accommodation of new arrivals.

For the majority of emigrants the journey was not over when the ship finally docked. Relatively few Scottish emigrants settled in Lower Canada, although large numbers of paupers, lacking resources, initiative and contacts, loitered about Quebec in the usually misplaced hope of finding work. These paupers were often forwarded westwards at the expense of the Canadian Immigration Department, whose chief agent, Alexander Buchanan, was particularly critical of landlords in the Highlands and Ireland, who in the mid-nineteenth century expelled impoverished tenants with minimal assistance, frequently only enough to enable them to reach Quebec. Emigrants with sufficient resources generally took the advice of guidebooks not to linger in the ports but proceeded at once to Upper Canada, where employment opportunities were allegedly much better than in the east, and where more fertile land was available for settlement.

For many, however, the onward journey was as long, arduous and expensive as the passage across the Atlantic. From Quebec they continued up the St Lawrence to Montreal, sometimes without disembarking or more commonly transferring to river steamboats. In 1820 the one–two-day journey cost 15s but in the 1830s, when inland steamship travel was more commonplace and there was more competition on the river, the steerage or deck price fell to 5s. Fire was a constant hazard and accidents were frequent. The steamer *Montreal*, for instance, was gutted on 25 June 1856, while carrying 500 Scottish emigrants up the river, and 253 lives were lost. Until the St Lawrence canal was completed in 1848 the Lachine rapids, west of Montreal, prevented the passage of steamboats. The emigrants could either walk or – like Alexander Muir – go by stagecoach across the nine miles between Montreal and Lachine, where at the head of the rapids they took to the more manoeuvrable bateaux or Durham boats to continue up the river to Prescott. The journey along this 160-mile stretch of water could take up to a week, with the passengers sometimes having to disembark and pull the bateaux when the river became impassable. During this time the crew and passengers either camped in the open or sought shelter in taverns and shanties. Emigrants who entered Canada from the USA could, after the completion of the Erie and Oswego canals in the 1820s, take a steamer up the Hudson River and then transfer to the 362-mile-long Erie canal for the northward journey to Oswego on Lake Ontario, from where they could take a steamboat to a variety of Canadian towns on the northern shore of the lake.

By whatever route the emigrants reached their final debarkation point, they generally faced yet another journey by stagecoach, oxcart and foot if their future home was a settlement in the bush. First impressions of the new home often fell far short of expectations, even for middle-class settlers like Susanna Moodie and her husband:

> About a mile from the place of our destination the rain began to fall in torrents, and the air, which had been balmy as a spring morning, turned as chilly as that of a November day ... Just then, the carriage turned into a narrow, steep path, overhung with lofty woods, and, after labouring up it with considerable difficulty, and

at the risk of breaking our necks, it brought us at length to a rocky upland clearing, partially covered with a second growth of timber, and surrounded on all
sides by the dark forest ... I gazed upon the place in perfect dismay, for I had
never seen such a shed called a house before ... The prospect was indeed dreary.
Without, pouring rain; within, a fireless hearth; a room with but one window,
and that containing only one whole pane of glass; not an article of furniture to
be seen, save an old painted pine-wood cradle, which had been left there by
some freak of fortune.[72]

Although by the second half of the nineteenth century steamships and rail-
roads had replaced sailing vessels, wagon trains and ox carts, improving technology did not solve all the emigrant's problems. New York's notorious
reputation gripped Robert Louis Stevenson's fellow passengers as they
approached the port in 1879:

As we drew near to New York I was at first amused, and then somewhat staggered, by the cautions and the grisly tales that went the round. You would have
thought we were to land upon a cannibal island. You must speak to no one in the
streets, as they would not leave you till you were rooked and beaten. You must
enter a hotel with military precautions; for the least you had to apprehend was to
awake the next morning without money or baggage, or necessary raiment, a
lone forked radish in a bed; and if the worst befell, you would instantly and mys-
teriously disappear from the ranks of mankind.[73]

When subsequently trying to book his railroad ticket, however, Stevenson was
forced to admit that the scene at the 'wretched little booking office' left a lot to
be desired, with 'a Babel of bewildered men, women, and children' being ver-
bally abused by a 'bearded, mildewed' emigration agent, 'his mouth full of
brimstone, blustering and interfering'. 'The whole system,' concluded Stevenson, 'if system there was, had utterly broken down under the strain of so many
passengers', an impression which was confirmed as he made his weary and
unpredictable way to the west, discovering in the process that 'haste is not the
foible of an emigrant train'.[74]

Just after the turn of the century, Aberdeenshire emigrant George Sangster
described his experiences on landing at Halifax after a transatlantic voyage on
the Allan Line's SS *Corinthian* from Glasgow:

We did not get a very favourable impression by our first view of Canada, for it is a very rocky and barren coast as you near Halifax. A steam launch came out to meet us with the medical inspector & a pilot. We got alongside the wharf at 10 o'clock. There were new immigration sheds built at Halifax last year, they are very large and finely fitted up buildings, you get into them from a gangway from the steamer. We had to go first and pass the medical inspector, in single file, he stamped our railway order with the word 'passed', then we went on to the immigration inspectors. We had to give up the cards we got on the steamer. They had shedules [*sic*] with all our names, they looked at the numbers on our cards, and turned to them for reference, then asked us the questions — 'Were ever you in Canada before?' 'What occupation do you intend to follow.' We next went and got our railway tickets, then we went and got our trunks and got hold of the customs officer to pass them. He asked what they contained, and then put a mark on them with chalk. We next got our luggage checked, they have a better system of checking luggage here, they tie a check with a number on your luggage, and you receive a duplicate and they will not deliver luggage to anyone unless they can produce this duplicate check. After this we went out to buy provisions for the railway journey and have a look of the place. Halifax is a very dirty looking place, the people were stepping off the cars into about four inches of mud. There are a good many coloured people in Halifax ... The train left Halifax at 4 P.M. the cars here are different, being seated, with two rows of seats along each side, each car is seated for 72. And you can get from one car to the other the whole length of the train. The seats can be made into beds, by pulling the seats together and letting the backs down. What serves as a luggage rack, during the day, can also be made into a bed, by placing the luggage under the seats. So where every four persons sit during the day they can lie down at night, two on the seats, and two up aloft in the scratcher. Although there are no cuschions [*sic*] on the seats one can make themselves pretty comfortable. The cars are all heated with steam pipes, and if there is any fault it is that they keep them too warm. There are stoves at the end of the cars where you can heat water ... We went via St John & Sherbrooke, through the state of Maine. It is a very desolate region, for from daylight on Friday until five O'clock in the afternoon we did not pass over twenty miles of cleared land altogether. We only saw one man the whole day except at the staitons [*sic*] and settlements. It was trees alongside the line nearly all the way, the most of them mere scrub, the timber has nearly all been destroyed by the forest fires traces of which are clearly to be seen by the number of charred logs lying on the ground and the bare stumps sticking up above the scrub.[75]

11. Scottish immigrants on board train, Quebec, c. 1911.

On the other side of the world, William Hamilton claimed on arriving at Sydney that he and his fellow ministers had been brought out to the colony under false pretences, for 'our prospects of emolument were not such as we had been led to expect'. Hamilton was almost immediately dispatched by the Presbytery of New South Wales to be the first Protestant minister in the district of Argyle, involving an arduous journey to Goulburn in an open mail coach. When John Sceales arrived in Sydney a year later, he and his family took rooms in the city for two months while he advertised in the press for employment, eventually accepting work as a stockkeeper at Bungonia, in the same area as William Hamilton. When Grahame Todd landed at the undeveloped site of Wellington in 1840, he purchased a tent, which was blown down during a storm on the second night after he pitched it. Jane Bannerman was slightly more fortunate when she arrived at Otago with her parents in 1847, for, although it was snowing and their blankets had not come, they had at least a house with a roof, some weather-boarding, windows and doors to protect them from the worst of the elements. After a long period of enforced idleness at sea, William Smith found it difficult to cope with even light manual tasks when he arrived at Dunedin in 1862. Some of his fellow passengers on the *Nelson* in 1862 found temporary lodgings in the Emigration Barracks at Dunedin, but after a night in the Exchange Hotel Smith managed to rent a house for his family while he searched unsuccessfully for work, rejecting the immigration agent's suggestion that he should go up country immediately.[76]

Some newly arrived emigrants became strangers in a strange land. Having forged friendships – or, at least, associations – during the voyage, they were obliged to disperse once the ship had docked, as they sought to make their solitary way as backwood or prairie farmers, pastoralists or gold miners, artisans or businessmen. Some, who had emigrated in extended family or community groups, settled communally in prearranged locations, while others teamed up with friends made on board ship. Still others joined kin, friends and neighbours who had previously emigrated in a chain movement that was a significant and enduring characteristic of the Scottish diaspora. For Scots, as for emigrants of many nationalities, the process of adaptation or assimilation was smoothed by employing a variety of settlement strategies which bridged the old life and the new, integrating memories of home into an unfamiliar environment.

THE EMIGRANT EXPERIENCE

'Everything is so much different, and so much easier than in the homeland.'[1]

If the transitional experience of the voyage gave some emigrants a sharp introduction to disparities between image and reality, in what ways were the ambitions of those who had been enticed overseas affected by the more protracted process of settlement? Although every emigrant's experience was unique, success and failure were influenced by factors such as the circumstances under which the move had taken place, the type of employment undertaken, the strength of support networks in the area of settlement, and the attitudes of both settlers and host societies. It is therefore possible to look beyond individual, family and community snapshots to identify continuities and changes in the emigrants' experiences during more than a century of Scottish settlement overseas.

Were farmers more likely than tradesmen to succeed, or is that a misleading stereotype fostered by agencies that had a vested interest in promoting agricultural settlement? Did the experiences of prairie farmers in the late nineteenth century echo or differ from those who pioneered the earlier settlement of Maritime or eastern Canada, or even the Antipodes? Were there significant differences between the experiences of Highlanders and Lowlanders, or those from rural and urban backgrounds? Did artisans who settled in the eastern United States enjoy better prospects than those who tried to make a living in the less developed countries of the British Empire? Where, and in what sort of enterprises, did investor-emigrants reap their greatest rewards? In what occupations and locations were emigrants most vulnerable to fraud and malpractice, and were these dangers lessened or intensified by emigrating under the auspices of sponsoring bodies? What were the particular concerns, strengths and weak-

nesses of female emigrants and how did their experiences overseas compare
with the adventures of their male counterparts?

Articulating the emigrant experience

Emigrants' impressions and experiences were described in their private and
published diaries and correspondence, and occasionally in commissioned reminiscences, as well as by agents, antagonists and neutral observers. By the end of
the century they were also being conveyed visually, in photographs. Sometimes
the request for information came from those who had stayed at home. Shortly
after Barbara Argo Watt had emigrated to Bon Accord in Upper Canada in 1836
with her husband, Alexander, the settlement's co-organizer, she was instructed
by her sister Margaret in Aberdeenshire to:

> begin a letter to me as soon as you get this and write something in it every day
> when you have time and write it very close so that I may have something in the
> form of a definite correspondence with you, write any thing, write every thing
> and I will do the same … I will expect a letter from you every six months, and
> oftener if any thing particular happens.

Margaret's own letters were full of family and community gossip, not least
about those who were emigrating, for, as she rightly predicted, 'among such a
wandering race you would not know who might alight at your house'.[2] Elizabeth
Connon, an Aberdeen shopkeeper who knew the Argos and whose nephew
Thomas, a wholesale grocer, also emigrated to the Bon Accord area in 1852, was
equally keen on maintaining a two-way correspondence, and it was because of her
advice – and financial assistance – that Thomas pursued a commercial rather than
a farming career, ultimately becoming a professional photographer in Elora.[3]

But letters were not as straightforward as they might seem at first glance.
The line between description and propaganda was often indistinct and, as we
saw earlier, letters were used to deter and attract their readers, as well as simply
to inform them about emigrant life. One emigrant from north-east Scotland
clearly saw the provincial newspaper back home as a means of updating his
acquaintances on his progress in Australia in the early 1850s:

> You will show this letter to as many of our friends as possible. I often think of
> you all; perhaps the best way would be to send it to the 'Aberdeen Journal', as all

our friends on the Dee, the Don, the Spey and the Deveron, will then have an opportunity of seeing that I am living and liking the Antipodes well.[4]

William Gibson, who emigrated from Auchinleck in Ayrshire to Wolseley on the Canadian prairies in 1886, and kept the *Ayrshire Post* supplied with a regular stream of letters over several years, did more than simply inform his readers. He repeatedly justified his decision to emigrate and encouraged others to follow his example, as well as reporting frequent encounters with other successful emigrants from Ayrshire.[5] But the private letters of John McBean, a Nairnshire farm labourer and journalist, were more equivocal about the benefits of prairie life. McBean wrote home frequently from Manitoba during an illness-ridden four-year residence, initially to deter his brother from joining him, but later to encourage him. Writing to his sister in March 1903, he declared, 'I would never think of advising Andy to sell out and come here, for I know he would hate the country, and the people he would never get along with.' Predicting that Andrew would 'die of homesickness' and 'never cease to blame me for misleading him', he continued to oppose his brother's emigration until an opportunity arose for John to purchase a prairie farm for $10,000. Since he was financially incapable of seizing the opportunity single-handedly, he began to correspond more regularly with his brother, in an attempt to persuade Andrew to invest the required capital and join him in the venture. Glossing over his earlier opinion that Andrew would rebel against the 'monotonous drudgery' of farm work, he had by April 1905 'no hesitation' in advising him to sell off the family farm

and come out here with all the money the sale will bring. If you remain there you will never, if you live a million years, be able to pay the lawful shares to the other members of the family. Out here I give you my guarantee that you can do so, with the same amount of exertion you would spend there merely to exist, in ten years or probably less.[6]

As these examples demonstrate, emigrant letters were shaped by the writers' objectives and sometimes had a hidden agenda. They therefore have to be used with caution, not least because they reflect only a very selective and self-conscious view of the emigrant experience, conveyed by a correspondent who might wish to impress a sceptical family with tales of success or paint a picture of need in order to obtain a remittance from home. Equally, recipients were more likely to preserve, and perhaps circulate, upbeat correspondence or letters that discussed arrangements for further family or community emigration. But only a handful of emigrants wrote letters. While the illiterate were obviously unrepresented, those who emigrated in family groups, who left no connections or dependants behind or who adapted quickly often had little need or inclination to retain links with home. It has been suggested that the most assiduous letter writers were the unassimilated and lonely, who longed for news from home, perhaps because they had failed to establish themselves successfully overseas.[7] John McBean certainly seems to have fallen into that category. Despite his faith in the future of western Canada, he did not have an easy life or enjoy great personal success, health or happiness. The restlessness, discontent and inconsistencies in his letters were probably due to his failure to achieve the independence he so desired; his whole brief career in Manitoba was spent in the service of others, often performing what he deemed to be menial or degrading duties, generally without any security of employment, and his premature death in 1906, as he was on the threshold of an independent farming venture, denied him the opportunity to prove whether in becoming his own master he would have achieved the security and success he craved.

If private letters were biased, those published by newspapers, periodicals and emigration agents were even more likely to reflect the outlook of the host publication. In reporting the deaths of most members of a Morayshire family in the United States in 1833, the anti-emigration *Elgin Courier* grumbled, 'When any person prospers in America, we are sure to hear of it; but it is seldom we hear of the miseries which many of our countrymen suffer when they go there, unless in cases such as here stated, where whole families are almost swept away.'[8] Forty years later, a correspondent of the *Shetland Times* in St Louis, Missouri, warned readers against going to the United States on the strength of misleading descriptions of 'large wages, light work, good homes &c' by young men in whose letters 'good fortune is brought too prominently forward, and evils are glossed over and made to look like blessings'.[9] From the opposite perspective, Henry Jordan's pamphlets on Queensland in the 1860s and James Adam's *Twenty Five Years of Emigrant Life in the South of New Zealand* (1873) were authored by professional agents with a remit to stimulate emigration, while the very titles of publications such as *Letters from Successful Scottish Ploughmen* (1909) and *Prosperity follows Settlement* (1911) leave little doubt about the tone of the correspondence selected by the Canadian immigration authorities to attract more emigrants. Letters and anecdotes quoted in the published reports of female emigration societies such as the British Women's Emigration Association or the Aberdeen Ladies' Union were, like those in the Barnardo and Quarrier propaganda, clearly biased towards success, not least for fund-raising reasons. Commissioned surveys, such as the questionnaires issued by the Saskatchewan Archives Board in the 1950s to settlers who came to the prairies between 1878 and 1914, give a colourful retrospective snapshot of pioneer life, although the advanced age of some of the respondents, and their tendency to recall achievements rather than failures, have to be borne in mind when evaluating the reliability of their reminiscences.[10]

The farming emigrant

Much of our evidence about the emigrant experience comes from the agricultural community, not only because farming was the career most frequently recommended and pursued, at least until the 1860s, but also because men and women on isolated farmsteads with uneven work patterns had the inclination and the opportunity to write home at fairly frequent intervals. In the early nineteenth century the farming emigrant from Scotland was most likely to be found in the backwoods of Upper Canada or, if he was a Highlander, in the Maritimes. Once first impressions, good and bad, had been dealt with, descriptions of daily life centred on work, wages, crop yields, business transactions, health and encounters with kinfolk and other fellow Scots. When the Stocks family emigrated from Paisley, they settled in the midst of acquaintances from the west of Scotland, in the vicinity of Sherbrooke, where Mary Stocks's skills as a midwife were much sought after:

> It is now more than a twelve months since we came on our land: We have Reaped a pretty fair crop … Our clearance Rises Gradually to the north and therefore it lies to the Mid-Day sun – we as well as the generality of our Neightbours are well pleased with our situations. We are very well off for Neightbours Robert Twidel, from Parkhead is our nearest it is not a quarter of a mile from us their clearence and ours is already mett against the Spring of the year our two families will have a clearence of 22 acre …
>
> Duncan McDugal and Daniel Ritche: Arch'd McDugal, Josiah Davies James Nisbet, John Porter, Alexander Young, Robert Simm, David Wilie, James and Robert Smith, Thomas Hall, Antony Mcbrid: James Eson: James Gilmour and son, Captan Elliot and George Watson are all around us and within two mile distance of us: and a little farther lies: 3: Brown Lee Lads; and a Crawford. Duncan and Arch'd Campbell, Ouen Creiley, William Cristilaw and many more too

tideous to mention. So you see we have maney neightbours and they are all agreeable and very helpful to each other ... most of the young girls are gone away to service and gets from it 2: to 4: dolars a Month: our Daughter Betty has been away too for about 4 months: she is about 60 miles down the country: Twidals, Gilmours and Wilies Daughters are further away: I fill the want of Betty in the family when I am from home: when we were in the ship Earel of Buckinghamshire I was caled along with the Doctor that came along with the ship to assist Women in child labour [and] delivered [a] sone. . . and I delivered severals before we landed: and some as we came up the river with the Boatuoos [bateaux] – and ever since we came to Shearbrook there is no other sought and I have been with a good maney.[11]

Elsewhere in her letter, Mary Stocks hinted that not all settlers were content with their land. In 1831 Robert Seton, a retired army officer from Oldmeldrum in Aberdeenshire, bought 100 acres near Lake Simcoe from the government at a cost of £70, payable in ten annual instalments at 6 per cent interest. Two years later he made use of his military background to acquire a further 500 acres at a substantial discount as a speculation, 'as land is increasing most amazingly in value from the great demand', and he anticipated a further rise once communications with Toronto had been improved. By 1838, however, he had moved elsewhere, having become disillusioned with a property whose remote location and expense of clearing outweighed the advantage of its cheapness, and he claimed that many others who, like him, had ignored the much-repeated advice of guidebooks to invest in cleared farms were also selling out as they discovered their mistake.[12] When William Webster, a joiner from New Deer, also in Aberdeenshire, took his wife, children and grandchildren to Zone Mills in the 1840s to join another daughter and son-in-law, he had difficulty in obtaining a title to his 143-acre purchase of uncleared Crown land, discovering – after he had built a house and made a partial clearing – that the government land agent had no authority to sell the Indian land which he had bought. But undeterred by these legal problems, he had no regrets, since 'I have had uninterrupted health since I left Scotland and my wife has been pretty well to [sic] ... I have not for a moment repented of coming to this country. I only wish I had been here when I was younger than now.'[13]

Some emigrants who lacked the means to purchase cleared land straight away preferred to work for wages until they could afford an improved farm. Ten years elapsed between James Thompson's emigration from Aboyne and his purchase of a farm in Edwardsburgh, Upper Canada, in 1854:

Since writing to you last I have purchased a farm, within ½ mile of this village. The farm contains one hundred and fifty acres, fronting on the River St Lawrence. There is a pretty good house and barn on it. I will give you a more lengthy description of it some other time. I have got the deed, but as I am busy with the Railroad, I do not intend to live on the farm this summer, nor do much with it farther than having a few acres ploughed and put under crop. I pay for the farm at the rate of five pounds fifteen shillings per acre in all £862, 10/ of which I have paid £500 and the balance in three equal yearly instalments.[14]

Although Michie and Mary Ewing, emigrants from the Castle Fraser estate in Aberdeenshire, aspired to rent rather than purchase a farm, they were still some way from achieving that goal when they wrote home from Upper Canada in 1857 to ask for an extension on the money loaned them by their former employer. But despite their indebtedness and some reservations about the 'sick soil of Canada', they too were content, not least that they had remained healthy in an environment where debilitating illnesses like malaria and epidemics of cholera or typhus were a constant concern:

It is now nearly two years since we left; it will soon be two years since we arrived in the land of our adoption; And God in his mercy hath blessed us with remarkable good health, both on our journey and since our abode in a foreign clime. And although I have not (in one point of view) been altogether so successful as I expected, yet I like the country, I like the climate, and am fully convinced that many a poor man would be much better here than in Scotland. Yet there are many come here, who would be much better at home than here. Wages are high, but much more work is expected, and unless a man be a good workman, few will employ him, at the same time people, manners, climate, work and all strange, A good many get disheartened, return home, go to drinking, or even lose their health and die. And although we have not had the same comfort as yet, that we had at Castle Fraser, being most of the time away from home, my only cause for complaint is having to pay from 10sh to 12sh Stg per week for Board. Being either with Farmers (who always board their hands) or so far off that I could not walk home. Yet I have great cause to be thankful, in having all the time got plenty of work, and sometimes two or three persons wanting me at the one time. Last winter I got several good offers of farms to rent. In summer I was paid with from 6d to 8d more a day, than other workmen, part of the time being intrusted with the charge of from 16 to 20 men and 3 or 4 span of horses, at the making of a gravel road, I felt as if on trial, did my best, both contractor and engineer were pleased, and I was just about to engage to go on to the branch of railway from St Mary's to London, to take charge of a squad of men, when all was brought to a stand still.[15]

Surviving accounts of the experiences of Lowland farmers in pre-Confederation Canada tend to be optimistic, perhaps because the decision to emigrate had usually been based on positive foundations. Conversely, removal to Canada apparently did nothing to alleviate the sufferings of cleared Highlanders, at least in the early stages of settlement. In autumn 1849 the anti-landlord *Inverness Journal* was repeatedly preoccupied with the plight of thousands of famine-stricken Highlanders who had been sent out in the midst of a cholera epidemic, to fall victim to 'pauperism and beggary ... amid the horrors of a Canadian winter'.[16] According to one correspondent, a Tain man living in Hamilton who raised a subscription to assist a contingent of emigrants from Mull and Tiree, and persuaded the city authorities to forward them to Fergus:

> They were landed at Quebec at a time when cholera raged in all our towns and cities. They were forwarded by the Government from port to port until they arrived here at the head of the Navigation, when, without any provision being made for them, they were thrown on our wharfs, weary, diseased, and destitute. Their numbers had been considerably thinning by the prevailing plague, many having died in Montreal, Kingston, and Toronto, another thinning was still in reserve for them here. The emigrant sheds being already filled to overflowing with the destitute sons of Erin, the poor Highlanders had to weather, as the best way they could, under the canopy of heaven, huddled together on the wharf, and on the commons that lie between the city and the bay; the greater part of them lay for the space of eight days, with nothing to screen them from the scorching rays of an almost tropical sun, or the cold damp dews of our Canadian night – what the sad consequences were may easily be conjectured. The first night after their arrival, thirteen were seized with cholera; on the second night, eight; in all, while they remained here, forty-eight; they were sent to the hospital, but as yet none of them have left it alive.[17]

Unlike the Lowland farmers who had found Fergus and the surrounding townships a profitable field for investment and labour, for the Highlanders it was a bleak, temporary halt en route to their final destination of Owen Sound, where

– despite having 'nothing necessary for a life in the bush' – they were to take up free grants of uncleared land.

But the Highland emigrants' experiences varied widely. Further east, in Cape Breton, the first wave of settlers, many of whom had some capital in reserve, secured Crown land freehold on generous terms, and were able to establish reasonably productive commercial frontland farms, on which they enjoyed a far higher standard of living than in Scotland. By contrast, the impoverished emigrants of the 1830s and 1840s found not only that most of the good terrain was already taken but that stricter regulations made it virtually impossible for them to acquire land legally. Often squatting without title on inferior backlands, they eked out a precarious existence on a meagre agricultural base, supplementing their incomes by part-time wage labour in mining and fishing. Following a lifestyle very similar to what they had left behind in Scotland, they were even dogged by the same potato blight they had sought to escape. Having obtained a substantial grant by virtue of his army service, Captain Donald McNeil of Mira River had been confident of securing his family's future until the economic crisis of the 1840s. Writing to his brother in North Uist – from whom he had just heard after a twenty-year period of unanswered letters – he was now pessimistic about his prospects in Cape Breton:

It is melancholy to what extent the failure of crop has effected [*sic*] the inhabitants of this Island, potatoes have almost altogether disappeared, and other crops, tho' not to the same extent, have been very backwards. I need not say that I feel the pressure of these times in Common with others. My Farm and Half Pay are the only means I have of supporting my Family and when the one fails, the other is by far too limited to be an equivalency for every demand. I have laid out a very large crop this season and Providence may become favourable, if otherwise I know not what be the result. I have a Grant of Five hundred acres & could I get for it as much money as would bring us up to Canada and purchase a small Farm there, I would not hesitate to try the change, but under present circumstances that is entirely out of the question. I have had to contend with greater difficulties and Kind Providence carried me through and his word directs me to trust him still and not dispair [*sic*].

I have Nine of a Family, four Sons & five Daughters (enough you say in hard times). My oldest Son Ewen I suppose will follow the Farming if better does not cast up to suit his inclination, but the second, Rory, of a different turn of mind,

gives me great concern not having it in my power to procure a situation for him
… Before the change of times I had every prospect before me, that my undertaking would be ultimately crowned with success and I did not in the least envy
even your larger possession at home, as my property was improving apace, all
my own, and to pass to my heirs & successors for ever. Such was my Consola-
tion, with a living in comfort, tho' not in luxury. The wheel may turn.[18]

McNeil's ambition to move west was not unique, for many Highland settlers
saw Cape Breton as a staging post on the way to Upper Canada, the American
Midwest or, later, the prairies. However, the remigration that became inevitable
for many backland settlers in the wake of the 1840s and 1870s depressions was
often to urban-industrial centres, notably Boston. It was a pattern that was replicated in another area of concentrated Hebridean settlement, the Eastern Townships of Quebec. There, as in Cape Breton, the emigrants were characterized by
widespread squatting, subsistence agriculture, a reluctance to cultivate large
parts of their holdings and eventual remigration to New England and the
prairies, while in both locations the abandoned marginal farms that had been
wrested from the bush reverted inexorably to their original state.

Highland settlers on the prairies came directly from Scotland, as well as from
eastern Canada. Lady Emily Gordon Cathcart's sponsored settlement of ten
Benbecula families at Wapella in 1883 was followed in 1888 and 1889 by the colonization of Killarney and Saltcoats by 100 families from Lewis, Harris and
North Uist with the aid of a £10,000 grant from the British government. Neither
venture was particularly successful, although William Gibson, who farmed only
fifty miles away from the Benbecula crofters, thought they were 'all doing fairly
well, and have no cause to regret coming to the North-West'.[19] One Saltcoats
settler with twelve cattle and almost twenty acres under crop after two years
claimed in 1891, 'I would not leave this country unless I am dragged from it by
ropes',[20] and the two pioneers who subsequently recalled their experiences for
the Saskatchewan Archives Board's survey in the 1950s were also fairly uncriti-
cal. In 1952 Norman McDonald (seventy-nine) was still living on the same
homestead in Wapella that his father had taken up when the family had emigrated from Benbecula in 1883. Their early experiences, he remembered, were a
mixture of triumphs and tribulations:

In 1883 we built a sod shack and it was burned down and we lost the most of our
clothes. We built a log house before winter set in. It was on 7th June that we

planted potatoes on land newly broken and had a very good crop. We also put in a few acres of barley and oats. The barley crop was good but oats were frozen. We were out here a year before we got our first cow.[21]

Six years after McDonald arrived in Wapella, Archibald Docherty emigrated from North Uist to Saltcoats in a party of forty-nine families, under the government's prairie settlement scheme. Both the Saltcoats settlement and its sister colony at Killarney had been hastily conceived and poorly implemented. Applicants had been given only a week between acceptance and embarkation to settle their affairs, and the Scottish Office, in its haste to set the scheme on foot, failed to reach a specific agreement with the Canadian government about the latter's responsibilities in terms of land allocation and the retrieval of loans. The crofters were dispatched on the strength of incomplete negotiations with various land companies and a vague assurance from the Canadian government that it would 'render every assistance' to the emigrants. Not surprisingly, both settlements, but particularly Saltcoats, were beset by practical, financial and administrative difficulties. Many of the settlers, brought up with the sound of the sea in their ears, were unwilling or unable to adapt to life on a land-locked prairie homestead, and often preferred to work as seasonal harvest labourers or railway navvies, sometimes in order to work their way to British Columbia. Their tardiness in paying Canadian taxes and in repaying their loans of £120 per head to the British government discouraged any extension of the scheme, which became 'the forgotten episode in the history of the Scots in Canada'.[22]

None of these problems was reflected in the reminiscences of Archibald Docherty. Like Norman McDonald at Wapella, he had farmed in the same location all his life and was also the first person in the community to buy a car, a Model T Ford, in 1914. Recalling, at the age of seventy-eight, how 'agents came to the Islands to induce the people to emigrate to Western Canada', he went on to describe various incidents from the family's emigration and settlement:

The Saltcoats district was the end of steel, and was then being opened up ... Some of my relations were also coming to Canada with the same party, but mostly they thought we were crazy to go so far. People came from all over the island, and with tears in their eyes tried to dissuade us ... We came by small steamer from the Islands to Glasgow, and from there to Halifax in the Allan Line *Scandinavian*. Then to Saltcoats by train. The chief thing I remember was that I was very seasick, as were most of the other children and most of the women. There was quite a large building in Saltcoats known as the Immigrant Shed. This was insufficient so a number of boxcars were used. Two families were housed in each boxcar ... My chief impression of the early years was the great loneliness of prairie life, after living in the Islands where people were crowded together. We went to Saltcoats about once a week, a day's journey by oxen. After the first church was built in the district in 1896, we went to church every Sunday. All travel was by ox wagon or on foot, as none of the settlers had horses in the early years.[23]

John Laidlaw, who emigrated from Ross-shire with his parents in 1882, travelled west from Brandon in a prairie schooner and lived for a time in a tent, confirmed that ox wagon was the customary form of transport for the pioneers. His father, having been attracted out by 'far from truthful' propaganda spread by the Canadian Pacific Railway, hoped to make enough money to retire back to Scotland, but it was not to be, and the family remained in Grenfell, where they first settled, for seventy years.[24]

Of the 285 responses to the questionnaire, sixty-two came from Scottish settlers, only a small minority of whom were Highlanders. Peter Fraser, who came from Kilsyth to Kamsack in 1891, and had a varied career as a homesteader, farm worker, cook at an Indian mission school and storekeeper, remembered the hazards of fording flooded rivers, the impact of Doukhobor settlement and the tragic death of one of his employees, a Barnardo boy who had accidentally shot himself. William Harkness, who emigrated from Johnstone in Dumfries-shire in 1892, recalled that during his first two summers he was 'nearly eaten by mosquitoes', while James Tulloch from Shetland had intended to go to Australia until an encounter with the mayor of Winnipeg in Dumfries changed his mind. Arriving in Winnipeg penniless in 1897, he worked for wages for three years until he was able to secure a homestead, and later paid the fares of several other emigrants from Shetland. George Bruce, who had already spent a harvesting season in western Canada before returning to the University of Aberdeen to continue his BSc course, emigrated permanently in 1904, having been unable to finance the completion of his studies. He was joined almost immediately by his parents and sisters, and both father and son took up homesteads.[25]

Many respondents had vivid memories of fires and frosts that threatened their livelihoods and sometimes their very lives. Although on one occasion Aberdonian Andrew Veitch's family lost their barn, granary, hay and an entire season's crop after threshing, he remembered not only the fear of being burned in his bed but also 'the beauty of watching fields of jumping flame in the various

12. Group of immigrants arrive at CPR Station, Winnipeg 1927. Winnipeg remained the major hub for the settlement of the West.

formations on hill tops, valleys and bluffs against a pitch black night'.[26] At the other extreme, Dundonians Robert and Jim Wood were given up for dead when, searching for missing cattle in winter 1899, Jim became lost forty-five miles from home in a blizzard and temperatures that plunged to sixty-four degrees below zero. Fifty-five years later, Robert recalled the adventure:

> The weather had been getting steadily colder since we left home and on the morning of the fifth day we decided we had gone as far as we could with the team. However we decided we would make one last cast with the riding horse and in the grey of that morning Jim left on Nipper, going north east, while I stayed in camp and chopped down dry poplar most of the day, cutting it into twelve foot lengths ... It was intensely cold and when darkness came that night and Jim hadn't got back I became very anxious. We had a shotgun with us and about a dozen shells. An hour or so after dark I fired a shot and thereafter every half hour or thereabouts I would fire another. In that time I went through all the emotions of the condemned man who was to be executed the next morning – for I had made up my mind that Jim was frozen and I had no intention of going back without him. But about nine o'clock that night Jim rode into camp.

He had a very remarkable tale to tell over the camp fire that night. Travelling north east in the morning for quite a few miles he had stumbled on an Indian Camp … The Indians, some of whom apparently knew a few words of English, told him that the cattle were safe and were only a few miles from their camp. The absence of snow had helped them and they were coming through alright. Jim did not go any further but late that afternoon took to the bed of the Carrot River, heading south west towards our camp. After travelling slowly for hours and for long after dark he had no idea whether he had passed the camp or was still approaching it. He had his heavy fur coat on and the collar up over his ears and could not hear anything. But suddenly he saw Nipper prick up his ears and knew he must have heard something. Scrambling up the steep bank at the first feasible place he gave Nipper his head and the horse walked back about a mile and some distance from the river and finally walked into the camp. He had heard one of my shots in the first place no doubt and had then located the camp by the smell of the camp fire …

That night Jim became very ill and in the morning I had a sick man on my hands. I knew it was going to be a close thing. My best chance would be to try and locate the Leather River ranch which would be, I thought, about thirty miles south of our camp – and this I decided to try for. Fortunately the sun was shining the next morning or I would have been lost in a very short time so far as going south was concerned. With Jim lying in the bottom of the sleigh and almost everything I had piled on top of him I travelled steadily south all that day. There could be no stopping. Darkness came and I then used the stars to guide me. Then on the snow I found a faint sleigh trail. How it had come there I did not know. As it seemed to be going south it might lead to the ranch but I had no idea as to this. I had to take a chance. Jim was still lying flat on the bottom of the wagon box. I put the reins in his hands and told him I was riding ahead but I doubt if he understood me. I slung the axe in my belt, swung on Nipper and made the race of my life for about two miles, following the faint trail. I rode finally into the yard of the Leather River ranch. I put Nipper into one of the open stables and tore into wood chopping for some stove wood, working like a fiend. There was a stove in the shack with a stovepipe going outside through the wall and protected by some tin. I had a fire nicely going when the team walked into the yard. They had been able to follow the trail in some way though in the dark it was hardly discernible.[27]

Like many of those who responded to the questionnaire, Robert Wood claimed to have written home regularly, and it was through correspondence that most emigrants described their experiences of pioneering on the prairies. In 1881 Peter Wallace (fifty-nine) left Glasgow with his sons, William (twenty-two) and Andrew (fifteen), to take up a homestead in western Manitoba, which was then experiencing a temporary land boom as a result of railway development. The Wallaces first purchased Canadian Pacific Railway land near Brandon, but in 1882 sold it in order to make a more speculative purchase to the north west, in the Shell River area, expecting that the railway would soon follow. This was a misjudgement, for it was not until 1909 that the railway reached their local town of Shellmouth, and for the first five years the nearest rail connection was forty miles from their farm. Despite the difficulty of selling their produce beyond the low-priced local market, they survived and made headway, probably through a combination of hard work and the possession of a sufficient cushion of capital to make an early purchase of land, implements and stock, which in turn generated more capital and allowed them to pay debts as they arose. Unlike some prairie settlers, they also enjoyed an active social life, regularly visiting neighbours and attending religious and secular events in town. Peter Wallace was president of the Russell Agricultural Society, William – who purchased a parlour organ in 1883 – served as organist and choirmaster in both the Presbyterian and Anglican churches and Andrew became a stalwart of the Masonic Lodge.

For twenty-three years the Wallaces' experiences were described in regular letters from William Wallace to his schoolteacher sister Maggie, letters which she preserved and brought with her when she and her husband emigrated in 1904. Two months after making their first land purchase, William described the pros and cons of frontier life:

> You already know all the particulars of our journey here, but will be curious to learn why we did not proceed farther and secure more land. The reasons were our oxen were unloaded, and this delayed us when travelling, and caused extra expense. When we arrived here our oxen were jaded and our purse very light, rendering it impossible to proceed much farther. The land we did take up is without doubt a good investment, By the end of the next summer season we could sell it and our stock at a sum that would refund the principal and pay our expenses coming here and also, if reckoned desirable, home again with possibly 50 or 100 [pounds] additional. Now all this considered, causes me to think over the fact of whether or not you should join us at the time agreed. I will try to inform you of both sides.

The climate, so far as we have experienced it, is simply unparalleled, but the winter will be, I am afraid, very unpleasant. All admit hereabouts that extraordinary precautions have to be taken, rendering travelling dangerous. Confined thus to the spot, I fear the long dark nights will be very monotonous. The soil is peculiarly and particularly rich, but the country's aspect is not very picturesque. Plain after plain is all that can be seen, with hardly a tree to relieve the scene. In the summertime it is very beautifully arrayed, with gorgeous and many-coloured flowers, but that is only for a comparatively short period. During winter it is just one flat after another of white snow. This, you can imagine, will be very dreary ...

The inhabitants, our neighbours, are our principal cause of dislike. Nearly every one of them came from Lower Canada. The stock question is 'what part of Ontario do you come from?' ... They as a class are very undesirable society. A good-going Yankee is pleasure compared to them. They are about the greediest, least thankful, unenthusiastic lot I could imagine. Their ignorance of everything but surroundings is awful, and renders intercourse wearisome and unentertaining. Boors and clodhoppers is exactly the term they deserve. You would think they imagined that all things were common. Into the house they will march without asking your leave, no matter whether Sunday or Saturday they take an unblushing inventory of everything, spit all around and talk commonplace. No things or articles are safe from their borrowing proclivities. Notwithstanding this horror they are [a] hardy, hardworking, fine-looking, rough-and-ready class of people, Now, how would you like ten years or so at the least of these surroundings and society with sometimes pretty hard work?

But this is not all. We are at present hampered for want of money, and before you come out we must borrow £50 to build a house. It is almost impossible to obtain logs. We will require to build of lumber or sawn boards. After two years we will be sure to have sufficient money, but at first we will be a little scrimped. Now the question before we do this is, will you care about coming out?[28]

The themes of relative impoverishment and the desirability of Maggie's emigration recurred frequently in William's letters. In June 1882, shortly after they had moved to Shell River, he asked her if she could spare £20, since 'there have been a number of unforeseen and unavoidable items of expenditures', but added that she should 'run no hazard of being short' in saving for her own emigration, since 'we could pull through more easily than you could'. At that time he was confident the railway would pass within two miles of their settlement, 'so our fortune is looming'.[29] Prosperity was usually anticipated rather than fully enjoyed, however, not least because of repeated disappointments over railway communication and an abortive attempt to build a permanent home-stead in a location where there was no water. Like many of his neighbours, William was also critical of the federal government's settlement regulations, as well as its heavy taxation of prairie farmers, and predicted a secession of the western provinces which would bring an end to railway monopolies and usher in free trade. Yet on the whole he was content with his own circumstances and the prospects of his adopted country. Although he regularly asked his sister to send out newspapers and journals from home, he had no desire to return to Scotland. 'I think I would get crazed were I to awake in Glasgow and find out that my Manitoban life had been all a dream. I could not live in the city smoke again,' he wrote in 1885.[30]

There are some parallels between the experiences of William Wallace and John McBean. Both men were alternately optimistic and pessimistic, depending on their circumstances at the time of writing, although McBean had a greater tendency to cynicism. He emigrated twenty years after the Wallaces, at a time when the federal government and the Canadian Pacific Railway were making a concerted effort to attract British emigrants through agency work and sponsor-ing tours by influential individuals from Scotland. 'The whole business is looked upon here as a huge swindle,' he wrote to his sister in September 1902. 'It is entirely the work of Lord Strathcona and the Canadian Pacific Railway, which dominates the Government of this country in every conceivable way.'[31] Like Wallace, McBean regarded the settlers as ill-bred and pretentious:

> The people have sprung up in a short decade from labourers, farm servants, and incapable mechanics, with a mixture of well educated penniless ne'er do weels, to farmers owning from a quarter to a mile and a half of land, with stock, imple-ments, and a buggy; and they feel that the position requires an assumption of dignity in accordance with the circumstances. The assumed dignity is foreign to their natures, is aggressively ostentatious, and its effect is disagreeable. Etiquette is studied from books, and a display of its most objectionable phrases go bandied about the table at every meal.[32]

John McBean was not enamoured of the 'drudgery' of working on the farm of a 'disagreeable tyrant' when he first arrived in Manitoba. Within six months, however, that career was cut short by illness and accident, and he was subsequently employed as an itinerant journalist by an agricultural period-ical, the *Farmers' Advocate and Home Magazine*. Although he enjoyed the writing assignments, which included articles of advice for would-be emigrants, he disliked touting for the subscriptions and advertisements on which he depended for payment of his expenses and salary. Nor was he fit enough for the rough life on horseback required for canvassing work on the prairie frontier, and after resigning his post in April 1904 he found similar work with the rival *Nor' West Farmer*. But he had jumped from the frying pan into the fire, for his duties were just as onerous, with even less job security and the 'lonely monot-ony of a new town every day and a new bed every night', as he traversed the prairie in sub-zero temperatures, waiting in small towns for farmers who never appeared. No doubt the hardships of his lifestyle contributed to his frequent ill-nesses and premature death, for in addition to the persistent fear of dismissal, he had to live on a salary which he regarded as inadequate and savings that were increasingly eroded by medical expenses. His travels were enlivened by encoun-ters with fellow Scots, who, he claimed, played a disproportionate role in the frontier life of Manitoba, as farmers, stock breeders, journalists and doctors, an impression not gained from William Wallace's occasional encounters with Scots a generation earlier. After becoming engaged to the daughter of a substantial farming family, he was persuaded to upgrade his view of prairie farming, and just before his death, as we have seen, he was negotiating both for the purchase of 640 acres near Killarney and for the emigration of his brother, whose joint investment would have allowed him to clinch the deal.

A contemporary of John McBean was much more disillusioned about prairie life, lamenting, four months after he arrived in Red Deer, that it was 'the last place on God's earth that I would care to remain in'. He was also much less san-guine than William Wallace about misleading information from railway pro-moters, claiming that he had been defrauded, as had the 400 other settlers who had accompanied him on the colonist train to Calgary, in the hope of making their fortunes:

> Fortunes, did I say? Well, if the truth were told, many of them come out to eke out a miserable existence ... This [Red Deer] is a little place with a little over 1000 inhabitants, and is just like many another little Western town. The people are sleepy, with no 'go' in them ... The other places are no better, and many of them much worse. Edmonton, the only town of importance north of here, is overdone, and property is up to famine price. Our idea in coming to this country

was to take up the free homestead land, and go in for farming and stock raising, but everything is so different to how it is coloured and puffed up in their pamphlets that I for one drew the line. For instance, we are told that splendid homesteads can be had within a mile or two of the railway for 10 dollars, which, in plain English, is a downright lie. The nearest homestead land I could get was about 35 miles, and to get land which was at all worth taking even at the price of 10 dollars (£2) for 160 acres, I have to go out from railway and town 60 to 80 miles.[33]

The experiences of Scottish farmers in the United States were equally mixed. 'I bless God every day that I followed your advice not to farm at home and that I had discrimination enough to decide upon the United States as my place of rest,' wrote wealthy brewer James Robertson in 1830, from his 300-acre farm on the banks of the Hudson River. He had a large frame and brick house with commodious outbuildings and staff accommodation, and generally enjoyed life with fishing, sailing, good wine and a well-stocked library. Recommending the area to any of his friends from Strathmore in Angus who could spare £1,000 to invest in a good farm, he thought it 'surprising that people are so blind as still to emigrate to Australia or over Canada'.[34] Shetlander Peter Tait too preferred his farm at Joliet, Illinois, to the tree-covered wilderness of Canada, as did Robert Young from Ayrshire, who in 1860 reconnoitred land on both sides of the border before bringing his family over to a largely Scottish community in North Tama County, Iowa. Unfortunately, within fifteen months of arriving, three of his ten siblings died, of pneumonia, drowning and typhoid, victims of the harsh pioneering environment.[35] James Alexander, who emigrated from Aberdeenshire to farm in Nebraska in 1873, disapproved of the idea that a 'Scotch Colony' should be formed in the state, arguing that the false security of communal settlement, as well as unmerited financial assistance, encouraged the wrong type of emigrant. A convinced individualist, he had, on arriving at Lincoln, parted company from his fellow Aberdonians, who, although 'neighbourly and agreeable', insisted on retaining their incomprehensible Doric dialect in conversation with Nebraskans.[36] Attempts by Scots to farm communally do seem to have been fraught with difficulty, if the story of the Victoria colony in western Kansas, founded in 1871–2, is anything to go by. Its creator, George Grant, a crofter's son who had made a fortune in the cloth business in London, attracted almost 200 fellow Scots and also introduced the first Aberdeen Angus cattle to the United States, but investors shied away when the colony was vilified in the Scottish press, subsequently crumbling in the wake of drought, grasshoppers and Grant's premature death in 1878.[37]

In the Antipodes, as we have seen, the emphasis was on sheep farming. In return for trivial licence fees, many Scottish pastoralists in Australia acquired huge acreages, flocks, bank balances and reputations. Philip Russell, who in 1821 left the family farm in Fife after his father had fallen on hard times and could no longer provide for his thirteen children, went to Van Diemen's Land to manage a retired East India Company officer's farm. His success induced his brother George to join him ten years later, until in 1836 George moved to Port Phillip to work for the newly formed Clyde Company of Scottish pastoralists. Within three years he was managing 8,000 sheep and almost 300 cattle at an annual salary of £100 and a share of the profits, and when he died in 1888 he left over £318,000.[38]

As settlement expanded, large numbers of Scots cattle and sheep farmers 'squatted' on land to which they had no legal title, until in 1836 the government allowed them to buy squatting licences for £10 a year. They came from the Highlands as well as the Lowlands. Godfrey McKinnon, who farmed at North Goonamba, had done well enough by 1864 to pay a brief visit home – not entirely willingly, for 'if my mother was not there to meet me I never would go back to Skye, nothing could persuade me to go home but to see her', he wrote to his friend John McDonald in Uist, in a letter which also outlined his achievements:

> I had very hard work of it the first three years that I was in the country but now I can take it a little easier ... I have done very well for all the time I have been in the Colony more than if [I] had been in Skye for the rest of my life tho' I would live for fifty years more. I have got a beautiful piece of country and first rate stock of both sheep cattle and horses. I have gone to great expense with my sheep purchases – imported rams. It will pay me very well in a few years. I had a splendid clip of wool this season and I expect a better next clip.[39]

The expansion of the farming frontier into the interior brought the pastoralists into unexplored territory. Although they were sometimes assisted in their expeditions by Aboriginal guides, the settlers increasingly came into conflict with the nomadic Aborigines, whom they displaced from their sacred lands and sometimes killed. In the Antipodes as in North America, European settlers saw the land as theirs for the taking, and its indigenous population was regarded as irrelevant or expendable. Moral and anthropological unease about the anticipated extinction of a whole race of people was slow to develop in Australia and New Zealand, where there was much less evidence of economic and cultural interaction than in the United States and Canada. 'Our natives have been much more quiet lately and I think every year they will become more accustomed to our ways if not civilised,' wrote D. S. Murray from China Farm, Canning River, to his mother in 1839.[40] When Angus McMillan, an emigrant from Skye, explored the Gippsland area of Victoria the following year, he was initially accompanied by an Aboriginal guide but in 1843 he, along with other Scottish settlers, played a leading part in the Warrigal Creek massacre, in which an estimated 60–150 Aborigines were killed.[41]

Sheep farming – and displacement of the Maoris – also dominated much of the emigrant experience in New Zealand. In 1878 George Wrey, of the Cunninghame of Thornton family in Ayrshire, after travelling throughout New Zealand, bought a 1,500-acre sheep farm for £10,500 and £3,000 worth of stock as an investment 'to improve and sell again for a price sufficient to cover any loss of interest or more if I can'. Such practices, he assured his aunt, were 'considered very safe and there are agents out here whose entire business consists in making these investments and collecting and remitting money home'. He also repeatedly wrote of the beauty of the landscape, on one occasion contrasting the lush foliage of the South Island with 'the dry arid appearance of Australia'.[42]

From time to time Scottish farmers settled in more obscure locations, not always with great success. In 1825 198 northern Scots, mainly demobilized soldiers, tradesmen and shepherds, sailed from Cromarty to Venezuela in order to establish an agricultural colony in the arid Topo Valley, between La Guaira and Caracas. The colony came into being as a result of the rash of speculative foreign investment in Venezuela which followed liberation from Spanish rule in 1821 and the creation of the centralized Republic of Colombia under Simón Bolívar's presidency. The government in Bogotá, bankrupted by a decade of war, desperately needed foreign capital and technology to stimulate economic development, and British mercantile houses, eager to exploit the new Latin American market, were happy to oblige. Huge loans were negotiated, and ambitious plans drawn up for agricultural development through the government's allocation of land to companies such as Herring, Graham and Powles. Shortly after that firm had been awarded 316,160 acres, in return for a promise to introduce settlers and promote cultivation, it founded a joint stock company, the Colombian Agricultural Society of London, to promote colonization, select settlers and finance the venture. John Ross, parliamentary correspondent of *The Times* and a former Church of Scotland minister, recruited and led a colony of Scots to one of the proposed locations near Caracas, where they were to grow cotton, coffee and indigo. Each colonist was promised up to fifty acres of rich agricultural land, free tools and seed, and eight months' provisions.

Within a short time of arriving at their snake-infested, cactus-covered, arid and stony destination, the colonists realized they had been deceived, but their demands for better land or compensation were rejected by the Colombian Society and by the British consul at Caracas, Sir Robert Ker Porter. Although the Caracas newspaper *El Colombian* (which was owned by Herring, Graham and Powles) initially praised the 'sober and industrious habits' of the settlers, Porter regarded them as a 'worthless, drunken set', responsible for their own misfortunes. His assessment may have been the more accurate, since excavations at Topo show numerous broken bottles and drinking vessels, and John Ross – who left the colony in July 1826 – had a reputation for heavy drinking. When a serious financial crisis in Britain in 1826 bankrupted the Colombian Society, the Topo colonists were in desperate straits. 'We have nothing now in our view but starvation and a lingering death to ourselves and families in a place where we can not get work or wages,' they wrote to Porter in April 1827, but it was only when their petitions reached the government in London that the consul was forced to take action. Since by that time the imminent disintegration of the Republic of Colombia had made it impossible to relocate the Scots safely in Venezuela, arrangements were made for their removal to Canada, where by the end of 1827 they were successfully resettled on Canada Company lands at Guelph.[43]

The trials and tribulations of the 250 Scots who founded the Monte Grande colony near Buenos Aires, also in 1825, echoed those of their countrymen at Topo. The newly independent Republic of Argentina, under Bernadino Rivadavia, was anxious to foster European ideas and institutions and, like its counterpart in Venezuela, sought to do so by offering substantial land grants to immigrants who would settle on the shores of the River Plate. Attracted by the apparently generous promise of assistance in establishing an agricultural colony, John and William Parish Robertson, two brothers from Kelso, recruited colonists, mainly from the Borders, and sent them out on the *Symmetry* from Leith in May 1825. By that time, however, the Robertsons had rejected the poor-quality land offered by the Buenos Aires government and had instead purchased 16,660 acres from two Scottish ranchers, George and John Gibson. Despite exaggerated promises and scanty planning, the colony prospered briefly, but soon fell victim to the political and economic instability brought about by Argentina's war with Brazil and the subsequent replacement of Rivadavia's Europeanized liberal regime by the nationalist dictatorship of Juan Manuel de Rosas. Although Rosas saw the importance of maintaining trade with Britain and therefore did not mistreat the Scottish colonists, civil unrest in the area in 1829 drove many of them out to Buenos Aires or other parts of the province, while those who stayed continued to face harassment from marauding soldiers throughout the two decades of Rosas's rule. Jane Rodger, who was only four when she emigrated from Scotland with her parents, had vivid (if perhaps embellished) recollections eighty years later of the lawlessness of an era when life was cheap:

> My father now joined in partnership with a Mr. and Mrs. G., and they carried on a large dairy farm. Father imported some pigs from home, had quite a large business and did very well … At this time the country was more and more unsettled. Rosas was outside, and Lavalle in, Buenos Aires. There were bands of Indians wandering about who were Rosas's men. Lavalle's soldiers were also wandering about, stealing, murdering and causing the greatest alarm. It was well named 'The Reign of Terror'. My father said that Mother must go with us children, but she said, no, if he could not go she would not leave him. So for a time we remained on, always in danger.[44]

It was only after they were attacked in their own home by sword-wielding intruders who hacked their dog to death that the family moved temporarily to Buenos Aires, returning a year later to find that their property had been ransacked and razed to the ground.

Danger to life and limb was also a hazard faced by the Scots who were brought out to the Eastern Cape between 1877 and 1883 to form agricultural settlements on border land from which the Xhosa population had recently been displaced. Before the end of 1877, while the Kaffir War raged, most of the first arrivals had fled their farms in the Gonubie district to settle in the towns, many never to return to the land in which some had invested savings of up to £100. When James Mackenzie from Stirlingshire ventured out to his farm after some months in East London, he found the buildings in flames, while the Bryson family from Loch Lomond spent two enforced years in East London before settling on their farm. Travel was hazardous not only on account of banditry but also because of the poor infrastructure, with few proper roads and hardly any bridges, so that on a number of occasions settlers were drowned when attempting to ford swollen rivers. Others were murdered, gored to death, decamped to the diamond fields or lost their lands through insolvency. Nevertheless, and despite his irritation with the Cape's London agent for sending out men with inadequate means to sustain themselves on the land, J. B. Hellier, Superintendent of Immigrants at East London, was optimistic about the prospects of the two contingents of Scottish settlers who had arrived by the time he penned his first report in 1881:

> Care has been taken to locate the immigrants on good arable land, and with a good supply of water whenever possible. All the immigrants appear to be satisfied with the land allotted to them, and many of them express themselves hopefully as to their future prospects. With scarcely an exception, those who have settled on their land have enjoyed most excellent health, and some of them say that they have got rid of ailments from which they used to suffer, and that they are getting quite young again. Several of them have been making inquiries, and some have made applications to get their relatives out to this country ... The Scotch immigrants who landed in 1877 and 1878, and who are settled in the East London districts, have also suffered much from the drought, but reaped the advantages of the present good season, the best they say, or rather the only good season they have had, since they came into the country. No doubt this better season will encourage these men to cultivate more ground; and a few more such seasons will lead most of the men now working on the harbour works and railway line to stay altogether on their farm, and give their undivided attention to its cultivation and improvement. Some of these immigrants who have lived altogether on their farms have done very well, and I think that they promise with better times to be a very prosperous part of our colonial population.[45]

In most locations, farmers' accounts of emigrant life were positive, particularly if they were looking back over a fairly lengthy period of settlement. Disappointment was most commonly expressed by unassimilated new arrivals, those who had acquired land precipitately and, especially, the victims of fraudulent, misleading or badly designed colonization schemes. From the pampas to the prairies, the forests of New Brunswick to the plains of Kansas, Lowland and Highland colonists alike deplored the disparities between agents' images and the harsh realities of pioneer farming, with the fires of doubt and disappointment often being fuelled further by the opportunity for collective grumbling afforded by these isolated, introverted communities. Yet family and community networks were also vital support mechanisms, and many emigrants – as their correspondence demonstrates – sought the practical assistance, or simply the company, of fellow countrymen.

Not surprisingly, success and contentment seem to have been more easily attained in the relatively settled society of eastern Canada than in the pioneering environments of the Antipodes and South America, although loneliness was a recurring complaint among some settlers on the prairies. Adaptability, health and perseverance, rather than previous experience, were the determinants of success; despite being a builder, not a farmer, William Gibson turned his hand successfully to prairie agriculture, whereas John McBean, who came from a rural background, had little enthusiasm or stamina for farm work. In other ways, however, the emigrants' backgrounds spilled over into their subsequent experiences. While self-confident Lowland farmers emigrated with a determination to make the most of overseas opportunities, the miseries of cleared Highlanders often followed them to the new world, at least initially. Yet inauspicious beginnings did not necessarily preclude successful settlement. Indeed, for Highland exiles, the achievement of prosperity in the face of adversity satisfied the demands of poetic – and sometimes retributive – justice, as in Alexander MacKenzie's juxtaposition of the wealth and comfort of the descendants of cleared Highlanders in Glengarry County with the bankruptcy of the 'grasping sheep farmer who was the original cause of their eviction' from the Scottish Glengarry.[46] Ironically – and unlike many of their Lowland counterparts – Highland emigrants seem to have found the transition to Australia easier than that to Canada, perhaps because they emigrated through carefully financed and monitored government schemes rather than under the auspices of parsimonious landlords.

The artisan experience

Emigrant farmers may have faced a life of unremitting toil, but they were generally their own masters. The same could not be said for many artisans, which perhaps explains why their experiences – at least those we know about – were more liberally peppered with reservations and complaints. For some tradesmen, however, lack of independence was less important than the anticipation of high wages, particularly if they were saving with a view to acquiring a farm or a business of their own. James Thompson, the Aboyne baker, emigrated in 1844 with no clear plan in mind other than a vague intention to go to the Toronto area, where a cousin was farming. Armed with a letter of introduction to Henry Essen, a Scottish minister in Montreal, who quickly found him a baking job with Scottish employers, he spent a comfortable winter under the roof of a fellow countryman. 'Since my arival [*sic*] in the city,' he wrote to his father on 14 June 1844, 'I have been living in a lodging house kept by Mr McHardy who twelve years ago was a coach guard on the Deeside road. We have always beef steak and potatoes to breakfast and also to tea and roast beef and potatoes to dinner besides a number of other dishes.'[47] At Essen's St Gabriel Street Church he could mix with many fellow Scots and also heard a number of visiting Scottish preachers, while one of his employers kept him well supplied with copies of the Aberdeen newspapers. Although he had to work harder than at home and, as a new arrival, was not paid at the top rate, he still managed to save £15 from his year's wages. He was impressed with the standard of living in Montreal, where servant girls 'dress almost as fine as their mistresses' and he had seen 'fewer ragged people than in Aberdeen'.[48]

In June 1845 Thompson moved west, where for four years he baked for the Irish navvies who were canalizing the St Lawrence near Edwardsburgh. Although his wages were lower than in Montreal, conditions were better, with no night work, and when construction work ceased for the winter Thompson worked in the local store. In October 1847 he took a fortnight's holiday, during which he visited his cousin's farm, Niagara Falls and Buffalo, but in 1849, 'on account of the dullness of business in Edwardsburgh and in Canada generally', he decided to seek pastures new and went to Chicago on the recommendation of Andrew Elliott, the canal contractor who had recently employed him.[49] He stayed eight months there, working as a lumber merchant's clerk, but by March 1850 he had decided to join the gold rush to California, where by 1853 had made enough money by a combination of mining, baking and logging to afford a trip home, and, on his return, the fulfilment of his goal, the purchase of a farm in Edwardsburgh.

James Thompson did not marry until a year after he had set himself up as a farmer. Artisans were more likely to be single men – or to leave their families behind – when they emigrated than those who went straight on to the land, not least because a family was often more of a liability than an asset to a tradesman whose employment opportunities fluctuated and whose lifestyle might well be itinerant. They were also, Charlotte Erickson has argued, more likely than farmers to seek support networks beyond the family, through workmates and acquaintances from their own ethnic communities.[50] Both traits were evident in the case of Thompson, who regularly remitted money to his family at home, and referred frequently in his letters to practical assistance he had received from fellow countrymen. They were also evident in the correspondence of James McCowan, a smith from Perthshire, who in 1819 told his correspondent of encounters with other Scots in Richmond, Virginia, and how he had tried unsuccessfully to use one of those contacts to remit money home:

> You know David Imrie Wright from Methven he was at the Wood of Trowen. He Came here about the 10 of July and Cant get no work here at his trade. He told me all the news about the Place but had no word about you as I expect that you did not no that he was comeing to it. And there was one from Perth by the Name of Buchen after som Maney and I wished to Send home some to My Father and Mother but he told Some of them that He did not no what time he wold get his Busnes settled, but I must try and get some opportunity of Sending Some to Them this fall … it is hard to get it Sent home at this time for you Do not know who to trust here for they are all Roges here.[51]

As Chapter 3 demonstrated, the United States, with a more developed economy than its northern neighbour, attracted significant numbers of Scottish tradesmen, factory operatives and manufacturers, not least to textile communities in New England. From the 1820s, emigrants from Paisley and Kilmarnock flocked to the carpet-manufacturing centres of Lowell, Massachusetts, and Thompsonville, Connecticut, respectively, while the workers brought out to Newark, New Jersey, and Pawtucket and Fall River, Massachusetts, by the Paisley thread-making firms of Clark, J. & P. Coats and Kerr, earned double the wages they had been paid in Scotland. By the end of the century, some of the Scottish artisans who were ultimately displaced by cheaper American workers had succeeded in moving into managerial positions and even proprietorship.[52]

But not all artisans had the assurance of employment or settled down immediately. Many spent several years 'on tramp', changing jobs in pursuit of higher wages and better working conditions, often with a view to investing in a farm or ultimately returning to Scotland. Adaptability was a prerequisite, and many new arrivals had to endure a period of low wages until they gained experience. While some complained of the irregularity of employment, loneliness and lack of assimilation were probably more serious consequences of their itinerant lifestyle, as they moved from town to town and boarding house to boarding house. David Laing, an unskilled day labourer, never fully adapted to life in the United States, despite emigrating (probably from the Edinburgh area) at the age of eighteen and marrying a woman from Pennsylvania. In 1858 he moved to Indiana, but by 1873 his marriage had foundered and he had moved to Logan-port. 'I am working in a large rail road shop at the machine busness,' he told his sister. 'We have 86 locomotive engins to keep in repair & four hundred miles of road to keep up. Our formen are nearly all English and Scotch men & many of the men also. I am running a machine & have good easy situation.' Despite his occupational progress, the recurring theme of Laing's letters was one of pro-found loneliness:

> I have read your letter at least twenty times since I received it … If I were only able, I should be so happy to go over to see you; but my health has not been good since I was in the Army, I have had several spells of illness. I think a trip *home* would do me good but I must not think of it. It only makes me more unhappy, but, Johan dear, I do want to see you all so much.[53]

Although he had good lodgings with a widow and her son, he bewailed having 'no home', and anticipated that the son's forthcoming marriage would require him to move, 'as he will not wish to trouble his bride with a lodger. Well such is life, so I have always been driven about in the world.'[54] By 1874 he was living with his daughter, the youngest of his five children, whose husband worked alongside him in the locomotive works, but after she died in 1876 her husband remarried and Laing, forced back into lodgings, feared losing touch with his infant grandson:

> I am prospering in life but still I am so *lonely*. The boys are grown up all men. They loved theyr sister, but cannot mourn her loss as I do, for all the love of a warm nature was concentrated on her. Charley & George are runing on the same railway that I am working for and are boarding at the same house that I do, rooming in the same room when in Logansport … I was promoted on the 1st of Aprial, am forman of a gang of twenty men receiving and shipping all the stores & material; have 20 men and locomotive engine under my charge.[55]

James Mouat Garriock fared even worse than Laing, despite coming from a relatively prosperous background in Shetland and having some training in medicine. In 1891, a year after he arrived in Vancouver, he wrote to his mother, expressing his bitterness at the misleading propaganda that had lured him to a city where there were up to 1,500 unemployed, wages were low, living costs high, and a succession of casual jobs had barely kept him above the breadline:

> The medical profession being a failure, I tramped the town in all directions searching for work of any kind. A month passed but nothing came of it. I applied to the C. P. Ry [Canadian Pacific Railway] for a situation & received a reply stating that my application had been received, & that it should be kept in mind, but tho' I have several times applied at the different departments I have had no success.
>
> At last, after being about six weeks here, I struck a job for two days with the City Engineer in surveying & measuring the foreshores of the harbour & bay. After this I had an attack of fever induced by gases given off from the sewage & other decomposing matter lying about the shore. A week or two after recovering from the fever I managed to get out with a surveyor for a fortnight, but for this I only received my 'keep', but for this I was thankful, altho' the travelling through the woods & underbrush was frightfully tiring in my not very strong state, & the felling of trees no joke.

Although building tradesmen could make money in the summer, their savings were 'swallowed up' during the enforced idleness of winter, and Garriock had only survived when he was paid thirty dollars for curing his former landlady of 'a bad leg & breast'. After she left for the United States, he and two fellow boarders had moved into a wooden shanty, but his companions – both English immigrants – were about to leave on a sealing trip to Alaska. Garriock, unable to join them on account of an eye condition, had spent his last dollar on the rent of the shanty, and was about to spend his last cent on posting his tale of woe. 'I have little more to say,' he concluded. 'You need not mention to outsiders that you have received a letter from me. Had I better news to convey it would have been different, but the outlook is so dark that it is better to keep it to yourselves.'[56] Garriock was never heard from again.

Unlike their farming counterparts, artisans were rarely satisfied with their circumstances unless they could make and save money quickly. Such higher expectations may have generated more frequent and acute disappointment than was evident in the farming community, where success was measured primarily in terms of long-term prospects for the emigrant and his family. The nature of artisans' work may also have made them prone to disillusionment, since they were at the beck and call of individuals and organizations that might be capricious, exploitative or downright fraudulent. Coal miners who were persuaded by Alexander McDonald, the Scottish miners' leader, to go to the United States in large numbers in the 1860s, found that, although wages and housing conditions were better, working hours were longer than at home, while both safety legislation and unionization were less advanced. At times colliers and foundry workers were even recruited as strikebreakers, as were granite tradesmen in both the USA and Canada. A particularly notorious strikebreaking incident, involving granite cutters from Aberdeen, occurred in Texas in 1886. After the State Capitol at Austin burned down in 1881, the building syndicate hired to construct its replacement employed 500 convicts from state penitentiaries to cut stone for the new building, creating a massive backlash of public opinion in Texas and a bitter dispute with the American Granite Cutters' Union about the use of cheap, non-unionized labour. When the union boycotted the project in a well-supported strike, the building syndicate sent its agent, George Berry, to Aberdeen, to recruit 150 cutters and fifteen blacksmiths to break the strike. His press advertisement and subsequent public meeting were disingenuous, for he made no mention of the strike, promising his audience of 300 a prepaid passage out and back and at least eighteen months' work at wages of up to $6 a day, with cheap board and lodging, in a pleasant environment. The eighty-six recruits who accompanied Berry back across the Atlantic were totally unprepared for the reception that greeted them in New York, where they were intercepted by three officials from the American union and apprised of the real state of affairs. While twenty-four men agreed not to proceed further but to look for work in the New England granite yards instead, the others were allegedly 'coaxed and coerced' aboard the ferry for New Jersey, from where they proceeded by train to Austin. Some, like Alexander Greig, were optimistic and disinclined to believe the union's warnings:

> While we were at New York, there were several of the society met us, and tried all that was in their power to get us to stop at New York; and I am sorry to say that there was a few fools amongst us who listened to what they had to say ... You can tell anybody that asks about us that everything is right, and that we have been treated well. I was told that I was growing fat upon it. I am in first class health and intend to stick in. This is the most splendid country I have ever seen. I have seen nothing to equal it through all the States.[57]

But not all the recruits were of the same mind, particularly once the work actually began, and they found they were working in blazing sun, with no shade, in
temperatures of over 100 degrees. The cutting yards were not at Austin, as they
had been led to believe, but at Burnet, seventy miles away, and the quarry was at
Marble Falls, a few miles from Burnet, in the middle of the Texan desert. The
lodgings – a fenced enclosure at Burnet – were cramped and uncomfortable,
with up to six men sharing a room ten feet square, and the food was described as,
at best, indifferent. 'Bitter feelings and homesickness are cropping out everywhere,' reported the *Galveston Daily News* on 13 May. There was also financial
disillusionment. The men had incurred unexpected extra expenses during their
seven-day journey from New York, and their hopes of high wages did not materialize, for when it was found that many of them had no previous experience of
granite cutting, they were unable to earn even $1 a day. By the end of October
1886 at least three emigrants had died, and by May 1887 only fifteen of the original recruits were still employed at Burnet. It was difficult for the Scots to get
away, since their prepaid passages were to be repaid from their wages before
they received a penny. Even if they absconded, as many seem to have done, their
prospects of employment were bleak, at least in the granite industry, for they
had been blacklisted as strikebreakers, and their names had been circulated to
every branch of the American Granite Cutters' Union. 'Give them no work,
and see that they get no work in your neighborhood' was the order in a circular
issued by the Austin Assembly of the Knights of Labor in August 1886, and
when the Capitol contract ended a year later, the granite cutters were left to fend
for themselves in a hostile labour market.[58]

Twenty years later Aberdeen granite tradesmen were involved in an
equally bitter dispute in Canada, when Alexander Robertson, a trade union
activist and former president of the Aberdeen Trades Council who had emigrated some years earlier, tried unsuccessfully to unionize the Toronto workforce of the Stanstead Granite Quarry Company, where he then worked. His
demands were rejected by the company, which instead tried to persuade
employees to sign long-term agreements and take out shares. When those
who refused to do so were dismissed, the remaining workers came out on
strike, both in Toronto and at the firm's quarries at Beebe Plain, Quebec.
Although Robertson and his fellow unionist James Duncan asked Aberdeen
granite masons to ignore advertisements for work in Toronto, several were
recruited by Stanstead Company agents who visited the city between 1906
and 1909, and their strikebreaking activities caused particular acrimony at

Beebe Plain, where many of the tradesmen who had downed tools were themselves emigrants from Aberdeen. The recruits were caught on the horns of a
dilemma: those who refused to take up their positions were, like the earlier emigrants to Austin, indebted to the company for their prepaid passages, while
those who carried on regardless were blacklisted by unions on both sides of the
Atlantic.[59]

The pursuit of wealth took Scottish artisans all over the world, sometimes to
a succession of destinations. In no industry was such itinerant fortune hunting
more clearly seen than in the search for gold, as Scots joined with other nationalities in flocking to the gold fields of three continents between 1849 and 1900.
Not surprisingly, optimism and disappointment were the hallmarks of their correspondence. James Thompson, whose objective in joining the California gold
rush was simply to make enough money to finance a visit home and the subsequent purchase of a Canadian farm, 'found some people making fortunes and
others scarcely making their board' when he arrived in Nevada City in 1850.
After working briefly in the supply of lumber for building, he and two partners
purchased a mining claim for $1,000. 'I cannot give a very favourable report of
my success, although the star of hope is still in the ascendent [*sic*],' he wrote to
his father in February 1851. By June 1852 the partnership had purchased several
mining claims, which were yielding a modest income, although Thompson was
making a living primarily at his original trade of baking. Ten years later, when
he joined the Cariboo gold rush in the hope of supplementing the meagre
income from his farm in Edwardsburgh, his letters reflected the homesickness of
a married man who had received no letters from the family he had left behind.
'Amidst all the toil and anxiety and privations experienced in this country that is
hardest of all to bear,' he wrote to his wife in July 1862, although his despon-
dency was perhaps exacerbated by pecuniary disappointment and the prospect
of returning home empty-handed, 'to be laughed at into the bargain'.[60] More
than thirty years later, Dunfermline emigrant James Dodds, writing from the
Klondike, remained optimistic in the face of difficulties and sought to reassure
his parents that his luck would turn. 'I believe this to be as rich a gold field yet
discovered,' he wrote in March 1898. Although his partner had been taken ill,
scurvy had affected 'a great many people' in Dawson City and one miner was
about to lose all his toes through frostbite, Dodds remained 'thankful to the
ruller of the universe for the health and strength I have been blessed with since
comming in here'.[61]

Meanwhile, Scots gold seekers had also been attracted to Australia in large numbers after the precious metal was discovered in Victoria and New South Wales in 1851. Some of the gold camps, particularly in Bendigo, were recognizably Scottish, and the Scottish press devoted many column inches to the varied experiences of the miners. For established settlers such as Dr William Sutherland, gold fever was 'a curse rather than a blessing' because of the disruption it had brought to the labour market, although, as he confessed to his sisters, he was still tempted to try his luck himself:

> You are aware that the great want in this country has been the scarcity of labour but now servants are fast becoming masters and heaven alone knows how matters will terminate. Nearly all the people who can handle a spade or pick axe are going or gone to the diggings. This township is nearly deserted and were it not for the unprotected state of my family I should feel very much inclined to try my luck also. The other two medicos of this place have gone and left the whole field to myself ... if we have not a most extensive immigration from home to make up for those leaving for the mines, we shall be at our wits ends. Female servants can scarcely be had for love or money. My poor wife, with four children to look after, and not at all strong, is obliged to do all the housework. We have only one little girl to whom we give £14 p. ann. whom you in Thurso would hardly give house room to. We are paying therefore dearly for our gold. The settlers or squatters are very much to be pitied, nearly all the shepherds having deserted their flocks for the mines.[62]

Like James Thompson in California, some Scots found they could make a more reliable income by following their own trade, capitalizing on inflated wage rates that paid carpenters, masons and plumbers from 25s to 30s a day. A correspondent of the *Inverness Advertiser* who emigrated to Geelong in 1854 to work as a shipping clerk for a Glasgow company documented the experiences of a long list of fellow passengers and other Scots 'who are all doing much better than ever they could at home'. Success was dependent on sobriety, according to another correspondent of the same paper, who, having abandoned his £90-a-year job as a shepherd to go to the diggings, had been too much 'in love with John Barleycorn' to make a fortune, although he still claimed to be better off than if he had stayed in Scotland. On the other hand, some who went to the gold fields painted an unequivocal picture of greed, lawlessness and squalor. 'Nothing but money, money, make money, either by fair our foul means,' wrote a store clerk at Mount Alexander to his friend in Forres in 1852: 'Tis nothing unusual for a tent to be robbed, and unless you be the first to fire your pistol or gun and bring the villains down, you stand a poor chance yourself, for they will shoot you with as little compunction as they would a wild dog. I never lie down without my pistols and gun in working order.' To make matters worse, the miners had been laid low by an outbreak of dysentery resulting from contaminated water, yet 'the fact that a few are making fortunes, is a sufficient inducement for them to brave all sufferings and dangers – each one hoping that he will be as fortunate as his more successful neighbour'.[63]

While most artisans whose experiences have been documented emigrated from the Lowlands, gold miners came from all parts of Scotland and all walks of life. Since the activities of the Highland and Island Emigration Society coincided with Australia's gold rush, it is not surprising that some of the emigrants sought their fortunes at the diggings, even though they were expected to replenish the labour that had been lost to the gold fields. Ewan 'California' Gillies was perhaps the most remarkable of these emigrants, at least in terms of his worldwide wanderings. One of thirty-six emigrants who left St Kilda for Victoria in 1852, he worked initially as a brickmaker. After six months he was dismissed for laziness and went to the gold fields, where over the next two years he made enough money to buy a farm, which later failed. Moving to Melbourne with his wife and children, he left them there while he dug for gold in New Zealand, returning within two years to discover that his wife had remarried. He then took ship for the USA, where he fought for the Union in the Civil War, deserting in 1861 to join a California gold rush, where within six years he made a fortune. After returning to Australia to claim his children, he went back briefly to his native island in 1871, but within four weeks returned to the United States, where he remained for the next eleven years. During another short spell in St Kilda he remarried, emigrating again to Melbourne with his second wife, whose homesickness prompted a return to St Kilda eight months later. But the St Kildans, who had turned against him on his return from America the previous year, forced the couple out and in 1889 they settled permanently in Canada.[64]

The female emigrant

The vast majority of farmers and artisans were, of course, men, although female gold miners and homesteaders were not unknown. One sheep-farming squatter who 'prospered exceedingly' was Anne Drysdale, a middle-aged spinster from Kirkcaldy who had farmed in Scotland before she emigrated in 1840 with capital of £3,000. Despite disparaging comments by the Russell brothers, who joked with each other about her matrimonial prospects and thought 'she should have invested her Money, and enjoied herself at home', she took up a 10,000-acre run at Boronggoop, near Geelong, in partnership with Caroline Newcomb. By 1844 the women had 6,000 sheep, as well as a few horses and cows, and five years later they replaced their rather primitive cottage with a more substantial stone house. Janet Richardson (twenty-three), who kept a diary of her voyage from Scotland to Geelong in 1848 in company with her brother and sister, remembered the discomforts of Anne Drysdale's first home:

> About 1 o'clock Miss Drysdale's phaeton came, and a note to me from her. The note assured us of a hearty welcome to her poor hut, such as it was: it also informed us that the heavy rains of the preceding day had flooded the house, so it was fortunate we had not come last afternoon ... At last we stopped at the white gate, barking dogs announced our arrival, and a very stout lady hurried out to meet us. This was Miss Drysdale; she led us into the cottage: we tried to restrain our wondering looks at the badness of the hut, but when shortly she took us to our room, and left us to prepare for dinner, it would have been amusing for anyone to have noticed our disappointed faces: our bedroom was scarcely larger than our cabin in the 'Hooghly', and besides the furniture and conveniences of the place were so different from what we had expected that we looked quite blank at the prospect of remaining here some months. Mr. Aitchison had indeed many times warned us not to expect too much, but the place was many degrees worse than in our blackest moments we could have conceived.[65]

Despite problems with drunken shepherds and the loss of labour to the gold fields, the partnership continued until 1854, when Anne Drysdale suffered a fatal stroke, and the property was henceforth run solely by Caroline Newcomb. Most women emigrated in families or to work for wages. Some were well known. The eloquent Strickland sisters, Catharine and Susanna, English emigrants married to Orcadians Thomas Traill and John Moodie respectively, recalled the experiences of pioneering before an international readership in their respective accounts *The Backwoods of Canada* (1836) and *Roughing it in the Bush* (1852). Catharine, who was stricken with cholera at Montreal almost as soon as she had arrived in 1832, subsequently settled with her husband on a lakeside bush farm near Douro, in the same neighbourhood as her brother, Samuel Strickland. By 1834 they were mingling in a 'highly respectable' society that

13. Jessie MacLaren McGregor (1863–1906), MD Edinburgh 1899, was one of the first women medical graduates of Edinburgh University. She emigrated to the United States but within a few days died as a result of spotted mountain fever following a tick bite.

included many former military and naval officers, although Catharine regarded with a mixture of amusement and irritation the egalitarian attitudes that 'the inferior class of Irish and Scotch' settlers soon acquired from their 'Yankee' neighbours. Susanna, who also arrived in 1832 and, like her sister, regarded emigration as an act of duty rather than pleasure, was horrified by her first glimpse through the dense forest of the 'miserable hut' where the family was expected to settle, although she too soon became not only reconciled, but enthusiastically devoted, to her adopted country.[66]

Most female emigrants were anonymous, however, offering only fleeting glimpses of their experiences in letters and diaries. Some, like Mary and Betty Stocks, emigrated in family groups as the wives, mothers and daughters of farmers or – less frequently – tradesmen. Maggie Wallace eventually went to Manitoba in 1904, more than twenty years after her brother William had first asked her to join him and his brother on their homestead 'to cook our meals, keep the house and dairy clean, and stitch our garments'. Beseeching her to 'give the country a trial for a year' and encouraging her that she could easily find work in her profession of teaching 'if at any time you should discover that you did not like the farm work', William also promised to arrange her return home if she did not like Canada. Until 1904, however, Maggie was unconvinced that there was any 'great necessity' for her to emigrate, and when she did at last agree to go, it was to take up a homestead which William had secured for herself and her husband.[67] Most of the Scottish women who feature in the Saskatchewan pioneers' questionnaire also came in family groups to settle on homesteads. They included Margaret Smith from Linlithgow, who recalled the difficulties of having to live in a tent with her husband and four children after they arrived in North Battleford in 1906 to find 'not a house, nothing but prairie ... no where to eat and no where to sleep'. That winter, according to another 1906 arrival, Jessie Ross from Aberdeen, brought temperatures of up to sixty degrees below zero. Six months after her husband emigrated, also in 1906, Margaret McManus from Lanark followed with her children and sister, only to find that her letters had gone astray and she had to remain in the immigration hall in Saskatoon for six weeks until he could collect her and take her on a two-week journey to their homestead, across a trail strewn with buffalo bones. Like Margaret Smith, she lived initially in an earthen-floored sod house, until after six years 'the walls began to give out, & the rain came in'.[68]

Women who emigrated in company with, or at the behest of, their families attracted far less contemporary attention than those who went out on their own. Large numbers of single women took up positions of domestic service or factory work, some in response to the advertisements of recruiting agencies and others under the auspices of employers and emigration societies. Others forged careers as teachers, governesses and nurses. Although British emigration was largely unregulated, there was a clear element of social engineering in the activities of female colonization societies, which steered women to the empire, where it was hoped they would both exert their 'hallowing influence' and redress the chronic gender imbalance. Indeed, perhaps the main distinguishing characteristic of British female emigration was the way in which it was explicitly harnessed to the cause of imperialism, particularly in the second half of the nineteenth century, although many of the emigrants may have been blissfully unaware of that wider agenda. Women were also less likely to be itinerant, and those who anticipated or experienced the loneliness of a backwoods farm or prairie homestead may – like Margaret Farquharson from Logie Coldstone – have been more prone than men to doubts and disillusionment.

The specific encouragement of independent female emigration began in the era of systematic colonization, when attempts were made by the British and colonial governments, assisted by a number of charitable societies and individuals, initially to repair the gender imbalance in Australia and then to send selected female emigrants to Britain's other settler colonies. From about 1870 the campaign took on a new lease of life in response to the economic depression in Britain, and for more than three decades after 1884 the British Women's Emigration Association dominated the organization of sponsored female emigration, supervising the work of many smaller provincial associations. The twin arguments that had produced the earliest schemes to assist women emigrants – 'civilizing' the colonies and reducing the chronic surplus of women in Britain – were re-emphasized, not only with respect to working-class women but also as a legitimate means of improving the status and prospects of 'distressed gentlewomen'. The widely publicized and chronic shortage of domestic servants overseas was commonly cited as a major justification for the societies' activities, though they also pointed out that in the colonies a competent woman who earned her own living was treated as a social equal by her employers, while women who still balked at the idea of domestic service were promised employment as teachers, nurses and mothers' helps. Women were also encouraged to believe that, as well as remunerative and congenial employment, they would stand a better chance in the marriage market than they would at home. By the turn of the century the case in favour of the emigration of educated women was greatly strengthened by the popularity of the eugenics movement and the upsurge of imperialistic sentiment. While the eugenicists recommended emigration as a short-term device for eradicating the ongoing surplus of women in Britain, they advocated it primarily as a means of promoting racial purity in the colonies. These ideas were readily adopted by the female emigration societies, which increasingly embraced a wider, imperial function, particularly after the Boer War. Recruits were told that they were 'missionaries of empire' who were setting forth not only to fill positions of employment but ultimately, and more importantly, to become the wives of British settlers and the mothers of a future British colonial generation.

Such arguments did not go unchallenged. While commission-hungry booking agents were criticized in the colonies for irresponsible, indiscriminate recruitment of unsuitable and shiftless women such as Mary Rait, Isabella Mitchell and Rose McIntyre, emigration societies were accused of a more insidious conspiracy to export a surplus female population from Britain. In the 1830s complaints had centred on the moral and physical shortcomings of workhouse girls sent from England and Ireland to Australia, but by the end of the century concern was also expressed about the attitude and aptitude of 'genteel' emigrants who were said to be pretentious and incapable, despite the societies' assurances that, once trained in basic domestic duties, they would be more adaptable, reliable and socially acceptable than working-class emigrants. From the home perspective, however, the insatiable colonial demand for domestic servants provoked much criticism that emigration societies which assisted the removal of these women were depleting Britain of a scarce, rather than a surplus, commodity.

The societies sought to counter domestic criticism by insisting that they recruited primarily from the ranks of shop and factory employees, or among middle-class girls who would never consider going into service at home. They also claimed that the highly specialized servants required for domestic service in Britain were unsuited to the more basic needs of colonial employers. At the same time, they tackled colonial criticisms of the girls' calibre by implementing rigorous vetting and training programmes. The British Women's Emigration Association worked through local committees, scattered across the country, made up of voluntary workers who made an initial selection of candidates, helped them complete their application forms and checked their references. The final decision lay with the BWEA's London headquarters, which booked the passages of successful applicants and authorized loans of the fare where necessary. Hostels were opened in Liverpool and London to house emigrants before they sailed, and reception centres at the debarkation ports looked after them on arrival and generally forwarded them to places of employment.

Scottish women were often recruited and assisted in their own localities. In 1850 nineteen young women from Shetland – where there was a gender imbalance of three to one – were sent to Adelaide with the assistance of Lady Franklin and a committee of philanthropists in Lerwick. All found work within twenty-four hours of their arrival, and the average wage of 5s per week represented untold riches to girls who had rarely earned more than 8s per quarter at home.[69] During the 1860s and 1870s several inmates of the Female School of Industry in Aberdeen were sent overseas, particularly to Otago and Victoria, thanks to the fund-raising activities of the school's governors, Farquhar Spottiswoode and his wife, who were convinced that assisted emigration relieved pauperism and snatched some of their most vulnerable recruits from the jaws of prostitution.[70] But perhaps the best-documented Scottish female emigration agency was the Aberdeen Ladies' Union, which between 1883 and 1914 oversaw the emigration of 330 women, primarily to Canada, under the patronage of the dynamic Ishbel Gordon, Countess of Aberdeen. The ALU did not concern itself solely with emigration. Its aim was to coordinate women's welfare work in the city of Aberdeen, and to that end it operated recreational and educational clubs, a servants' training home and an employment registry. But the sponsorship of emigration was always integral to its work, and was reinforced by Lady Aberdeen's three-month sojourn in Canada in 1890, followed by a five-year residence from 1893, during her husband's tenure of office as Governor-General.

When the Aberdeen family first visited Canada in 1890, they were accompanied by eight household servants, all of whom remained in the Dominion with their employers' blessing. During their travels in 1890 and 1891 they encountered several girls who had emigrated from their own estates, including one who, despite the birth of an illegitimate child, was still in service with her original employer in Kingston and another who was farming with her husband in British Columbia, raising fruit and vegetables to sell to the miners and railway construction workers in their area. Lady Aberdeen was particularly satisfied with the operation of her seven-year-old emigration scheme, which had initially seen her recruits dispatched under the care of her friend William Quarrier, along with his parties of home children. After 1889 she utilized the facilities of the BWEA to transport the girls and secure repayment of their loans, while at Quebec and Montreal the Women's Protective Immigration Society generally found immediate work for the new arrivals. Contacts were also established with the YWCA and the Girls' Friendly Society, and from 1897 the Girls' Home of Welcome in Winnipeg made particular efforts to attract Scots. Although more generous donations and prompt repayment of loans would have allowed the scheme to expand, there were advantages to a small-scale operation, which – if we are to believe the union's annual reports – met with the approval of both employers and recruits. 'Nice healthy sensible girls' was the verdict of Jane Evans, secretary of the Women's Protective Immigration Society in Montreal, on a contingent that arrived in June 1886, while Robert Acton, immigration chaplain at Montreal, who supervised a large transatlantic emigrant party in 1889, singled out seven Aberdeen girls for particular commendation, and wrote to the Ladies' Union committee that 'we could readily place 500 more of the same kind'. Several girls encouraged friends and relatives to join them, including a group of Winnipeg hospital ward maids who returned to Aberdeen in 1895 to persuade their friends to accompany them back to Canada, while another Winnipeg recruit reported in 1896 that 'everything was much better than we expected'.[71]

It is difficult to know whether such sentiments were representative, and whether the experiences of the majority of female emigrants exceeded or disappointed their expectations. Glowing testimonials reproduced in fund-raising reports are clearly suspect, as are formulaic letters in promotional magazines such as *The Imperial Colonist*. Lady Aberdeen's perception of the treatment of female emigrants at Quebec was very different from that of some of the new arrivals. Visiting the reception centre in 1893, she described the facilities:

> The arrangements are all v. well made. There is a large long central sort of hall where they go on arriving with their baggage & sit & rest. In this place there are stalls where they can buy provisions for their journey & also socks, books etc. We asked what they bought most & found it was cheese – then tins of condensed milk, coffee, tongues, sausages etc. Out of this room there is the dining room, where preparations for very comfortable meals, breakfast, dinner were being made. Each meal can be had for 25c. Then there are a limited number of rooms upstairs where girls arriving without friends or who are not well can stop for a few days free, or are found places for. Then there is the place where all the steerage passengers baggage have to be fumigated, with the exception of articles of leather, & books, & then we looked through one of the colonists sleeping cars where the seat makes into berths for which bedding can be purchased for $2.25.[72]

Lady Aberdeen's impressions were corroborated by the booking agent H. W. J. Paton, who described the care taken of the girls on board ship as well as the careful arrangements made for their reception and employment by the Toronto lady superintendent, Mary Carmichael, and her colleagues in Quebec and Montreal. Chaperoned from the time they left home, they were put under the watchful eye of the chief stewardess on the Atlantic crossing. 'The girls wear a distinctive badge,' he reported proudly. 'They are all berthed together on the steamer and are looked after specially in *every* way till they arrive at Landing Port.'[73]

A much more negative picture of the segregation and supervision of female emigrants was painted by two women whose complaints appeared in the Aberdeen press in 1913. According to the daughter of William Miller, a jeweller in Aberdeen, her party, which had sailed from Liverpool to Quebec in May, had been treated no better than cattle, confined in a customs shed for a day on arrival and then dispatched to Montreal without food. There they were accommodated ten to a room, and the following day prospective employers 'came to interview the live-stock', with those who did not receive appointments being sent on to Toronto, where the procedure was repeated. Meanwhile, a domestic servant recruited by a local booking agency alleged that inadequate liaison between the Scottish booking agent, Isabella Stewart, and Mary Carmichael had left her temporarily stranded in Toronto, with no papers and no employment. Potentially more serious was the plight of those who fell victim to fraudulent agents, such as Joseph Christie, an erstwhile town councillor, alcoholic and failed businessman, who in 1909 induced nine young Aberdeen women to emigrate to Nova Scotia. When the promise of a free return passage, accommodation and a year's employment as herring filleters and gutters in Halifax did not materialize, the destitute girls were taken under the wing of the local Society for the Prevention of Cruelty to Children and the North British Society while jobs were found for most of them in domestic service.[74]

Most emigrant accounts bore out agents' assurances that conditions for domestic servants were better abroad than at home. Elspet Knowles wrote home enthusiastically to her local newspaper shortly after she emigrated from Stonehaven to New Brunswick:

> You may tell all the servant girls about Stonehaven that I never was so well off. The people here are not so proud, and their servants live as they do themselves. You get a nicely-furnished room for yourself – a mirror you can see yourself in from top to toe. You could have your clothes warm every morning if you chose, for there is a stove that burns all night, and pipes running through the house to keep it warm. The servants in Stonehaven do not enjoy the same comfort as the servants in St John's, although they work for little more than half the wages.[75]

Elspet's appreciation of modern conveniences and social equality was echoed by Maggie Masson, who in 1913 emigrated from Whitehills in Banffshire, with no complaints about the situation secured for her by Isabella Stewart. Everything was 'so much easier than in the homeland', she wrote to Mrs Stewart. 'We have a lovely electric washing-machine, so we can sit and eat breakfast and have the washing going on at the same time. We dine at the same table as the master and mistress, and travel first-class with them. I cannot thank you enough for recommending me to a good family.'[76]

Elspet Knowles and Maggie Masson had emigrated to better themselves, and would have been disappointed if their experiences had not matched their expectations. For Mary Williamson, however, a convict transported from Aberdeen to Australia in 1845, the experience of enforced emigration was on the whole more positive than she had expected, as she explained in a letter to the governor of the East Prison:

> We had a prosperous voyage, and my child, little Margaret, was permitted to accompany me. She is in the Orphan School, a most excellent institution; and, let me tell you, Government is our best friend, for settlers in these parts are selfish in the extreme; for, regardless of our toil, they 'spur a free horse to death.' For want of discrimination they confound the good with the bad, and, by this means, we are glad to fly to the female factory at Paramatta for shelter, gladly accepting of an asylum there to shield us from the tyrannical oppression of our merciless mistresses; but as there is never a rule without an exception, so there are some good ladies who get bad servants. If we were not prisoners, this colony would delight us.[77]

Conclusion

Although the uniqueness of each individual's experience defies generalization, there are undoubtedly recurring themes that link emigrants of various backgrounds and occupations who came from different parts of Scotland and settled throughout the world in the entire course of the nineteenth century. The huge influence of family, friends and community in choosing and consolidating a settlement was clearly and consistently evident, and emigrant letters were frequently characterized by references to the exploits of known fellow countrymen who were located in the area and sometimes extended a helping hand to the new arrivals. The need for resilience and perseverance was also repeatedly stressed, whether the emigrant was clearing a bush or prairie farm, shepherding in the outback, labouring in industry or cooking, cleaning and homemaking on the frontier. At the same time, there were obvious differences of emphasis in the way that experiences were evaluated. Farmers tended to invest for the future and measured success through a longer telescope than many artisans, who preferred to make and save money quickly and were more prepared to move on if their immediate expectations were not fulfilled. These different priorities were also reflected in the tendency of artisans to send money home, perhaps to support families who had remained behind, whereas farmers, who were more likely to have emigrated with their families, sometimes sought remittances from relatives at home to shore up or enhance their investments. While all emigrants ran the risk of being defrauded, and farmers had to be wary of the wiles of land speculators, particularly in undeveloped areas, the self-employed, independent emigrant was generally less vulnerable than the wage worker, particularly the contract labourer.

Most emigrants probably played a long-term game of snakes and ladders, as setbacks alternated with achievements. In some cases, however, the emigrant experience was unexpectedly and tragically cut short. Victims of accident, disease or foul play rarely left a personal record, but their fate was sometimes mentioned in the letters of their fellow countrymen or in the press. In 1872 granite mason Peter Adam was about to return from a two-year sojourn in Maine to be married in Aberdeen. He got no further than Boston. According to the newspaper in his home town:

> He changed his bank bills for gold, then buying a ticket for New York, he started on the night express train, intending to take a steamer at New York. This was the last seen of Peter Adam till his dead body was found in the Quaboag river, seven days later, eighty miles west of Boston, in the town of Palmer, Mass. There were two stabs in the neck, one of which had severed the jugular vein. It is supposed that he was followed by the murderers to the broker's office, and from there to the train; that he had put his gold in his boots, and, as he was passing from one car to another, he was seized and murdered, his boots cut open, the gold secured, and his body thrown into the river while passing over one of the numerous open bridges between Brookfield and Palmer.[78]

Fourteen years later, in the cemetery at Burnet, Texas, the Aberdeen granite cutters who had gone to cut stone for the new State Capitol erected a headstone in memory of three of their workmates who died during the job. Suicide was not an uncommon response to the trauma of homesickness, disappointed expectations or failed endeavours of emigrants from all walks of life, although it was not always mentioned publicly. Christina McMillan, Argyll-born widow of the Gippsland sheep farmer Angus McMillan, who himself died in penury in 1865, drowned herself in the La Trobe River in 1884. Two years earlier William Wallace had reported the suicide of a Scottish settler in his neighbourhood in western Canada:

> A young man, a licentiate of the Edinburgh College of Surgeons, came out to Manitoba with his young wife and family to get more scope but he did not

succeed in getting an opening ... Some influential persons knowing his circumstances secured for him the mastership of a small school, but he seems to have
felt his inferior condition acutely. He one day astonished the children by asking
those of them who wanted a new teacher to hold up their hands, and immediately after took poison, and before he could stagger to the door he was dead.
Subscriptions are being asked to enable his family to go back to the old
country.[79]

The repatriation of the surgeon's family was precipitated by tragedy, but by
no means all return migration was the result of death or disappointment. Temporary sojourning overseas, as opposed to permanent settlement, was an important dimension of the emigrant experience, particularly among artisans,
contract workers and those who sought their fortunes in climatically inhospitable regions. Its causes, characteristics and consequences are examined in the
following chapter.

THE TEMPORARY EMIGRANT

'The Scot ... never loses his attachment to his native land ... Whenever fortune smiles on him he returns to his native village and the drama of his life closes where it commenced.'[1]

Although more than a third of Scotland's emigrants in the second half of the nineteenth century came back to their homeland, the phenomenon of the returning exile has long been the Cinderella of Scottish diaspora studies. Emigrants returned home for a variety of reasons. Probably only a minority came back with their tails between their legs, since those who were bankrupt, ailing or disillusioned often lacked the financial, physical and psychological resources to retrace their steps. Much more commonly the decision to return was a carefully planned part of the whole emigration strategy from the start, and demonstrated success rather than failure. A significant number of Scots went overseas with no intention of settling permanently in the new land, but with the objective of repatriating the profits they hoped to make in a range of enterprises, from managing plantations in the tropics to fur trading in the Arctic. Others, such as soldiers and missionaries, sojourned overseas out of duty or vocation, while a professional élite of doctors, teachers, clerics and administrators capitalized on an international demand for their expertise as they pursued their careers round the globe. Even more adept at exploiting the internationalization of the labour market were tramping artisans, particularly in the United States, who emigrated in pursuit of higher wages and moved on – or back across the Atlantic – when opportunities dried up or they had saved enough money to return home without loss of face. While temporary and seasonal emigration was undoubtedly given a huge boost by the technological revolution in sea and land transport after 1850, as well as better telegraph and postal communications, it was by no means unknown in the age of sail, and the sojourning Scot had been a familiar figure in many overseas locations in the seventeenth and eighteenth centuries.

How did the motives and characteristics of the sojourner conform to or diverge from those of the settler? Both utilized the same communications media and transportation facilities, both developed overseas networks that influenced the timing and location of their emigration, and both struggled to reconcile harsh realities with overblown images. But there were also significant differences. Temporary emigrants – at least, those who emigrated for economic reasons – were probably characterized by a more speculative and detached approach than their counterparts who put down permanent roots overseas. Many of them were young men, either bachelors or married men whose dependants had stayed at home. Their focus remained very much on Scotland, and wages were either remitted home or saved against their ultimate return. Their expectations were higher, and they were often more impatient for quick and substantial returns than permanent settlers, who judged success and failure by longer-term, and perhaps more modest, criteria. Since they did not anticipate putting down roots, sojourners were also more likely to be found in climatically inhospitable or socially undeveloped regions, provided the economic prospects were favourable for exploitation, than those who had invested their entire future in relocation overseas. But it was probably in the long-term consequences of sojourning, particularly the repatriation of capital, labour and ideas, that the difference was most marked. However long they stayed, or however many times they returned to the same location, sojourners were transient visitors, not committed home-makers and nation-builders, and while they undoubtedly stamped their presence on their host societies in a variety of ways, the most lasting legacy of their overseas experience was generally the application of its fruits to their places of origin in Scotland.

Plantation life

Sojourning did not suddenly become a feature of Scottish emigration in the nineteenth century. We have already seen that long-standing European connections were overtaken after 1700 by a growing focus on the American continent, as middle-class career emigrants, frustrated by limited horizons at home, flocked to the southern mainland colonies and the Caribbean. Most did not intend to stay for good, but hoped to exploit lucrative openings in the Chesapeake tobacco industry or the sugar plantations of the West Indies, generating income for profitable investment back in Scotland. To buy a colonial estate yielding a steady return was regarded as a legitimate stepping stone to the ultimate, and more prestigious, acquisition of land in Scotland, and up to 10,000 ambitious Scots may have sojourned in these plantation colonies in the second half of the eighteenth century. While those who went to the Chesapeake were generally involved in tobacco factoring and storekeeping for merchant houses in Glasgow, the Caribbean provided more varied openings in conjunction with possibly greater physical and ethical challenges. Doctors, lawyers, merchant-planters and estate managers in Jamaica, Antigua and the Windward Islands of Grenada, Dominica, St Vincent and Tobago sometimes struggled to reconcile their image of professional integrity not only with the temptations of the flesh and the bottle but also with their ambition to bring home a fortune as quickly as possible before their health gave way. In both locations the Scots cultivated complex transatlantic patronage networks which fostered a sense of ethnic solidarity and – by maintaining clear links with the homeland – reduced the likelihood of assimilation.

Caribbean capital had a more diffused impact on agriculture and industry across Scotland than the profits of the tobacco trade, which were invested primarily in and around Glasgow. By the end of the eighteenth century 'the great influx of money from the East and West Indies' had contributed markedly to the 'increasing prosperity' of Inverness, while at Logie Pert in the county of Forfar 'there is an increase both of splendour and luxury in many places of the neighbourhood, occasioned chiefly by the influx of wealth from the East and West Indies'. At least two landowners in the Kincardineshire parish of Fetteresso had, on returning from the West Indies, invested in substantial new dwelling houses, as well as agricultural improvements, while 'several young men of spirit' who had gone to the Caribbean from Kells in Kirkcudbright had reappeared after sixteen or seventeen years, 'with genteel fortunes'.[2] In the early nineteenth century the Gordons of Buthlaw applied Jamaican revenue to land purchases which made them one of Aberdeenshire's largest landowning families, while the Baillies of Inverness achieved a similar status in the west Highlands by the 1830s, investing their Caribbean money in the improvement and extension of their estates, as well as diversifying into the business and political sectors. In Argyllshire the Malcolms of Poltalloch used profits from their Jamaican enterprises to improve their properties between the 1780s and the late 1840s, while in the vicinity of Glasgow merchants with Caribbean interests frequently invested in the processing of cotton and sugar, the products on which many of their fortunes were based. West Indian money was also channelled into Scottish educational and philanthropic ventures, further reflecting the attitude of the donors that the Caribbean was a place of short-term sojourn rather than a new home in which to put down roots.[3]

But by no means all who went to the plantations succeeded in making and repatriating fortunes. In the mainland American colonies growing resentment of foreign moneylenders culminated in the wholesale expulsion of Scottish loyalists in 1776. Many returned to Scotland empty-handed, and after the American Revolution they received minimal compensation for their loyalism. The obituary columns of the Scottish press testify to the rapidity and frequency with which sojourners in the Caribbean succumbed to tropical diseases, while those who did earn enough money to purchase large estates and numerous slaves discovered that these assets could not always be translated into the acquisition of land in Scotland, where the economy was expanding rapidly and land values were rising beyond their calculations. Paradoxically, the more successful the sojourners became, the greater the difficulty they experienced in extricating their fortunes, and some became permanent settlers by default, repeatedly postponing their return in pursuit of ever-expanding but elusive ambitions.

The abolition of slavery in the British Caribbean between 1834 and 1840 and the accompanying economic dislocation rendered the islands a less attractive prospect for Scottish investors. Some sought to replace the slaves with wage labourers recruited at home, either as permanent settlers or under indentures reminiscent of the recruitment of artisans in the eighteenth century, while advertisements for plantation overseers, governesses and tutors also appeared occasionally in the Scottish press. In 1836 John Anderson, an Edinburgh lawyer, called on the patronage of the Colonial Secretary, Lord Glenelg, to secure the position of Special Magistrate in St Vincent, with responsibility for adjudicating disputes between former slaves and their masters during the transitional 'apprenticeship' period. When he was killed in a riding accident three years later, the Colonial Office defrayed the return fare of his wife and family to Scotland, where they took up residence in Inverness. During his brief sojourn in St Vincent Anderson kept a journal which reflects the difficulties of implementing meaningful manumission in a context where even liberal abolitionists like himself continued to assume the servility of the former slave. It also declaims against the vulgarity and depravity of West Indian society which made the Caribbean a place to sojourn rather than settle, lamenting – among other evils – the general absence of civilized society:

He who treads these Western shores, will soon be reminded he has parted with
them, to be a denizen of a land, where discomfort & luxury; where desolation &
hospitality, oddly assort. The badly paved, or metaled dirty streets, where
broken bottles, – hoops of iron, & other rubbish lie huddled before the doors;
the mean appearance of the low roofed stores, and huckster shops; – the
defaced, & mouldering houses; the naked appearance of the planked, uncovered
floors & walls of even the best and inhabited tenements; – whether in town or
country, the scanty & illkept furniture; – the rarely seen objects of books or
musical instruments; – the barefooted, shirted menials; – bring in painful contrast to the recollection, all the harmonised comforts of home! word, sacred
even here; where the Planters would fain have no abiding spot, – but still yearn
at some distant day for that 'home' they recognize only over the blue Atlantick.

While genteel emigrants would find that 'the life of a planter at the best, is but
an apology for life', for the 'sensitive European female' the sense of desolation
and imprisonment was even greater, so that it was little wonder, declared
Anderson, that she 'lolls on a settee all day long … [and] vegetates a death of
life'.[4]

Some of those who sojourned in the Caribbean moved on to other overseas
pastures before returning to Scotland. As we saw earlier, Robert Boyd Tytler,
who was initially sent from Aberdeenshire to Jamaica in 1834 to serve an apprenticeship on a family friend's sugar plantation, removed three years later to
Ceylon, where his name became a household word in both commercial and political circles. Having established a family dynasty among the island's planters, he
retired to Aberdeen to enjoy the fruits of a labour which had made him pre-
eminent among the island's pioneer planters. He was not unique in cashing in his
return ticket. Many of the handsome granite mansions that sprang up in the city's
west end testified to fortunes made on eastern plantations, and in 1875 a dinner of
planters and ex-planters held in Aberdeen in Tytler's honour attracted over 100
men, half of whom had current or past commercial connections with Ceylon. All
were well-to-do, according to one of those who attended, and 'thoroughly enjoy-
ing a well-earned furlough. The Lord Provost congratulated us, and drank continued prosperity to coffee, whilst some of us waxed eloquent in declaring our
implicit faith that, so long as heather grew on Benachie, coffee and Scotsmen too
would thrive on the hills of Ceylon.'[5] Although, even as those words were being
uttered, Ceylon's coffee industry was being brought to its knees by the double
blow of a destructive fungus and the increasing popularity of the healthier

Brazilian product, many planters simply switched their attention to tea, which in turn provided a comfortable income for these Scottish career-emigrants well into the twentieth century.

The corn chest for Scotland?

Scottish sojourners' connections with the Indian subcontinent were not confined to plantation investments. Two of Robert Tytler's brothers were in the service of the East India Company well before he went to Ceylon, and many Company officers bought plantations on the island during the first coffee mania in the 1830s and 1840s. In the eighteenth century the expanding East India Company had become a rich source of patronage for soldiers and administrators, well before 1784, when Henry Dundas, Scottish Solicitor-General and first Senior Commissioner of the Company's Board of Control, dispensed Indian appointments liberally to those who were prepared to pay the political price for such favours. Even in the era of Warren Hastings, India had become, in Sir Walter Scott's memorable words of a later date, 'the corn chest for Scotland', a place where the younger sons of the Scottish gentry and merchant classes sought their fortunes, as well as a field of service for recently created Highland regiments. Successful soldiers sometimes moved on to political, administrative or commercial careers, but whatever their employment, and however long they stayed in India, most Scots kept their eyes firmly fixed on the homeland, to which they intended to return. Like their counterparts in the Caribbean, many of them anticipated that their eastern fortunes would purchase not only landed estates but also the accompanying social prestige which would have eluded them if they had stayed at home. Many achieved their goal, and the Scottish landscape is dotted with reminders of the Indian connection. Looming 1,500 feet above the village of Evanton in Easter Ross is the Fyrish monument. Commissioned by Sir Hector Munro of Novar in 1792 to relieve local unemployment, it was intended to be a replica of the temple gate at Negapatnam, the scene of one of Munro's greatest victories during his military service in India. On the other side of the Moray Firth, over £90,000 of Indian capital was invested in the town of Elgin between 1815 and 1924, when Dr Gray's Hospital and the Anderson Institute were founded on the bequests of local men who had made fortunes in India. Meanwhile, in Aberdeenshire the Bombay free merchant John Forbes (1743–1821) bought back his ancestral estates in Strathdon, where he poured large sums of money into the development of agriculture and forestry, as well as leaving £10,000 to Aberdeen Royal Infirmary.[6]

The image of India as an El Dorado for the enterprising Scot persisted throughout the nineteenth century, fuelled by the exotic tales of those who returned with fortunes to invest or – more realistically – by continuing opportunities in the military and civil service. By the 1850s the prospect of fortune-making had been rendered negligible by much stricter regulation of East India Company servants' independent trading activities, and by the transformation of the Company from a mercantile to a largely administrative organization. If, however, the curtailment of opportunities for freebooting had rendered Scottish nabobs something of an anachronism, it still remained commonplace for ambitious young Scots to flock to India as soldiers, surgeons and civil servants in the vast imperial bureaucracy that increasingly enveloped the subcontinent.

Yet India had an ambivalent impact on the Scottish psyche, for, as contemporary commentators emphasized, it posed threats as well as provided opportunities, and was often a place of violence and tragedy, where dreams and illusions were shattered rather than fulfilled. Certainly, neither Sir Walter Scott nor his contemporary John Galt highlighted the attractions of the Orient when they touched on the subject in two novels in the 1820s; on the contrary, both were preoccupied with the corruption and immorality induced by the unrestrained ambition that characterized many nabobs and would-be nabobs, and none of their fictional emigrants was enriched by the Indian experience. The tone of Scott's novel *The Surgeon's Daughter* (1827) was set by the narrator's preface, in which those who went to India were portrayed as a 'gallant caste of adventurers, who laid down their consciences at the Cape of Good Hope as they went out to India, and forgot to take them up again when they returned'.[7] The villain of his novel, Richard Middlemas, having been duped by a fraudulent recruiting agent into enlisting in an East India Company regiment, resorted to murder and treachery as part of a complex plan to restore his fortunes and win Bangalore for the Company. By the time he died under the hoofs of a ceremonial elephant, he had blighted the lives of all around him, notably his fiancée, who returned to Scotland to live in sad seclusion after a series of Indian misadventures sparked off by Middlemas's betrayal of her trust.

John Galt, like Scott, had mixed feelings about emigration. While on the one hand he claimed that 'every man of sense and talent seeks his fortune abroad, and leaves only the incapable and those who are conscious of their deficiencies at home',[8] he was concerned at the ruthless acquisitiveness of many who returned to flaunt their wealth. He too used the medium of fiction to demonstrate the damaging effects on Scottish society of Indian riches unfairly won and unwisely spent. Malachi Mailings and Mr Rupees, the main characters in his novel *The Last of the Lairds* (1826) epitomize the conflict between the old Scotland of traditional values, where probity and a good name counted for more than possessions, and the brash new Scotland whose commercial priorities were inextricably linked with burgeoning overseas enterprise. At first Mailings, the laird of Auldbiggings, managed to thwart Rupees, who had returned from India determined to buy his way into the landed gentry:

> Ye see, when Mr Rupees the Nawbub came hame frae Indy, and bought the Arunthrough property frae the Glaikies, who, like sae mony ithers o' the right stock o' legitimate gentry, hae been smothered out o' sight by the weed and nettle overgrowths o' merchandise and cotton-weavry, he would fain hae bought Auldbiggings likewise, and sent that gett o' the deil and the law, Caption, to make me an offer; but I was neither a prodigal son nor an Esau, to sell my patrimony for a mess o' pottage, so I gied him a flea in his lug, and bade him tell the Nawbob to chew the cud o' the sin of covetousness, the whilk is disappointment.[9]

But after Mailings had been tricked into borrowing money from Rupees, he faced the threat of losing his entire estate to his avaricious and flamboyant creditor when Rupees called in the loans, leaving the reader with the clear message that, while Mailings may have won a series of moral battles, he and his contemporaries were losing the war against the encroachment of wealth without responsibility represented by Rupees and his ilk.

It was not only in fiction that the high hopes of an Indian sojourn could turn sour. In 1975 the University of Aberdeen was bequeathed 'the diaries, papers, pictures, letters, swords, chests, instruments and medals relating to the family of Chalmers'.[10] Hidden in that bequest is an absorbing tale, not only of adventure and tragedy in the Indian Empire around the time of the Mutiny, but also of the networks of Aberdeen-based patronage, friendship and chain migration which sustained and enlivened the overseas sojourns of a significant number of the sons of north-east Scotland in that era.

'Mamma must not give way, but remember that we have all promised to come back rich Nabobs, or at least with half a dozen Medals of which she shall be proud,' wrote John Chalmers to his father in 1857.[11] As sons of a leading public figure in Scotland's third city, John and his brothers were well placed to set foot on a more solid – if potentially less rewarding – Indian career ladder than had been available in the era of Henry Dundas. Their father, Alexander Wallace Chalmers, was for thirty-seven years governor of the Bridewell and East Prisons, Aberdeen. His marriage to Mary Jamson, the daughter of a local shipmaster, produced two daughters and then five sons, three of whom pursued careers in the military wing of the East India Company. Like many of their contemporaries, two of the Chalmers brothers undertook preliminary academic training at the city's Marischal College, the records of which are peppered with the names of men – the sons of merchants and tradesmen, as well as those of the gentry and professional classes – who found military, medical and administrative careers in the East India Company. This trend continued after the fusion in 1860 of the two Aberdeen colleges, Marischal and King's, into the University of Aberdeen, which during the first twenty years of its existence produced 458 graduates who worked abroad at some stage in their careers, mainly in India. They included seventy-seven recruits to the Indian army, fifteen missionaries and twelve civil servants, as well as seventy-nine men who joined the Indian medical service, eleven of them in 1865 alone.[12]

While Mary Chalmers may have been proud of the medals bestowed on two of her sons, she must surely have bewailed the cost at which they were won, for the history of the Chalmers family was repeatedly punctuated by premature death. First to succumb was the eldest boy, Richard, a civil engineer and the only son to remain in Scotland, who died in Aberdeen in 1852, aged twenty-three. Six years later twenty-five-year-old Samuel succumbed to brain fever at Calcutta, and was buried in the military cemetery at Bhowanipore. John, who, like Samuel, was awarded the India Mutiny Medal, was invalided home in 1860 and died in Wales also aged twenty-five, less than a year later. William too was invalided home from service as an assistant surgeon in India, and died of consumption in 1863, at the age of twenty-nine, while Alexander, a chief engineer in the Royal Navy, also fell victim to tuberculosis in 1868, three years after being invalided out of the service.

Samuel was the only one of the five Chalmers boys who did not attend Marischal College. His entry into the employment of the East India Company differed from that of his brothers in other ways too, since it took place for reasons of expediency rather than ambition, and under a cloud of unidentified disgrace that he felt barred his ultimate return home. After working as a druggist in Aberdeen, Sam left in February 1854 to seek greener pharmaceutical pastures in London, armed with a testimonial of competence from his employer and a somewhat unenthusiastic character reference from his minister, given more as a favour to Sam's father than out of any high regard for the son himself. Perhaps these doubts were justified, for after writing home regularly during his first four months in London, Sam then fell silent for a year, until May 1855, when he wrote to his mother from Bengal, where he had sailed under an assumed name. 'Look on me only as a pecuniary exile,' he urged her, in a veiled reference to the financial misdemeanours that had probably led to his hasty departure:

> I have no intention of recalling to myself scenes that are past and gone, and which cannot be amended now, but merely consider it my duty ... to let you know that, however unfortunate I may have been in my native country, fortune is smiling on me in this one abundantly ... I have played the part of the prodigal, no doubt, but after all it was more misfortune than fault ... Keep my being in India a secret, not that I care a pin, but then it is just as well that people don't know. I may only expect to be pestered with Bills etc.[13]

Unlike most of the 'unfortunates' who shared his 'dreadful passage', he had secured employment. Having enlisted in the East India Company's artillery, he was one of a draft of recruits sent from Calcutta to Meerut, where he was appointed an assistant in the Indian Telegraph Department under Dr W. B. O'Shaughnessy, the Irish Superintendent of Electric Telegraphs in India. The medical officer in charge of the draft was William Watson, the son of Aberdeen's distinguished sheriff, who honoured Sam's request not to mention him in his letters home, but who passed on domestic news, including that of John Chalmers's imminent arrival in India.

Throughout his three years in India, Sam kept in regular communication with Watson, who on one occasion nursed him through a dangerous attack of cholera contracted in Agra. 'It is an awful thing,' he wrote to his mother while convalescing, 'to be sick in India among natives, who care no more for you than a Dog; yet I have every reason to be thankful for having been cast among dear friends in the hour of my afflictions.' Chief among those friends were William Watson and another Aberdonian, Dr Farquhar, with whom he could also share 'old school anecdotes' and speak 'broad Scotch'.[14] Equally kind to him were two other acquaintances of his parents, Dr and Mrs J. P. Walker, with whom on one occasion, still convalescing, he enjoyed a rare 'taste of home ... a splendid dinner and tea, and then Mrs Walker favoured me with a selection of Scotch songs, and while she sang and played the piano, the Dr and I gave chorus'.[15]

The preservation of links with home and family meant a great deal to Sam, who wrote to his parents at least once a month, as well as to his brother John in the Punjab. Although the brothers never met in India, they clearly looked after each other's financial and career interests. 'What is mine is his and that his is mine is an agreement we have formed till we get wives,' wrote Sam to his parents in 1857, by which time he evidently anticipated that his exile would not be permanent, for he continued, 'Don't mourn for us, we are both well and happy, and hope soon again to see you.'[16] They maintained and exploited links with the Aberdeenshire community, which in Agra included not only Watson, Farquhar and the Walkers, but also Dr Murray from Peterhead, who was Farquhar's superior, and Dr Clarke from Ballater, the Acting Postmaster General, whose assistance John Chalmers tried unsuccessfully to secure in having Sam appointed to a more remunerative post in his department. The brothers also kept a finger on the pulse of events at home by regular scrutiny of the *Aberdeen Herald*, sent out by their parents and also circulated among the Aberdeenshire exiles. 'We enjoy the papers much,' Sam told his father in 1856, just as his parents in Aberdeen perused the Indian press keenly, exchanged news with neighbours whose sons were also in India, and put new recruits in touch with their own boys.[17]

As the first member of the Chalmers family to go to India, Sam often imparted advice and information to his younger brothers who followed in his footsteps. 'Always sleep with your drawers on,' he instructed John, when the latter arrived in Calcutta in 1855, courtesy of a Company cadetship gifted by a former rector of Marischal College. Sam – who frequently assured his parents that their youngest son was a first-rate scholar who would 'turn out a great Officer if he is spared'[18] – also recommended that John enhance his chances of promotion and good remuneration by learning Hindustani, 'because he cannot get charge of a Native Regt. until he passes an examination on it, and moreover he gets 1000 Rupees as a gift of the Company if he speaks well'.[19] When William Chalmers – who in 1855 was pursuing a commercial career in Edinburgh and Glasgow – sought Sam's advice about openings in India, the response was qualified. While on the one hand 'situations here are as thick as mites in a cheese', and the rapidly expanding railway network in particular offered numerous remunerative openings, on the other hand Sam reminded his brother that there was 'no place like home', advising him to bide his time and not rush out to India prematurely. 'Don't let yourself believe I don't want you out here,' he continued. 'I shd be very glad of it, but it is a long road to come on chance and maybe be disappointed.'[20] Nine months later, by which time William had returned to

Aberdeen to study medicine at Marischal College, Sam was still ambivalent in his encouragement, perhaps because his brush with death was still fresh in his mind: 'Tell Bill to grind away, and that there is a good field for him yet in India, but if he can do well where he is, to stay. Rupees are tempting, but think of Cholera. A man of talent should not be in India.'[21] By December, however, he was more optimistic, urging his brother to 'Go ahead as you are doing, and a Superintending Surgeoncy may be yours yet in India'.[22]

Like many emigrants all over the world, Sam Chalmers's opinions of India fluctuated according to his health and circumstances. In September 1855 he succumbed to an attack of fever, along with a fit of depression and homesickness:

> I suppose you will wonder what sort of a place this India really is, and form I have no doubt very fine ideas regarding it, but alas, how miserable is the reality, for in two lines I can picture India to you from the Cape to the Himalayas as one vast semi-cultivated plain covered with Mud Houses not one built straight, and the inhabitants beggars living many of them in filth and hardly a rag to cover their bodies. When you see two miles of India and one village, you may say you have seen it all. Meerut, Delhi, Agra, Lahore, Benares are no doubt fine-looking places at a distance and because there are Europeans there, but give me my choice and Scotland for me. I am now in what is considered a dangerous part of India. The mail is frequently robbed here and the men murdered; and 25 miles from this there is a place where they lately looked on it as sport, to knock one another's heads off as an offering to their gods, but the Govt has put a stop to it. I go to bed with my cudgel and gun every night, independent of a Guard outside, but they are blacks, and as they are not Company's Sepoys and very corpulent, I don't much fancy their protection.[23]

By November, however, when he had recovered his health and spirits, he believed that his decision to come to India was 'a dispensation of Providence fraught with good to me', for 'no man cd be more comfortable or better off than I am at present'.[24] His contentment was short-lived. Although initially happy to be transferred to Seepree in January 1856 at increased pay, he soon found the work so hard, the food so unpalatable and the inspector of his division so hostile that in April he requested a transfer to Agra and from there to the Punjab. By this time he was determined to purchase his discharge from the army and resume his previous occupation as a druggist, perhaps prompted by his encounter with a son of the Thurso manse who, having run away from home to military service, had 'at least freed himself of that yoke', succeeded in business and 'assured me could any day go home with 30,000 hard cash'.[25]

In fact Sam Chalmers never left the service of the Indian Telegraph Department. By April 1857 John had purchased his brother's discharge and, with the help of Dr Walker, Dr Clarke of the Post Office and another Scot, the Reverend John Milne of Calcutta, secured his admission to a three-year course at Calcutta Medical College, 'with a view to obtaining a Sub-Assistant Surgeoncy'.[26] But Sam's plans were thwarted when he became caught up in the events of the Mutiny, during which he was present at the siege of Delhi. 'I cannot describe to you the scenes I have been an eye-witness of during the past five months,' he wrote to his father on 18 October 1857:

> The account furnished in newspapers is a mere shadow of the reality. I came inside the city on the 17th, three days after the attack, but it was not to view the Delhi I saw last year; it was to cast my eyes on a heap of ruins, deserted houses, starving inhabitants, and putrid corpses of man and beast. Misery was the watchword. Plundering went on to a terrible extent, shops and goods of all descriptions blocked up the roads, and here and there dead Sepoys. Not a European house is fit to be occupied, they were burned to the ground. Shall I reveal to you the horrors of the 8th, 10th and 11th of June? Ladies butchered at the breakfast table, children torn from their mothers arms and dashed upon the flags, husbands tied to the wall and saw their wives ravished, spat upon, vivisected, and had their throats cut, maddened Sepoys rushing here and there and calling for the Europeans to come out and be tortured.[27]

Although Sam made his way to Calcutta in 1858, his health was broken and he died on 14 August 1858, just as his brother was promoted to an assistant commissionership in the Punjab, at an enhanced salary which John had earmarked to help finance Sam's medical studies.

John Chalmers, like Sam, made the acquaintance of several fellow Scots during his five years in India. When he arrived in Calcutta in December 1855 the Reverend John Milne, at the request of his friend Alexander Wallace Chalmers, took the newly arrived recruit under his wing and recommended him to his commanding officer before he was posted to the 39th Native Infantry at Jehlum in the Punjab. Acutely aware that India was 'a dangerous country for soul as well as for body', Milne – who returned to Perth in 1858 – felt that 'parents at home do not know what they are sending their children to, when they rejoice at getting them into the Civil or Military Services', and he reminded Alexander Chalmers of the continuing importance of patronage if John was to succeed. 'You must,' he urged, 'try to interest any influential friends at home in his behalf.'[28] During his time at Jehlum, where his house-mate and almost all the officers were also Scots, John studied hard for the language qualification which would open up the adjutancy of his regiment. Like Sam, he also enlisted the help of his fellow Aberdonian Dr Walker, whose powerful connections could smooth the way to such an appointment, and he was more consistently optimistic than Sam that India was still a rewarding outlet for Scottish sojourners. 'In two or three short years,' he wrote encouragingly to William in 1856, 'we three shall stretch our legs under the same mahogany table in some part of the Gorgeous East.' He frequently encouraged William to persist in his studies, not least because of the promise of a Company salary of at least £60 a month, coupled with the prospect of being able to retire on a pension of £500 after seventeen years' service. Subsequently, however, he advised William to enlist in a royal regiment which, while it did not offer such a good retiring allowance, would not exile him for so long to a country which he might not like.[29]

By 1858 John's optimism had been shattered, first of all by the severe arm wound he sustained during the Mutiny and then by Sam's death, which plunged him into depression and sharpened his desire to return to the bosom of his family. 'Everything in this country seems changed to me, and I hope only for the day when I may rejoin you all at home,' he wrote to his sister in November 1858.[30] The passage of time did not alleviate his homesickness. A year later, attributing his tardiness in writing home to ongoing grief at his brother's death, he explained, 'Home is a subject of contemplation I generally avoid. It brings up painful memories, & excites vain wishes of return.'[31] Correspondence with an acquaintance who, 'like everyone else here regrets the hour he came to India' reinforced his disillusionment with the 'Gorgeous East'[32] and, like Sam, he was acutely aware of the way in which an Indian sojourn accelerated the ageing process. Although John was not due a furlough until 1865, he was invalided home in 1860 after an unsuccessful attempt to recuperate in Kashmir, aiming to return to his post – passage paid – after fifteen months. It was not to be, for he died in Wales in August 1861, in straitened circumstances and still struggling to obtain the arrears of pay from his Indian sojourn.

William had the shortest Indian career of all three Chalmers brothers. After completing his studies, he followed John's advice and became an army surgeon, on the grounds that the reorganized East India Company was no longer such an attractive proposition:

> I rather think that the days of having any chance of civil employ in India are gone, as I see by the papers that the Power has been taken from the East India Coy, and conferred upon one of the Secretarys of State … Therefore, the pay of a Medical Officer in John Co's Service unless much increased will never counterbalance the disadvantages of the £300 out of pocket for outfit and passage, and such a number of years of exile. Compare with that the 10/- of a day now given in the Queen's Service, the small outlay for outfit, for the passage money to India alone wd fit a man out for the Queen's, besides his drawing pay within a few days after passing, instead of a few months, as in John Coy's. Such being the case, you can hardly wonder at my having changed my mind in regard to which Service I am to honour with my talents. And besides all the above, Jack is a Company's Officer, Alick is a Queen's Naval one, and I think I cant do better than become a Queen's Army man; and thus the family will be pretty well divided among the different Arms of War, as they are called.[33]

After working briefly in England, William was posted to India in 1861. But just as Sam's death had taken the gilt off the attractions of the Orient, so John's death made William disillusioned and anxious to come home almost as soon as he had arrived. 'What a shock I got yesterday evening on reading at the Mess the English Telegraphic News and finding that Poor Johnny had died,' he wrote to his father on 11 September. 'How I hated these niggers before and now it will be a deeper hatred. I can't settle to anything since and shall write by next mail.'[34] Although his father thought it 'not likely that you will be allowed to return after so short a sojourn',[35] William was to get his wish sooner than he expected, like his brother, on the grounds of ill-health. By December 1862 he was back in London, from where he wrote a last letter to his aunt, asking her to find cheap lodgings for him in Aberdeen. 'Don't be alarmed, it is only I wish to be amongst you,' he reassured her, less than a month before he died.[36]

William's death brought to a close the Chalmers's futile efforts to 'come back rich nabobs'. For all three brothers, sickness had been a constant concomitant of life in India, and their experiences provided a solemn reminder of the risks, as well as the opportunities, of sojourning in a hostile environment. Equally notable is the way in which both Sam and John, who went overseas under very different circumstances, not only maintained strong links with home but also identified and exploited Aberdeenshire connections in India in their efforts to secure promotion, or, in Sam's case, a complete change of career. Like many other temporary emigrants, they demonstrate that the creation of ethnic networks was not the preserve of permanent settlers but extended to sojourners, who, it could be argued, found them an even more vital lifeline if they had only a limited period in which to make their mark, or, more ambitiously, their fortune.

Arctic adventures

Many Indian sojourners returned home after a single prolonged spell overseas. By contrast, those who pursued their careers in the equally inhospitable Arctic, either as whalers or in the service of the Hudson's Bay Company, were more commonly episodic emigrants, the former coming and going annually and the latter usually undertaking a series of five-year sojourns in the north. In the eighteenth century over thirty ports, mainly in England, had sent vessels to the Greenland Sea and the Davis Strait in pursuit of the Greenland Right Whale. By the 1830s, however, falling prices, combined with a series of disastrous seasons, had caused many of them to drop out of the business and by 1849 Hull was the only English port still involved in whaling. The more tenacious and adaptable Scots, meanwhile, continued to send vessels to the Arctic, but alternated whale fishing and seal hunting as conditions dictated. These industries were centred on north-east Scotland, particularly on Peterhead, which soon became Britain's leading whaling port, in 1857 sending out over half the entire British whaling fleet. One native of the town, born in 1853, later recalled that in his childhood as many as thirty-three whaling and sealing ships had left Peterhead each spring, providing work not only at sea but also in the shore-based activities of shipbuilding and sailmaking and in the rendering yards.

This picture of Peterhead in the 1850s and 1860s was recalled sixty years later by David Cardno, no casual observer but a lifelong diarist and by the 1920s a veteran of numerous journeys to the Arctic. He was only thirteen when he made his first trip in 1866, after stowing away on the *Lord Saltoun*. To stow away successfully on Arctic whaling vessels was, he recalled, the ambition of almost every small boy in Peterhead in the 1850s, and some straight talking from his mother after he had failed in two previous attempts did nothing to alter his resolve. His grandfather and father were both second mates of whaling ships, and his father, who had sailed with the *Lord Saltoun* in 1865, had remained in the

Arctic at the end of the season to manage one of the whaling stations in Cumberland Sound. David's desire to be reunited with his father made him all the more determined to succeed, and so on 14 June 1866, instead of going to school, he directed his steps towards the harbour, dropped his redundant schoolbooks into the revolving bucket of a dredger and concealed himself in a barrel aboard the *Lord Saltoun*. There he remained, undetected, during the customary search for stowaways, and only when the ship was well out to sea did he make himself known, as hunger got the better of him. The captain's first reaction was to put him ashore at Orkney and have him sent straight home, but the ship's owner, who was on board, interceded on David's behalf when he heard that the boy had stowed away in order to join his father. As a result David Cardno was given his first job on a whaling vessel, that of ship's boy, launching an Arctic career that was to continue for more than half a century.

It was not long before the new recruit was exposed to the dangers and discomforts of the Arctic. On its way up the Davis Strait the ship became trapped in ice for ten days, during which time it only just escaped destruction by an iceberg. When disaster seemed imminent the captain ordered all the whaleboats to be unlashed and hauled on to the ice, clear of the imprisoned ship. Provisions and men were allocated to each boat and the crew watched as the iceberg bulldozed along the port side of the *Lord Saltoun*, tearing away part of the stern, davits, bulwarks and about twelve feet of sail. But the damage was not irretrievable and the carpenters immediately set to work to make repairs before the ice broke. Having spent a fruitless few weeks hunting, the ship was then forced to winter in Niantilik harbour in Cumberland Sound after the ice barrier closed early. There David had his first encounter with the Inuit, who gathered at the whaling stations and worked for the visiting Scottish and American ships. As well as joining in baseball games on the ice with the crews of six other Scottish and American whaling vessels, he made friends with an Inuit family who lived on Niantilik Island and spent much of his free time in their company, tobogganing with their children and sharing their food:

> We got a skin from their Mother and we had some great fun going up to the top
> of the hill, and laid the skin down on the snow and sat down on the skin, and we
> did come down that hill with some speed – our faces used to be covered with
> loose snow, the rate we came down. I may say I was nearly as much in their
> house as I was in the ship. When the father came home at night there was always
> a pan of boiled seal ready for him, so I came in for my share just the same as their

own two, and I was picking up a word or two of their lingo, and when I felt very hungry I used to go to other Igloos on Niantilik Island, as all the natives nearby lived there that was engaged to the ships. After we had dinner if there was any soup left, I got [it] from the cook into a beef tin and took it ashore and gave it to the children, and they did think a lot of that, as they are very fond of all our meats.[37]

But an Arctic winter was by no means all fun and games. Since the *Lord Saltoun* had been provisioned only for the autumn fishing, the captain put all crew members on to half-rations as soon as it became clear that the ship would be detained, but by January supplies had become so depleted that six crew members and four Inuit had to be sent on a dangerous fifty-mile trek across the ice to Kekerten Island Station to replenish stocks. The outward trip was made without incident, but on the way back one of the Peterhead men went missing from the sledge. When he was found by the others several hours later he was in a state of collapse, badly frostbitten and unable to speak. He was taken back to the supply station, where the cooper used his seal knife to saw off both feet, without the luxury of an anaesthetic. A worse fate was to befall James Kynoch and James Reid, two other crewmen from the *Lord Saltoun*, who were sent on a second expedition to Kekerten before the first party had returned. Accompanied by an Inuit couple and their young son, the men set off by sledge, but when they were just over halfway to their destination, the weather deteriorated and the Scots soon became exhausted. The native couple constructed an igloo, where they left Kynoch and Reid, along with their own son, while they struggled on and reached Kekerten. But the weather then worsened still further, and during the next ten days, when it was impossible to mount a rescue mission, it became clear that once the trio's small supply of stove oil ran out, it was only a matter of time before they froze to death. In fact, the bodies were not discovered until the following summer, lying huddled together, several feet down, in clear ice.

The *Lord Saltoun* returned empty-handed to Peterhead in August 1867. David Cardno had not been deterred by the hardships of his fourteen-month inaugural voyage, and in 1868 he again signed on as a ship's boy on the same vessel. During that trip he had his first experience of helping to capture one of the four whales killed during the voyage, and during the next few years he served regularly on whaling and sealing vessels. The constant hazards of the whaler's life meant that much of his journal was taken up with gruesome descriptions of accidents, many of which occurred as the whalers, in twenty-five-feet rowing boats, pursued a quarry that could be sixty feet long and weigh 100 tons. For most of the nineteenth century, however, the profits of whaling outweighed the risks, as oil from the blubber continued to be used as an illuminant, lubricant and ingredient in soap, while whalebone was in demand for corsets, umbrellas and a variety of other goods.

David Cardno's last voyage as an active member of a whaling crew was in 1898. He then spent four years at herring fishing and trawling, followed by a spell as a barge skipper engaged in harbour construction at Peterhead. But the lure of the Arctic was too strong, and in 1910 he accepted an offer to manage Kekerten Island Station, supervising the seal-hunting activities of the Inuit and the storage of the skins until the return of the storeship. His first tour was uneventful, but in 1914 he returned to Kekerten for a second tour, with a year's provisions and the promise of a store ship in the spring. No such ship arrived, and for the next three years he was forced to exist on a diet of seal meat and venison, the only European among 300 Inuit, completely unaware of the outbreak of the First World War. By the time he retired in 1923, the whaling industry had become little more than a memory. Profits had dropped steadily in the face of competition from alternative products, and in 1893 the last whaling vessel had sailed out of Peterhead. For a while the industry survived in Dundee, where whale oil was still used to heat hemp in the jute mills, and most of Cardno's later voyages were made out of that port. But by 1913 only two whaling ships sailed from Dundee to the Arctic, and the First World War drove the final nail into the industry's coffin.

While whaling played a part in the life of ports such as Peterhead and Dundee, it was never the crucial hinge of the local economy. Further north, in the Orkney islands, it was a more significant source of employment and income, recruiting an average of about 500 men a year in the 1840s. But it was the Arctic fur trade that provided perhaps the most vital and enduring lifeline to many communities in the Northern and Western Isles, as Scots came to dominate the ranks of both the North West Company and the Hudson's Bay Company in the eighteenth century. Chartered in 1670, the Hudson's Bay Company soon became one of the largest and most consistent employers of Scottish sojourners, whom it regarded as 'submissive and industrious'. Orkney was initially a fertile recruiting ground, not least because until 1891 Stromness was the last port of call for outgoing Company ships and the base of an agent who received a commission on each employee engaged. As the minister of St Andrews and Deerness explained in the *Statistical Account*, the Hudson's Bay Company began to recruit in Orkney in the 1740s, and by the end of the century it engaged up to 100 islanders a year. Around three-quarters of its 400–500 men in the field were Orcadians, 'as they find them more sober and tractable than the Irish, and they engage for lower wages than either the English or Irish'.[38]

From 1783 until 1821 the Hudson's Bay Company was challenged by the Montreal-based North West Company, which was described by one English pedlar as being 'overrun with Scotchmen'. Operating initially as a loose federation of traders who swarmed across the Canadian wilderness and solicited furs from the Indians, its approach necessitated a similar response from its rival, which until then had adopted the more passive policy of establishing bases on Hudson's Bay, to which the Indian trappers brought their furs. Increasing rivalry culminated in a bloody battle in 1816, five years after Lord Selkirk, backed by the Hudson's Bay Company, had purchased the huge Red River tract, intruding into the North West Company's territories and threatening its pemmican supplies. In 1821 the rivals amalgamated in what was effectively a defeat for the North West Company, although it did bring valuable wilderness survival skills to the enlarged Hudson's Bay Company, which now controlled vast territories stretching from the shores of Hudson's Bay to the Pacific coast.

Scots continued to dominate the new company throughout the nineteenth century. The most notable – indeed notorious – character was George Simpson. Born on the wrong side of the blanket in Lochbroom, Wester Ross, he joined the Hudson's Bay Company in 1820 and was immediately sent out to Athabasca, where he was pitched into the heat of the war between his employer and the North West Company. So skilfully did he conduct himself during the conflict that when hostilities ended he was appointed to govern the important Northern Department of the remodelled Hudson's Bay Company. In 1826 he added the Southern Department to his jurisdiction, presiding over the reorganization of the fur trade following the merger until his death in 1860, and being knighted for his services in 1841. No armchair governor, Simpson travelled extensively on regular trips of inspection, making epic canoe journeys to remote parts of the Company's domain, in order to assess conditions and requirements. These were not simply administrative reconnaissance trips. He also aimed to open up new regions of fur trading, in order to allow conservation in the older areas, and by the 1830s the Company had extended its activities much further north, along the eastern shore of Hudson's Bay itself, to Labrador, and to the west in the region of Great Bear Lake. As well as opening up new fur trading posts in the outback, Simpson was also gripped by the polar exploration mania, in particular

the challenge of being the first to discover the much sought-after Northwest
Passage between the Atlantic and the Pacific.

A workaholic who did not suffer fools gladly, Simpson's autocratic manner,
ruthless efficiency and Napoleon-like appearance led to him being dubbed 'The
Little Emperor of the Plains'. His 'Character Book', kept during the winter of
1831–2, is full of acerbic remarks about many of the eighty-eight clerks, whom he
clearly thought were a drain on the Company. He was particularly scathing about
Colin Robertson, 'a frothy trifling conceited man, who would starve in any other
Country and is perfectly useless here'. Having been apprenticed to his father's
trade of weaving in Perth, he was 'too lazy to live by his Loom, read Novels,
became Sentimental and fancied himself the hero of every tale of Romance that
passed through his hands'. After a brief spell in New York, he had found himself
in the service of the North West Company, but despite being dismissed, he had
reappeared on the books of the Hudson's Bay Company at the unusually old age
of fifty-five. Simpson clearly wished to bring his prolonged sojourn to an end:

> To the Fur Trade he is quite a Burden, and a heavy burden too, being a com-
> pound of folly and extravagance, and disarranging and throwing into confusion
> whatsoever he puts his hand to in the shape of business. The concern would gain
> materially by allowing him to enjoy his situation a thousand Miles distant from
> the scene of operations instead of being taxed with his nominal Services in the
> Country.[39]

Although George Simpson continued to recruit employees in northern Scotland, he preferred Lewismen to Orcadians, as he explained in his annual report
to the board in 1832:

> With regard to Servants, we beg to request that thirty Orkneymen … be sent
> out by the ship of next year. The Orkney servants we have lately had were
> weak, undersized, many of them Sickly and nearly the whole of them half
> starved in appearance so that for the two first years of their contracts many of
> them were ineffective. They are however generally speaking, quiet, orderly well
> behaved men. The Lewis islanders are preferable in many points of view, being
> strong hearty active and fit to be immediately employed on laborious service;
> but although steady well behaved and generally of a serious turn of mind, we
> find them exceedingly stubborn and difficult of management and so clannish
> that it is scarcely possible to deal with them singly. Under those circumstances

we are not desirous of having any more of them in the country than at present, and highlanders are equally objectionable from the same cause. I therefore beg leave to recommend that instructions be sent to your Honors' agent at Orkney, sufficiently early to enable him to make his selection before the Agents of the Davis Straits fisheries begin to engage these people.[40]

Simpson's reservations were not without effect, for whereas the Orkneys provided 88 per cent of the Northern Department's servants in 1830, the figure had dropped below 50 per cent by 1855, and recruits from Lewis outstripped Orcadians by the early 1870s.

Shortly before he died near Montreal in 1860, George Simpson corresponded with a countryman who was later to fill his shoes but who, unlike him, ultimately returned home. Donald Smith, who emigrated from Forres in 1838 with a letter of introduction to Simpson, is probably the best example of an enterprising sojourner who worked his way up through the ranks of the Company to its top office, progressing from a thirty-year isolation as a trader in the frozen wastes of Labrador to become not only governor of the Company from 1889 to 1914 but also one of the financial masterminds behind the construction of the Canadian Pacific Railway, a member of the Dominion Parliament and, in 1896, Canadian High Commissioner to Great Britain. Created Baron Strathcona and Mount Royal in 1897, he purchased an estate in Glencoe and was also a major benefactor of the University of Aberdeen.

Simpson and Smith were high-profile figures who rose to the highest echelons of the Hudson's Bay Company. Most servants, clerks and even the better-paid factors had a much more mundane and anonymous experience. The ideal employee, from the Company's perspective, was a young single man aged at least twenty-one. Youths were not thought to have reached their full strength, and married men, it was thought, were unlikely to renew their contracts after the end of the mandatory five-year contract. If the Company records showed that employees had been healthy, financially prudent and of good character during their first Arctic sojourn, the benefits of re-engagement, even at slightly increased wages, were reckoned to outweigh the risks and costs of recruiting new men. Despite the preference for young bachelors, many recruits were in fact married men who were beyond the first flush of youth. Some, like Orcadian Alexander Kennedy, spent their entire working life in the Arctic but remained mindful of their responsibilities at home. After thirty-one years' service, Kennedy retired in 1829 from his post as a chief factor, dying in London three years later. His will, drawn up in 1831, left £300 to each of his two sisters and the residue to his wife and nine children in South Ronaldshay, although his wife was only to be paid an annuity out of the interest on the capital.

While some recruits may have been attracted by romantic images of the frontier peddled by Edinburgh-born children's author R. M. Ballantyne, who spent seven years as a clerk in Rupert's Land, most enlisted because of economic necessity arising from overpopulation and estate reconstruction. In famine-stricken Lewis in the 1840s and 1850s, for example, service in the Hudson's Bay Company was a recognized outlet for the surplus and rent-defaulting tenants of Sir James Matheson, whose cousin, Alexander Matheson, MP, was one of the Company's governors. Information about conditions was transmitted in correspondence, as well as word-of-mouth reports from those who returned. Recruits and their relatives were painfully aware of the hazards of an Arctic sojourn, which, as in the whaling industry, included frostbite and drowning, particularly among inexperienced canoeists, as well as the obvious dangers of exploring uncharted territory. But poor communications meant that bad news sometimes took a long time to reach home, and it was not uncommon for families in Scotland to continue writing to their sojourning brothers and sons long after they had died.

A high mortality rate was not the only difficulty faced by the Hudson's Bay Company's Arctic sojourners. Internal rivalries, power struggles and administrative breakdowns posed a variety of problems. Particularly perplexing were the circumstances surrounding the death of Thomas Simpson, the Dingwall-born cousin of Sir George Simpson, who in 1840, after surviving three polar expeditions, died in mysterious circumstances on the Dakotan prairie. It was no surprise that in 1829, on graduating from Aberdeen's King's College, Thomas followed in the footsteps of a brother and half-brother and joined the Hudson's Bay Company. His appointment as Governor's Secretary was on the invitation of his powerful cousin, who in 1836 sent Thomas on a polar expedition as second-in-command to Peter Warren Dease, the veteran explorer who had accompanied Sir John Franklin on his second overland Arctic journey in 1825. Thomas had already demonstrated qualities of leadership and scientific expertise, and these were reinforced during both the 1836 expedition and a follow-up trip in 1839. By then Dease was in poor health, and although both men submitted a joint recommendation to the Company for permission to resume their search for the Northwest Passage the following season, it was likely that command of any expedition would fall to Thomas Simpson.

At that juncture, however, George Simpson intervened to ensure that his ambitious young cousin would not forge the final decisive link in the chain of northern polar exploration. Instead of granting him permission to return to the Arctic in 1840, he ordered him back to Fort Garry and thence to Britain on leave, while at the same time promising that plans would be drawn up for a future expedition. Thomas, acutely disappointed that the directors in England had apparently failed to overrule the governor and sanction another expedition, set off for London on 6 June 1840, carrying with him the narrative and maps of his recent travels, as well as a determination to petition the directors personally. He was never to know that the directors had, on 3 June, mailed a letter containing the authorization he craved, for only nine days into the journey Thomas Simpson met a violent death just over the American border, in Dakota.

The official explanation of his death was that he committed suicide while of unsound mind after murdering two of his four Métis companions. That interpretation rested primarily on the testimony of one of the two surviving Métis, James Bruce, who claimed that Thomas had, without warning, shot dead John Bird and Antoine Legros senior, believing that they had intended to murder him and steal his papers. When the two survivors returned the next day with reinforcements, Thomas allegedly shot himself through the head as they approached, whereupon the witnesses buried all three bodies in the same unmarked grave at the place where they had fallen and several weeks later reported the incident to the authorities. Thomas's insanity was attributed to a growing obsession with finding the Northwest Passage, aggravated by a volatile temper and a depression brought on by too many 'lonely Arctic winters'.

The fact that Thomas Simpson killed Bird and Legros was never disputed. But the allegation that he launched a frenzied, unprovoked attack on them and then killed himself was hotly denied by his brother Alexander. He argued that Thomas had acted in self-defence after being attacked by the Métis, who bore a long-standing grudge against him following a dispute over wages six years earlier, and who perhaps also intended to steal and sell the secret of the Northwest Passage, which they thought was contained in Thomas's papers. Having been wounded in the first skirmish, Thomas was then murdered the next day by one of the other Métis who returned to the scene with Bruce. Alexander also refuted the insanity theory, claiming that Thomas had good reason to revile his despotic cousin, who had failed to honour a promise to promote him, withheld letters from London informing him that he had been awarded the Royal Society's Gold Medal and a government pension for his discoveries in 1837, and

blocked his efforts to persist in Arctic exploration. It is significant that the governor – described by Thomas in 1834 as 'a severe and most repulsive master'[41] –
did not release his personal effects to Alexander Simpson for almost three years,
by which time all George's letters to Thomas had been removed. Nor was the
explorer's diary ever recovered, although the Governor's attempts to suppress
publication of Thomas's record of his expeditions, in favour of incorporating
them in a book of his own, came to nothing. Alexander was convinced that the
Governor had removed from Thomas's papers all correspondence relating to
his promised promotions and his repeated attempts to make the Company pay
into his brother's estate the share of profits due to him as a Chief Trader and
then as a Chief Factor (up to £3,000) met with a blank refusal.

Alexander Simpson's financial dispute was a matter of principle, but at a
lower level any breakdown in the transmission of earnings could cause serious
hardship to dependants at home. In 1857 Christina Anderson in Shetland made
an unsuccessful appeal to the Hudson's Bay Company's London office after her
husband, a labourer who had been in the Company's service since 1848, accidentally defaulted on his remittances:

> My husband Edward Anderson ... wrote me Some time ago Stating that he had
> Sent me Five Pounds which has not yet come to hand and as I am very needful
> at present it would oblige me very much if you could advance me the Five
> Pounds on his account. I am led to believe that he has omitted to enclose the
> check and the more so from his regularity in Sending me Small Sums annually.
> If you comply with my request please to Send it on to Mr Peter Williamson Jr
> Merchant Lerwick Shetland as I have been receiving Some Supplies from him
> for my Family and had it not been for Mr. Williamson's humanity Since my
> husband left here I and my children could not have been alive.[42]

Arctic earnings were a vital part of the household economy of many
sojourners' wives and parents and also helped to stimulate trade in the Northern and Western Isles. More substantial fortunes made in the service of the
Hudson's Bay Company were reflected in the tendency of some sojourners –
like their countrymen in the Caribbean – to bequeath money for schools and
poor relief in their home parishes. Sojourning could also pour oil on the troubled waters of family conflict, for 'when a man and his wife cannot live in
peace together, the parties and the parish are relieved from such disquiets, by
the husband's retreat to the Hudson's Bay settlements'. But some commenta-

14. William Tomison's School, Orkney. William Tomison (1739–1829) was a Scottish sojourner who spent 47 years in the service of the Hudson's Bay Company. He founded a school for poor children in his native island of South Ronaldshay and Burra and also bequeathed £200 to the poor of his native parish.

tors deplored the deleterious social and economic effects of overseas service in 'this infernal settlement' on the sojourners themselves and the local economy. 'The money which they have earned,' complained the minister of Kirkwall and St Ola in the *Statistical Account*, 'instead of furnishing the means of industry, is almost always spent in idleness, and often in dissipation.' Although there was no explicit criticism of the tendency to take native 'country wives' while overseas, in the 1790s sojourners were criticized for abandoning their families, ignoring their patriotic duty to serve in the navy, and depleting the farming, fishing and kelping labour force. 'Many … bring home with them all the vices, without any of the virtues of savages … and at the same time a broken constitution,' complained the minister of Orphir, who was also not alone in accusing the returners of inflating rents by displacing small farmers from their holdings until they too, having failed in agriculture through inexperience, were similarly displaced a few years later.[43]

For three centuries Scots were predominant among all ranks of men employed in the Canadian fur trade. Life in these northern climes was no less hazardous than in their tropical counterparts, for although fortunes could be made, it was often at considerable cost, and there were many sojourners who never came home. For most recruits, making a modest living was more important than winning a vast fortune, but while they were generally unable to flaunt their wealth and left no architectural legacy of their sojourn, their accumulated earnings had a considerable and prolonged influence on the economy of the Northern and Western Isles in particular.

Transient tradesmen in North America

All parts of Scotland felt the impact of wages earned by temporary emigrants in more familiar locations. The United States in particular attracted large numbers of itinerant artisans who sought to capitalize on the demand for skilled labour in textiles, mining, construction and a host of other developing industries. John Ronaldson (twenty-nine), the flax heckler from Fife, arrived in 1852 with a list of contacts and the intention of securing work not only for himself but also for his new wife and other female relatives who had stayed in Scotland. Despite periods of unemployment during his two-year sojourn, he was able to save some money from wages earned at his trade in Schagticoke, New York and Braintree, Massachusetts. He could therefore go home with his head held high and avoid the 'jeering of their relations and shopmates' experienced by disappointed sojourners who returned with empty pockets. 'I have not rued coming to this country,' he assured his wife shortly before he went home, even though he admitted that he had enjoyed only moderate success, and 'change of climate has been sore against me in health and money affairs'. His decision to return was based not only on wages and job prospects, especially the lack of opportunities for his wife, but also factors such as working conditions and lifestyle. Remuneration, he felt, was 'not in proportion to the work performed', and he disliked the pressure to become a rolling stone, covering huge distances in a constant search for better-paid employment.[44]

After the American Civil War, the episodic emigration of artisans developed apace, thanks to a continuing demand for their labour, coupled with readily available transatlantic steamship passages. Many tradesmen made a conscious decision to play the international wage market as peripatetic or seasonal emigrants, and while some, such as the iron moulders who reapplied for membership in their Scottish trade union in the 1860s, were disappointed in their American expectations, most came and went in pursuit of the best wages. According to miners' union leader, Alexander McDonald, in 1873:

One of the causes at the present moment reducing the price of coal in Scotland
… is that a large number of our young men have returned home. The high rate
of wages at home has attracted quite a number. I should say that I know at the
present moment at least 500 young men that have returned; but over all I estimate that at least 1,500 men have returned from the United States. Not to
remain, however. We have hundreds of youths in Scotland that have got the
habit of coming home in the winter season; they go out for the run in the
summer season in the United States; it is only a matter of 16 days and 6l passage
money; then they go by the emigrant cars, and 2l will take them to the coal field;
the whole thing is done from 10l to 12l; they take the run, as they call it, and they
can in some instances make 20l a month. They return in October, and they work
here. In other cases they come back here and they do not work at all. But at the
present time an immense number have returned, and are located here for a time.
Many of them have their return passage tickets; and whenever the wages come
to 4s. or 5s. or 6s. a day again they will not be found here, but will be off.[45]

While the miners came largely from the coal-rich central belt of Scotland,
seasonal or episodic emigration was also practised by large numbers of
Aberdeenshire granite tradesmen who played a key part in establishing a flourishing granite industry in the USA, particularly in New England. They too were
enticed by the offer of high wages, for when the United States began to exploit
its granite deposits after the Civil War, it had to purchase the skills of experienced quarrymen and cutters who could instruct a native labour force. Scottish
masons were in particular demand, and in the 1870s and 1880s it was not unusual
for around 200 granite tradesmen to be lured away from Aberdeen each spring
to the American quarries and stoneyards. Some settled down permanently, but
many returned to Aberdeen each winter and became long-term seasonal emigrants, going back to the USA each spring when the quarries and yards
reopened; others might remain abroad for some years before returning to
Aberdeen with their nest-egg.

  Both permanent and temporary emigrants were effective recruitment agents.
From time to time men were recruited by American granite companies or building contractors who sent agents to Scotland to engage labour for specific contracts, perhaps with the added incentive of a free two-way transatlantic passage;
at other times men simply responded to advertisements in the local press. A
large number, however, went to the USA either with no guarantee of employment or under a private arrangement. Many had friends who had crossed the

pond and they used these connections to secure jobs. Tradesmen who settled down and established their own businesses in the USA played an especially significant part in the origin and maintenance of the links between America and Aberdeen. Not only did reports of their success arouse general interest in the USA's prospects; even more importantly, granite quarries and yards opened by Aberdonians in various parts of New England and in New York State often acted like a magnet to subsequent seasonal emigrants. For instance, several Aberdonians were employed by the New York firm of Booth Brothers, which was established in 1887 by William and John Booth of Kemnay and subsequently won a number of large contracts, including the stone work for the St Louis Post Office and the Boston Court House. The mechanical polishing of granite – already developed in Aberdeen – was introduced into the USA in 1869 when Aberdonian John Westland, along with Gordon McKenzie and George Patterson from Huntly, set up a polishing yard at Quincy, having had machinery on the Scottish model manufactured in Boston. After Westland's death in 1872, the firm was carried on by his surviving partners, who had by 1885, according to the *Boston Post*, 'absolutely carved their fortune out of granite'.[46]

Emigration and trade went hand in hand, and Aberdeen's flourishing American export trade in polished granite owed much to the activities of entrepreneurial granite tradesmen. Although American orders were generally negotiated by agents who paid regular visits to Aberdeen, temporary emigrants also brought back American orders for home yards, while those emigrants who set up granite yards of their own on returning to Aberdeen were particularly influential in cementing trade links, using the capital they had saved in the United States to become manufacturers on their own account, and their American contacts to sustain their order books. Stonecutters also had their interest in the USA aroused through the preparation of American orders, as well as through their conversations with returned emigrants, who often worked on these export orders at home during the winter before re-emigrating in the spring. The huge return wash of emigrants undoubtedly helped to swell the subsequent outflow, since advice and encouragement could be imparted personally, doubts and enquiries could be answered on the spot, and enthusiastic emigrants might persuade friends and colleagues to accompany them on their next transatlantic trip. Particularly strong links were forged with New England, and Scottish communities began to form in such places as Quincy, Massachusetts, Concord, New Hampshire, Vinalhaven, Maine, and most notably Barre, Vermont, with many granite workers returning to the same location year after year:

Those who settled wrote their friends and relatives or gave the information personally – especially when revisiting Scotland. For there were numerous such journeys in those days ... Not uncommon was the intention on such departures to remain permanently in the homeland – with goodbye here accordingly. But that was usually in the early winter with a complete right about face in the spring. Many a sudden decision then – the wanderlust developing over a week end or even on the way to work Monday morning. The announcement of that resolution to a fellow workman and by night it was all through the different yards ... that so-and-so was going to America. Before the close of that week a group would likely be well on the broad Atlantic headed Barre-ward for they invariably travelled in groups both going and coming.[47]

Scottish granite tradesmen were in demand not only in the north-eastern United States. 'From the Atlantic to the Pacific comes the cry for more men,' wrote one correspondent of the *Granite Cutters' Journal* in 1902.[48] It was answered by cutters and masons who turned their steps to such far-flung locations as Alabama, Texas, California and Vancouver, as well as by those who cut stone for the Mormon Temple in Salt Lake City and by the many who moved freely and frequently between Vermont and Quebec, or between Maine and New Brunswick.

Railway construction also gave temporary labouring work to Scots in various parts of the world. James Gordon, from Lumphanan in Aberdeenshire, arrived in Montreal in June 1886, but spent only two days in the city before securing a six-month contract with the Canadian Pacific Railway and moving west to British Columbia. After spending two weeks working in a sawmill, he found the labour too strenuous and moved on to another job, building snow sheds to protect the newly completed line. The workforce was international and the job hazardous, as he recalled in his diary:

I am sorry to say that many a young man lost his life that summer in the Rockies there was accidents nearly every day I myself came to an accident in the end of the year a piece of wood fell on my back that finished my work in the Rockies I lay about two weeks in the tents when I took very bad with rehumitism [*sic*] some friends of mine singled the train to stop I was then carried with a blanket to the train I had to go 40 miles to the hospital it was kept up by the men working on the railway we had to pay 2/- per mounth There was one Docter in the Hospital he did not put himself to much trouble with the patients.

After spending three weeks in hospital, Gordon collected his wages and cashed in his free rail pass back east. In an attempt to cure his rheumatism, he spent another six weeks in a Toronto hospital at a cost of 15s a week. He then worked on the Welland Canal briefly before going on strike, suffering a relapse and returning to Toronto, where he found three months' work digging out house foundations. Other temporary jobs in various parts of Ontario followed, often among fellow Scots, before the death of his parents, within nine weeks of each other, dictated the return of the rolling stone to Aberdeenshire. Accompanied by his brother, who by autumn 1889 was working alongside him in Toronto, James took ship at Montreal, observing that 'on the journey homeward there is little amusements the people are not so hearty as when going out'.[49]

Sojourning tradesmen, we have seen, were sometimes given a rough ride by workmates and unions. But it was not just unwitting strikebreakers who felt they had been misled by disingenuous recruiting agents. Perhaps temporary emigrants, particularly contract labourers, were more vulnerable to fraud and malpractice than those who emigrated under no obligation, or alternatively perhaps the speculative, 'get rich quick' approach of some of those who played the international labour market engendered an impatient, critical spirit that could not brook disappointment or delay in achieving their anticipated goal.

When looking at the recruitment of emigrants, passing reference was made to the vilification of R. B. Arthur, a booking agent from Aberdeen, by a group of labourers whom he had sent out to Quebec on a six-month contract with a lumbering company. Many of the 100 men recruited for the North Shore Power Railway and Navigation Company at Clarke City were disappointed in their expectations of sending home money to their families, who as a result had begun to suffer severe hardship. Not only were their earnings to be just 8½d per day for a nine-hour day; like the granite cutters in Austin twenty years earlier, they were not to receive any payment at all until the passage money had been repaid in full, and men with families, who had been promised a £2 bonus on arrival, were never given this gratuity. The men were not employed indoors, as they had been led to believe, but were labouring in the open air, in a remote, inaccessible location 350 miles from Quebec City, where weather conditions and poor communications ensured that they would be effectively prisoners until the spring. Some of their wives back home had been forced to apply for parish relief, and one of the local newspapers, the *Evening Gazette,* waged a crusade on their behalf:

Husbands have left their wives and families at home, and as the promises which induced them to give up their situations have not been fulfilled, they are barely able to keep themselves far less to send money home for support of those near and dear to them. The unfavourable reports which have come home have had a deterrent effect on several young men who intended to leave for Canada shortly, and some official statement would be welcomed to allay the feelings of many as to the prospects which Canada affords for the industrious artisan.[50]

R. B. Arthur was quick to defend himself against his accusers and in a letter to the *Aberdeen Journal* on 30 October he blamed the 'misleading information' published two days earlier on a few 'hysterical' wives. Insisting that he had made full enquiries into the Clarke City firm's business standing before sending out any emigrants, he noted that recruits who had gone out in spring 1907 – and their dependants – had so recommended the arrangements that around 200 men left behind were eager to join them as soon as work became available, and some wives too had made plans to join their husbands once the St Lawrence reopened. Arthur's position was supported by both the Canadian government emigration agent for northern Scotland, John MacLennan, and the editor of another local paper, the *Evening Express*. The former claimed that many people who emigrated by means of advanced passages were 'careless and indifferent respecting those they leave behind', while the latter felt that it was easy for emigrants with unrealistic expectations of a land 'overflowing with milk and honey' to blame their disappointment on misinformation by agents, pointing out that few agents were likely to risk the heavy penalties imposed on those who wilfully deceived clients, just for the sake of a few shillings' commission. At the same time, though, the editor thought the complaints coming back from Clarke City were of more substance and merited the official inquiry which by that time had been promised by the Canadian immigration authorities.[51]

Letters from disillusioned emigrants began to appear in the press from late October. On 31 October the *Evening Gazette* published two such letters, from a boxmaker and a sawyer who had found conditions at Clarke City intolerable. The boxmaker, in a hastily written note, complained that recruits were not even told when there was to be a postal collection, for fear they would abscond on the mail boat. He went on bitterly:

God knows when we are to get any money. They don't even pay us on pay day. It is always a week or so past the time before we get paid. There are some boys here getting all their passage money kept off them this pay day, so they will be left without a penny, but ... if they don't watch themselves there will be a riot here, for we are getting played on too much now. I have been seriously thinking of doing a bolt before the snow comes here, as everybody that is here is leaving with the last boat. It is sickening working here, as the gaffer is a French Canadian, and he gives all the best work to his countrymen, and they all speak French, so we don't know what they are saying, and can't follow them with the work. We have been digging out trenches every day we have been working, and my legs and feet are soaking wet every night. It is an awful place. It is always raining in torrents, so bad that we cannot work. We have lost four days already since we started.

Another recruit, James Troup, in an interview with the *Evening Gazette* on 20 November, described Clarke City as nothing more than a collection of wooden huts in the bush, where the men were housed in rough bothies:

On the second day after arrival most of the men commenced to work. They were divided into squads; some worked at concrete, some filling holes in the river ... Work had not been in operation but a few days when a great many of the men complained of illness, due to the water, and a general feeling of discontent as to the class of work at which they were engaged, the belief having been that they were to be employed at a pulp mill.

A delegation of up to fifty recruits had then marched on the site manager, complaining that they had been employed under false pretences, but although the manager promised to redeploy them at more congenial work, many grievances remained, particularly over the non-payment of wages. Troup went on to relate how after three weeks – by which time he had earned £9 but had not received a single payment – he had returned to Quebec along with three companions. By then it was too late in the season to find work, and they were forced to seek help from the St Andrew's Association, which arranged for them to be fed by the Salvation Army and then sent them on by steamer to Montreal. But employment prospects were even worse there, and after pleading unsuccessfully for a passage on several transatlantic vessels, Troup stowed away in the coal bunkers of a Dundee steamer and in that way returned to his home in Aberdeen.

On 9 January 1908 John MacLennan wrote a lengthy letter to the *Aberdeen Journal* in support of his beleaguered booking agent, refuting the allegations made by Troup and other complainants. He denied that the men had ever been

promised either wages of 11s per day or a £2 starting bonus. The misunderstanding had apparently arisen because one of the June recruits had written
home saying he was earning 11s per (twelve-hour) day, and another had sent
home a £2 bonus to his wife before he had even begun work. But MacLennan,
having scrutinized all the Clarke City company's correspondence with Arthur,
said the bonus was never intended to be the universal right of all employees; it
was to be granted at the company's discretion, while it had also been made perfectly clear that no wages would be paid until the fare had been fully recouped.
Nor were the men ever promised anything other than general labouring work,
despite the claims of some that they had been engaged to work indoors at specialist tasks. MacLennan also pointed out that the company had incurred substantial financial losses as a result of the desertion of some recruits and the
incompetence of others. Of ninety-eight men who had sailed from Glasgow,
twenty-three had refused to proceed from Quebec to Clarke City, and although
denied their services, the company was still obliged to pay £126 10s to the
steamship company for their fares. Some of the other recruits had never done a
day's manual labour in their lives, and MacLennan ventured to suggest that emigrants who sought prepaid passages were often less committed, less adaptable
and much more ready to complain than men who paid their own way.

These criticisms did not go unchallenged. Within two days MacLennan's
claims had been contradicted by an anonymous correspondent, who followed
up his letter of 11 January with a second onslaught four days later. Pointing out
that there were more ways of misleading people than telling out-and-out false-
hoods, he insisted that the full conditions of their employment had not been ade-
quately explained to the Clarke City recruits. If they had really been told – as
MacLennan claimed – that they would not be able to send home any funds until
their fares had been paid off, then clearly they would not have abandoned their
families without the means of support. And if, as MacLennan also suggested,
the men were shiftless and lazy, then surely this reflected badly on R. B. Arthur's
selection procedure. In his second letter, the unnamed correspondent went on to
complain that MacLennan's statement had replaced the original promise of an
impartial Canadian government inquiry into the grievances of the Clarke City
recruits. Instead of taking evidence on the spot, from the men actually involved,
the Canadian immigration authorities had simply commissioned a report from
their man in Aberdeen, who had reached his conclusions without a full knowledge of the facts, and largely on the evidence of two witnesses, one of whom
had never been to Clarke City.

The last public word on the dispute went to R. B. Arthur, whose advertisements had initiated the whole controversy. On 27 January he wrote to the *Aberdeen Journal*, again denying that the men had been misled in any way. While interviewing applicants, he insisted, copies of an official circular, quoting a minimum wage rate of 15c and a weekly boarding charge of $3, had been clearly displayed on his desk; he had also pointed out the position of Clarke City on the map and had passed around letters from previous recruits. In response to Arthur's request of October 1907 that the company should investigate the complaints that had been appearing in the Aberdeen press, some recruits had taken it upon themselves to defend their employers' interests, and Arthur cited two such items of correspondence. Both letters were written by George Robertson. While the first praised the increasing accessibility and prospects of Clarke City, the other, which was countersigned by five of his workmates, described the favourable way that the Aberdeen recruits had been received, despite the inability of some men to perform manual labour. All employees who had requested an advance had been promised that this would be allowed once they had got some time in, and during November most of the married men had in fact been able to send home $35–40 (£7–8) to their families.

Remittance men and investors

Remittances did not flow in only one direction. Indeed, the late Victorian era was the heyday of the 'remittance man', a figure who fuelled the pens of emigration agents, journalists and satirists for more than a quarter of a century. Coined initially in Australia but employed most extensively in western North America, it was a disparaging term that conjured up images of eccentricity, ineptitude and idle dissipation, going well beyond its literal meaning of an emigrant who received regular allowances from family or friends at home. Remittance men were frequently depicted as supernumerary younger sons, victims of primogeniture or the black sheep of aristocratic families who were exiled because they had failed in academic, business or military life, or had been tainted by moral scandal. As traditional career outlets at home became either less popular, overcrowded or too competitive, they might well be dispatched across the Atlantic to seek their fortunes or to pursue their profligate and leisured lifestyles at a safe distance.

The notoriety of the remittance men was not entirely their own fault. Some were predisposed to failure as a result of misleading advice from the pens of promoters eager to exploit untapped potential in the emigration market by painting western North America as a sportsman's paradise. Some were victims of their own erroneous perceptions of Western society, and their place in it, for the youth of late Victorian Britain was reared on a diet of romantic adventure stories about the North American frontier, beckoning those who could afford it to a lifestyle seemingly more exciting and unrestricted than they could expect to find at home. But some had only themselves to blame for the high-handed attitudes, misplaced priorities and inflated expectations which they imported along with their hunting rifles, fishing rods and tennis racquets, and which simultaneously amused and infuriated those with whom they came into contact.

Only a handful of remittance men were Scots, and some of them settled, rather than sojourned, overseas. But the experiences of men like William Drummond Stewart and the Marjoribanks brothers allow us to test the validity of the stereotype and assess the impact of aristocratic sojourning on the American West. William Drummond Stewart had served at Waterloo and toured the Middle and Far East before he set off for the United States in 1832. As a second son, he did not expect to inherit his father's 32,000-acre estate, but was able to use remittances, and his contacts with Scottish fur traders, to join the annual rendezvous of Rocky Mountain fur trappers and their suppliers in Wyoming. During his seven-year American sojourn, he returned regularly to the rendezvous, where the debauched atmosphere probably suited his own promiscuous lifestyle. More importantly, towards the end of that time he also commissioned Alfred Jacob Miller, a Baltimore artist who had recently moved to New Orleans, to accompany him on an expedition with a view to painting the West 'before civilisation closes in'.[52] From over 280 drawings, Miller produced a pictorial history of the West that rapidly won him critical and public acclaim and an exhibition in a New York gallery. Stewart, meanwhile, had returned to Perthshire to claim his estate after the death of his elder brother, although he returned to the United States in 1842 for a final two-year Western expedition, and continued to remind himself of the wilderness he loved by decorating the walls of Murthly Castle with many of Miller's large oil paintings. He also initiated an exchange of plants, birds and animals with his fur-trader friends, sending out hogs and cattle in return for grizzly bears, antelope and buffalo, and lining the entrance drive to his home with giant yew trees, western hemlock, Douglas firs and sequoia. Most of the livestock that he imported did not survive, but the buffalo, which he shared with his neighbour Lord Breadalbane, thrived and in 1840 attracted the attention of Queen Victoria, who remarked on the 'strange humpbacked creatures from America'.[53] Stewart died in 1871, after an unsuccessful legal battle to bequeath the Murthly estate to his adopted son from Texas, Frank Nicols, rather than his own brother Archibald. But although 'Frank the Yank' did not inherit the land, he stripped the castle of its valuables, including many of Miller's paintings, and returned to Houston, where much of his treasure was destroyed by floods in the early 1900s.

Stewart and his countryman Charles Augustus Murray were remittance men in the era before such aristocratic adventures became the subject of public comment. Indeed, it is possible that their writings helped to popularize the romantic images that attracted subsequent generations of wealthy young men to the American West, for both wrote inferior novels based on their experiences, while Murray also published a more straightforward travel account. The second son of the Fifth Earl of Dunmore, he went to St Louis in 1835 after failing twice in his bid to win a parliamentary seat. During his brief sojourn he spent a month in Kansas with a band of about 150 Pawnee Indians, an experience which disabused him of a romantic view of America's native people derived largely from James Fenimore Cooper. Before returning home – to London rather than Scotland – he also invested in a 20,000-acre estate in Wisconsin, an example that was to be followed by many later remittance men or their parents.

It was because of family investment in American land that Coutts and Archie Marjoribanks arrived in the United States in the 1880s, each armed with an allowance of £400 per year. The two youngest sons of a newly ennobled Scottish family, they were sent out to manage their father's ranching interests in North Dakota and Texas respectively. Caught up in the ranching mania that swept the West in the 1880s, their father, the First Earl of Tweedmouth and a long-serving Liberal MP, was one of a number of British investors who became involved, individually and corporately, in the promotion of the American beef cattle industry. After buying a small ranch near Towner in North Dakota for £6,000 in 1882, he put the property in sole charge of his son Coutts, and went on to make a much biggest investment the following year, when he bought 150,400 acres in the Texas Panhandle for $553,000 and constituted the Rocking Chair Ranch Company Limited. Archie, his youngest son, became co-manager along with John Drew, an experienced cattleman who already had ranching interests in the area and who had persuaded the earl to finance the venture. In 1887 Archie's eldest brother, Edward Marjoribanks, became joint owner of the Rocking Chair Ranch along with his brother-in-law, the Seventh Earl of Aberdeen, the same year in which Lord Aberdeen's wife,

Ishbel, paid a brief visit to both her cowboy brothers while on a world tour with her husband.

Ishbel Marjoribanks Gordon had been a prolific diarist since childhood, and much of the evidence about her brothers' lifestyle comes from her pen, supplemented by her husband's observations, and Archie's voluminous progress reports and correspondence. It was to Texas that the Aberdeens first directed their steps on arriving at San Francisco in June 1887. On reaching the end of the Southern Kansas Railway – still under construction – they were met by Archie and taken on a three-day journey by buckboard over the remaining 100 miles to the ranch. Despite the heat and dust, Archie was not neglectful of etiquette. 'Of course shirt-sleeves were the style for such conditions', his brother-in-law recalled. 'But he was always very neat and natty in his arrangements, and never adopted a casual "out-west" mode, and I noticed that when we were approaching Fort Elliott, where we were to stay with some friends of his, he carefully put on his coat.'[54]

On arriving at the ranch, Ishbel declared herself 'charmed with the place from our first glimpse of it ... It was a lovely evening when we arrived and there was a pervading feeling of peacefulness and freedom.'[55] She praised her brother's housekeeping, commenting on his practice – common among remittance men – of adorning the interior walls with illustrations and photographs from the London newspaper *The Graphic*. Although the ranch house had four rooms and four outhouses, there was only one bedroom, which Archie and Drew vacated in honour of their visitors. It was a very brief visit, especially for Lord Aberdeen, who left with Drew the next day to keep an appointment in Kansas City. After a day's sketching, Ishbel followed on with Archie, and before leaving Kansas City she introduced him to the secretary of the YMCA, in a vain attempt to interest her brother in religion.

The Aberdeens then took the train 1,500 miles north to St Paul, Minnesota, where they were met by Coutts Marjoribanks. Not having seen her second-youngest brother for five years, Ishbel felt 'quite a pang to find how much of an American and of a ranchman he has become',[56] to the extent that he had begun to take out application papers for American citizenship. While Lord Aberdeen remained in St Paul, Ishbel accompanied Coutts on a four-day visit to her brother's ranch, travelling in a private car loaned to them (at Coutts's request) by the president of the St Paul and Manitoba Railway Company. The Horse-Shoe Ranch, five miles from Towner, boasted a two-bedroomed log house, an expert foreman, and 500 head of cattle, including a number of pedigree

Aberdeen Angus bulls. There was a livestock catastrophe the day after Ishbel arrived, when a new pure-bred bull worth $800 died of heart disease, but despite this setback, the oppressive heat, and the voracious mosquitoes, Ishbel was just as optimistic about Coutts's prospects as Archie's, and greatly welcomed the fact that his nearest neighbour was another well-bred remittance man, E. H. Thursby, the son of a Scottish baronet.

It was not long before Ishbel was forced to revise her positive assessment of the capabilities and prospects of both her brothers, as the ranches began to lose alarming amounts of money, exposing their managers to the wrath of the irascible Lord Tweedmouth. One of Ishbel's motives in making her first visit to Canada in 1890 was therefore to purchase a ranch or farm in the West which could be managed by Coutts, who would move from 'the dreary place in Dakota … where bad luck had dogged his steps and that of his pure-bred Aberdeen Angus cattle which my mother had sent out to him'.[57] It was with this in mind that the Aberdeens purchased a 480-acre property in the Okanagan Valley in British Columbia, a province that was explicitly promoted as a haven for British gentlemen at the end of the nineteenth century. The new property was named Guisachan, after the Marjoribanks family's sporting estate in Inverness-shire, and by the end of the year Coutts had been installed as manager. His responsibility, initially at Guisachan, then from 1891 at Coldstream Ranch, a much bigger second purchase made by the Aberdeens at the northern end of the Okanagan Valley, was to promote commercial fruit farming as well as to continue cattle ranching, in the hope of revitalizing the economy of that part of the dry belt of British Columbia.

Coutts's record in Canada suggests that his sister may have been too charitable in attributing his earlier failure in Dakota to 'bad luck' and the malevolent influence of American society. Residence under the British flag did not improve his fortunes, and the severe losses suffered by Lord Aberdeen's Okanagan Valley ventures were due in part to mismanagement and financial profligacy on the part of Coutts. His priority on moving to Guisachan was to pull down the existing house and build a bigger one, at the same time as he sold off the ranch's cattle at rock-bottom prices. Remembered in the area as 'quite a gay blade', who liked to be addressed as 'The Major',[58] he was more interested in breaking horses and frequenting the saloon than in balancing the books or studying the techniques of fruit cultivation, while his incautious generosity led him to employ too many workmen at excessive wages. After his father's death he returned to Britain, but came back to the Okanagan with his

English wife in 1910, purchasing an orchard property of his own. He continued to be dogged by ill-fortune, for some years later the ranch house was destroyed by fire, and although Coutts, having sojourned in various locations, remained in Canada until his death in 1924, he never achieved the wealth and status for which his sister had striven on his behalf.

Coutts's problems were matched by those of his brother Archie. The 'peacefulness and freedom' which Ishbel had enjoyed during her fleeting visit in 1887 were probably illusory even then, for others were mockingly critical of Archie's management style and general competence from the very moment of his arrival in the Panhandle. He apparently introduced himself by telling his cowboys 'My name is Sir Archibald Marjoribanks', a name rapidly and permanently converted into 'Old Marshie' by his workforce.[59] An article in the *Fort Worth Star-Telegram* a generation after Archie's death took the caricature of the newly arrived eccentric remittance man even further:

> Well, you bally old tin of fruit [he is reputed to have said to co-manager Drew], what's this deuced Godforsaken wilderness of flatness you've brought me to? Tweedmouth and Aberdeen will have to come through with the fiz if they expect me to stay here. Cheerio, who are you, old bean? Eh?
>
> Archie carefully polished a correct monocle, adjusted it crookedly to his bloodshot eye and gazed upon a tall cowboy who had come out of the house.[60]

Is that cutting caricature a fair representation of Archie Marjoribanks, the aristocratic adventurer? The reference to his bloodshot eye at least is probably accurate, for Archie, like Coutts, was reputed to have liked his liquor, and to have spent much time in Mobeetie, forty-five miles away from the ranch, drinking, playing cards and carousing in any of its thirteen saloons. He was also remembered for having used an English saddle, keeping company with his hounds rather than his cowboys, and keeping the ranch books.

But it was his bookkeeping that demonstrated a puzzling paradox in his character. On the one hand he was meticulous in submitting progress reports to his brother in London, and impatient with what he felt were the haphazard business practices of suppliers, failing to accept that merchants on the frontier often had no control over the quality of the goods they received and distributed. In 1892 his range boss, Sam Balch, was reprimanded for acting on his own initiative in placing an order, as severely as the merchant himself was censured for supplying allegedly unusable products. These included molasses that were 'unfit to eat', bacon that was 'execrable' and flour that was 'musty and black'.[61] Yet while criticizing others for careless business practice, Archie himself was guilty of much more serious neglect. His failure to have the Rocking Chair brand and the ranch Articles of Incorporation recorded meant that, in law, the business was operating illegally, and therefore could not prosecute in the event of any cattle theft. This was to prove Archie's undoing, for it was theft, much of it perpetrated right under his nose by his co-manager Drew, that brought the ranch into serious financial difficulties. The fraud came to light only in 1893, when the Rocking Chair's London management, alarmed at huge cattle losses over the previous three years, called in the state rangers to investigate why 12,000 head of stock carried on the books translated into only 2,500 on the ground. Although Drew's guilt was quickly uncovered, the unwitting Archie had co-signed every annual report and was therefore equally culpable in the eyes of the law.

In disgust at this fraud and incompetence, the London management stopped payments on all cheques signed by the two co-managers, dispensed with their services and in 1896 sold the ranch at a substantial loss, which forced the Second Baron Tweedmouth to sell his London home, the Marjoribanks family's sporting estate in the Scottish Highlands and his late father's art treasures. As for Archie, his lifestyle had by that time caught up with him and he was in declining health. His appointment in 1895 as an aide-de-camp to his brother-in-law during Lord Aberdeen's term as Governor-General of Canada was little more than a nominal position, and when he died in 1900, three years after marrying a Tennessee heiress and setting up home near Bath, England, it was rumoured that his death was brought about by his own hand.

Lady Aberdeen always blamed her brothers' problems on arbitrary bad luck and the eagerness with which unfriendly interests defrauded gullible but well-intentioned young men. The evidence suggests, however, that both Archie and Coutts played a more active part in their own downfall than their sister was willing to admit, and were badly out of touch with the realities of Western life, laying themselves wide open to ridicule and failure. Less culpable, but also unfortunate in his experience of the West, was her own husband, the Earl of Aberdeen. Although not a remittance man, he lived in Canada for five years, when from 1893 to 1898 he served as Governor-General. During that time the family escaped as often as possible from the pressures of Ottawa to the peace and quiet of their British Columbian bolthole. But they did not regard the Okanagan Valley ranches simply as upmarket holiday homes or even as a tool in

15. Apple tasting, 1890s, at Coldstream Ranch, Vernon, British Columbia.

the attempted reformation of Coutts Marjoribanks. George Grant Mackay, the Vancouver-based Scottish real estate agent who first directed the Aberdeens' attention to the Okanagan in 1890, persuaded the earl of the benefit he would bestow on the whole area if he would subdivide large parts of the property into orchard units of between twenty and 100 acres for sale to small investors.

Significant sums of money were duly invested, but, as Lady Aberdeen later recalled ruefully, 'the golden age predicted always receded'[62] and in 1903, after more than a decade of deficits, Guisachan was sold and Coldstream incorporated as a limited company. The earl's Scottish estates could not supply capital for the British Columbian venture indefinitely. In 1921 the company was dissolved, Lord Woolavington of Petworth became sole owner of the estate and Lord Aberdeen's involvement with British Columbia came to an end. His financial embarrassment had been due not to laziness or dereliction of duty, but to naïvety, marketing problems and the myriad hazards of introducing a new type of agriculture to an unfamiliar environment, as well as the mismanagement of employees like his brother-in-law. Ironically, however, the emergence of the Okanagan Valley as one of Canada's major fruit-growing regions in the twentieth century was in no small way due to the pioneering efforts of the former Governor-General in redirecting the regional economy from cattle ranching to fruit farming, as well as actively promoting immigration and employment.

The Great War was also to prove the decisive watershed in the history of the remittance man. For the unsuccessful who felt themselves trapped in uncongenial locations or occupations, enlistment seemed to provide – ironically – a glorious opportunity of escape. Of those who survived the conflict, only a minority returned in a largely futile attempt to take up the threads of their old life in a radically altered social and economic climate. What epitaph should be written on the collective headstone of the remittance men? Some undoubtedly did represent the flotsam and jetsam of British aristocratic society, transients and dilettantes who sowed their wild oats and deserved the harvest of ridicule and financial embarrassment that they often reaped. Others, however, made a positive contribution to the development of the American West, as ranchers, farmers and administrators, while even those who became notorious were generally regarded as eccentric anachronisms rather than a serious threat to the fabric of the society in which they sojourned.

Conclusion

Sojourners have always constituted a significant part of the Scottish exodus, although the technological revolution of the 1850s undoubtedly brought a considerable acceleration in the volume of return movement. Temporary emigrants came from a variety of backgrounds and displayed a range of ambitions. Like permanent settlers, some sojourners fell victim to death, disease, disappointment or destitution. Others, who had intended to settle abroad permanently, changed their minds when the economic climate became too chilly, or family circumstances necessitated their return. Even those who persevered sometimes found it difficult to repatriate wages or savings, a problem that could be particularly serious for families who depended on regular remittances from overseas. Sojourners could also be controversial figures whose effect on their adopted country was not always positive. Caribbean planters were notoriously promiscuous and intemperate, a reputation that they shared with some fur traders and remittance men, while tradesmen who worked as temporary contract labourers in North America were often castigated for strikebreaking and generally undermining the nascent labour movement. In Africa too they were sometimes perceived as money-grabbers who 'too often think the Colonies exist to yield them a rapid and fat fortune'. Scotsmen, observed an editorial in the *South African*

Scot in 1905, 'are too apt to go abroad like honey bees, and to return home laden with wealth …They forget the duties and responsibilities they owe to the country of their adoption.'[63] Whether temporary emigrants generated more controversy than permanent settlers is a moot point, although it might be argued that some sojourners displayed a particularly ruthless acquisitiveness, while the absence of females from many types of sojourning could have had a destabilizing social effect. What is clear is that career emigrants and casual sojourners alike cultivated networks of fellow Scots with the aim of developing an ethnically based social life as well as enhancing their economic prospects. The significance of such issues in the overall story of Scottish emigration and settlement is the subject of the next chapter.

ISSUES OF IDENTITY

'I'll do everything all proper here in America, but, at heart,
I'll always be Scottish.'[1]

'We'll take Scotland with us, a kingdom of the mind,' declared Daniel Munro, the patriarch of the Highland emigrant family in Frederick Niven's western Canadian novel *The Flying Years*.[2] Emigrants' expectations, we have seen, embraced much more than the practicalities of finding a farm or a job, making a living and passing on a material inheritance to the next generation. Equally important to the fictional Munro, and to many real emigrants, was the planting of ethnic anchors which bridged the old world and the new and allowed them to integrate memories of home into an unfamiliar environment. Nostalgia for the institutions of the homeland and a desire to seek out fellow countrymen were sentiments by no means unique to expatriate Scots, but in many parts of the world they seem to have cultivated memories of home with a persistence and effectiveness that persuaded not only the emigrant community itself but also the donor and host societies of the cultural vitality and economic vigour of the Scottish diaspora.

A Scottish identity overseas could be fostered in many different ways, both deliberately and subconsciously. Even place names demonstrated specific patterns of movement and sometimes helped to foster ongoing emigration to areas of perceived familiarity. Emigrants who settled in isolated frontier locations, often in colonies of their fellow countrymen, were not forced to confront and conform to other cultures, but could pursue their old way of life virtually unhindered. In Highland settlements, memories of home were manifested most obviously in the preservation of the Gaelic language, but emigrants from all parts of Scotland reproduced the architecture, the hierarchies, the folkways and the institutions of their former life as they sought to establish a new identity in strange surroundings. In many emigrant communities priority was given to the early establishment of a church and a school, institutions frequently perceived – at home and abroad – as the key symbols of Scottish identity. The role of the church was particularly crucial and wide-ranging. Clergymen of all denominations promoted and maintained the cohesion of Scottish communities throughout the world, sometimes by initiating and leading an exodus, but more commonly by simply ministering to the spiritual needs of their uprooted and dislocated compatriots. Although church adherence could offer emigrants cultural and material, as well as spiritual, benefits, there were also many secular vehicles through which Scots could demonstrate and nurture their identity overseas, as well as be helped up the economic ladder. Burns clubs, along with other literary, musical, sporting and piping associations, were usually purely social in function, but the St Andrew's societies and Caledonian clubs out of which many of them arose often had a charitable as well as a social purpose, offering assistance to Scottish emigrants in difficulty. Freemasonry too offered an avenue of assistance and advancement, while the informal mechanisms of correspondence, family and community networks and chain migration were of incalculable importance in creating a home from home.

The construction of a Scottish identity overseas was shaped by the emigrants' background. In particular, the sense of exile that pervaded much of the Highland exodus may have predisposed some emigrants to create an image of communal solidarity and stoicism that their Lowland counterparts felt less need to cultivate. That image of a community forged in adversity was then perpetuated and given retrospective coherence through the mythologizing of Highland emigration in a powerful oral and literary tradition that was absent from the more comfortable Lowland narrative. Lowlanders, particularly from urban areas, lacking the Highlanders' vision of a kin-based racial solidarity, and pulled rather than pushed into emigrating, often integrated more easily and imperceptibly into their new environment. The effect of these different priorities was that the interpretation of Scottish emigration as an unwilling and self-conscious diaspora – which belonged primarily to a traumatic era in west Highland emigration – came to be misleadingly applied to the entire Scottish exodus. Meanwhile, in the host societies, opinion was divided over whether communal settlement was a blessing or a curse, and from time to time there were allegations that Scots were characterized by exclusive clannishness, pride, tight-fistedness and debauchery, rather than the positive stereotypes of hospitality and sobriety. Literary as well as historical sources are relevant in the quest to disentangle real and ersatz identities, as we try to understand what 'Scottishness' meant to both emigrants and host societies across the world.

Highland colonies and coteries

The prospect of a reconstituted Scotland, with evils expunged but treasured institutions preserved and old relationships restored, was emphasized by those who promoted specifically Scottish colonies. The most visible examples were probably the frontier settlements of Gaelic-speaking Highlanders created in two different parts of Canada in the 1830s and 1880s. The thickly wooded landscape encountered by the Hebrideans who flocked out to the British American Land Company's territories in Quebec's Eastern Townships between the 1830s and the 1880s was strikingly different to the treeless, sea-girt homes they had left, but they carried with them many of the place names of their native island – Stornoway, Tolsta, Galson and Ballallan, among others – and collaborated with their French neighbours in building their new, but distinct, communities. They also compensated for the physical dislocation by emigrating in extended family groups and settling in close proximity to each other in an agricultural environment where mutual aid was a prerequisite for survival. Centenarian Maryann Morrison, who emigrated from Harris as a child in 1888, reminisced in 1976 about her family's emigration to Marsboro:

> We sailed from Tarbert on a little boat … a little steamer from Tarbert to Glasgow, and from Glasgow on a one called the *Siberia*. There was lots of immigrants coming over with us. In our family there was my mother, father, sister, and myself, and my grandfather, and my auntie, and she had three children. Her husband was dead, but she come with us. And my grandfather came with my father because his wife died when the children was young and he stayed with my father and mother. So he followed them over to Canada.[3]

Despite joining an uncle who had emigrated some years earlier, homesickness almost overwhelmed the family, and she recalled that in the early days her father would happily have returned home if he could have afforded the passage.

Homesickness and the difficulties of making a start were overcome by the proximity of fellow Scots, as well as the settlers' willingness to work together in logging bees, barn raisings, harvesting and many other homesteading activities.

'I am very comfortable in the midst of the old settlers,' wrote Angus Young of Lingwick to his father in Lewis in 1851. Thirteen years later eleven heads of families settled in the same area declared that on arriving at Lingwick they had been treated with 'the greatest kindness' by their fellow countrymen, 'who invited us to their houses, where we enjoyed their hospitality till we took up land for ourselves and had houses of our own to live in'. And in 1866 John Macdonald, mayor of Whitton, wrote to Sir James Matheson, thanking him for sending him and his fellow islanders to a country 'wholly governed by Scotchmen or of Scotch descent'.[4]

While they had to sacrifice some of the staples of their native diet – notably mutton and fresh fish – the Eastern Township Highlanders bought in large quantities of salt herring and continued to follow traditional Hebridean recipes, notably scone making, although the end product was thinner than the Scottish scone. Other imported practices included the spinning and weaving of cloth, using spinning wheels and looms brought with them from Scotland, and participating in waulking bees, when the wet cloth would be beaten to the rhythm of Gaelic waulking songs. Folk remedies for conditions ranging from toothache to tuberculosis were also part of the imported culture, as was the tradition of the *taigh céilidh*, when settlers would gather in each other's homes to exchange accounts of emigration and adventure, as well as historical events, anecdotes, ghost stories and tales of the supernatural, including many narratives from the homeland:

> Night after night, during the long winter evenings, people would gather, first at one place, then at the other. Around a crackling brush fire they would congregate ... and would swap stories, joke and sing the folk songs of their old homeland. In the meantime the women would prepare vast quantities of food ... [Some evenings] the women quilted ... [other times] all the moveable pieces of furniture would be thrust out of the way, and, as the fiddlers ground out their gay Scotch melodies, all hands would temporarily abandon their cares to join in joyful dances.[5]

One of the most frequently told stories in later years concerned Donald Morrison, the Megantic Outlaw, and reflects the ethnic tensions between British Protestants and French Catholics in Quebec. Morrison, a native of Lewis, returned from the prairies in 1888 to find that, although he had been sending back regular remittances, his father's homestead had been lost to a creditor and was occupied by French-speaking owners. After shooting dead the American law officer deputized to arrest him for harassing the new owners, he was sheltered for ten months by fellow Highlanders in a gesture of community solidarity and opposition to what they felt was the takeover of the Megantic area by French speakers. Morrison was eventually arrested during Easter weekend 1889, convicted of manslaughter and sentenced to eighteen years in prison, where he died of tuberculosis in 1894.

Donald Morrison's seven-year Western sojourn reflected the prairie fever that drew many Hebrideans to Manitoba and the North West Territories in the 1870s and 1880s, directly from Scotland as well as from the Eastern Townships. 'I am very glad for my change from the old Benbecula to the new Benbecula,'[6] wrote Angus MacCormic from Wapella in the North West Territories, although the Benbecula colony of ten Long Island families created by Lady Emily Gordon Cathcart in 1883 was in fact the product of proprietorial duress more than the participants' desire. Five years later continuing Highland poverty and land congestion were reflected in the settlement of seventy-nine Hebridean families at Killarney and Saltcoats, after the Napier Commission had recommended that state-subsidized emigration should constitute part of the economic rescue programme for the Highlands. To the Highlanders the barren prairie presented a topography as hostile as that of the wooded Eastern Townships had done earlier, but the distance between homesteads made it more difficult for them to seek solace and support from their fellow colonists. The Countess of Aberdeen, on an official visit to Killarney in 1890, was so struck by the settlers' lonely isolation and the 'inexpressible dreariness of these everlasting prairies'[7] that she subsequently spearheaded the formation of a society that aimed to bridge the gulf between their old and new worlds. During a stopover in Winnipeg a month later, she addressed a 1,400-strong women's meeting at Knox Church. After recalling her distress at the homesteaders' plight, she urged her audience to organize local collections of magazines, books and newspapers and at regular intervals to dispatch parcels of this reading material, along with flower seeds and small ornaments, to isolated prairie homesteads. So was born the Aberdeen Association for the Distribution of Literature to Settlers in the West. Its members – initially only in Winnipeg but before long in other cities across Canada and Britain – corresponded regularly with hundreds of prairie settlers right up until the First World War, assisted by the subsidies Lady Aberdeen secured from a number of transatlantic shipping companies, as well as the Canadian Pacific Railway, which transported the literature parcels free of charge.

It was not only in formal colonies that Highlanders tried – or were assisted – to re-create their lost homeland. As we have seen, their eighteenth-century predilection for emigrating in extended family or community groups was continued into the nineteenth century, when whole districts were sometimes depopulated at one fell swoop under the auspices of government agencies, specialist societies or individual landlords. Highland identity was most visible in Atlantic Canada. For much of the nineteenth century Gaelic remained the working language of large parts of Nova Scotia and in 1871 Scottish origin was claimed by over 79 per cent of the population of the four eastern counties of the province.[8] Numerous cemetery inscriptions bear testimony to the fact that Highlanders continued to flock to Cape Breton Island in particular, not just for reasons of eighteenth-century precedent but also because its topography reminded many of them of their Hebridean origins. Prince Edward Island too attracted a significant influx from the north of Skye, following in the footsteps of Lord Selkirk's colonists of 1803. The eighty-four families who arrived in 1829 commemorated their area of origin by founding the settlement of Uigg adjacent to Selkirk's Belfast settlement. Throughout the 1830s and 1840s they were joined by many others from Lord MacDonald's estates in Kilmuir, Snizort and Portree, though Skye emigrants were also drawn to established Scottish communities in other parts of the island. For these emigrants, the prospect of preserving their identity overrode the better land, climate and employment opportunities available in Upper Canada, a priority that did not go unnoticed by John Bowie. In 1841 he explained to the select committee on Highland emigration why 1,250 of the 1,850 emigrants whose removal from Skye he had organized since 1837 had gone to Prince Edward Island and Cape Breton:

> The parties preferred those districts in consequence of many of their countrymen having previously settled there; and in consequence of the representations sent home to them, last year there were 700 or 800 went from Skye; and the parties had not been long in their new country before they wrote home such favourable accounts to their friends, that parties are now anxious and many are now actually arranging to go out as soon as they can procure the means.[9]

Wherever they went, from Canada's Atlantic seaboard to Antipodean locations like the Hunter Valley in New South Wales and Waipu in New Zealand, Highlanders were enabled to retain their distinctiveness partly by the concentrated and often isolated nature of much of their settlement, but more explicitly by the Gaelic language, which some commentators regarded as the major hall-mark of their identity. In Glengarry, Ontario, 'they retain many of the habits of their native country; they generally converse in the Gaelic language, some of them use no other,' declared a Canadian witness to the select committee on Highland emigration in 1841.[10] As we have seen, Gaels were encouraged to emi-grate to Canada by the publication of promotional literature in their own lan-guage, notably Robert MacDougall's guidebook, *Ceann-Iuil an Fhir-Imrich do dh'America Mu-Thuath* (*The Emigrant's Guide to North America*) (1841) and Dr Norman McLeod's periodical, *Cuairtear nan Gleann*. Readers were reminded of more than the material benefits of emigration. *Cuairtear* assured them that they could continue or reinstate their old way of life among welcoming compatriots, with the harshness of the Canadian winter mitigated by the opportunity to socialize, 'visiting and ceilidhing between homes, plenty to be had and to be spared, and the friendliest entertainment and hospitality to be had'.[11] Mac-Dougall, who relied heavily on familiar Scottish analogies to describe Canada and the Canadians, was lost for words when it came to the cold of winter: 'My ears have felt it, but though they have, I have no words to describe its harshness, as in truth, the Gaelic language is not capable of describing it.'[12] MacDougall also instructed emigrants on how to preserve their culture and their morals, as well as their fingers and toes, in the new land:

> Since I am now about to bid farewell to everyone and everything on this side of the Ocean, and to take one leap forward without reservation, in order to smooth out everything which might cause the emigrant to stumble when he arrives, I would pray of the Gaels, before we part, that they leave in groups, as I have directed them; for, in so doing, the youth will not be in danger of falling into bad company, which is much too commonly seen in America.[13]

He urged emigrants to look out for each other's moral welfare, for 'the decent man will protect the man who seeks good companions' in a country where 'in the everyday speech of some persons there are curses as repulsive as any ear has ever heard'.

It was not the mere survival of the Gaelic language that allowed Highlanders to retain and reinforce their identity in areas like Cape Breton even after they had ceased to be numerically dominant. Their cultural vitality was achieved and sustained in no small part by the way in which memories of home were cele-brated, manipulated and at times invented in Gaelic sung poetry, which was the main vehicle of Gaelic literary expression and public articulation of the emigration experience. As Chapter 2 demonstrated, the traumatic context of much Highland emigration meant that it was frequently portrayed as involuntary exile, the unhappy consequence of the erosion of the Highlanders' traditional economy and way of life through landlord-instigated modernization policies. Deliberately or unwittingly, emigrants and commentators conflated arbitrary nineteenth-century evictions with the very different estate policies of the eighteenth century, portraying the whole history of Highland emigration as an uninterrupted tragedy of brutal eviction and wholesale clearance. While this was historically inaccurate, it was a powerful weapon in the construction of an enduring sense of identity and solidarity in the emigrant community. That community, it was perceived, had been forged in the fires of adversity and persecution, and it was incumbent on the emigrants to restore traditional clan loyalties, put people before profits and help each other adjust to the new environment that had been imposed on them.

Yet there was no common interpretation of emigration, even Highland emigration. The emigrants' varied backgrounds and experiences ensured that Gaelic song celebrated as well as lamented their experiences. Two cousins from Lochaber, John MacDonald (Iain Sealgair) and Allan MacDonald (Ailean an Rids), both settled in Mabou Ridge in Cape Breton, but saw their emigration through different ends of a telescope. John, consumed with the bitterness of exile when he arrived in 1835, wrote a Gaelic lament, in which he looked back longingly:

> *I left my country, I left my heritage;*
> *my mirth remained over there.*
> *I left the friendly, hospitable place,*
> *and my beloved relatives there.*
> *I left the beauty and the place where it was seen,*
> *land of the hollow and the cairn.*
> *It is the cause of my reflection that I could not*
> *stay there forever.*[14]

Allan MacDonald disagreed vehemently with that interpretation. 'You have put down lies and boasts about many subjects in your song,' he accused his cousin, claiming that 'the land that you left is the land without kindness, without humanity for the tenantry'.[15] To Allan, who had emigrated twenty years earlier,

Cape Breton offered hope for the future, a sentiment even more prominent among those Highlanders who, having discovered that the commercialization that had forced them from home could work to their advantage in the new world, integrated into the colonial élite and celebrated their identity primarily in terms of the martial tradition and loyalty of generations of Highland settlers.[16]

Michael Kennedy is adamant that the public perception of Highland emigrants as being 'in a constant state of nostalgic mourning for a lost Highland homeland' is attributable to a misleadingly selective and distorted reading of the folklore by non-Gaelic authors. As a result, 'only those songs which confirmed the romantic interpretation of the Highland emigrants as victims were selected, translated and incorporated into the dominant English language tradition'.[17] He singles out for particular criticism the (in)famous 'Canadian Boat Song', which first appeared in *Blackwood's Edinburgh Magazine* in 1829, purporting to have originated among Highland boatmen on the St Lawrence. It includes the following emotive lines:

> *When the bold kindred, in the time long-vanish'd,*
> *Conquer'd the soil and fortified the keep -*
> *No seer foretold the children would be banish'd,*
> *That a degenerate Lord might boast his sheep:*
> *Fair these broad meads – these hoary woods are grand;*
> *But we are exiles from our fathers' land.[18]*

Pointing to the lack of any evidence of a Gaelic version, and the technical disparities between the poem and other contemporary Gaelic literature, the anonymous 'Canadian Boat Song' was, says Kennedy, 'a work of the imagination and of English, and not Gaelic, literature'[19] which reinforces the myth that Highland emigrants invariably lamented, and never celebrated, their translation to the new world.

The negative identity criticized by Kennedy is certainly evident in the declamations of the two best-known contemporary Scottish polemicists, reinforcing the overall image of an ill-starred, hapless company of unwilling exiles. Both Donald McLeod and Alexander MacKenzie castigated Lord Selkirk's treatment of his Red River colonists and highlighted the plight of the large contingent of Barra emigrants sent to Canada in 1851. According to MacKenzie, Selkirk's colonists had been 'deceived and deserted ... and left to their fate in an inclement wilderness', where, said McLeod, they had undergone 'unparalleled sufferings', with their descendants in the 1850s still allegedly 'subject to the grasping insatiable avarice of the Hudson Bay Company'.[20] Almost forty years later, the newly arrived Barra emigrants were identified with destitution and potential starvation, both at Quebec and after they reached their final destination in Ontario. MacKenzie drew on an editorial in the *Dundas Warden* to demonstrate how at one and the same time they were set apart and drawn together in shared misery:

> We have been pained beyond measure for some time past, to witness in our streets so many unfortunate Highland emigrants, apparently destitute of any means of subsistence, and many of them sick from want and other attendant causes. It was pitiful the other day, to view a funeral of one of these wretched people. It was, indeed, a sad procession. The coffin was constructed of the rudest material; a few rough boards nailed together, was all that could be afforded to convey to its last resting-place the body of the homeless emigrant. Children followed in the mournful train; perchance they followed a brother's bier, one with whom they had sported and played for many a healthful day among their native glens. Theirs were looks of indescribable sorrow. They were in rags; their mourning weeds were the shapeless fragments of what had once been clothes. There was a mother, too, among the mourners, one who had tended the departed with anxious care in infancy, and had doubtless looked forward to a happier future in this land of plenty. The anguish of her countenance told too plainly these hopes were blasted, and she was about to bury them in the grave of her child.[21]

In other cases documented by MacKenzie or reconstructed from oral tradition, Highland emigrants had fallen victim to shipwreck, disease or misrepresentation by agents. The 178 passengers aboard the *Hector*, which left Loch Broom in July 1773 for Pictou, allegedly endured squalid accommodation, storms and disease during the voyage. Eighteen children died, 'and were committed to the deep amidst such anguish and heart-rending agony as only a Highlander can understand'. Having been promised 'splendid farms', these emigrants from the treeless west coast of Scotland were aghast to be put ashore into a dense, unbroken and uninhabited forest, where they would clearly have to learn skills of axemanship before they could even begin to cultivate their lands. Yet after enduring 'unspeakable suffering', the remnant of the *Hector*'s passengers who remained at Pictou ultimately – and surprisingly – emerged 'prosperous and happy'.[22] A party of 229 emigrants from Lewis to the Eastern

Townships of Lower Canada in 1841 experienced a similar reversal of fortune when, after being saved from starvation and a 'horrid death' only by timely financial assistance from the St Andrew's Society of Montreal, they settled down in 'easy circumstances', and founded what by the 1880s was a 'happy and prosperous community' at Lingwick and Winslow.[23]

It is therefore misleading to claim that English-language sources depicted the identity of Highland emigrants in unequivocally negative, defeatist terms. Ultimate success in the new world was a common theme even in the most nostalgic literature. Indeed, the achievement of prosperity in the face of adversity satisfied the demands of poetic – and sometimes retributive – justice, as in Alexander MacKenzie's juxtaposition of the wealth and comfort of the descendants of cleared Highlanders in Glengarry with the fate of the 'grasping sheep farmer who was the original cause of their eviction … [who had] died ruined and penniless'.[24] These images of an identity forged by exile and entrepreneurship also became part of colonial folklore, with Canadian novelists such as Ralph Connor and Hugh MacLennan taking up and reinforcing the stereotype. Connor's 'Glengarry' novels, published at the turn of the nineteenth century, depict a tenacious people, 'bound together by ties of blood', but also by the isolated, inhospitable nature of the land they had to tame. 'Driven from homes in the land of their fathers, they had set themselves with indomitable faith and courage to hew from the solid forest, homes for themselves and their children that none might take from them', and in their ultimately successful struggle with nature, 'their brittle Highland courage [was] toughened to endurance'.[25] MacLennan, writing in the 1950s about a Highland mining community in Cape Breton Island, used similar imagery to explain the Highlanders' emigration:

> Then across the ocean in the Highlands of Scotland a desperate and poetic people heard of her [Cape Breton Island]. They were a race of hunters, shepherds and warriors who had discovered too late that their own courage and pride had led them to catastrophe, since it had enabled them to resist the Saxon civilization so long they had come to the end of the eighteenth century knowing nothing of the foreman, the boss, the politician, the policeman, the merchant or the buyer-and-seller of other men's work. When the English set out to destroy the clans of Scotland, the most independent of the Highlanders left their homes with the pipes playing laments on the decks of their ships. They crossed the ocean and the pipes played again when they waded ashore on the rocky coast of Cape Breton Island.[26]

The bagpipe, another familiar icon of Highland identity in emigrant fiction, also appeared in Margaret Laurence's flashback novel of the legacy of joint Highland and Indian ancestry in Canada, *The Diviners*. In a more upbeat interpretation of the Sutherland clearances than that presented by Donald McLeod and Alexander MacKenzie, Laurence used the figure of Piper Gunn to represent the proud spirit in which Lord Selkirk's pioneers came to Red River in 1813:

> Then Piper Gunn spoke to the people. *Dolts and draggards and daft loons and gutless as gutted herring you are*, he calls out in his voice like the voice of the wind from the north isles. *Why do you sit on these rocks, weeping?* says he. *For there is a ship coming*, says he, *on the wings of the morning, and I have heard tell of it, and we must gather our pots and kettles and our shawls and our young ones, and go with it into a new world across the waters* ... Then Piper Gunn changed his music, and he played the battle music there on the rocks ... Then what happened? What happened then, to all of them people there homeless on the rocks? They rose and followed! Yes, they rose, then, and they followed, for Piper Gunn's music could put the heart into them and they would have followed him all the way to hell or to heaven with the sound of the pipes in their ears.[27]

Faith communities

While the sound of the pipes might rally exiled Highlanders, whose cultural vitality was also nurtured by Gaelic song and story and whose confidence was enhanced by the communal nature of much Highland emigration, there were many formal institutions through which emigrants from all parts of Scotland could demonstrate and reinforce their identity in unfamiliar environments. Probably the most vital – certainly the most familiar – was the Church. For innumerable Scots the cultivation of religious roots was the crucial way to maintain memories of the old country, and until the end of the nineteenth century founding or joining a Scottish church was probably the major mechanism through which Scots throughout the world acknowledged their origins and anchored themselves in a new community. There was no common religious identity, for Scots exported their sectarianism, while some changed their religion as well as their domicile when they emigrated. Irrespective of denomination, however, many emigrants, clergy and observers recognized that the Church provided a strong social cement, offering both spiritual and practical support to its adherents.

Clergymen were often seen as the keystones of emigrant communities. One of the Canadian witnesses to the select committee inquiry into emigration in 1841, when asked whether Highland emigrants to Canada should be accompanied by a clergyman, replied emphatically:

Most unquestionably; I deem this of the utmost importance ... nothing tends so much to keep a community of persons going to a strange land together, as having some one person of superior intelligence, prudence, and benevolence among them, who being possessed of their confidence and respect, they can look up to as their adviser and friend, and who by his counsel and example will encourage them to persevere in overcoming difficulties which without such advice and encouragement they might regard as insurmountable. A clergyman is evidently the person most likely to answer these purposes, and the performance by him of the religious services to which the emigrants had been accustomed would, more than anything else, probably diminish the natural feeling of regret at leaving their native country.[28]

By 1841 there was some precedent for clergymen organizing and accompanying emigrant parties, particularly from the Highlands to British North America. In the late eighteenth century several Roman Catholic clergy had been actively involved in west Highland and Hebridean emigration, though not always with the explicit backing of the Church hierarchy. In 1772, for instance, Father James MacDonald accompanied 210 emigrants from South Uist, Arisaig and Moidart to Prince Edward Island, after the Uist tenants had been ordered to renounce their faith for Presbyterianism on pain of expulsion from their lands. The exodus was devised and financed clandestinely by two Scottish bishops, who hoped to stem the spread of Protestantism among Highland landlords by threatening to depopulate their estates, at a time when landlords still fiercely opposed emigration. The bishops also hoped that the isolated location of the settlement would help to preserve the Catholicism of the settlers, Bishop George Hay suggesting in 1770 that 'being all together on an Island, they would be the easier kept together & Religion the more flourish among them'.[29] Fourteen years later there was another priest-led exodus from the Highlands, when 520 tenants who had been evicted from their lands in Knoydart emigrated to Glengarry County under Father Alexander McDonell. There they re-joined their countrymen and co-religionists, 600 of whom had emigrated in 1773, initially to the Mohawk Valley in New York. In 1804 there was a further substantial addition to the Glengarry community, when 1,000 Highlanders, members of the disbanded First Glengarry Fencibles and their families, settled there under the auspices of their chaplain, also Alexander McDonell.[30]

It was not only Catholic clergymen who accompanied Highland emigrants overseas. Perhaps the best-known example of this kind of exodus is the departure of a boatload of Presbyterian emigrants from Assynt to Nova Scotia in 1817, under the leadership of Norman McLeod, a rusticated theological student and separatist preacher who had been thwarted in his attempt to become parish schoolmaster in Ullapool. Talented but autocratic, McLeod had spoken out against the Established Church's lack of zeal and discipline. When the litigious minister of Lochbroom blocked his appointment as schoolmaster and had his salary stopped for unlicensed preaching to separatist congregations which he had established at Assynt and Ullapool, he was prompted to emigrate, along with 400 supporters from those districts, in a self-built boat. At Pictou he upset both the Presbyterian Church of Nova Scotia and the local secessionist clergy by fomenting dissent among Highland settlers, large numbers of whom were attracted to his unlicensed preaching. 'So great was the fame of Norman as a preacher,' wrote the Reverend G. Patterson, 'that people went so much further to hear him than any other minister ... by thoughts so wildly fanatical he was a man of great power and gained influence over a large portion of the Highlanders such as no other man in the country possessed.'[31] The Presbyterian establishment was no doubt relieved when, three years later, McLeod persuaded 200 followers to build another boat and set sail on the first stage of a journey to a Highland colony which he had been invited to found in Ohio. That invitation provided McLeod with a timely excuse to move on, since by 1820 he was in bad odour with the civil authorities, having been charged with libel and defamation after levelling an accusation of bigamy at the Reverend Donald Fraser, the Church of Scotland minister at East River. When McLeod and his followers were stormbound off Cape Breton Island, the party abandoned plans to go to Ohio and instead applied for government land grants in the isolated location of St Ann's. Here the 'Normanites', as they were known, established the first Presbyterian church on Cape Breton Island, and in 1826 McLeod was ordained by Genessee Presbytery in New York State. As magistrate, schoolmaster and minister, McLeod had unassailable authority, and he ruled his colony with an iron rod akin to that exercised by many Hebridean churchmen back in Scotland.

The settlement at St Ann's did not see an end to the colonists' wanderings, however. Between 1851 and 1860 McLeod persuaded about 900 of his followers to leave Cape Breton for South Australia, Victoria, and ultimately for New Zealand, in six vessels which they again built themselves. Following encouraging letters from McLeod's son in Adelaide, the first two ships sailed for that port in 1851 and 1852. Unimpressed with prospects there, and McLeod junior having disappeared to Victoria, the pioneers, led by their minister, halted briefly at Melbourne, where McLeod was distinctly unimpressed with the moral tone of a society convulsed by gold fever. After making a reconnaissance trip to New Zealand, the Normanites finally settled on a 30,000-acre tract at Waipu, north of Auckland, where they were subsequently joined by other shiploads direct from St Ann's. By 1860 there was a 1,000-strong Highland community at Waipu, and McLeod had successfully reconstituted the unique, cooperative, Gaelic-speaking community which he had first created and presided over at Pictou fifty years earlier.

Fourteen years before McLeod set foot in Australia, an equally magnetic and controversial Scottish cleric had organized the removal of nearly 4,000 impoverished Highlanders to New South Wales. John Dunmore Lang had originally emigrated in 1823 on his brother's advice that Sydney's settlers needed a Presbyterian minister, and from 1826 until his death in 1878 he pastored the Scots Church which he founded there. He was also an assiduous writer, traveller and emigration agent, establishing three newspapers and publishing almost 300 books and pamphlets. His first major work, *An Historical and Statistical Account of New South Wales*, was completed during the third of nine trips back to Britain, undertaken to recruit ministers and Christian settlers and to seek government and public support for religious, educational and colonization projects. Lang advocated selective Protestant emigration in order to relieve poverty in Britain and effect the moral regeneration of Australian society, dominated by convicts and Catholics. The success of his first recruits, fifty-four 'Scotch Mechanics' and their families who accompanied him to Sydney in 1831 to build a Presbyterian college, led him to organize several further emigrant parties, including the Highland contingent of 1837, many of whom were given land grants on his brother's extensive estate in the Hunter Valley. Although Lang's outspokenness in ecclesiastical and political affairs provoked hostility and four times landed him in prison, he was for fifty years Australia's best-known Scot, a firm advocate of the transfer of Presbyterian identity, and his funeral in 1878 brought the city of Sydney to a complete standstill.

Some clergymen were initially reluctant to accompany emigrant parties, as Donald Meek has demonstrated in the case of a number of Congregational and Baptist pastors who left the Highlands for Canada in the first half of the nineteenth century. One of these men, Dugald Sinclair of Lochgilphead, refused regular requests from former members of his congregation to join them in Upper Canada, until in 1831, 'finding ... that a great part of the church had determined to follow their friends and brethren this year, he saw it his duty to accompany them, along with his family'.[32] Dissenting pastors may have actually found it easier than Established Church ministers to emigrate with their flocks, suggests Meek, partly because their removal did not have to be sanctioned by any central body and partly because their meagre stipends and lack of manses and glebes forced them to take secular employment alongside their people, which further cemented their identification with them. The decision to throw in their lot with their congregations was also influenced by the concept of spiritual kinship that was particularly highly developed within evangelicalism – both dissenting and Presbyterian – which encouraged a particular affinity between ministers and members of churches, as well as within the membership. For these brothers and sisters in faith, the emigrant experience was a spiritual, as well as a physical, journey to a land where members of the pilgrim family were covenanted to support each other in re-establishing their corporate identity.

It is neither coincidental nor surprising that the foregoing examples all relate to Highland emigration. Most recorded instances of clergymen accompanying Scottish emigrants come from the Highlands, where the communal nature of much emigration made it likely that the clergyman, a pivotal figure in the local community, would play an integral part in the planning and implementation of an exodus. Catholic priests, Presbyterian ministers and dissenting pastors alike stood with their people in deploring the economic and social dislocation that had necessitated emigration, but at the same time they often sanctioned the decision to leave as a means of both escaping from deteriorating conditions at home and reconstituting the old way of life overseas. Their crucial role was further enhanced by the way in which Highland emigration was sometimes equated with Old Testament accounts of the Israelites' enslavement in Egypt and their subsequent exodus under Moses into the Promised Land. This analogy was not made because the Highlanders' departure stemmed from religious persecution; even the South Uist emigrants of 1772 were provoked more by economic and social pressures than by attempts to convert them to Protestantism. Yet, as we saw in the context of Gaelic poetry, the portrayal of emigration as an enforced

exile, and its endowment with a religious symbolism, enabled a deeply conservative people to legitimize what for them was a very radical reaction to the
secular challenges of modernization, a reaction which would otherwise constitute the betrayal of traditional loyalties. The trauma of leaving home also made
the emigrants particularly responsive to eve-of-departure sermons which
assured them of God's protection during the coming trials of voyage and settlement. 'Casting all your care upon him; for he careth for you' (1 Peter 5:7) was
the theme of the parting sermon preached by the Congregational minister of
Sannox, Arran, to a Canada-bound contingent of cleared islanders in 1829. And
when a shipload of Skye emigrants embarked at Greenock for Melbourne in
July 1852, they were addressed by the Reverend Dr Norman McLeod, whose
Gaelic exhortations were witnessed and reported on by the *Glasgow Constitutional*:

> At great length … the 23rd Psalm was sung, amidst much sobbing, and under
> very deep impressions … Not one bitter word was spoken against landlord or
> factor. They declared, in very touching language, that they went forth trusting
> in God, as did Abraham of old, not doubting that he was sent of God for pur-
> poses of good.[33]

Highland emigrants did not have a monopoly on either clerical leadership or
specially created Christian colonies. As Chapter 4 demonstrated, the province
of Otago in New Zealand, founded by the Reverend Thomas Burns and
Captain William Cargill, was the brainchild of the Free Church of Scotland,
and was unambiguously promoted as a Christian colony for Lowland Presbyterians. In the event, however, religious enthusiasm was more apparent among the
promoters than the settlers, and Otago did not become a church settlement in
the manner its founders had envisaged. Once in the colony, the settlers refused
to follow Cargill's advice to keep Presbyterianism as 'the religion of the place'
and in 1854 the Provincial Council insisted that colonists should be invited from
the whole of the British Isles, with an emigration agent being appointed in
England.[34]

Settlements such as Otago and individuals such as Thomas Burns, Norman
McLeod and John Dunmore Lang were the exception rather than the rule.
Most clergymen went overseas as a result of pleas from Scottish settlers in scattered locations, rather than on their own initiative or at the head of a Christian
colony. In new emigrant communities high priority was often given to the estab-

16. Scottish Church, Collins Street, Melbourne, 1874, from Melbourne Views *, 1880*

lishment of a church, and would-be settlers kept an eye open for evidence of this pivotal symbol of Scottish identity. When George Elmslie was sent to Nichol Township to purchase land on behalf of his friends in 1834, he was instructed to ensure that church and school were both within 'reasonable distance'. In 1866 Charles Farquharson was persuaded to join his Deeside relatives in Tilbury East partly because of the proximity of church and school, as well as the induction a

year earlier of the Reverend William Troop from the Deeside village of Ballater.[35] Emigrants often looked to their home communities to supply them with
pastors. In 1831 Donald Hendry left Sannox in Arran to minister to a group of
emigrants from his home church who had settled in Megantic County, Quebec,
while the second pastor of Breadalbane Baptist Church in Glengarry County,
Ontario, Duncan Cameron, came, like his flock, from Lawers in Perthshire.
When Peter MacLean went to Whycocomagh in Cape Breton in 1837 at the
request of his fellow islanders from Lewis, he presided over a notable revival in
the district before returning to Lewis four years later. And Alexander Mac-
Fadyen of Tiree, a Baptist minister who emigrated to Canada in 1867, initially
struggled as a missionary among the Roman Catholics of Quebec, but eventually (in 1884) found his spiritual home among a substantial community of fellow
islanders at Tiverton Baptist Church, Bruce County, Ontario.[36]

   From time to time emigrants grumbled about the lack of church provision.
An unsigned appeal for a Presbyterian minister made by a group of early settlers in Cape Breton between 1780 and 1809 asked for 'a pastor to tak care of our
souls we have non of our Way heir only of the church of ingland and We was
never Brought up in that Way'.[37] And Aberdeenshire emigrant George Forbes
complained to his father in 1846 that demand vastly exceeded supply, at least in
his township just north of Toronto, where 'we have preaching every 2 sabbaths
in the free church'. Both the Established and Free Churches were vacant, and
only occasionally did they hear a visiting minister from Scotland. 'There are,' he
lamented, 'so many congregations and few ministers.'[38]

   The Scottish churches were acutely aware of the needs and were sometimes
more anxious to supply clergymen than the settlers were to receive them, recognizing that not all emigrants gave priority to the preservation of their religion. As early as 1785 Catholic clergy in both Quebec and Nova Scotia
expressed concern that inadequate provision of Gaelic-speaking priests was
encouraging apathy, drift and loss of religious identity among the Scottish settlers. In Quebec, reported Father Roderick MacDonell of Culachie, 'All the
Highlanders and others from Scotland are doing very well in all respects except
in that of religion.'[39] In Nova Scotia, alleged Captain John MacDonald, up to
4,000 Catholics – Irish, Acadian, Indian and Scot – were 'exceedingly ill off
from the want of a Missionary'. He discouraged further emigration until a clergyman had been settled in Halifax, adding perceptively, 'I fear Religion is at any
rate too apt to become an inferior concern with the most that leave their own
Country to try their fortunes any other where; certain I am they will not put

themselves to great inconvenience for it.'[40] Things had not improved greatly a generation later. Angus Bernard MacEacharn, who emigrated from the Small Isles to Prince Edward Island in 1790 and thirty-nine years later became Bishop of Charlottetown, tried to address the Highlanders' spiritual needs in their own tongue, but complained for over thirty years of the persistent difficulties under which he laboured. The death of a colleague in December 1807 left him with sole responsibility for the island's scattered Catholic population of almost 2,000, and he was aware of similar problems in Cape Breton and Lower Canada:

> It is a dreadful thing to see so many thousands, so scattered, I may say over these kingdoms, depend and look for all spiritual assistance from two hands now much the worse of the wear. Old men are not fit for these wild countries. It requires youth, and activity to move in all weathers by sea and by land in N America ... I beg and beseech of you by all that is sacred to endeavour under God to send us two or three such men as you best know would suit these mixed Missions, where every person enjoys all the advantages of the British Constitution, but where at the same time, that equality, which is not so well understood anywhere, as in America, entitles every man to censure even an imaginary fault in his neighbour.[41]

By 1819 he was still ploughing a solitary furrow, aided only by a Canadian priest 'who knows no Gaelic, and very little English', and in 1820 he appealed again for assistance for his expanded sphere of duty:

> I have no less than 9 chapels, besides the French ones, very distant the one from the other, to attend. Fillin himself with all his speed and agility, would find himself hard put to in three or four feet of snow. The French Gentleman who is stationed on the Island, speaks little English, and not a word of the language of Morven [sic]. They have thought proper also to attach New Brunswick to my charge. St Johns, Frederickton, and Maramichie [sic] in the said extensive Province are without a Priest. I wish for the sake of Our Maker you could spare me one who can speak French, and if possible Gaelic.[42]

More than sixty years later the Reverend George Corbett of St Andrews, Ontario, was motivated more by cultural than religious priorities when he canvassed the Bishop of Oban to send out Gaelic-speaking Highlanders to replace those who had been lured from Eastern Canada to the prairies:

I perceive, by the papers, that some of the tenants in Scotland are likely to emigrate this year. No doubt many of them are Catholics. I therefore take the
liberty of stating that Ontario is as good a section of the Dominion as I know
of. Labourers of every class are scarce and the children of those who speak
little but gaelic will run great danger of loosing [sic] the faith unless they settle
where their language is spoken. There have always been a few gaelic speaking
priests in Stormont and Glengarry, Ont. Within the last twenty years numbers
have been going away to the province of Manitoba and to the Western States
… Many of them are returning, convinced that no place can compare with
Ontario. Still there is room for more and I should prefer some of the Highland
Class to fill up the vacancies and help to keep up the old gaelic language
among us.[43]

Perhaps Corbett's comments about the exodus to Manitoba led Bishop Mac-
Donald to enquire about provision for Scottish Catholics on the prairies. At any
rate, in May 1884 he received a letter from the Archbishop of St Boniface,
informing him that there was 'no priest talking Gaelic' within his archdiocese
and petitioning him 'to send one of his good priests to reside amongst these poor
people. They are in the midst of Protestants and they cannot safely be left a long
time, without a pastor speaking their own language.'[44] Two years later, the Reverend David Gillies, writing to MacDonald from the North West Territories,
where he had recently taken up a charge among Gaelic-speaking crofter emigrants, reiterated the fear that his flock would be proselytized by neighbouring
Protestants:

The people are very good, full of faith, yet they are greatly exposed to loose [sic]
it here unless they are looked after, as they are surrounded by protestant ministers on all sides, and who have funds to enable them to build churches and
schools, while we must strive very hard, with empty hands, to get up small
buildings wherein to assemble on Sundays.[45]

Unlike the Catholic Church, the less centralized Presbyterian denominations depended heavily on freewill offerings from Scottish congregations to
meet overseas commitments. Until 1825 the Church of Scotland had no auxil-
iary body to support members in the colonies, but in that year a group of evangelical clergy and laity in the Synod of Glasgow formed the Society for
Promoting the Religious Interests of Scottish Settlers in British North

America, more commonly known as the Glasgow Colonial Society. Its President was the Tory MP and former Lord Provost of Glasgow Kirkman Finlay, who, as we saw earlier, helped to orchestrate the emigration of destitute weavers to Upper Canada in the 1820s. Through its branches all over Scotland, the society aimed to publicize the spiritual needs of Scottish emigrants, and raised funds to supply them with ministers, catechists and schoolmasters, who, it was hoped, would strengthen the commitment of the emigrants to their mother church. Like their Catholic counterparts, the Presbyterians were frustrated by lack of personnel and funds, and also seem to have had difficulty in persuading Scottish churchgoers to identify with their colonial brethren. In 1835, two years after he had been sent to minister to the Gaelic-speaking congregation at St James, New Brunswick, the Reverend P. McIntyre wrote to the society in some frustration:

> I trust that your most useful and benevolent Society will continue to prosper, and extend its sphere of usefulness. Your labours of love are so duly appreciated on this side of the Atlantic, that it is a matter of wonder to us that you are not better patronized by the Scottish public. Why not write circular letters to every minister in Scotland, and earnestly urge them to bestir themselves, and procure for you – men and money? Surely the religious wants of America need only be told in order to excite the sympathy of every true-hearted Scotchman. Could the people of Scotland only cast an eye over the dense and unmeasured forests of America, and behold their expatriated countrymen, and their youthful offspring, immersed in the bosom of the trackless wilderness, and, like trees and plants that surround them, left to the care of nature, without the labour of a single vine-dresser to prepare them for the vineyard above; could they behold many of them growing up in heathen ignorance and utter unconcern about their immortal spirits; and hear others, with tears in their eyes, lamenting the loss of those religious privileges which they once enjoyed, but from the enjoyment of which poverty and iron-hearted oppression expelled them; could the people of Scotland, I say, witness such scenes, a tide of sympathy would roll from Johnny Groat's to Galloway, and thousands instead of hundreds would flow into the coffers of the Colonial Society. But alas! Scotland knows neither our wants nor her own privileges.[46]

For over a decade the Glasgow Colonial Society was almost solely responsible for providing Presbyterian facilities throughout Upper and Lower Canada and the Maritimes, and by 1840 it maintained over forty ministers. Most were in Upper Canada, although a branch of the society, the Edinburgh Ladies' Associ- ation, took a particular interest in the neglected Highlanders of Cape Breton, holding monthly simultaneous prayer meetings on both sides of the Atlantic to demonstrate the spiritual link between the old and new worlds. Under the lead- ership of Isabella Gordon Mackay, the association sponsored the emigration of Gaelic-speaking ministers, catechists and teachers to such an extent that by the early 1850s it had 'provided the scaffolding and framework for the whole edifice of Presbyterianism in Cape Breton'.[47] After 1840 the Glasgow Colonial Society merged with the General Assembly's Colonial Committee, a standing committee which had been appointed in 1836 as part of the Church's greater commitment to overseas missions. A similar commitment by the Free Church of Scotland after 1843 meant that the second half of the nineteenth century saw considerable attention and resources devoted to colonial needs, not just in Canada, but all over the world. In 1862, for instance, the Reverend Martin Ferguson was sent from Inellan in Argyll to Chascomus, near Buenos Aires, 'where a large and influen- tial Scotch population are resident, and have built a handsome church and manse'. This development, in the opinion of the Church of Scotland,

> speaks volumes for the religious liberty enjoyed by our fellow-countrymen who have emigrated to this and the other numerous fertile plains of the district watered by the Rio de la Plat, where a liberal and enlightened government are desirous of promoting all the social and religious institutions which those who may adopt this country have previously enjoyed at home; and we cannot doubt therefore, that a large and respectable class of emigrants will seek this new and splendid field for their capital and labour.[48]

The search for religious identity took some emigrants down unorthodox pathways. The Mormon Church, established in 1836, found central Scotland a fertile recruiting ground in the 1840s and 1850s. By the end of the century approx- imately 9,200 Scots had joined the Church and over 5,000 converts had emigrated to Utah, as required by Mormon theology. The first missionaries to Scotland were Alexander Wright from Marnoch in Banffshire and Samuel Mulliner from East Lothian, both of whom had been converted to Mormonism after emigrating to Canada in the 1830s. They arrived in Scotland in December 1839 and while Wright travelled north to preach in and around Banffshire, Mulliner concentrated on the central belt, where in January 1840 he baptized his first converts in the

Clyde. The troubled textile town of Paisley, which had already featured prominently in the story of Scottish emigration, was the location for the first branch of
the Mormon Church in Scotland, and also supplied one of the first three recruits
to go to America, in September 1840. Perhaps not surprisingly, Mormonism, like
Chartism, made its greatest appeal in the economically volatile industrial counties of Renfrew, Lanark and Ayr, notably among coal miners and textile operatives, and despite some assistance offered by the Church through its Perpetual
Emigrating Fund, several Scottish converts who were 'weary to go home to Zion'
were allegedly unable to do so for lack of funds.[49]

The missionaries' activities did not go unchallenged. When the orthograph-
ically challenged Alexander Wright tried to preach near Inverness in 1842 he
reported that 'the pregadeous was so great that I could not get another heren.
They spoke the galek and are very much pregadiced against anything but the
tradition of their fathers.'[50] Although no attempt was made to publish the Book
of Mormon in Gaelic, some Highland Baptists were persuaded to change their
faith. One Argyllshire convert, Daniel Mackintosh, nephew of the pastor of
Lochgilphead Baptist Church, was berated by his uncle for violating both his
religious identity and his family responsibilities by following a 'fatal delusion'
and emigrating to Salt Lake City, where by 1851 he was editing a Mormon magazine. After charging Daniel with responsibility for the 'cruel injuries' and
'agony of soul' that his apostasy had inflicted on his parents, the Baptist pastor
turned his polemic on the Mormon creed:

> By their own speeches I am thoroughly convinced that your leaders know not
> God. They were never converted. They may have a good moral character but
> they never experienced a change of heart. They do not love Christ, and there-
> fore they do not speak of Christ. Their religion consists, apparently, in external
> economies and in show. If you are doing justice to their speeches in your peri-
> odical, there is little or nothing of Apostolic doctrine or scriptural religion to be
> found there ... Your Leaders, your Elders, your Bishops, your Apostles, as you
> call them, appear to me to be a set of infidels, and their deluded followers moral
> Pharisees, of whom the Law said that publicans & harlots should enter the
> Kingdom of God before them. Oh how it pains me that my dearest Nephew is
> associated with such people.[51]

Other denominations were equally critical. In March 1852 the *United Presbyterian Magazine* publicized the Mormon recruitment drive in the hope that it 'might

perhaps do good in warning some thoughtless persons meditating emigration to the great theocratic settlement in America' to think again, and when William McLaughlin of Dumfries, who had been converted in London, announced his intention of going to Utah, his father responded that it was 'all nonsense [*sic*]' and offered him a job in his home town. Richard Ballantyne recalled that when he had left Selkirk in 1843:

> As we parted with the people of Earlston many of them wept and promised us help if we should ever again return to sojourn with them. They thought we were deceived in leaving our home and country to serve our God. They said why cannot you serve Him in this country as well as in America. We told them it was the command of God that we should go.[52]

Some Scottish Mormons sojourned temporarily in the eastern United States, accumulating sufficient funds for the final trek to Utah, while others went straight to the West. Among the first arrivals, in 1847, were twenty-four Scots who came not directly from home but from the Lanark settlement in Upper Canada, and they were followed by 130 arrivals from Scotland in 1848. By 1890 there were 3,474 Scots in Utah, some of them successful businessmen but many of them artisans whose skills were used in the physical construction of the Mormon colony. Although they sought out fellow Scots and imported national celebrations such as Hogmanay and Burns Night, they seem to have been happy to obey the Mormon exhortation to disavow nationalism in favour of assimilation and concentration on the ingathering of the nations to the new Zion. The Scottish Mormons who organized Utah's first pipe band in 1939 were anxious to point out that the purpose was not to foment a national spirit, 'because first, last, and all the time we are AMERICANS',[53] a sentiment that was probably encouraged both by the family nature of most Mormon emigration and by the Church's portrayal of America as a favoured land with a divinely inspired constitution.

If Mormonism discouraged the expression of national sentiment, the mainstream churches, to which most Scottish emigrants belonged, made a significant contribution to the forging of Scottish identity overseas. In practical terms, as we have seen, the various denominations provided money and personnel to build and staff churches in emigrant communities. Melville Church in the 'Scotch Colony' of New Kincardineshire, for instance, was opened in 1878 with the aid of a £100 grant from the Colonial Committee of the Free

17. Melville Church, The Scotch Colony, New Brunswick, 1878. The Kintore and Kincardine settlements which comprised the Scotch Colony were founded in 1873 by over 700 settlers from north-east Scotland under the auspices of William Brown.

Church of Scotland, and its longest-serving minister – who held the charge for fifty-two years from 1896 – was a Scot, Gordon Pringle. The existence of a church was also used by emigrants to reassure those still at home – particularly in Gaelic-speaking Highland communities – that their religious identity could be reconstituted overseas. 'The greatest blessing of all,' wrote Norman Mackenzie of Lake Megantic to his brother in Back, Lewis, in 1866, was that 'we have the Gospel preached to us in our own tongue', while John Macleod, writing to thank Sir James Matheson for his assistance in helping him emigrate from Lewis to Richmond, noted that the Highland settlers 'have two churches, with Gaelic ministers settled over them, and form the two largest Protestant congregations in the eastern townships'.[54] Clergymen often became community leaders, offering advice on everything from medical problems to farming methods, as well as mediating in disputes and generally acting as agents of social control. Religion was woven into daily life, not least among the Presbyterians of the eastern townships, where land grants were allegedly marked out by 'singing the survey' – that is, settlers repeatedly singing the Twenty-third Psalm in Gaelic as they walked through the woods, marking the boundaries of

each family's plot.[55] The annual or biannual Communion season was celebrated with the same fervour as it was in Scotland, often drawing crowds of
several thousand, although, as in the old country, only a fraction of those who
attended felt able to take the sacrament. Its significance was highlighted in Sir
Andrew MacPhail's autobiographical novel of life in the Gaelic-speaking community of Orwell, PEI, where, even among second- and third-generation settlers in the 1860s, 'the way of life, religious customs, and hierarchy of values
were those of the old country':

> The Sacrament was the event of the year. It lasted from Thursday to Monday.
> People came fifty miles. All work was suspended. Every house was filled, and
> many visitors were billeted in barns. Thursday was fast-day; Saturday for
> preparation; Monday for thanksgiving. The church windows were removed, so
> that those outside could hear the sermon and the Master's splendid voice as he
> led the singing. The tables were 'fenced' and 'tokens' taken up. An elder was
> once seen to drag an unworthy person from the table lest he eat and drink
> damnation to himself. In early days the service would not be finished before the
> sun had set. We still do what we can to keep alive the spirit of the Sacrament. It
> brings us in contact with old men of rich and beautiful nature.[56]

As MacPhail's novel demonstrates, the iconic significance of the church,
particularly in Highland settlements, is powerfully reflected in fiction as well as
the historical record. For Ralph Connor's Glengarry settlers, life revolved
around the church and the school, which respectively form the primary themes
of *The Man from Glengarry* and *Glengarry Days*. For Connor it was Presbyterian godliness, taught in church and reinforced in school, that made the Highland
settlers and their descendants successful and fulfilled. Hugh MacLennan,
however, portrayed the Highlanders' Calvinist heritage as a curse, holding its
victims in thrall to a restrictive and inhibiting past, from which they made futile
attempts to escape either through drunkenness and dissipation, or through an
excessive – and obsessive – pursuit of knowledge:

> To Cape Breton the Highlanders brought more than the quixotic gallantry and
> softness of manner belonging to a Homeric people. They also brought with
> them an ancient curse, intensified by John Calvin and branded upon their souls
> by Knox and his successors – the belief that man has inherited from Adam a
> nature so sinful there is no hope for him and that, furthermore, he lives and dies

under the wrath of an arbitrary God who will forgive only a handful of His elect on the Day of Judgment.

As no normal human being can exist in constant awareness that he is sinful and doomed through no fault of his own, the Highlanders behaved outwardly as other men do who have softened the curse or forgotten its existence. But in Cape Breton they were lonely. They were no part of the great outer world. So the curse remained alive with them, like a somber beast growling behind an unlocked door. It was felt even when they were least conscious of it. To escape its cold breath some turned to drink and others to the pursuit of knowledge. Still others, as the Puritans of New England had done earlier, left their homes, and in doing so found wider opportunities in the United States or in the empty provinces of western Canada.[57]

Schools and societies

Whether its effect was perceived as positive or negative, and largely irrespective of denomination, the preservation of their religious heritage was undoubtedly one of the main vehicles for demonstrating and reinforcing the identity of Scottish emigrants, particularly Highlanders, in their transplanted overseas communities. Closely allied with the church in this respect was the school. Emigrants like George Elmslie and Charles Farquharson were concerned to ensure the proximity of both institutions, the Scotch Colony boasted four schools by 1877, the year before its first church was opened, and for Ralph Connor the two institutions worked hand in glove in the promotion of spiritual and material well-being. Ministers like Norman McLeod were also schoolmasters and organizations such as the Glasgow Colonial Society dispatched teachers as well as clergymen. Emigrant guidebooks too emphasized the importance of teacher and minister working in tandem. Robert MacDougall was in no doubt that both should accompany emigrant parties:

It would not only be ministers who would vouchsafe my hope for the Gaels. There is another special group of gentlemen that I would like to send along with them, that is the schoolmasters ... The school is the hearthstone of the house of knowledge and information; and if the hearth of the house does not get swept clean and is not kept in good order, what hope do we have at all of gathering at the threshold? It is the schoolmasters who gird us up and prepare us to make our way through life as is proper for heroic men, and for Christians. It is they who make the ministers' yoke, to a large extent, tolerable.[58]

In the realms of higher education too, Scottish ministers and teachers played an important – and overlapping – role. As early as 1693, the Reverend James Blair, a product of Marischal College, Aberdeen, and the University of Edinburgh, founded William and Mary College, where, as president, he introduced the concepts and curriculum familiar to him from his time in Aberdeen. The influence of the Scottish Enlightenment's tradition of common-sense philosophy on eighteenth-century American education, culture and politics is well known. It is exemplified most clearly in John Witherspoon, president of the College of New Jersey and signatory of the Declaration of Independence, but is also evident in the careers of men like William Smith from Aberdeen, first president of the University of Pennsylvania, and in the careers of several American students who returned to the United States after spending time in the Scottish universities in the course of the eighteenth and nineteenth centuries. Scottish academics were head-hunted to help develop scientific instruction at Johns Hopkins University in the late nineteenth century, and in the same era a number of Scottish academics taught in American state universities.[59] Similarly in Canada, Scottish clergymen were prominent in the foundation and administration of institutions like the University of Manitoba. The powerful but paradoxical impact of a Scottish religious and educational heritage was also evident in both the life and fiction of Sir Andrew MacPhail. A graduate of McGill University in both Arts and Medicine, he was English Canada's leading intellectual at the beginning of the twentieth century, first editor of the *Canadian Medical Association Journal* and, through the mouthpiece of the *University Magazine,* which he founded, edited and financed from 1907 to 1920, a fierce critic of the social disintegration that he claimed resulted from the urbanization and industrialization of Canada. But although in *The Master's Wife* he celebrated the stability of a traditional way of life based on the imported Scottish values of church and school, he recognized that education was also the gateway through which bright boys could expand their horizons and 'escape from the land and the ice', as well as from the stifling sabbatarianism of rural Scotland transplanted to rural Canada.[60] MacPhail himself exemplified this tension, for while he spent much of his life in the secular, humanist academic world of Montreal, his heart remained in Orwell, to which he regularly returned and whose values he never repudiated.

The interconnectedness of church and school was also demonstrated in Australia, where in 1826 John Dunmore Lang founded the Caledonian Academy, a primary school attached to the Scots Church in Sydney. This was to be supervised by a licentiate of the Church of Scotland and each day was to include prayer, Bible reading and religious education. That particular venture was short-lived, but by 1844 there were thirteen primary schools in the vicinity of Sydney, nearly all with Scottish teachers. Thirteen years earlier Lang had opened his Australian College, staffed by three licentiates of the Church of Scotland, and of the 500 boys who passed through the college in its twenty-three-year existence, several went on to hold influential positions in the colony. The Scotch College in Melbourne, opened in 1851, performed a similar function for the sons of wealthy squatters in Victoria, particularly under Alexander Morrison of Morayshire, who, as principal from 1857 to 1903, modelled its curriculum on the lines of Elgin Academy, where he himself had been educated. Among the leading advocates of secular education – and a co-founder of the Sydney Mechanics' School of Arts in 1833 – was Henry Carmichael, who had been brought out by Lang to teach in the Scots College but opposed his sponsor's divisive denominationalism. Higher education in Australia benefited from a stream of Scottish professors, particularly at the University of Sydney, as well as from gifts and bequests from a variety of Scottish philanthropists. Aberdeen-born William Ormond, for example, a self-made pastoralist who left an estate of nearly £2 million, donated more than £100,000 to Ormond Theological College in the University of Melbourne, while the University of Adelaide benefited from the donations of Sir Thomas Elder from Kirkcaldy, another successful pastoralist, and the engineering school at the University of Sydney was developed with the aid of donations from Sir Peter Nicol Russell, another Fife emigrant, who had made his money as an engineer and ironfounder in Sydney.[61]

In New Zealand education was accorded less of a priority among Otago's Presbyterian pioneers, with fewer than 100 out of a possible 270 children living in and around Dunedin attending school in 1853. Schooling was controlled by the provincial government, rather than – as the founding fathers had hoped – by the Church, and there were periodic complaints that the colonists were more interested in making money than in making provision for their children's education.[62] In due course, however, educational development throughout New Zealand received, in the opinion of historian Tom Brooking, 'greater assistance from the Scots than any other immigrant group'.[63] Aberdeen-born James MacAndrew, who became a leading merchant and politician in Dunedin, was instrumental in establishing training colleges and schools, as well as the University of Dunedin. Thanks largely to him, over 100 schools had been established by 1871, and that year also saw the establishment of the first girls' secondary school in New Zealand. Two years earlier New Zealand's first university had been founded at Dunedin and both it and the Victoria University of Wellington were administered and staffed largely by Scots. After MacAndrew's death in 1887, the people of Otago commemorated this founding father by instituting a £500 scholarship in his memory, to be used to send deserving medical students from Otago to the University of Aberdeen to complete their training.

For many emigrants, church and school were clearly much more than simply institutions that met their spiritual and intellectual needs. They were powerful symbols of a transplanted identity – 'a rallying-point for Scottish sentiment and tradition', as the Church of Scotland reported of the Scots Kirk in Colombo, Ceylon, in 1920.[64] But emigrants could also demonstrate their identity and solidarity through a range of purely secular institutions, notably the St Andrew's societies and Caledonian clubs that sprang up wherever Scots congregated. The Scots Charitable Society of Boston, founded in 1657, was the oldest Scottish society in North America, while that of Halifax, founded in 1768, was the oldest in Canada. Some associations were based on precise local origins. The Fraserburgh Society of Winnipeg, for instance, was formed in 1911, although by the end of the year that definition was soon found to be too narrow and, under the new name of the Aberdeenshire, Kincardineshire and Banffshire Association of Winnipeg, it opened its doors to a wider membership. Antipodean Scots were slower to follow suit. Although Sydney had a St Andrew's Club in the 1820s, Caledonian societies began to appear in other parts of Australia, mainly Victoria, only in the 1850s, but by the 1890s there were Scottish societies in almost all the Australian states. In New Zealand these societies were even slower to develop, partly because the colonists were more concerned with material issues and the forging of a new nation than with the preservation of their identity. Gaelic was disparaged as the language of backwardness, and although Caledonian societies existed from the 1850s, they did not really take off until the 1890s, which was also when Burns clubs began to be founded. By 1905 there were over forty Highland and Caledonian societies in South Africa, and in November of that year *The South African Scot* was founded as a monthly journal, to give the societies greater coherence and promote 'all that is worth preserving in the heritage of the Scottish people'.[65]

The function of these élite associations, particularly in North America, was partly philanthropic, at times even repatriating those who had fallen on particularly hard times and frequently offering practical assistance to needy settlers.

18. Statue of William Wallace, Druid Park, Baltimore, Maryland. The statue was presented to the city by Wallace Spence, a Scot who emigrated in 1833, and unveiled on St Andrew's Day 1893, with 12,000 spectators, the St Andrew's Society of Baltimore, pipers and marching bands.

A party of 229 Lewis emigrants had reason to be grateful for such assistance when, in 1841, a handout from the St Andrew's Society of Montreal allegedly saved them from starvation and enabled them to reach their final destinations in the Eastern Townships. Similarly, the 'Scotch Colonists', whose disembarkation at Saint John in May 1873 had been celebrated by the St Andrew's Society in that town, were less than a year later given a $100 grant by the same society after around seventy settlers had fallen victim to sickness, unemployment and destitution in their isolated, unprepared settlement in the heart of New Brunswick. Following the foundation of the Order of Scottish Clans at St Louis in 1878, Scottish granite tradesmen in New England were among those who upheld their national identity by forming branches of this mutual benefit and insurance society in the towns where they worked. In Barre, Vermont, the Scots' social life revolved around Clan Gordon Number Twelve, established in 1884, which provided financial aid to disabled members and to the dependants of men who had died. But the Scottish organizations did not help only settlers in distress; in 1863 the Guelph St Andrew's Society donated £20 to the Lord Provost

19. Past Presidents of the Caledonian Society, Montreal, 1889.

of Glasgow for unemployed cotton spinners in that city, while the Vancouver St Andrew's and Caledonian Society, founded in 1886, donated money raised by its 1893 tug-of-war with the St George's Society to the indigent citizens of Vancouver, and in 1909 helped to sponsor the St Andrew's and Caledonian Society Ward in the city's General Hospital.

Some of the Highland societies, particularly in Canada, were also anxious to erase memories of poverty and enforced clearance in favour of a more sanitized interpretation of Highland emigration that reproduced the social hierarchies of the homeland. The prominent and successful Scots – non-Gaels as well as Highlanders – who ran these societies fostered an identity based on the settlers' military prowess and conservatism, particularly in the wake of the war of 1812 and the 1837 rebellions. 'In the hands of the colonial élite,' says Rusty Bitterman, 'the construction of Highland traditions and their public celebration went hand in hand with affirmations of loyalty and deference to authority.'[66] The icons of that carefully constructed identity were bagpipes, plaids and banners displaying the arms of the parent society, the Highland Society of London. On the other side of the world, the proliferation of Scottish societies, newspapers, magazines and statuary in Australia at the end of the century was in part a rearguard action against the perceived 'homogenization of Scots' into a predominantly English culture.[67]

But by no means all Scottish societies were so self-conscious or defensive. Many simply gave their members the opportunity to celebrate their national origins through a range of social functions. While picnics and sporting fixtures were popular, St Andrew's Day Balls on 30 November and Burns Night dinners on 25 January were generally the two highlights of the social calendar. In 1800 the St Andrew's Day celebrations in Wilmington, North Carolina, drew an approving comment from the local newspaper:

> Sunday last being St. Andrew's Day, the same was observed on Monday, when the NATIVE and SONS OF NATIVE BRITONERS, residing in Town, having previously invited all fashionable company within twenty miles, gave a most splendid Ball and Supper. Upwards of two hundred Ladies and Gentlemen were entertained during the evening, to their most perfect satisfaction, not a single cloud hovering near the sun of Festivity. A set supper was given, exhibiting all the luxuries of the season, at which Robert Muter and Henry Urquhart, Esquires, presided, and drank the usual Toasts, viz. 'The Immortal memory of St. Andrew,' 'Land of Cakes,' 'Beggar's Bennison,' 'Land we live in,' etc. etc. Between the set dances, the Ladies and Gentlemen entertained themselves with Scotch Reels in an adjoining room.[68]

And the normally austere John Dunmore Lang responded in verse when invited to an anniversary ball by members of the St Andrew's Club in Sydney in 1823:

> *Friends of St Andrew and the Thistle,*
> *Accept, I pray, this short epistle.*
> *In answer to your invitation*
> *To the Grand Ball and Cold Collation.*
> *I wish you well as well may be,*
> *Long may you live in harmony.*
> *And every year in hot November*
> *The Caledonian Saint remember![69]*

Scotland's National Bard was even more enthusiastically commemorated than her patron saint. As early as July 1787 copies of Burns's *Poems* were on sale in the United States, and were snapped up like hot cakes. Two American editions appeared the following year, and the nineteenth century saw the sprouting of statues of Burns all over the world, the largest crafted by the Aberdeen granite

20. *Curling on the St Lawrence, composite, 1878.*

masons of Barre, Vermont. Burns clubs, as well as sporting and piping associations, were usually purely social in function, and shinty, curling or Highland
dancing contests were usually followed by dinners at which people recited or
sang of a Scotland many of them had either never seen or could not remember.
Curling, shinty, golf and dancing were exported largely by Scottish regiments.
The Montreal Curling Club was allegedly 'the first organized sports club in
British North America', promoting a sport which soon became – and remained
– hugely popular in Canada.[70] Although shinty did not generally survive
beyond the first generation of emigrants, it contributed to the subsequent development of ice hockey and was played in some surprising locations. In 1842, for
instance, the *Inverness Courier* reported on a shinty match at Montevideo on the
River Plate:

> The fourth of April being a holiday, the sons of the mountains, resident in this
> province, had determined to try a game of shinty for auld lang syne. Though
> the weather was very threatening in the morning, the players were not to be
> daunted, but crossed the Bay in boats, and marched to the ground ... under the
> inspiring strains of the bagpipes, to the tune of 'The Campbells are Coming,'
> where they were greeted by a large concourse of people, assembled to witness
> the game.
>
> After sides were called, and a few other preliminaries arranged, playing
> commenced, and was carried on with great spirit till four P.M., when the players
> sat down on the grass and partook of an asado de carvo con cuero (beef roasted

with the hide on,) and plenty of Ferintosh [whisky] (Aldourie and Brackla being scarce.) Dancing then commenced, and the Highland Fling danced by Messrs Maclennan and Macrae; Gille Callum, by Captain MacLellan; Sean Truise, by Mr MacDougall; and several other Scotch reels were greatly admired.

At half-past seven o'clock, the bagpipes struck up the 'Gathering' and the whole, forming two deep, marched from the field to the place of embarkation, to the tune of 'Gillean na Feileadh,' amidst loud cheering, and still louder vivas from the natives.

At nine o'clock, the players sat down to a comfortable supper at the Steamboat Hotel; and, after the cloth was removed, and bumpers quaffed for the Royal family, and the President of the Republic, Don Frutuoso Rivera, the Chairman called for a special glass for the toast of the evening and, in a neat and appropriate speech, interspersed with Gaelic, proposed, 'Tir nam bean, 's nan gleann, 's na gaisgich,' which was drunk with great enthusiasm amidst deafening cheering.

Several Gaelic and other songs were sung during the evening, and the health of our chairman, Captain Maclellan, of the ship Orpheus, being proposed, and the thanks of the company returned him, for the spirited manner in which he conducted the proceedings of the day, the whole separated at two in the morning, after drinking 'Deoch an dorus,' highly delighted with the day's amusement.[71]

The aim of those who founded the New York Highlanders' Shinty Club in 1903 was 'to keep alive in the land of their adoption the game which in their youth, afforded them such delight, and which in some measure at least gave them that grit and pluck which are essential in fighting the stern battle of life'. One of their players, Angus MacPherson, an emigrant from Laggan, was not only expert at shinty but was also 'in the very forefront of pipers and dancers'.[72] Piping and dancing performances usually took place under the umbrella of the Highland or Caledonian Games, a phenomenon that provided the model for the later development of the professional athletics circuit. Although such gatherings were not actually exported from Scotland – the first Highland Games in Canada and Scotland both took place simultaneously, in 1819 – they rapidly became part of the invented Scottish identity overseas. 'On the whole the result of the Highland gathering is good', reported the *Celtic Monthly* of a Canadian meeting in 1893. 'The national sentiment is stimulated, and the best phases of our national character are the more easily reached and cultivated because of the manly exercises and the games of the old home being kept alive.'[73]

Intermarriage between expatriate Scots was common throughout the Scottish diaspora, and many people met their partners through Scottish churches and secular societies. Wedding celebrations themselves offered a further opportunity to celebrate old country customs, not least in that notable but neglected Scottish outpost in the South Atlantic, the Falkland Islands:

> On Thursday August 4 [1892], the marriage of Mr Archibald McCall (Superintendent of the North Area Section of the Falkland Island Company's Camp) and Miss Jennings, of Darwin, was celebrated.
>
> ... About 150 gathered in from the Camps, some on horseback, others in cutters and a few, from the near neighbourhood, on foot. As there are but 12 inhabited houses in Darwin, much wonder will be felt as to where they all managed to find room: but the Darwinites were equal to the occasion and opened their doors most hospitably to all friends and acquaintances. The eve of the wedding was devoted to the peculiar Scotch custom of 'washing the bridegroom's feet', namely, giving them a brilliant polish with blacklead brushes &c. The opportunity for carrying out this custom occurs so seldom, that all who have been married within the last ten years had to submit to the ordeal. The evening was closed with a dance which was vigorously kept up from 6 P. M. until broad daylight.[74]

Loss of identity

We have seen how, all over the world, Scots emigrants strove to preserve or recreate the linguistic, religious and social symbols of their national identity. Frequently, however, these efforts were made in the face of overt or insidious challenges, not the least of which came from within the Scottish settlements themselves. In Canada, for example, where Confederation provided a new focus for allegiance and where sports such as curling had virtually lost their Scottish identity by the end of the century, Wilfrid Campbell was led to lament in 1911 that the Scots had become 'ever afraid to act as a community and uphold their most sacred ideals'.[75] Like many other commentators, he equated the preservation of ethnic identity with material comfort and moral integrity, but perhaps more scholarly attention should now be paid to the other side of the coin – namely, the desire and ability of numerous Scots to assimilate imperceptibly and successfully into their host societies.

Loss of identity was perhaps most noticeable in Gaelic-speaking communities. In the Eastern Townships of Quebec, some of the Hebridean place names imported by the settlers were replaced by French names, and Stornoway, the hub of the Scottish community, became entirely French-speaking. 'Bienvenu à Scotstown' or 'Stornoway vous Acceuille' are the messages greeting modern visitors to that corner of Quebec, where the Hebridean component of the population dropped from over 20 per cent to 6 per cent between the 1880s and 1931. Out-migration, particularly to New England, led to the closure of churches and schools, while the use of Gaelic was eroded by exogamous marriages, the loss of community resulting from material success and a perception among the settlers that English was the language of progress. 'Guard the Gaelic' was a poem written at the end of the nineteenth century by Angus MacKay (Oscar Dhu), a bard from the Eastern Townships, who, as this extract shows, lamented the cultural effects of the haemorrhage of Highlanders to the Boston States:

> *Lads and lasses in their teens*
> *Wearing airs of kings and queens –*
> *Just a taste of Boston beans*
> *Makes them lose their Gaelic!*

> *They return with finer clothes*
> *Speaking 'Yankee' through their nose!*
> *That's the way the Gaelic goes,*
> *Pop! Goes the Gaelic.*[76]

More bitter opprobrium was reserved for emigrants who turned their backs on their religious heritage. Chapter 1 demonstrated how would-be emigrants were warned about the irreligion and sharp business practice of American society,[77] but Scots could just as easily fall prey to such temptations when surrounded by their own countrymen. Preaching in the Perth district of Upper Canada in the 1820s, the Reverend William Bell was disappointed, not only at the clannishness of the Scottish settlers, who wanted him to confine his services entirely to them, but also at evidence of their spiritual backsliding:

On looking round me ... I saw a moral as well as a natural wilderness requiring my cultivation. With regard to a great majority of the settlers, religion seemed to occupy no part of their attention. The Sabbath was awfully profaned, and drunkenness, swearing, and other vices, were thought matters of course. The number of those inclined to attend public worship was small, and of those possessing real piety still smaller ... In going to and returning from the place of worship, I could not help making comparisons between my native country and this. Many were at work at their ordinary employments, and I began to see that religious instruction, by a great part of the population, so far from being considered a privilege, would be considered a great hindrance to the prosecution of their plans.[78]

It was not only clergymen who were critical of Sabbath-breaking. Thirty years later a correspondent of the *Inverness Advertiser*, who had emigrated reluctantly to Upper Canada to find work, complained that he had not heard a Gaelic sermon since he left home, and confirmed Bell's impression with the following anecdote:

They are not keeping the Sabbath here at all. They are shooting and cutting firewood the same as on other days. I saw a man one Sabbath-day cutting a tree with an axe. He was a shoemaker. When I was speaking to him about the Sabbath-day, he said he was so busy through the week he could not cut fire-wood. I went into his house, and one of his boys came in and said, Father, you must mend my shoes to-morrow. The old man said, you can mend them yourself. Yes, said the son, but I have no time, as I must be early to my work. You can mend them to-day, said the old man. I'll not mend them on Sunday, said the son; on which the father took a stick and made the poor boy break the holy day of rest by mending them on the Sunday.[79]

Further south, the tropical climate of the Caribbean seems to have undermined the morals, as well as the health, of Scottish emigrants. In British Guiana, they won striking material success but lost both their inhibitions and their integrity, as self-indulgence replaced sobriety, and their clannishness became the subject of local derision:

there is perhaps no class of European emigrants that has undergone such changes in their natural habits. The reserve, the temperance, the zeal for religion which characterised them in their own country, became gradually obliterated in their translation to this colony. They still associated together, and sustained each other in the true spirit of nationality, carrying this principle of cohesion indeed so far that the shrewd negroes applied the term of Scotchmen to the large shrimps which they were in the habit of hawking about for sale, because of the habits of these creatures in clinging one to the other. But, separated from the austere influence of domestic examples at home, and cast into a community very differently organised, they plunged as readily as others into the vortex of dissipation. In reference to a great many, it may be observed, that much of this change was owing to the fact of their being introduced on their arrival to a footing in society, and to a mode of living to which they had been previously strangers in 'Auld Reekie'. Mingling in more pretending and extravagant circles, and living in a style superior to that in which they had been brought up, they soon came to lose that simplicity and sobriety of character which, as a nation, they have so meritoriously maintained. They have been more successful in business notwithstanding than most of the other settlers from England and Ireland, but they have also encountered greater reverses, and although forming a majority of the white population, they have failed to impart their nationality to the colony.[80]

Elsewhere in the Caribbean too, the legendary frugality, industry and business acumen of the Scots were coupled with debauchery, boorishness and the complete absence of the cerebral symbols of Scottishness so lauded in other emigrant destinations. Lady Maria Nugent, whose husband served as Lieutenant-General of Jamaica for four years at the beginning of the nineteenth century, recalled an encounter with an unsavoury but successful Scottish plantation overseer:

The overseer's chere amie, and no man here is without one, is a tall black woman, well made, with a very flat nose, thick lips, and a skin of ebony, highly polished and shining. She shewed me her three yellow children, and said, with some ostentation, she should soon have another. The marked attention of the other women, plainly proved her to be the favourite Sultana of this vulgar, ugly, Scotch Sultan, who is about fifty, clumsy, ill made, and dirty. He had a dingy, sallow-brown complexion, and only two yellow discoloured tusks, by way of teeth. However, they say he is a good overseer; so at least his brother Scotchmen told me, and there is no one here to contradict him, as almost all agents, attornies, merchants and shopkeepers, are of that country, and really do deserve to thrive in this, they are so industrious.[81]

Particularly reprehensible – but unpunished – was the conduct of one of his

fellow countrymen recounted by the Scot John Anderson, Special Magistrate in
St Vincent:

> A Scotsman – (I blush to write it) who resided to Leeward was on another occa-
> sion being rowed to Kingstown in his canoe, on board of which was a runaway
> slave, whose neck for greater security he had encircled with an iron collar,
> attached to a heavy weight – which the unfortunate wretch supported in his
> hands, or on his head, when in motion. As they coasted along, he seized as he
> conceived, a favourable moment for escape, and leapt into the waves. 'Hout
> away mon' said Sawney, 'are ye gaen that gait? Then tak it a wi you'; – & suiting
> the action to the word, he threw over the ponderous ball – and as the poor slave
> was sucked into the vortex the momentary bubble of water announced that an
> immortal spirit was struggling to be free. The reins of authority were too
> loosely held, to bring retributive Justice on the tyrant. The deed – and the per-
> petrator became known, but the murderer was never called to account.[82]

But even if Scots retained their religious and cultural identity, it could still be
a source of discord or a stumbling block rather than an asset. Distinctiveness
was certainly interpreted negatively in a stinging diatribe against the Scots of
Pictou in 1859 which disparaged them as 'a canting, covenanting, oat-eating,
money-griping tribe of second-hand Scotch Presbyterians; a transplanted,
degenerate, barren patch of high cheek-bones and red hair, with nothing cleav-
ing to them of the original stock, except covetousness and that peculiar cuta-
neous eruption for which the mother country is celebrated'.[83] Further west, in
Killarney, the sabbatarianism of the Hebridean emigrants in the 1880s irritated
their less legalistic Protestant neighbours, who could not understand why men
did not shave on Sunday, or why the potatoes remained unpeeled, the cream
unseparated and the lakes unfished on the Sabbath.[84] The Gaelic language too
isolated these emigrants unhelpfully from their more experienced neighbours.
'Gaelic may be a very nice and expressive dialect but you cannot raise wheat
from it, and these people had nothing else,' commented T. J. Lawlor, the Killarney merchant who supplied the new arrivals with seed corn and seven years
later reflected on the reasons for the colonists' limited success.[85] His views
echoed those expressed a generation earlier by the *Dundas Warden*, in respect of
the 1,100 emigrants sent from Barra to Ontario in 1851. While the inability of all
but a handful of the emigrants to speak English may have reinforced their ethnic
identity, the newspaper was of the opinion that their monolingualism seriously

impeded their ability to capitalize on any of the benefits emigration might offer them, concluding as a result that, for these impecunious Hebrideans, 'emigration is more cruel than banishment'.[86]

Contemporary opinion was divided over whether specially created ethnic colonies were a blessing or a curse. Some, like William Brown, were utterly convinced of their value, especially as a social cement, but others were concerned that they encouraged an isolating introspectiveness that prevented the settlers interacting with their more experienced neighbours and rendered them vulnerable to economic failure. By remaining socially distinct, the Killarney settlers missed the opportunity to learn crucial new skills from earlier settlers, and their poor agricultural techniques were heavily criticized by the Imperial Colonisation Board. Ethnically autonomous settlements could also be disputatious settlements, another charge levelled at the Killarney emigrants, whose assimilation was made more difficult by their history of collaborative political agitation in the crofters' war, and their tendency to look to Scotland for redress of the grievances that they identified and discussed in their new Canadian environment. In the opinion of A. M. Burgess of the Canadian Department of the Interior:

> The Crofters and the Highland people generally are excellent settlers when they emigrate of their own accord, and are placed alongside of people of other nationalities, but when settled in compact body they are like the Indians in that they spend a great deal of time in talking over their grievances, real or fancied ... they are content to make very little progress when left to themselves.[87]

Finally, we have to address the issue of spurious identity. Did Scots overseas, deliberately or subconsciously, filter out memories of home that did not fit the prevailing orthodoxy of either brutal expulsion or the sentimentalized 'kailyard' image of rural domesticity? Inevitably, emigrants' memories of their homeland – frozen in their minds at the time of departure – became increasingly divorced from reality as the years passed, but in some cases the image and the reality had never coincided. Perhaps the preservation or refashioning of their ethnic identity overseas was only sustainable if the emigrants exaggerated either the evils that had driven them away or the attributes of Scotland that made its memory worth celebrating. As a result, the Scotland they remembered in exile was generally larger than life, or even a complete figment of their imagination. While for some the construction of such an ersatz identity was the means of giving a corporate rationale to a dislocating experience, for others it was simply a piece of occasional fun. As E. J. Cowan has suggested, 'Whether attending balls or Burns suppers, there was an element of the carnivalesque involved; one or two annual wallowings in Scottish culture, bathos and nostalgia enabled people to act like normal human beings ... throughout the rest of the year.'[88]

But there was also a commercial dimension to the fashioning of a Scottish identity overseas. Scotland's growing tourist industry in the nineteenth century owed much to the romantic lure of an invented Highland landscape promoted in word and picture by Sir Walter Scott and Sir Edwin Landseer respectively. Although — or because — such images distorted the reality of a country where, by the end of the century, four-fifths of the population lived in the urban-industrial central Lowlands, they were immensely popular overseas, where they further exacerbated the 'tartanization' of the Scottish emigrant culture. Nowhere was this more evident than in Nova Scotia, which in the late nineteenth century began to recognize the commercial value of its Scottish connections. Later, during the 1930s depression, it 'began parading its Scottishness ... as a calculated and self-conscious promotion for the tourist industry'.[89] Premier Angus L. Macdonald coupled his personal enthusiasm for Scotland with a drive to promote the Gaelic heritage of economically vulnerable areas, even if that meant ignoring the existence of other ethnic groups. The result was the simultaneous creation of the Cabot Trail and the Cape Breton Highlands National Park, to which was later added the Lone Sheiling, a completely spurious replica of a Highland settler's home, built of stone and thatch (rather than the wood that the emigrants actually used) along the most northerly stretch of the Cabot Trail. Elsewhere too Caledonian games and Scottish societies were used as tourist bait, particularly in the wake of the burgeoning interest in genealogy in the second half of the twentieth century. Grandfather Mountain Highland Games in North Carolina is currently the biggest — and most Disneyfied — gathering on the international circuit of such events.

In the headlong rush to claim and capitalize on Scottish origins, accurate analysis has sometimes been sacrificed to a fuzzy stereotype in which all Scots were portrayed as brothers, marching forth in honourable poverty from the land of the but and ben to win fame, fortune and universal respect as explorers, fur traders, soldiers, farmers, businessmen, clerics, educators and politicians from the Arctic to the Antipodes. The uncomfortable truth that evicted Highlanders in turn displaced Native Americans and Australian Aborigines is conveniently forgotten, as is the fact that Scots did not always bury their differences when they emigrated. No doubt it is true that in the melting pot of the emigrant experience, different motives for remembering home, different mechanisms of remembrance, and different memories – real and artificial – converged to some extent into a single stream of Scottishness. Robert Louis Stevenson certainly claimed that when Scot met Scot overseas, differences of origin, language and religion were forgotten, and 'Highland and Lowland, all our hearts are Scottish.'[90] But not always, for Scots exported their prejudices and their quarrels as well as their brotherly affections, as is evident from even a cursory glance at the colonial manifestations of Scottish theological disputes and Highland–Lowland rivalries. Lowland Scots such as John Galt and William Gilkison actively discouraged Gaels from settling in Guelph and Elora, the towns they respectively founded in Upper Canada, and although refugees from the Highland famine were initially given relief in Fergus, by the early 1850s they had become an embarrassment and were being pushed south to townships around Lake Erie.[91]

Conclusion : a Scottish diaspora?

The predominance of Canadian examples in this book is not accidental. It is attributable partly to the longer history of Scottish settlement in Canada, at least in comparison with Australia and New Zealand, where the influence of Wakefield's principles of systematic colonization, the different socio-economic structure and the emphasis on creating a new national identity may have made it more difficult to establish distinctive Scottish communities. But that does not fully explain why Scottish identity was far more visible in Canada than in the United States, since North America as a whole had a strong eighteenth-century tradition of Scottish settlement. One clue, as we have suggested, lies in the ease with which a skilled Scottish workforce, the product of an advanced economy and a literate society, could respond to the requirements of American industry. But also important was the fundamental difference in the immigration philosophies developed by the two countries. Whereas the preference of the United States for the concept of a melting pot perhaps tended to obscure the visibility of individual immigrant groups – particularly those who, like the Scots, were not consistently oppressed or victimized – the mosaic approach favoured by Canada allowed the Scots, like other immigrant groups, to retain and promote their ethnicity with confidence. Perhaps we can therefore claim that in Canada, to a greater extent than in other areas of Scottish settlement, issues of identity, isolation and integration were easily recognizable, hotly debated and even definable in terms of a diaspora.

On closer examination, however, the definition of Scottish emigration as a diaspora may be more widely applicable. While it clearly cannot be defined in the Jewish sense of the complete scattering of a nation under persecution, many emigrants not only brought cultural, social and economic ideas from the homeland but also nurtured and replicated them with such tenacity that key features of the Scottish psyche became deeply embedded in the culture of the host societies. Dr Johnson's assertion that communities of emigrant Scots in the 1770s 'change nothing but the place of their abode' was equally true of the nineteenth century, as many emigrants, consciously or otherwise, created enduring ethnic colonies on the North American prairie, the South African veld and the Antipodean or Falkland Islands sheep station. Yet this was not true of all who left Scotland. Johnson's observation was confined to those who emigrated in neighbourhood parties, whose 'departure from their native country is no longer exile' and who 'carry with them their language, their opinions, their popular songs, and hereditary merriment'. Solitary emigrants, on the other hand, he believed, lacked any ability to imprint their identity on the new land, since 'their power consisted in their concentration: when they are dispersed, they have no effect'.[92] This trend too was evident in the nineteenth century, among those whose main objective was to put the past behind them and capitalize on the opportunities of a new land by integrating into the host society as quickly and as imperceptibly as possible.

The extent to which emigrants wished to remember seems to have depended not on factors such as gender, occupation or location *per se*, but on whether they regarded themselves as passive exiles or active adventurers. Exiles remembered in song and story in order to commemorate and justify a traumatic experience, while adventurers remembered in practical collaboration if it was in their individual interest to do so. On the basis of this definition, it might be argued that the cultivation of memory – including spurious memory – was primarily the preserve of Highlanders. Their culture and experiences combined to create in them a greater psychological need to remember, and therefore a particularly potent image of a diaspora, which predated their settlement overseas, and was couched in terms of enforced removal rather than positive choice. Their predilection for group settlement in isolated locations facilitated the transfer of their corporate identity, since they were not compelled to adjust to other cultures, but could reconstruct the world they had lost, with all its memories, real and invented.

Lowlanders' attitudes, on the other hand, tended to be pragmatic rather than romantic. Caribbean planters who cultivated business and social links with fellow countrymen, timber merchants who monopolized the Maritime and St Lawrence trade in the early nineteenth century, tradesmen who competed for skilled jobs on the USA's industrial frontier and wealthy pastoralists who endowed educational and religious institutions across Australia generally played the ethnic card in pursuit of individual economic betterment rather than cultural solidarity. Most Lowlanders were not burdened with a sense of guilt about abandoning the land of their fathers and therefore felt little need to justify their decision to emigrate by attributing it exclusively to negative factors beyond their control. Their more individualistic, ambitious approach made them less inclined overtly to cultivate memories of home, and that in turn inhibited the development of a clear concept of diaspora or even shared experience. The consequence of this has been the misleading – but persistent – application of the powerful Highland memories and definition of diaspora to the overall Scottish exodus.

But Scottish emigrants did not fall into watertight compartments. While Highlanders may have been more inclined to kin-based concentrated settlement and the cultivation of memory, and Lowlanders to individualistic dispersal, the experience of uprooting often engendered, even in individualists, an unexpected desire to proclaim their identity and erase regional and cultural differences. If they differed in the way they remembered home, in practice there was often little difference in the ways that they demonstrated and capitalized on their identity overseas. Highland emigrants might be set apart by language, and might have regarded the cultivation of Celtic contacts primarily as a means of preserving their culture, but that did not prevent them from using those contacts in pursuit of their economic and social betterment. Remembering and forgetting were moulded to fit their changing circumstances and ambitions and, as we have seen, there was no common memory or single mythology of emigration, even among cleared Highlanders. Conversely, Lowlanders who might have been more inclined to highlight the practical economic applications of the emblems of diaspora often came to value the cultural functions of those emblems, particularly if the experience of emigrating had provoked in them a feeling of rootlessness. And the emblems themselves were often identical, for both Highlanders and Lowlanders made equal use of the formal mechanisms of church, school and Scottish society, and the informal mechanisms of place names, correspondence, family and community networks and chain migration to preserve, articulate and even invent their memories and identity. The Aberdonians who settled in Nichol Township in the 1830s christened their settlement Bon Accord, after the motto of their native city, while their neighbours in Fergus constructed dormer-windowed stone houses in the style of the homeland and put a high priority on the early establishment of church and school. Further east, Scots in Montreal's mercantile community not only did business with each other but also paraded their origins through the thistle and saltire iconography engraved into their commercial buildings, while the 900-strong Scotch Colony in the forested depths of New Brunswick displayed many of the features more commonly associated with the isolated group settlements favoured by Highland emigrants.

The decline of many of the symbols of ethnicity in the early twentieth century suggests that the preservation of Scottish identity was also generational, at least in the United States, where by the 1920s the once thriving Scottish immigrant press had disappeared and only two Highland Games remained. In this the Scots overseas differed markedly from their Irish counterparts, whose defensive ethnic solidarity, forged in the nineteenth century, remained strong throughout the twentieth century. The largely skilled, Protestant Scots – 82 per cent of whom came from urban areas by the 1880s – were welcomed by host societies for their occupational ability and adaptability, while the emigrants themselves did not harness their diaspora to political grievances or folk memories of English oppression. Their national, regional and clan societies were often élite clubs rather than – as in the Irish case – political and cultural pressure groups which have continued to cultivate a self-conscious ethnic alienation and sharp diasporic profile, with significant commercial, as well as social, implications in the global business world of the twenty-first century.

NOTES

Abbreviations

AUA   Aberdeen University Archives

NAC   National Archives of Canada

NAS   National Archives of Scotland

NLS   National Library of Scotland

NRA(S)   National Register of Archives (Scotland)

NSA   *New Statistical Account of Scotland, by the Ministers of the Respective Parishes, under the Superintendence of a Committee of the Society for the Benefit of the Sons and Daughters of the Clergy* (Edinburgh, 1834–45)

NLNZ   National Library of New Zealand

OSA   Sir John Sinclair (ed.), *Statistical Account of Scotland, 1791–1799*, edited by D. J. Withrington and I. R. Grant (East Ardsley, 1981, originally published 1791–9, arranged by county and republished 1972–81)

PP   Parliamentary Papers

PRO   Public Record Office

SCA   Scottish Catholic Archives

Chapter 1: Traditions of Emigration

1. *Blackwood's Edinburgh Magazine*, vol. CXXXVI (October 1884), p. 468.
2. Ivan Doig, *Dancing at the Rascal Fair* (New York, 1987), p. 94.
3. G. T. Bisset-Smith, *Vital Registration: A Manual of the Law and Practice Concerning the Registration of Births, Deaths and Marriages, Registration Acts for Scotland* (1907), p. 168.
4. *OSA*, vol. XVII (Inverness-shire, Ross and Cromarty), pp. 63, 517–18.
5. Ibid., vol. XVI (Banffshire, Moray and Nairnshire), p. 327. See also ibid., vol. XVII (Inverness-shire, Ross and Cromarty), pp. 117, 342.
6. Ibid., vol. XVI (Banffshire, Moray and Nairnshire), pp. 492–93.
7. Ibid., vol. VII (Lanarkshire and Renfrewshire), p. 466; ibid., vol. XX (The Western Isles), pp. 140–41.
8. *NSA*, vol. XII (Aberdeenshire), p. 117.
9. J. A. Galloway and I. Murray, 'Scottish Migration to England, 1400–1550', *Scottish Geographical Magazine*, vol. 112 (1996), pp. 29–38; J. Donaldson, *Money Increased and Credit Raised* (Edinburgh, 1705), p. 19.
10. *OSA*, vol. XX (The Western Isles), p. 307; ibid., vol. V (Stewartry of Kirkcudbright and Wigtownshire), p. 148.
11. E. M. Riley (ed.), *The Journal of John Harrower* (Williamsburgh, Va, 1965).

12. J. H. McCulloch, *The Scot in England* (London, 1935), pp. 74–5; Arthur Redford, *Labour Migration in England, 1800–50* (Manchester, 1926), p. 119.

13. T. W. H. Crosland, *The Unspeakable Scot* (London, 1902), pp. 190, 193, 194.

14. Charles Knight (ed.), *London*, vol. III (London, 1842), pp. 325, 335.

15. McCulloch, *The Scot in England*, p. 125.

16. Marjory Harper and Peter Payne, *Aberdeen University Students, 1860–1920* (6621 records, Economic and Social Science Research Council Data Archive, 1994).

17. Crosland, *The Unspeakable Scot*, p. 62.

18. Redford, *Labour Migration in England*, p. 118.

19. AUA, MS 2884/1/3/1–2, Samuel Chalmers to Alexander Wallace Chalmers, 12, 14 March 1854, letters 24 and 27.

20. Knight (ed.), *London*, p. 32.

21. S. Murdoch and A. Grosjean, *Scotland, Scandinavia and Northern Europe, 1580–1707*, http://www.abdn.ac.uk/history/datasets/ssne (Aberdeen, 1998).

22. David Dobson, *Scottish Emigration to Colonial America, 1607–1785* (Athens, Ga), p. 13; Nicholas Canny, *Europeans on the Move: Studies on European Migration, 1500–1800* (Oxford, 1994), pp. 80–82.

23. James Gammack, 'An Aberdeen Graduate in Virginia', *Aberdeen University Review*, vol. IX (1921–2), pp. 146–7; Gammack, 'Aberdeen University Men in Virginia', ibid., vol. X (1922–3), pp. 147–8.

24. NAS, RH15/1/95/30, Roderick Gordon of Carnoustie to Hon. William Duff of Braco, MP for the Shire of Banff, 28 June 1734.

25. *OSA*, vol. II (The Lothians), p. 541.

26. Ibid., vol. XVII (Inverness-shire, Ross and Cromarty – Glenelg), p. 76; ibid., vol. XX (The Western Isles – North Uist), pp. 117–18; (Jura and Colonsay), p. 375.

27. Ibid., vol. IV (Dumfries-shire), pp. 507, 69; ibid., vol. V (Kirkcudbright and Wigtownshire), pp. 202, 547; ibid., vol. XIV (Kincardineshire and South and West Aberdeenshire), p. 480; ibid., vol. XVI (Banffshire, Moray and Nairnshire), p. 493.

28. Ibid., vol. XII (North and West Perthshire), pp. 156–57.

29. Samuel Johnson, *A Journey to the Western Islands of Scotland* (London, 1875), edited by R. W. Chapman (Oxford, 1924), pp. 87, 120.

30. *The South Australian Handbook*, advertised in the *Aberdeen Journal*, 30 January 1839.

31. *Counsel for Emigrants – Sequel* (Aberdeen, 1834), p. 35, letter dated 9 March 1834; *Chambers' Edinburgh Journal*, vol. 8, no. 406 (9 November 1839), p. 333.

32. Patrick Shirreff, *A tour through North America; together with a comprehensive view of the Canadas and United States. As adapted for agricultural emigration* (Edinburgh, 1835), p. 410.

33. *Chambers' Edinburgh Journal*, vol. III, no. 112 (22 March 1834), p. 63.

34. Ibid., vol. I (9 June 1832), p. 149.

35. *Aberdeen Herald*, 20 September 1845.

36. *Tait's Edinburgh Magazine*, vol. V (1838), p. 780; *Aberdeen Journal*, 16 September 1840; *Chambers' Edinburgh Journal*, vol. IX, no. 233 (17 June 1848), p. 395.

37. *Aberdeen Journal*, 25 June 1873 and 17 June 1874; *Shetland Times*, 18 May and 8 June 1874.

38. University of Cape Town Library, Department of Manuscripts and Archives, BC 1038, Laburn Collection, A4.4, McNaughton to John Walker, 13 December 1881. See also pp. 140–1.

39. National Library of South Africa, South African Letters (Miscellaneous) Collection (2), 6040 MSB 744.2 (8), Andrew Murray senior to his sons, 20 January 1842.

40. *Aberdeen Journal*, 17 November 1852.

41. See, for instance, *Gentleman's Magazine*, vol. CI (February 1831), p. 109; *Blackwood's Edinburgh Magazine*, vol. 31 (June 1832), pp. 907–27; *Quarterly Journal of Agriculture*, vol. III (1832), p. 548; *Tait's Edinburgh Magazine*, vol. IX (January 1842), pp. 2–5.

42. *Counsel for Emigrants – Sequel*, p. 49; *Counsel for Emigrants* (Aberdeen, 1834), p. ix; ibid., p. 40, letter dated 4 December 1833.

43. *Counsel for Emigrants*, p. 138, letter dated 16 February 1834; *Toronto Leader*, quoted in *Aberdeen Journal*, 30 October 1857; *Aberdeen Herald*, 23 June 1855; *Aberdeen Journal*, 24 August 1864.

44. AUA, MS 2138, pp. 199–200, Patrick Bell's Journal.

45. *Shetland Times*, 1 May 1875.

Chapter 2: Expelling the Unwanted

1. PP 1826–27 (550), V, 23, *Third Report from the Select Committee appointed to inquire into the expediency of encouraging emigration from the United Kingdom*, petition by the President of the Kirkfieldbank Emigration Society, Lanarkshire.

2. David Dobson, *Scottish Emigration to Colonial America, 1607–1785* (Athens, Ga, 1994), p. 93.

3. Dumfries and Galloway Archives, jail books, GF4.

4. William Kennedy, *Annals of Aberdeen*, vol. I (London, 1818), p. 294.

5. Peter Williamson, *The Life and Curious Adventures of Peter Williamson, who was carried off from Aberdeen and sold for a slave* (Aberdeen, 1801). See also pp. 113, 161.

6. PRO, CO386/154, Register of Applications for Passages to the Colonies for Convicts' Families, 1848–1871. For discussion of Scots and transportation, see Ian Donnachie, 'Scottish Criminals and Transportation to Australia, 1786–1852', *Scottish Economic and Social History*, vol. 4 (1984), pp. 21–38; 'The Convicts of 1830: Scottish Criminals Transported to New South Wales', *Scottish Historical Review*, vol. 65 (1986), pp. 34–47.

7. AUA, MS 3004/7/5, Fraser of Philorth Papers, 24 May 1832, Lord Saltoun's factor to William Stuart, advocate in Aberdeen.

8. *Aberdeen Journal*, 26 February and 2 April 1834, and *Aberdeen Herald*, 24 May 1834.

9. *NSA*, vol. IV (Dumfries-shire, Kirkcudbright and Wigtown), p. 552.

10. NAS, CH2/492/1, Minutes of Greyfriars Kirk Session, Aberdeen, vol. 1, 4 August 1845; Aberdeen Industry School, Admission Minute Book, 1867–74, entry nos. 2532, 2676, 2687, 2775, 2794, 2816, 3099, 3184, 3391; ibid., 1874–7, entry nos. 3301, 3353, 3425, 3429.

11. PRO, T47/12, quoted in Viola R. Cameron, *Emigrants from Scotland to America, 1774–1775* (Baltimore, 1965), pp. 1–5, 28–9, 35–6, 37–40, 57–60, 61–2.

12. *Scots Magazine*, vol. 78 (July 1816), p. 549.

13. PRO, CO 384/1, John Campbell to Lord Bathurst, 11 March 1817; McDermid to Lord Bathurst, 18 March 1817; CO 384/3, enclosure in Navy Office to Henry Goulburn, 10 July 1819. All quoted in Helen Cowan, *British Emigration to British North America: The First Hundred Years* (Toronto, 1961), p. 45.

14. *Hansard's Parliamentary Debates*, second series, vol. 1, cols 40–43, 28 April 1820, speech by Lord Archibald Hamilton.

15. NRA(S) Survey no. 2177, Duke of Hamilton Papers. James Muir, Clerk of the Society, to Robert Brown, 24 January 1820; Charles Baillie to Lord Archibald Hamilton, 22 April 1820. Both quoted in Michael E. Vance, 'The Politics of Emigration: Scotland and Assisted Emigration to Upper Canada, 1815–26', in T. M. Devine (ed.), *Scottish Emigration and Scottish Society* (Edinburgh, 1992), p. 50.

16. NRA(S) Survey no. 2177, Duke of Hamilton Papers. William Granger to Lord Archibald Hamilton, 4 May 1820.

17. PRO, CO384/7 fo.425, Robert Beath to Lord Bathurst, 30 January 1821.

18. PRO, CO384/4, 16 March 1819, petition of Robert Brown, John Couper, John Reid and Gabriel Wilson.

19. Ibid., 8 and 16 July 1819.

20. Robert Lamond, *A Narrative of the Rise and Progress of Emigration from the Counties of Lanark and Renfrew to the New Settlements in Upper Canada* (Glasgow, 1821), pp.12, 13–14.

21. *Scots Magazine*, vol. LXXXVIII (July 1821), p. 81. See also Carol Bennett, *The Lanark Society Settlers, 1820–1821* (Renfrew, Ont., 1991).

22. Lamond, *A Narrative of the Rise and Progress...*, p. 64.

23. PP 1826–7 (237), V, *First, Second and Third Reports from the Select Committee on Emigration from the United Kingdom with minutes of evidence, appendix and index*, QQ. 150, 724, 221–6, 247–55.

24. PP 1826 (404), IV, 112–14, *First Report from the Select Committee appointed to inquire into the expediency of encouraging emigration from the United Kingdom.*

25. *Paisley Advertiser*, 19 April and 23 August 1828; James Cameron, 'A Study of the Factors that Assisted and Directed Scottish Emigration to Upper Canada, 1815–1855,' (unpublished PhD thesis, 1970), p. 97.

26. PP 1841 Sess. 1 [296], X, 273, *Report of the Commission for Inquiring into the Condition of the Unemployed Handloom Weavers in the United Kingdom*, evidence of Mr Symons and Dr Harding, 119–20.

27. PP 1843 (115), VII, 1, *Select Committee to Inquire into the Treatment of Unemployed and Destitute Inhabitants of Paisley since 1841*, QQ. 422–3.

28. PP 1844 (557), XX, 1, *Report from HM Commissioners for Inquiring into the Administration and Practical Operation of the Poor Laws in Scotland, Report and Appendix*, Part 1, Q. 8476.

29. J. Hector St John de Crevecoeur, *Letters from an American Farmer* (London, 1782, 1904 edition), p.102.

30. Cameron, *Emigrants from Scotland to America*, pp. 25–7, 54–5, 30–4, 41–3, 77–9, 88–92.

31. PRO, CO384/3, 20 November 1818, Donald Sinclair to Lord Bathurst.

32. Ibid., 4 November 1818, Donald Logan to Lord Bathurst.

33. PP 1826–27 (550), V, 223, *Third Report from the Select Committee on Emigration from the United Kingdom, Appendix 14, Abstracts of All Petitions Transmitted to the Colonial Department, since 1st January 1825, from persons desirous of emigrating from the United Kingdom, Scotch Petitions and Memorials.*

34. Ibid., petition dated 24 May 1827.

35. J. L. Campbell, 'Eviction at First Hand. The Clearing of Clanranald's Lands', *Scots Magazine*, (January 1945), pp. 297–302.

36. PP 1826–27 (550), V, 223. *Third Report from the Select Committee on Emigration from the United Kingdom*, question 2952. See also Eric Richards, *A History of the Highland Clearances*, vol. 2, *Emigration, Protest, Reasons* (London, 1985), p. 230, and James Hunter, *A Dance Called America: The Scottish Highlands, the United States and Canada* (Edinburgh, 1994), p. 114.

37. PP 1841 (182) (333), VI, *First and Second Reports from the Select Committee on Emigration, Scotland, together with minutes of evidence, appendices and index* [hereafter PP 1841, *Select Committee on Emigration*], Appendix I, Robert Graham, Return of an Address to the House of Commons, June 1837.

38. Ibid., *Second Report.*

39. PP 1844 (557), XX, 1, *Report from H.M. Commissioners for Inquiring into the Administration and Practical Operation of the Poor Laws in Scotland* [hereafter *Royal Commission on the Poor Laws*], *Appendix, Part I*, QQ. 11656 (McLeod), 12758 (Bowie).

40. T. M. Devine, 'Landlordism and Highland Emigration', in Devine (ed.), *Scottish Emigration and Scottish Society*, p. 94.

41. PP 1851 [1397], XXVI, *Report to the Board of Supervision, by Sir John McNeill, GCB, on the Western Highlands and Islands* [hereafter *McNeill Report*], *Appendix*, pp. 4, 35–6, 61, 74, 82.

42. *Inverness Courier*, 30 May 1838.

43. T. M. Devine, *The Great Highland Famine: Hunger, Emigration and the Scottish Highlands in the Nineteenth Century* (Edinburgh, 1988), p. 252.

44. Ibid., pp. 201, 212-13, 235; Richards, *A History of the Highland Clearances*, pp. 253–5, 275.

45. PP 1841, *Select Committee on Emigration*, QQ. 188 (John Bowie), 445 (Robert Graham), 1505 (Thomas Rolph).

46. PP 1844, *Royal Commission on the Poor Laws*, QQ. 11656, 12760.

47. PP 1851 [1397] XXVI, *McNeill Report*, pp. xxiv, xxvi, 73.

48. Richards, *A History of the Highland Clearances*, p. 240.

49. PP 1841, *Select Committee on Emigration*, Q. 2647, Duncan Shaw. The estate management won the battle in 1841–2, when a total of 631 people agreed to emigrate. (Richards, *A History of the Highland Clearances*, p. 245).

50. PP 1844, *Royal Commission on the Poor Laws*, QQ. 13211, 13258, 13834.

51. PP 1851, *McNeill Report*, pp. 2, 75, 79, xxi, xxiii, xxxv, 67; PRO, CO384/5, 22 February 1819.

52. *Scotsman*, 25 August 1849.

53. *Inverness Advertiser*, quoted in *Stirling Journal and Advertiser*, 14 September 1849 and in Richards, *A History of the Highland Clearances*, p. 264.

54. PP 1849 [1025], XXXVIII, *Papers Relative to Emigration to the North American Colonies*, extracts from notes appended to the periodical reports of arrivals of passenger ships at the ports of Quebec and Montreal in the season of 1848, no. 9, 31 August to 15 September.

55. PP 1851 (173) XL, *Papers Relative to Emigration to the North American Colonies*, extracts from notes appended to the periodical reports of arrivals of passenger ships at the ports of Quebec and Montreal in the season of 1849, no. 5, 1 to 31 August.

56. Ibid., 1 October to 2 November.

57. PP 1851 (348), XL, *Papers Relative to Emigration to the North American Colonies*, extracts from notes appended to the periodical reports of arrivals of passenger ships at the ports of Quebec and Montreal in the season of 1850, no. 6, 1 to 31 August.

58. PP 1852 [1474] XXXII, *Papers Relative to Emigration to the North American Colonies*, extracts from notes appended to the periodical reports of arrivals of passenger ships at the ports of Quebec and Montreal in the season of 1851, Alexander Buchanan to J. Leslie, 2 September 1851; Alexander Buchanan to J. Fleming, 26 November 1851.

59. *Quebec Times*, n.d., quoted in Alexander MacKenzie, *The History of the Highland Clearances* (Inverness, 1883), pp. 257–8.

60. Donald McLeod, *Gloomy Memories in the Highlands of Scotland: versus Mrs Harriet Beecher Stowe's Sunny Memories in (England) a Foreign Land: or a faithful picture of the extirpation of the Celtic Race from the Highlands of Scotland* (Toronto, 1857), p. 164. James Cameron suggests that in only twenty cases were Gordon's emigrants actually manhandled aboard the ships. James Cameron, 'A Study of the Factors that Assisted and Directed Scottish Emigration to Upper Canada', pp. 345–56, quoted in Richards, *A History of the Highland Clearances*, p. 254.

61. MacKenzie, *The History of the Highland Clearances*, pp. 285, 268.

62. PP 1884, XXXII–XXXVI, *Report of H.M. Commissioners of Inquiry into the Condition of the Crofters and Cottars in the Highlands and Islands of Scotland* [hereafter Napier Commission], Q. 14301.

63. Ibid., Appendix A, pp. 117, 119.

64. Ibid., Report, p. 8. See also Wayne Norton, *Help Us to a Better Land: Crofter Colonies in the Prairie West* (Regina, Sask., 1994).

65. 'The Large Farm System', *Free Church Magazine*, vol. V (1848), p. 112; C. Hope, *George Hope of Fenton Barns: A Sketch of his life, compiled by his daughter* (Edinburgh, 1881).

66. Comment of a Fife minister in *Free Church Magazine*, vol. VIII (1851), p. 249; see also Ian Carter, *Farm Life in North-East Scotland, 1840–1914: The Poor Man's Country* (Edinburgh, 1979), p. 157.

67. PRO, CO384/3, 25 May 1818; CO384/5, 20 March 1819; *NSA*, vol. IV, p. 539; E. J. Cowan, 'From the Southern Uplands to Southern Ontario: Nineteenth-century Emigration from the Scottish Borders', in Devine (ed.), *Scottish Emigration and Scottish Society*, p. 72.

68. NAS GD 224 511/20/5, 8 November 1842, William Ogilvie to the Duke of Buccleuch; Cowan, 'From the Southern Uplands ...', pp. 69, 62, from James Hogg, *The Works of the Ettrick Shepherd*, vol. 1 (London, 1865), p. 426.

69. James Leslie (of Aberchirder), *Willie and Meggie's Marriage; with a hundred cuts of homespun yarn therewith interwoven* (second edition, Aberdeen, 1837), pp. 32–3, 35.

70. *Aberdeen Herald*, 4 December 1852.

71. Ibid., 3 June 1854.

72. NAC, RG 76, C-10294-5, vol. 405, file 590687, Report of John MacLennan, in Department of the Interior, *Annual Reports on Immigration, 1909–10*.

73. PP 1906 [Cd 3273], XCVI, 583, pp. 15–16.

74. A. D. Hall, *A Pilgrimage of British Farming 1910–1912* (London, 1913), pp. 383–4.

75. *Aberdeen Journal*, 23 January, 22 March and 10, 13 and 14 April 1888, 28 May 1889; Jill Wade, 'The "Gigantic Scheme": Crofter Immigration and Deep-sea Fisheries Development for British Columbia, 1887–1893', *BC Studies*, no. 53 (Spring 1982), pp. 28–44.

76. *Fraserburgh Herald*, 14 February 1888.

77. *Aberdeen Journal*, 27 December 1889.

78. Ibid., 26 December 1890.

79. Aberdeenshire Archives, MS 6/27/23: Fraserburgh Parish Council, Record of Applications, 1907–1911, p. 24.

80. *Aberdeen Journal*, 9 January and 26 December 1911.

81. Ibid., 10 May 1912.

82. PP 1914 Cd. 7462, XXXI, *Report of the Scottish Departmental Committee on the North Sea Fishing Industry, Part II, Evidence*, QQ. 928–31.

83. Ibid., QQ. 4051–2 , 4058–65.

84. Ibid., Q. 4648.

85. Ibid., QQ. 5758–60, 1798.

Chapter 3: Attracting the Adventurous

1. *Counsel for Emigrants* (Aberdeen, 1834), p. 30.

2. PP 1857 (14), X, Sess. 1, *Despatches relating to emigration to the North American Colonies*, p. 28, Report for 15–21 July 1855.

3. Viola R. Cameron, *Emigrants from Scotland to America, 1774–1775* (Baltimore, 1965), pp. 44 (*Magdalene*), 50–51 (Sally), 67–9 (*Friendship*).

4. Ibid., pp. 53, 73–5.

5. *Dumfries Weekly Magazine*, vol. 1 (1772), p. 135, quoted in Ian Adams and Meredyth Somerville, *Cargoes of Despair and Hope: Scottish Emigration to North America, 1603–1803* (Edinburgh, 1983), p. 120.

6. Quoted ibid., p. 114.

7. Witherspoon and the Pagans were also behind the land speculation that brought the *Hector* and its Highland passengers to Nova Scotia in 1773. See pp. 115, 198–9, 200, 335.

8. Cape Archives Depot, A 394, Benjamin Moodie's notes on his experiences in Cape
    Colony, 1817–21, typescript, 18; Lieutenant J. W. D. Moodie, *Ten Years in South Africa*
    (London, 1835), 2 vols.

9. Carol Bennett, *The Lanark Society Settlers, 1820–1821* (Renfrew, Ont., 1991), p. 49.

10. Ibid., p. 52. Boag died in 1830.

11. Quoted in Eric Richards, *A History of the Highland Clearances*, vol. 2, *Emigration,
    Protest, Reasons* (London, 1985), p. 272, from *An Teachdaire Gaidhealach*, 1 August 1857.

12. PP 1826–27 (550), V, 223, *Third Report from the Select Committee appointed to inquire into
    the expediency of encouraging emigration from the United Kingdom*, extracts from
    correspondence quoted in the evidence of William Spencer Northouse. William Davie to
    his sons and daughters, 25 November 1821; Andrew Angus to his parents, 12 January
    1822; James Dobbie to his father and friends, 24 April 1826; Dobbie to his cousin, 26 June
    1826.

13. Anon., *A statement of the satisfactory results which have attended emigration to Upper
    Canada, from the establishment of the Canada Company until the present period; comprising
    statistical tables, and other important information, communicated by respectable residents in
    the various townships of Upper Canada, with a general map of the province; compiled for the
    guidance of emigrants* (London, 1841), p. 14.

14. Napier Commission, Appendix A, p. 138, letters dated 23 and 20 September 1851.

15. The six townships were originally in Buckingham County, later renamed Sherbrooke
    County, which in 1853 became Compton County. Laurel Doucette (ed.), *Cultural
    Retention and Demographic Change: Studies of the Hebridean Scots in the Eastern
    Townships of Quebec* (Ottawa, 1980), pp. 10, 22.

16. Robert MacDougall, *Ceann-Iuil an Fhir-Imrich do dh'America mu-Thuath (The Emigrant's
    Guide to North America)* (Glasgow, Oban, Inverness and Dingwall, 1841), translated and
    edited by Elizabeth Thomson (Toronto, 1998).

17. Margaret Bennett, *Oatmeal and the Catechism. Scottish Gaelic Settlers in Quebec*
    (Edinburgh, 1998), p. 9, interview with Duncan McLeod.

18. Ariel Dyer, *The Laird of Woodhill* (Waterdown, Ont., 1983), p. 30. See also Adam
    Fergusson, *Practical Notes, made during a tour in Canada and a portion of the United States
    in 1831* (Edinburgh, 1833) and *Practical Notes ... second edition, to which are now added
    notes made during a second visit to Canada in 1833* (London, 1834).

19. PRO, CO384/1, 21 April 1817, William Shaw to John Campbell, on behalf of Robert
    Weir; CO384/3, 13 April 1818, Francis Hall to John Campbell; CO384/3, 14 November
    1818, John Campbell to Henry Goulburn; CO384/3, 1818, James Whyte to Colonial
    Department; CO384/4, 6 November 1819, John Haldane to Lord Bathurst.

20. *Quarterly Journal of Agriculture*, vol. IV (1832–4), p. 216.

21. *Counsel for Emigrants* p. 45.

22. Ibid., p. 124. Letter dated 22 October 1833.

23. *Chambers' Edinburgh Journal*, vol. III, no. 112 (22 March 1834), p. 64. Letter from a
    former naval officer to his brother in Edinburgh.

24. Ibid., vol. I, no. 19 (19 June 1832), p. 150, quoting from Martin Doyle, *Hints on*

Emigration to Upper Canada (Dublin, 1832).

25. Ibid., no. 456 (21 September 1872), p. 594, quoting a report by the Canadian Minister of Agriculture.

26. Napier Commission, XXXII, Appendix A, 125–6. Emigration from the Long Island. Letters of emigrants from the property of Lady Gordon Cathcart, letter dated 17 June 1883.

27. Ibid, p. 129, letter dated 11 August 1883.

28. *Chambers' Edinburgh Journal*, vol. VI, no. 292 (2 September 1837), p. 252.

29. *Counsel for Emigrants* pp. 35–7, letter dated 9 March 1834.

30. Eric Richards, Alexia Howe, Ian Donnachie and Adrian Graves, *That Land of Exiles: Scots in Australia 1788–1914* (Edinburgh, 1988), pp. 70–71.

31. *Edinburgh Evening Courant*, 23 November 1822; *Quarterly Journal of Agriculture*, vol. III, p. 356. See also James Dixon, *The Narrative of a Voyage to New South Wales and Van Diemen's Land in the ship* Skelton *during the year 1820. With observations on the state of these colonies and a variety of information, calculated to be useful to emigrants* (Edinburgh, 1822).

32. Quoted in Richards et al., *That Land of Exiles*, p. 75.

33. *Paisley Advertiser*, 14 May 1842. James McDonald to Rev. Dr Thomas Burns.

34. *Aberdeen Herald*, 3 July 1852.

35. NRA(S), Survey no. 1150, Drummuir Castle MSS, bundle 203, letter from Alexander Walker of Elgin to his uncle in Scotland, 13 March 1867.

36. *Chambers' Edinburgh Journal* (18 July 1874), p. 464, written by an Aberdeenshire woman from an unspecified part of New Zealand.

37. Rae Bailey, *Old Keys: An Historical Sketch of Clear Creek Township, Ashland County, Ohio, and of Savannah, the Township's Only Village* (Washington, 1941), pp. 27–8. See also A. J. Baughman (ed.), *A Centennial Biographical History of Richland County, Iowa* (Chicago, 1901); *The History of Cedar County, Iowa* (Chicago, 1878); *The History of Poweshiek County, Iowa* (Des Moines, 1880); Marjory Harper, *Emigration from North East Scotland*, vol. I, *Willing Exiles* (Aberdeen, 1988), pp. 249–53. Thanks to Paul F. McWilliams of Fallbrook, California, for genealogical information relating to the Ohio and Iowa Scots.

38. Galbraith correspondence (eleven letters), courtesy of Mrs F. E. Young, Grant House, Main Street, Tomintoul, John C. Galbraith to George Galbraith, 16 May and 15 July 1881. See also A. C. Bellamy (ed.), *Tauranga, 1882–1982: The Centennial of Gazetting Tauranga as a Borough* (Tauranga City Council, 1982).

39. NRA(S), Survey no. 1345. Private correspondence in the possession of Mrs J. J. Grant of Banchory, Kincardineshire. David Fletcher to William Fletcher, 13 April 1845.

40. Ibid., David Fletcher to John Fletcher, 6 August 1849.

41. Ibid., Charles Farquharson to John Fletcher, 21 January 1851.

42. Ibid., John Fletcher to Charles Farquharson, 24 October 1861.

43. Ibid., John Fletcher to Charles Farquharson, 27 March and 13 July 1865.

44. Donald R. Farquharson, *Tales and Memories of Cromar and Canada* (Chatham, Ont., n.d. [1930s]), p. 164.

45. Ibid., p. 165.

46. NRA(S) 1345, William Fletcher to Charles Farquharson, 1860 (n.d.).

47. Arthur W. Wright, *Pioneer Days in Nichol: Including Notes and Letters Referring to the Early Settlement of the Township of Nichol and its Villages* (Mount Forest?, Ont., 1932), p. 96.

48. Ibid., p. 26.

49. John R. Connon, *Elora* (Elora, Ont., 1930), pp. 70–71. Elmslie's diary, preserved in the Wellington County Museum near Fergus (A 984.15 MU 59), describes in full the pioneers' search for a suitable tract of land.

50. *Counsel for Emigrants* (Aberdeen, 1838), p. 105, letter dated 13 September 1834.

51. Guelph University Library, Special Collections, XS1 MS A099. Correspondence and rental accounts relating to the Beattie family of Broomhill farm, Strathdon, John Beattie to George Beattie, 29 October 1838. See also William Beattie senior to George Beattie, 13 June 1836 and William Beattie junior to George Beattie, 10 June 1837.

52. William Chambers, *Information for the People*, nos. 4, 5. Quoted in *Counsel for Emigrants* (Aberdeen, 1834), p. 20.

53. PP 1841 [298], vol. XV, 86, week ending 11 July 1840; PP 1857 (125), vol. XXVIII, Sess. 2, 31 July to 16 August 1856; PP 1854–55 (464), vol. XXXIX, 27, 16 to 23 June 1855, dispatches relating to emigration to the North American colonies.

54. *Illustrated London News*, 25 April 1857, p. 384.

55. James Thompson, *For Friends at Home: A Scottish Emigrant's Letters from Canada, California and the Cariboo, 1844–1864*, edited by Richard A. Preston (Montreal and London, 1974), pp. 199–200.

56. Lord Teignmouth, *Sketches of the Coasts and Islands of Scotland* (London, 1836), pp. 85, 86.

57. *North British Daily Mail*, 17 and 21 June 1847; Napier Commission, Q 44731. See also T. M. Devine, *The Great Highland Famine. Hunger, Emigration and the Scottish Highlands in the Nineteenth Century* (Edinburgh, 1988), p. 199.

58. *Scotsman*, 26 July 1848, 21 July 1849.

59. Napier Commission, Appendix A, pp. 130, 131, letters of emigrants from the Long Island. John McCormick to Salina McDonald, 20 August 1833; Lachlan McPherson to his brother, 24 August 1883.

60. Eric Richards, 'Australia and the Scottish Connection, 1788–1914', in R. A. Cage (ed.), *The Scots Abroad: Labour, Capital, Enterprise, 1750–1914* (London, 1985), p. 128. For discussion of New Zealand and South American enterprises, see ibid., pp. 172–7, 230–3.

61. AUA, MS 2580/639, Walter Davidson to William Leslie senior, 30 June 1836. Information on the Leslies has been quarried partly from this archive and partly from additional correspondence in the private collection of Mr and Mrs W. de Falbe of Somerset. In addition, use has been made of K. G. T. Waller, 'The Letters of the Leslie Brothers in Australia' (unpublished BA thesis, University of Queensland, 1956), the original letters being in the John Oxley Library, Brisbane. The reference to 'surplus younger sons' is taken from Malcolm D. Prentis, *The Scots in Australia. A Study of New South Wales, Victoria and Queensland, 1788–1900* (Sydney, 1983), p. 30.

62. De Falbe letters, Patrick to William and Jane Leslie, 24 February 1837.

63. Waller/Oxley collection, George to William and Jane Leslie, 10 July 1839.

64. Waller/Oxley collection, Walter Leslie to Mary Anne Davidson, 15 December 1839.

65. AUA, MS 2580/705, Patrick Leslie to William Leslie senior, 29 May 1839, written from Vineyard.

66. Waller/Oxley collection, Patrick Leslie to William and Jane Leslie, 9 October 1838.

67. AUA, MS 2580/705, Patrick to William Leslie senior, 29 May 1839.

68. De Falbe letters, L1 19E, William Leslie senior to Walter Leslie, 20 August 1840.

69. De Falbe letters, Jane Leslie to Walter Leslie, 28 August 1839.

70. Waller/Oxley collection, Patrick Leslie to William and Jane Leslie, 11 September 1840.

71. De Falbe letters, L1 13D, William Leslie to George Leslie, 23 March 1841.

72. AUA, MS 2580/812, Francis Middleton to William Leslie senior, 19 January 1845.

73. AUA, MS 2580/1/876, William Leslie junior, to William Leslie of Warthill, 3 May 1844.

74. Sir John Fleming, *Looking Backwards for Seventy Years, 1921–1851* (Aberdeen, 1922), p. 185.

75. AUA, MS 2580/1/876, William Leslie junior, to William Leslie of Warthill, 3 May 1844.

76. *Blackwood's Edinburgh Magazine*, vol. 146 (October 1884), p. 468.

77. Paul Edwards, 'Scottish Investments in the American West', in *Scottish Colloquium Proceedings,* vols 4–5 (University of Guelph, 1973), p. 73.

78. Ferenc M. Szasz, *Scots in the North American West, 1790–1917* (Norman, Ok., 2000), pp. 103, 106.

79. See, for instance, Joseph Frazier Wall, *Andrew Carnegie* (New York and Oxford, 1970).

80. 'The emigrants from Scotland were respectable tradesmen and farmers; 104 were mechanics, principally connected with railroad work,' reported Alexander Buchanan of the arrivals at Quebec during May 1853 (PP 1854 [1763] vol. XLVI, papers relating to emigration to the North American Colonies, p. 32.)

81. Adams and Somerville, *Cargoes of Despair and Hope*, p. 112.

82. R. T. Berthoff, *British Immigrants in Industrial America, 1790–1950* (Cambridge, Mass., 1952), p. 19.

83. Ibid., pp. 30–46; Bernard Aspinwall, 'The Scots in the United States', in Cage (ed.), *The Scots Abroad*, pp. 96–7.

84. *Chambers' Edinburgh Journal*, vol. II (1833–4), 356–7, 364–5, 374–5, 381–2, 405–6, 413–14; ibid., vol. IX (19 December 1840), p. 379; ibid., vol. XI (17 December 1842), pp. 282–3.

85. NLS, Acc. 11416, Kerr correspondence, 1820–83.

86. Charlotte Erickson, *Invisible Immigrants: The Adaptation of English and Scottish Immigrants in Nineteenth-century America* (Ithaca and London, 1972), pp. 229, 231.

87. Connon, *Elora*, p. 85.

88. *Aberdeen Herald*, 23 July 1836.

89. NRA(S), Survey no. 1345, Charles Farquharson to John Fletcher, 3 July 1865.

90. *Cuairtear nan Gleann*, vol. 2 (1840), p. 31, quoted in Sheila Kidd, 'Caraid nan Gaidheal & "Friend of Emigration": Gaelic Emigration Literature of the 1840s', *Scottish Historical Review*, vol. LXXXI, 1: no. 211 (April 2002), pp. 52–69.

91. See pp. 134, 331, 339–40.

92. J. H. Tremenheere, 'New Zealand: Its Progress and Resources', *Quarterly Review*, vol. CVI (October 1859), p. 355.

93. *Aberdeen Journal*, 22 November 1837. See also Harper, *Emigration from North East Scotland*, vol. I, pp. 320–30.

94. Donald McLean to Norman Macdonald, 20 September 1851, in Napier Commission, Appendix A, p. 164.

95. Kidd, 'Caraid nan Gaidheal & "Friend of Emigration"'. The poster was produced by Nahum Ward.

96. *Counsel for Emigrants*, pp. 128–9. See also *Counsel for Emigrants – Sequel* (Aberdeen, 1834), p. 51.

97. See, for instance, ibid., p. 33; William Thomson, *A tradesman's travels in the United States and Canada in the years 1840, 41 and 42* (Aberdeen, 1842), pp. 39–40, 197–207.

98. Charlotte Erickson, *Invisible Immigrants*, p. 32.

Chapter 4: The Recruitment Business

1. Canadian Sessional Papers [hereafter CSP], vol. 6, no. 6 (1873), *Annual Report of the Department of Agriculture for the Dominion of Canada for 1872*, appendix 23, Report of Proceedings in England and Scotland, March to August 1872, by special agent, James Ross.

2. See pp. 34, 161.

3. *Aberdeen Journal*, 17 January 1749.

4. Ibid., 5 February 1751, 2 January 1753, 28 May and 16 July 1754.

5. Ibid., 26 July 1773, 5 July 1784.

6. Ibid., 24 December 1751.

7. The Pictou enterprise was also promoted by sub-agents at Inveraray, Maryburgh (Fort William), Portree, Fort Augustus and Inverness (*Glasgow Journal*, 17 September 1772).

8. Anthony Parker, *Scottish Highlanders in Colonial Georgia: The Recruitment, Emigration and Settlement at Darien, 1735–1748* (Athens, Ga, 1997), p. 39.

9. *The Colonial Records of Georgia*, vol. 21, pp. 13–14.

10. For discussion of the relationship between military recruitment and emigration, see Andrew Mackillop, *More Fruitful than the Soil: Army, Empire and the Scottish Highlands, 1715–1815* (East Linton, 2000), pp. 139–67.

11. *The Collected Writings of Lord Selkirk, 1799–1809*, edited by J. M. Bumsted (Winnipeg, The Manitoba Record Society, 1984), introduction, p. 32. Advertising poster dated 22 October 1802, NAS GD 112/61/1.

12. Alexander Irvine, *An Inquiry into the Causes and Effects of Emigration from the Highlands and Western Islands of Scotland, with Observations on the Means to be Employed for Preventing it* (Edinburgh, 1802).

13. Thomas Douglas, Earl of Selkirk, *On the Necessity of a More Effectual System of National Defence and the Means of Establishing the Permanent Security of the Kingdom* (London, 1808).

14. Aberdeen, Alloa, Ayr, Campbeltown, Cromarty, Dumfries, Dundee, Glasgow, Grangemouth, Greenock, Inverness, Irvine, Isla, Kirkcaldy, Leith, Leven, Montrose, Peterhead, Port Glasgow, Stornoway, Stranraer, Thurso and Tobermory.

15. Lucille H. Campey, 'The Regional Characteristics of Scottish Emigration to British North America, 1784 to 1854', 2 vols. (unpublished PhD thesis, University of Aberdeen, 1998), vol. II, p. 240.

16. *Inverness Journal*, 17 February 1832.

17. *John O'Groat Journal*, 15 June 1849.

18. NAC, RG 76, C-10261, vol. 358, file 410827, James Scott, Ayr, 8 August 1906, 7 October 1911; *Aberdeen Journal*, 25 July 1907, 1 April 1911, 28 February and 1 March 1912, 2 June and 1 September 1913; NAC, RG 76, C-10269, vol. 369, file 497599, Walter Easton, Jedburgh; NAC RG 76, C-10311, vol. 430, file 636689, Mary J. Farnon, Falkirk, 8 February 1908.

19. NLS, MS 11976. Thanks to Dr Lucille Campey for drawing this and the following two references to my notice.

20. *Inverness Journal*, 28 December 1810, from *Beacon Light*, a periodical published in Edinburgh. Robertson refuted the allegations in a letter published in the *Inverness Journal* on 1 February 1811.

21. NLS, SP Dep 313/1468, 349. See also letter to James Stuart, Writer to the Signet, Edinburgh, 21 July 1819.

22. NAS, CS235, Box 391, S/47/11, Unextracted Processes, Somerville v. Hemmans, 1844.

23. NAS, CE87/1/30, 21 May 1855.

24. *Chambers' Edinburgh Journal*, vol. XV, no. 388 (7 June 1851), p. 360.

25. *Aberdeen Journal*, 5 April 1912; NAC, RG 76, C-10621, vol. 530, file 803485, part I: W. G. Maitland, Longside, Aberdeenshire, booking agent, lists, 1910–19. In the 1912 court case Maitland claimed in his defence that he had withheld the tickets because of uncertainty over the sailing date, owing to a dockers' strike, but the sheriff ruled that the payment of a deposit constituted the making of a definite contract and that Maitland was bound to issue the tickets in return. NAC, RG 76, C-10325, vol. 450, file 686431, Andrew Spalding, Blairgowrie, newspaper clipping dated 9 May 1914.

26. NAC, RG 76, C-10644, vol. 564, file 809010, MacKay Brothers, Aberdeen, lists, 1910–19.

27. NAC, RG 76, C-10644, vol. 564, file 809010, letter dated 2 May 1913. Rait was actually deported on the grounds of insanity a year after coming to Canada.

28. NAC, RG 76, C-10627, vol. 538, file 803839, part 2: correspondence between Paton and the Department of the Interior; letters from J. Mitchell, Inspector Employment Agents, Toronto to W. D. Scott, 15 February, 12 April and 9 May 1917.

29. NAC, RG 76, C-10294, vol. 405, file 590687, part I, J. Obed Smith's report on British agencies, 15 March 1909.

30. Thomas Rolph, *Emigration and Colonization: embodying the results of a mission to Great Britain and Ireland, during the years 1839, 1840 and 1842* (London, 1844), pp. 23–5.

31. For a biography of Lang, see D. W. A. Baker, *Days of Wrath* (Melbourne, 1985). James MacDonald's involvement in emigration is described in J. M. Bumsted, *The People's*

Clearance: Highland Emigration to British North America, 1770–1815 (Edinburgh, 1982), pp. 60, 75, and Norman McLeod's odyssey in Flora McPherson, *Watchman against the World* (Toronto, 1962).

32.   PRO, CO 208/124, extract minute of a meeting of the Otago Association, 11 January 1850.

33.   James Adam, *Twenty-Five Years of Emigrant Life in the South of New Zealand* (Edinburgh, 1876), pp. 9–10.

34.   Henry Jordan, *Queensland: emigration to the new colony of Australia, the future cotton field of England, its geography, climate, agricultural capabilities, and land laws* (London, 1862); 'Bush Life in Queensland', See also W. R. Johnston, 'The Selling of Queensland', *Aberdeen Journal*, 17 August 1865. 'Henry Jordan and Welsh Immigration', *Journal of the Royal Historical Society of Queensland*, vol. XVI, no. 9 (1991), pp. 379–92.

35.   CSP, vol. 8. no. 8 (1875), *Annual Report of the Department of Agriculture, 1874*, appendices 21, 28. Not all commentators agreed that Queensland was stealing a march on Canada. In 1910 a correspondent of the *Aberdeen Journal*, lamenting Queensland's continuing dearth of population, claimed that most of the emigrants who were flocking from Scotland to Canada had never even heard of Queensland, and urged that agents of the Canadian calibre should be sent to Scotland by the Queensland government to redirect the emigrant tide to the Antipodes (*Aberdeen Journal*, 23 June 1910).

36.   CSP, vol. 34, no. 10 (1900), *Annual Report of the Department of the Interior, 1899*, appendices 6 (H. M. Murray, Principal Agent for Scotland) and 8 (Thomas Duncan); NAC, RG 76, C-10324, vol. 450, file 682150, Malcolm McIntyre, Glasgow, J. Obed Smith, Assistant Superintendent of Emigration, London, to W. D. Scott, Ottawa, 15 March 1909. See also J. Camm, 'The Hunt for Muscle and Bone: Emigration Agents and Their Role in Immigration to Queensland in the 1880s', *Australian Historical Geography Bulletin*, vol. 2 (1981), pp. 7–29.

37.   Wilbur S. Shepperson, *The Promotion of British Emigration by Agents for American Lands, 1840–1860* (Reno, 1954).

38.   CSP, vol. 6, no. 6 (1873), *Annual Report of the Department of Agriculture, 1872*, appendix 30, Angus G. Nicholson, 'Report of Proceedings in the Highlands of Scotland'; appendix 17, report by W.J. Patterson to J.H. Pope, Minister of Agriculture, dated 13 December 1872.

39.   University of Cape Town Library, Manuscripts and Archives, B 1038, Laburn Collection, A3.4, *Cape Mercury*, 20 November 1876; A7, *Report on Cape Immigration for the year 1877*.

40.   Ibid., A3.5, *East London Daily Despatch*, 8 and 15 November 1877.

41.   Ibid., A4.4, Public Works Department, 2/66, J. B. Hellier to John Laing, Commissioner of Crown Lands, 25 February, 2 and 10 June 1880.

42.   Ibid., A3.5, *East London Daily Despatch*, 10 December 1881.

43.   Ibid., A4.4, J. X. Merriman to John Walker, 17 December 1881.

44.   Ibid., A3.6, Department of Crown Lands and Public Works, McNaughton to J. B. Hellier, 5 August and 12 December 1882; *East London Daily Despatch*, 19 August and 20 October 1882, 2 February 1884, 1 July 1885; John Walker to John Laing, Commissioner of

Lands, Public Works Department, Cape Colony, 5 May 1881; A4.6, W. Burnet to John Walker, 8 February 1882.

45. *East London Daily Despatch*, 1 March 1882. Walker apparently stayed on at Kei Mouth after the collapse of his settlement, but by 1883 had become involved in railway construction in Cape Colony, which occupied his attention for the next two decades (ibid., A14).

46. Martin Hewitt, 'The Itinerant Emigration Lecturer: James Brown's Lecture Tour of Britain and Ireland, 1861–2', *British Journal of Canadian Studies*, vol. 10, no. 1 (1995), 103–19. The quotation is taken from Brown to S. L. Tilley, 26 March 1862, James Brown Papers, MC 295/3/256, Provincial Archives of New Brunswick.

47. CSP, vol. 6, no. 6 (1873), *Annual Report of the Department of Agriculture, 1872*, appendix 17, report by W. J. Patterson.

48. Ibid., appendix 30, Report of Proceedings in the Highlands of Scotland by Angus G. Nicholson.

49. Ibid., vol. 9, no. 7 (1876), *Annual Report of the Department of Agriculture, 1875*, appendix 45, Report of Special Immigration Agent, Angus G. Nicholson, 14 February 1876, p.186.

50. Ibid., vol. 31, no. 9 (1897), *Annual Report of the Department of the Interior, 1896*, appendix 7, report of W. G. Stuart.

51. Ibid., appendix 6, report by Peter Fleming. Temporary agent Thomas Duncan thought that Fleming's selective canvassing of agriculturists through the valuation rolls excluded the general public and resulted in lower – although perhaps more attentive – audiences at lectures than was the case in W. G. Stuart's area (ibid., CSP, vol. 32, no. 10 [1898], *Annual Report of the Department of the Interior, 1897*, appendix 8).

52. NAC, RG 76, C-10294-5, vol. 405, file 590687, MacLennan's reports for weeks ending 26 October 1907, 16 January and 20 March 1909. For a discussion of MacLennan's activities, see Marjory Harper, *Emigration from North East Scotland*, vol. 2, *Beyond the Broad Atlantic* (Aberdeen, 1988), pp. 28–31.

53. NAC, RG 76, C-10318, vol. 440, file 662655, J. Bruce Walker to W. D. Scott (Superintendent of Immigration, Ottawa), 26 November 1907; *Aberdeen Journal*, 8 September 1908;NAC, RG 76, C-4747, vol. 80, file 6968, part 2, J. Obed Smith, Assistant Superintendent of Emigration, to W. D. Scott, Superintendent of Immigration, 18 March 1909.

54. *Highland News*, 8 April 1911.

55. NAC, RG 76, C-10324, vol. 450, file 682150, Malcolm McIntyre, Glasgow, report for week ending 18 February 1912.

56. CSP, vol. 32, no. 10 (1898), appendix 8.

57. NAC, RG 76, C-10294-5, vol. 405, file 590687, MacLennan's report for week ending 4 February 1911.

58. Ibid., report for week ending 22 February 1908. See also pp. 312–16 for the Clarke City dispute.

59. Ibid., MacLennan's report for week ending 16 October 1910.

60. CSP, vol. 6, no. 6 (1873), *Annual Report of the Department of Agriculture, 1872*, appendix 23.

61. Ibid., vol. 34, no. 1 (1900), *Annual Report of the Department of the Interior, 1899*, appendix 6.

62. NAC, RG 76, C-10291-2, vol. 401, file 572933, J. Obed Smith to W. D. Scott, 28 November 1911. The request was granted, and W. D. Scott himself later admitted, 'I do not think there is a single paper in the British Isles which has been more friendly towards Canada than the Aberdeen Free Press and there is no doubt but that the publicity already secured through this paper has been highly advantageous to Canada' (ibid., 9 January 1919).

63. Reprinted in the *Stonehaven Journal*, 26 June 1873.

64. NAC, RG 76, C-10644, vol. 564, file 808836, J. Obed Smith to W. D. Scott, 15 March 1909; NAC, RG 76, C-10294-5, vol. 405, file 590687, MacLennan's report for week ending 4 May 1907.

65. NAC, RG 76, C-10414, vol. 479, file 742357, MacLennan's report on Bredin; NAC, RG 76, C-10425, vol. 191, file 760771, MacLennan's report on Grant's visit to Scotland.

66. NAC, RG 76, C-10324, vol. 450, file 682150.

67. NAC, RG 76, C-10294-5, vol. 405, file 590687, MacLennan's report for week ending 13 February 1910; *Press & Journal* (formerly the *Aberdeen Journal*), 20 September 1924.

Chapter 5: Helping the Helpless

1.   Syrie L. Barnardo and James Marchant, *Memoirs of the Late Dr Barnardo* (London, 1907), p. 154.

2.   Canada, House of Commons, *Journals* (1888), 'Report of the Agriculture and Colonisation Committee', p. 10.

3.   Peter Williamson, *The Life and Curious Adventures of Peter Williamson, who was carried off from Aberdeen, and sold for a slave* (Aberdeen, 1801), p. 124. See also pp. 34, 113.

4.   PP 1914–16 [Cd 7886], XXXIV, 491, 76; *Report of the Departmental Committee on Reformatory and Industrial Schools in Scotland*. For lists of British reformatories and estimated emigrant numbers, see http://ist.uwaterloo.ca/~marj/genealogy/children/Organizations/reformatory/html.

5.   Phyllis Harrison (ed.), *The Home Children* (Winnipeg, 1979), p. 16.

6.   Gillian Wagner, *Children of the Empire* (London, 1982), p. xv.

7.   Gillian Wagner, *Barnardo* (London, 1979), p. 237.

8.   Quoted on the front cover of every annual report of Quarrier's Orphan Homes of Scotland, *A Narrative of Facts relative to work done for Christ in connection with the Orphan and Destitute Children's Emigration Homes, Glasgow* (hereafter *Narrative*).

9.   Ibid. (1872), pp. 9, 28.

10. Alexander Gammie, *A Romance of Faith: The Story of the Orphan Homes of Scotland and the Founder William Quarrier* (London, 1936), p. 105.

11. *Narrative*, vol. 26 (1905-6), p. 19.

12. Quarrier's Orphan Homes of Scotland, case files, vol. 9 (1887-8), p. 256.

13. Ibid., vol. 13 (1891–2), p. 354.

14. Ibid., vol. 28 (1903–4), p. 142.

15. Ibid., vol. 6 (1884–5), p. 223.

16. Ibid., vol. 10 (1888–9), p. 32.

17. Ibid., vol. 11 (1889–90), p. 38–9.

18. Ibid., vol. 27 (1905–6), p. 32.

19. Ibid., vol. 6 (1884–5), pp. 210, 139.

20. Ibid., vol. 7 (1885–6), p. 188; vol. 14 (1892–3), p. 179.

21. Ibid., vol. 7 (1885–6), p. 177.

22. Ibid., vol. 12 (1890–91), p. 78.

23. Ibid., vol. 20 (1898–9), p. 29.

24. Ibid., vol. 9 (1887–8), pp. 22, 23.

25. Ibid., vol. 11 (1889–90), p. 5.

26. Ibid., vol. 6 (1884–5), p. 230.

27. Ibid., vol. 10 (1888–9), p. 29.

28. Ibid., vol. 29 (1908–9), p. 117; vol. 30 (1909–10), p. 124.

29. Ibid., pp. 88–9.

30. Ibid., vol. 14 (1892–3), p. 24.

31. Ibid., vol. 16 (1894-5), p. 7.

32. Ibid., vol. 23 (1901–2), p. 103.

33. Ibid., vol. 34 (1913–14), p. 75

34. Ibid., vol. 11 (1889–90), p. 94.

35. Ibid., vol. 14 (1892–3), p. 328.

36. Ibid., vol. 15 (1893–4), p. 154.

37. Ibid., vol. 8 (1886–7), p. 127, quoting from an undated cutting from an unnamed newspaper attached to the case file.

38. Ibid., vol. 31 (1909–10), p. 60, quoting from the *Evening News*, 25 January 1910.

39. Ibid., vol. 32 (1910–11), p. 58, quoting from an undated cutting from an unnamed newspaper attached to the case file.

40. Ibid., vol. 33 (1911–12), pp. 66–7, evidence from the court case from an undated cutting from an unnamed newspaper attached to the case file.

41. John Urquhart, *The Life Story of William Quarrier: A Romance of Faith* (Glasgow, 1900), p. 270.

42. Ibid., pp. 296–314; James Ross, *The Power I Pledge* (Glasgow, 1971), pp. 69–70.

43. Urquhart, *The Life Story of William Quarrier*, pp. 286, 288.

44. William Garden Blaikie, *An Autobiography: 'Recollections of a Busy Life'* (London, 1901), pp. 318–19.

45. Emma M. Stirling, *Our Children in Old Scotland and Nova Scotia. Being a history of her work by Emma M. Stirling, the founder of the Edinburgh and Leith Children's Aid and Refuge Society, founded 1877* (London, 1892), p. 38. See also Philip Girard, 'Victorian Philanthropy and Child Rescue: The Career of Emma Stirling in Scotland and Nova Scotia, 1860–95', in Marjory Harper and Michael E. Vance (eds), *Myth, Migration and the Making of Memory: Scotia and Nova Scotia, c. 1700-1990* (Halifax and Edinburgh, 1999), pp. 218–31.

46. NAS, GD 409/1, RSSPCC Fonds, Minutes of Meeting of the Directors of the Edinburgh and Leith Children's Aid and Refuge Society, 6 November 1885.

47. Ibid., Minutes of Meeting of 6 October 1887, quoting letter from Miss Stirling of 25 August 1887.

48. Stirling Council Archives, PD41/1/1, Whinwell Children's Home, Stirling, Annual Report, 1910, p. 10.

49. Blaikie, *An Autobiography*, p. 330.

50. Ibid., pp. 329–30.

51. Stirling, *Our Children in Old Scotland and Nova Scotia*, p. 146.

52. For discussion of emigration from Catholic institutions, see http://www.parliament.the-stationery-o...9798/cmselect/cmhealth/755/8061.htm, House of Commons, Select Committee on Health, Minutes of Evidence. Two girls emigrated from Nazareth House in Aberdeen in 1899 and a further two in 1900, but after that no such departures are reported in the annual returns (Marjory Harper, *Emigration from North East Scotland*, vol. 2, *Beyond the Broad Atlantic* [Aberdeen, 1988], p. 208).

53. *Narrative* (1872), pp. 11–12.

54. Ibid., p. 14.

55. Ibid. (1888), p. 49.

56. Ibid. (1872), p. 13.

57. Blaikie, *An Autobiography*, pp. 320–23; *Narrative* (1886), p. 32.

58. Ibid., pp. 15–16.

59. Whinwell Children's Home, annual report, 1904, p. 11.

60. Ibid., 1906, p. 10.

61. *Narrative* (1904), p. 18.

62. Stirling Council Archives, PD41/4/15, Whinwell Children's Home, Reports from Canada, no. 3 (1920); letter from Louisa Birt to Annie Croall, 1 March 1921; undated letter from Mr Merry, Superintendent of Marchmont Home.

63. J. L. Churcher, Bancroft, Ontario, quoted in Harrison (ed.), *The Home Children*, pp. 37–8. See also Quarrier's Orphan Homes, case files, vol. 8 (1886–7), p. 52, and vol. 14 (1892–3), p. 96. Churcher, who came from a broken home in Leith and whose sister had preceded him to Canada in 1887, settled happily into his first placement. He remained there until 1906, and in the Bancroft area for the rest of his life.

64. The Orphanage and Home, Aberlour, Craigellachie, *Journal*, vol. VI, no. 7 (14 October 1887), p. 80.

65. Ibid., vol. VII, no. 4 (July 1888).

66. Ibid., vol. VII, no. 1 (April 1888).

67. Ibid., vol. IX, no. 110 (May 1891), p. 24.

68. Whinwell Children's Home, Annual Report, 1910, p. 11.

69. *Narrative* (1886), pp. 12, 24.

70. Joy Parr, *Labouring Children: British Immigrant Apprentices to Canada, 1869–1924* (London/Montreal, 1980), p. 105.

71. *Narrative* (1912), p. 4.

72. NAC, RG 76, C-4709, vol. 46, file 1532, 13 January 1898, L. Pereira, Dept of the Interior, Ottawa, to James Burges, Superintendent, Fairknowe Home; Burges to Pereira, 14 January 1898.

73. Blaikie, *An Autobiography*, pp. 314–16.

74. *Glasgow Herald*, 28 February 1883.

75. Canadian home child's daughter, interviewed on *The Little Emigrants*, BBC Radio Scotland, 25 December 1996.

Chapter 6: Leaving and Arriving

1. *Counsel for Emigrants* (Aberdeen, 1834), p. 59.

2. Robert Louis Stevenson, *From Scotland to Silverado* (Cambridge, Mass., 1966), pp. 10–12.

3. John MacDonald to —, n.d., but 1803, Public Archives of Prince Edward Island, 2664, quoted in J. M. Bumsted, *The People's Clearance: Highland Emigration to British North America, 1770–1815* (Edinburgh, 1982), pp. 59–60.

4. NLNZ, Alexander Turnbull Library [hereafter NLNZ, ATL] , qMS-0370, Jessie Campbell diary, 5 December 1840.

5. Ibid., 88–222, Isabella Ritchie Henderson diary, 28 July 1863.

6. *Aberdeen Journal*, 21 January 1835.

7. Ibid., 17 November 1852.

8. *Aberdeen Herald*, 16 June 1855; *Aberdeen Journal*, 18 June 1856.

9. NLA, MS 596, diary of William Shennan, 1870, typed transcription by Mrs M. R. Shennan, 1987.

10. *Illustrated London News*, 6 July 1850, p. 21.

11. *Chambers' Edinburgh Journal*, vol. I, n.s., no. 15 (13 April 1844), p. 229; vol. XV, no. 388 (7 June 1851), p. 360.

12. E. C. Guillet, *The Great Migration: The Atlantic Crossing by Sailing Ship since 1770* (Toronto, 1963).

13. Thomas Fowler, *The Journal of a Tour through British North America to the Falls of Niagara* (Aberdeen, 1832).

14. *Counsel for Emigrants*, p. 70.

15. *Chambers' Edinburgh Journal*, vol. 8, no. 406 (9 November 1839), p. 334.

16. *Counsel for Emigrants*, p. 59.

17. Robert MacDougall, *The Emigrant's Guide to North America*, translated and edited by Elizabeth Thomson (Toronto, 1998), pp. 14–15.

18. *Counsel for Emigrants*, p. 57.

19. *Aberdeen Journal*, 9 August 1854; Andrew Picken, *The Canadas, as they at present commend themselves to the enterprise of emigrants, colonists and capitalists* (London, 1832); W. H. Smith, *Canada; past, present and future* (Toronto, 1851), vol. II, p. 541.

20. F. S. Buchanan, 'The Emigration of Scottish Mormons to Utah, 1849–1900' (MSc thesis, University of Utah, 1961), pp. 82–3, from Matthew Rowan, *Journal*, p. 55.

21. John Ronaldson to Eliza Ronaldson, 21 May 1852, quoted in Dallas L. Jones, 'The

Background and Motives of Scottish Emigration to the United States of America in the period 1815–1861' (unpublished PhD thesis, University of Edinburgh, 1970), p. 142. See also p. 308.

22. NLNZ, ATL, qMS-0131, Jane Bannerman (née Burns), retrospective account of a voyage from Scotland to Otago in 1847.

23. Ibid., MS Papers 4275, Agnes MacGregor diary, 26 July 1881.

24. John Mann, *Travels in North America, particularly in the provinces of Upper and Lower Canada and New Brunswick, and in the States of Maine, Massachusets [sic] and New York* (Glasgow, 1824), pp. 1–2.

25. Fowler, *The Journal of a Tour ...*, p. 13.

26. NLNZ, ATL, Jessie Campbell diary, 31 August 1840.

27. NLA, MS 685, diary of John Mackenzie, 23 September 1841.

28. William Wallace, *My Dear Maggie: Letters from a Western Manitoba Pioneer*, edited by Kenneth S. Coates and William R. Morrison (Regina, Sask.,1991); The Countess of Aberdeen, *Through Canada with a Kodak*, new edition, introduction by Marjory Harper (Toronto, 1994), pp. xxxvi–xxxvii, 3.

29. NLNZ, ATL, Isabella Ritchie Henderson diary, 19 July 1863.

30. PP 1854 (296), LX, *Report on the wreck of the Emigrant Ship* Annie Jane *and alleged grievances of the Emigrant passengers on board; with appendices.* See also Bob Charnley, *Shipwrecked on Vatersay!* (Portree, 1992).

31. NLA, MS 1412, Rev. Mr Tait diary, 1837.

32. NLNZ, ATL, Jessie Campbell diary, 12 September 1840.

33. NLNZ, ATL, MS Papers 2534, diary of a passage from Glasgow to Otago by John Anderson, steerage passenger.

34. William Gordon Tulloch, 'John Scott Tulloch – an Early Emigrant to New Zealand', *New Shetlander*, no. 165 (Hairst 1988), pp. 6–8; NLNZ, ATL, Isabella Ritchie Henderson diary; ibid., MS Papers 1678, Jane Findlayson diary, typescript.

35. Wellington County Museum, Fergus, Ontario, Journal of Robert Cromar, MU 8 975.82.1.

36. Diary of Mrs D. Bonthrow, Wed., 29 July; Sabbath, 30 August 1863. Typed transcription, given to author by Len Gray of Auckland in 1997.

37. NAC, MG 24 I 193.

38. NLA, MS 685, John Mackenzie diary, 8 November 1841.

39. NLNZ, ATL, Isabella Ritchie Henderson diary, 8 October 1863.

40. NLNZ, ATL, Jessie Campbell diary.

41. Ibid., 30 August 1840.

42. Ibid., 5 and 10 September, 7 November 1840.

43. NLNZ, ATL, Isabella Ritchie Henderson diary, 31 July 1863.

44. NLNZ, ATL, Jessie Campbell diary, 6 September 1840.

45. Ibid., 29 October 1840.

46. NLNZ, ATL, John Anderson diary, 13 August 1862.

47. Stevenson, *From Scotland to Silverado*, pp. 6, 23, 52.

48. NLNZ, ATL, Jessie Campbell diary, 15 December 1840.

49. Ibid., 6 September 1840.

50. NLNZ, ATL, Isabella Ritchie Henderson diary, 2 August 1863.

51. NLNZ, ATL, Jane Findlayson diary, 8 October 1876.

52. Alexander Muir, *From Aberdeen to Ottawa in 1845: The Diary of Alexander Muir*, edited by George A. Mackenzie (Aberdeen, 1990), p. 3.

53. NLA, Rev. Mr Tait diary, 1 September 1837.

54. NLNZ, ATL, John Anderson diary, 30 July 1862.

55. NLNZ, ATL, Jane Findlayson diary, 4 October 1876.

56. NLA, William Shennan diary, 15 February 1870.

57. NLA, MS 2117, Rev. William Hamilton diary, 1 and 12 May, 1, 2 and 13 June 1837; MS 1412, Rev. Mr Tait diary, 1837.

58. NLA, MS 2717, 'Log kept on board the *North Briton* from Leith to Sidney [*sic*] 1838 by John Sceales, late of Gardner Crescent, Edinburgh'.

59. NLNZ, ATL, Jessie Campbell diary, 27 August, 12 September, 21 November, 31 December 1840.

60. AUA, MS 2884/1/5/2, 2 September 1855, John Chalmers to his parents.

61. NLNZ, ATL, Jessie Campbell diary, 3 September 1840.

62. NLNZ, ATL, Jane Findlayson diary, 12 November 1876.

63. NLNZ, ATL, John Anderson diary, 18 August 1862.

64. NLNZ, ATL, Isabella Ritchie Henderson diary, 1 and 6 August 1863.

65. NLA, William Shennan diary, 21 and 31 March, 19 April 1870.

66. NLA, John Mackenzie diary, 30 November 1841.

67. NLNZ, ATL, MS Papers 3427, Dr G. Todd letter; Jessie Campbell diary, 27 December 1840.

68. NLNZ, ATL, MS Papers 3609, William Smith diary, 12 August 1862.

69. *Lord Durham's Report on the Affairs of British North America*, edited by C. P. Lucas, 3 vols, (Oxford, 1912), vol. II, pp. 243–4.

70. Susanna Moodie, *Roughing it in the Bush, or Forest Life in Canada* (London, 1852), edited by Carl Ballstadt (Ottawa, 1988), p. 46.

71. NLNZ, ATL, John Anderson diary, 24 September 1862.

72. Moodie, *Roughing it in the Bush*, pp. 83–4.

73. Stevenson, *From Scotland to Silverado*, p. 86.

74. Ibid., pp. 100, 120.

75. George Sangster of Belhelvie, Aberdeenshire, manuscript diary (photocopy), given to the author by Mr Sangster's family.

76. NLA, William Hamilton diary; ibid., John Sceales diary; NLNZ, ATL, Dr G. Todd letter; ibid., Jane Bannerman diary; ibid., William Smith diary, 12, 13, 15 and 16 August 1862.

Chapter 7: The Emigrant Experience

1. *Aberdeen Evening Gazette*, 30 May 1913, Maggie Masson to Isabella Stewart.
2. Wellington County Museum, Fergus, Ontario, MU 33 A 981.26, Watt/Argo Family Papers, 1836–44, 4 October 1836, Margaret Argo Duthie, Tarves, Aberdeenshire, to Barbara Argo Watt, Bon Accord, Upper Canada.
3. Wellington County Museum, Connon Collection, Elizabeth Connon to Thomas Connon, 3 March 1853, 1 January 1855, 26 November 1856.
4. *Aberdeen Journal*, 12 May 1852.
5. Saskatchewan Archives Board, S-A83; William Gibson Papers, *Ayrshire Post*, 1884–92.
6. AUA, MS 3184, McBean correspondence: John McBean to Margaret McBean, 10 March 1903; John McBean to Andrew McBean, 7 April 1905. See also Marjory Harper, *Emigration from North East Scotland*, vol. 2, *Beyond the Broad Atlantic* (Aberdeen, 1988), pp. 77–94.
7. Lloyd Reynolds, *The British Immigrant, His Social and Economic Adjustment in Canada* (Oxford, 1935), p. 211; Charlotte Erickson, *Invisible Immigrants: The Adaptation of English and Scottish Immigrants in Nineteenth-century America* (Ithaca and London, 1972), pp. 5–6.
8. *Elgin Courier*, quoted in *Aberdeen Journal*, 20 November 1833.
9. John McEachrin, *Shetland Times*, 22 December 1873.
10. Marjory Harper, 'Probing the Pioneer Questionnaires: British Settlement in Saskatchewan, 1887–1914', *Saskatchewan History*, vol. 52, no. 2 (Fall 2000), pp. 28–46.
11. NAS, GD1/814/5/3, 10 December 1823, Mary and Arthur Stocks to John Colquon, c/o Betty Boyd, Well Meadow Street, Paisley.
12. AUA, MS 2787/5/2/18/15 and 16, Robert Seton to Alexander Anderson Seton, 21 November 1831, 2 July 1832, 19 May 1833, 31 December 1838.
13. NRA(S), North-East Survey, MS 2844, undated letter from William Webster to James Webster, Alehousehill, Aberdeenshire.
14. James Thompson, *For Friends at Home: A Scottish Emigrant's Letters from Canada, California and the Cariboo, 1844–1864*, edited by Richard A. Preston (Montreal and London, 1974), pp. 209–10, James Thomson to Alexander Thomson, 11 April 1854.
15. AUA, MS 3470/8/274, Castle Fraser Papers, Michie and Mary Ewing, Township of Downie, to Colonel Charles Fraser, 14 March 1857. Thanks to Myrtle Anderson-Smith for drawing this reference to my attention.
16. *Inverness Journal*, 2 October 1849.
17. Ibid., 23 October 1849.
18. NAS, GD403/27/2, Captain Donald McNeil to Captain William McNeil, June 1849. For details of Highland settlement in Cape Breton and the Eastern Townships of Quebec, see, respectively, Stephen J. Hornsby, *Nineteenth Century Cape Breton: A Historical Geography* (Montreal and Kingston, 1992) and J. I. Little, *Crofters and Habitants: Settler Society, Economy and Culture in a Quebec Township, 1848–1881* (Montreal and Kingston, 1991).
19. Saskatchewan Archives Board, William Gibson Papers, 'Further Experience of Farming Life in Manitoba', 15 December 1887, p. 63.
20. NAS, GD40/16/57, Lothian Muniments, Report on Killarney and Saltcoats.

21. Saskatchewan Archives Questionnaire, no. 2, Pioneer Experiences: A General Questionnaire, x2/2 [hereafter SAQ] (1883), Q. 23, Norman McDonald.

22. Wayne R. Norton, *Help Us to a Better Land: Crofter Colonies in the Prairie West* (Regina, 1994), p. xiii.

23. SAQ (1889), QQ. 10–11, 13–15, 23–4, Archibald Angus Docherty.

24. Ibid. (1882), Q. 10, John Laidlaw.

25. Ibid. (1891), memorandum dated 17 April 1953 Peter Fraser; 1892, Q. 23, William Harkness; (1897), Q. 10, 21, 24, 33, James Davison Tulloch; (1904), QQ. 14, 22, George Bruce.

26. Ibid. (1903), Q. 23, Andrew M. Veitch.

27. Ibid. (1892), Q. 23, Robert Golder Wood.

28. William Wallace, *My Dear Maggie: Letters from a Western Manitoba Pioneer*, edited by Kenneth S. Coates and William R. Morrison (Regina, Sask., 1991), pp. 20–22, letter dated 29 June 1881.

29. Ibid., pp. 84 (26 June 1882), 81 (15 June 1882).

30. Ibid., pp. 209 (18 March 1885).

31. AUA, MS 3184, McBean correspondence. John McBean to Margaret McBean, 2 September 1902.

32. Ibid., John McBean to Margaret McBean, 20 August 1902.

33. *Aberdeen Journal*, 11 August 1903.

34. NAS, GD16/35/68, Airlie muniments, James Robertson, Still Water Village, Easter County of Washington, to Patrick Kennedy, 17 January 1830.

35. *Shetland Times*, 1 May 1875; Janette Stevenson Murray, 'Lairds of North Tama', *Iowa Journal of History and Politics*, vol. XL (1942), pp. 256–60.

36. *Aberdeen Daily Free Press*, 3 January 1873.

37. Ferenc M. Szasz, *Scots in the North American West, 1790-1917* (Norman, Ok., 2000), pp. 83–4; James L. Forsythe, 'George Grant of Victoria: Man and Myth', *Kansas History*, vol. 9, no. 3 (Autumn 1986), pp. 102–14; Brian P. Birch, 'Victoria Vanquished: The Scottish Press and the Failure of George Grant's Colony', ibid., pp. 115–25.

38. Eric Richards, Alexia Howe, Ian Donnachie and Adrian Graves, *That Land of Exiles: Scots in Australia, 1788–1914* (Edinburgh, 1988), p. 34; Margaret Kiddle, *Men of Yesterday: A Social History of the Western District of Victoria, 1834–1890* (Melbourne, 1961), p. 469.

39. NAS, GD403/36/1, Mackenzie Papers, Godfrey McKinnon to John McDonald, 18 March 1864.

40. NAS, GD68/2/140/1, Lintrose Writs, D. S. Murray to Mrs Murray, Woodside Cottage, Couper [*sic*] Angus, 1 January 1839.

41. Don Watson, *Caledonia Australis: Scottish Highlanders on the Frontier of Australia* (Sydney, 1984), pp. 166–7.

42. NAS, GD21/482/1/86, Cunninghame of Thornton Papers, George Wrey to his aunt, 23 December 1877; GD21/482/1/119, Cunninghame of Thornton Papers, George Wrey to his aunt, n.d. [1878].

43. Hans P. Rheinheimer, *Topo: The Story of a Scottish Colony near Caracas, 1825–1827* (Edinburgh, 1988), pp. 60, 112, 115. See also Sir Robert Ker Porter, *Caracas Diary: A British Diplomat in a Newborn Nation* (Caracas, 1966).

44. Iain A. D. Stewart (ed.), *From Caledonia to the Pampas. Two Accounts by Early Scottish Emigrants to the Argentine* (Phantassie, East Linton, 2000), p. 80.

45. Annual Report of the Superintendent of Immigrants at East London, 21 March 1881, *Cape Town Directory* (1882), pp. 2, 383–7. See also University of Cape Town Library, Manuscripts and Archives, Laburn Collection, B 1038, A6, *Gonubie Presbyterian Church Centenary Booklet* (n.p., n.d.), pp. 24, 27–8.

46. Alexander MacKenzie, *The History of the Highland Clearances* (Inverness, 1883), p. 313.

47. Thompson, *For Friends at Home*, p. 45.

48. Ibid., pp. 67–8, James Thompson to Helen Thompson, 3 November 1844.

49. Ibid., 125, James Thompson to Alexander Thompson, 16 July 1849.

50. Erickson, *Invisible Immigrants*, p. 243.

51. NAS, GD50/186/125/3/3, James McCowan to James McGregor, July 1819.

52. R. T. Berthoff, *British Immigrants in Industrial America, 1790–1950* (Cambridge, Mass., 1952), pp. 39, 44, 46. See also pp. 104–5.

53. David Laing to his sister, 19 February 1873, quoted in Erickson, *Invisible Immigrants*, p. 362.

54. Ibid., p. 363, letter dated 8 June 1873.

55. Ibid., p. 366, letter dated 13 July 1876.

56. Shetland Archives, SC.12/6/1915, James Mouat Garriock to Mary Garriock, 9 June 1891. Thanks to Dr Brian Smith for this reference.

57. *Aberdeen Evening Gazette,* 17 May 1886.

58. *Austin Daily Statesman,* 11 August 1886. For further details on this incident, see Marjory Harper, 'Emigrant Strikebreakers: Scottish Granite Cutters and the Texas Capitol Boycott', *Southwestern Historical Quarterly*, vol. 95 (April 1992), pp. 465–86.

59. The Stanstead Company dispute is discussed in Harper, *Emigration from North East Scotland*, vol. 2, pp. 163–5.

60. Thompson, *For Friends at Home*, pp. 136, 141, 156, 166, 297, 303.

61. NLS, Acc 6655, James M. Dodds to Mr and Mrs Jas. Dodds, Dunfermline, 18 March 1898, Dawson City, North West Territory, Alaska.

62. NAS, GD139/455/2, Sutherland of Forse Muniments, Dr William Sutherland, Portland, Victoria, to his sisters, 11 April 1852.

63. *Inverness Advertiser,* 20 June 1854, 11 July 1854, 29 June 1852.

64. Tom Steel, *The Life and Death of St Kilda* (London, 1975), pp. 35–6.

65. Janet Richardson, 'Journal of our Voyage to Port Phillip', in Philip L. Brown (ed.), *The Clyde Company Papers*, 7 vols. (London, 1941–56), vol. V, pp. 617–18. See also ibid., vol. II, pp. 241, 270–1; vol. III, p. 77; vol. V, p. 291; and Richards et al., *That Land of Exiles*, p. 92.

66. Catharine Parr Traill, *The Backwoods of Canada* (Ottawa, 1997), pp. 64, 185–8, 194–5; Susanna Moodie, *Roughing it in the Bush, or Forest Life in Canada*, edited by Carl Ballstadt (Ottawa, 1988), pp. 83–4.

67. Wallace, *My Dear Maggie*, pp. 121, 214–15, letters dated 2 March 1883, 24 April 1885.

68. SAQ (1906), Margaret Smith, Jessie Mathieson Ross, Margaret Thomson McManus.

69. *Inverness Advertiser*, 24 June 1851.

70. Marjory Harper, *Emigration from North East Scotland*, vol. 1, *Willing Exiles* (Aberdeen, 1988), pp. 145–8.

71. Aberdeen Ladies' Union, *Emigration Reports*, 1886, 1889, 1896.

72. *The Canadian Journal of Lady Aberdeen*, edited by J. T. Saywell (Toronto, 1960), pp. 15–16, entry dated 1 October 1893.

73. NAC, RG 76, C-10627, vol. 538, file 803839, part 2, Paton to the Canadian government emigration agent, Aberdeen, 14 January 1914.

74. Harper, *Emigration from North East Scotland*, vol. 2, pp. 241–2.

75. *Stonehaven Journal*, 13 March 1873.

76. *Aberdeen Evening Gazette*, 30 May 1913.

77. *Inverness Journal*, 20 June 1845.

78. *Aberdeen Journal*, 30 October 1872.

79. Wallace, *My Dear Maggie*, p. 53, letter dated 12 January 1882.

Chapter 8: The Temporary Emigrant

1. Thomas Hamilton, *Men and Manners in America* (Edinburgh, 1833), p. 125.

2. *OSA*, vol. XVIII (Inverness, Ross and Cromarty), p. 96; ibid., vol. IX (Logie Pert), p. 51; ibid., vol. XII (Fetteresso), pp. 593, 594; ibid., vol. IV (Kells), p. 264.

3. Douglas J. Hamilton, 'Patronage and Profit: Scottish Networks in the British West Indies, *c.* 1763–1807' (unpublished PhD thesis, University of Aberdeen, 1999), pp. 290–322; NAS, vol. V (Ayr), p. 81; ibid., vol. VII (Glenurchy), p. 102.

4. Roderick A. McDonald (ed.), *Between Slavery and Freedom. Special Magistrate John Anderson's Journal of St. Vincent during the Apprenticeship* (Philadelphia, 2001), pp. 66, 133, 142, 145, 183.

5. Sir Arthur Sinclair, *In Tropical Lands. Recent Travels to the Source of the Amazon, the West Indian Islands, and Ceylon* (Aberdeen, 1895), p. 164.

6. L. Mackintosh, *Elgin Past & Present: A Guide and History* (Elgin, 1891), pp. 26–8, 41; A. A. Cormack, *More About the Founder of Fordyce Academy* (Banff, 1957), pp. 2–4. For discussion of the employment of Scots in India in the eighteenth century, see Linda Colley, *Britons: Forging the Nation, 1707–1837* (London, 1992), pp. 127–9.

7. Sir Walter Scott, *The Surgeon's Daughter* (Edinburgh, 1903), p. 226.

8. John Galt, *The Last of the Lairds* (Edinburgh, 1976), p. 73.

9. Ibid., pp. 25–6.

10. AUA, MSS 2884, Letters and Papers of the Family of Alexander Wallace Chalmers.

11. Ibid., MS 2884/1/5/3, John Chalmers [JC] to Alexander Wallace Chalmers [AWC], 6 January 1857.

12. Marjory Harper, 'The Challenges and Rewards of Databases: Two Decades of Aberdeen Students, 1860–*c.* 1880', in J. J. Carter and D. J. Withrington (eds), *The Scottish Universities System: Distinctiveness and Diversity* (Edinburgh, 1992), pp. 147–55.

13. AUA, MS 2284/1/3/1–2, no. 39, 20 May 1855.

14. Ibid., Samuel Chalmers [SC] to Mary Chalmers [MC], no. 62, 21 July 1856.

15. Ibid., SC to William Chalmers [WC], no. 63, 4 August 1856.

16. Ibid., SC to his parents, no. 76, 7 February 1857.

17. Ibid., SC to AWC, no. 65, 5 September 1856; AWC to SC, no. 78, 21 February 1857; JC to WC, no. 37, 29 August 1856.

18. Ibid., SC to his parents, no. 69, 23 October 1856.

19. Ibid., SC to JC, no. 43, 9 November 1855; SC to MC, no. 39, 20 May 1855.

20. Ibid., SC to WC, no. 42, 4 October 1855.

21. Ibid., SC to AWC, no. 61, 17 July 1856.

22. Ibid., SC to his parents, no. 73, 22 December 1856.

23. Ibid., SC to AWC, no. 42, 4 October 1855.

24. Ibid., SC to JC, no. 43, 9 November 1855.

25. Ibid., SC to AWC, no. 50, 17 December 1855.

26. Ibid., Dr Walker to SC, no. 70, 12 November 1856.

27. Ibid., SC to AWC, no. 88A, 18 October 1857.

28. Ibid., John Milne to AWC, no. 19, 8 December 1855.

29. Ibid., MS 2884/1/5/3, JC to WC, no. 23, 30 January 1856, and no. 23, 27 February 1858.

30. Ibid., JC to Elizabeth Cardno, no. 117, 5 November 1858.

31. Ibid., JC to AWC, no. 58, 13 November 1859.

32. Ibid., JC to AWC, no. 20, 4 October 1860.

33. Ibid., MS 2884/1/4/3, WC to SC, no. 119, 27 April 1858.

34. Ibid., WC to AWC, no. 68, 11 September 1861.

35. Ibid., AWC to WC, no. 79, 24 February 1862.

36. Ibid., WC to Elizabeth Jamson, no. 91, 24 December 1862.

37. AUA, MS 3090/1, fo. 33, David Cardno, Journals of whaling voyages, 1866–1919.

38. *OSA*, vol. XIX (Orkney and Shetland), p. 246.

39. Hudson Bay Company Archives, Provincial Archives of Manitoba [hereafter HBCA, PAM], A.34/2.

40. Ibid., D.4/99, fos. 3–5, Official Reports (by Governor George Simpson, York Factory), to the Governor and Committee in London, 10 August 1832.

41. Vilhjalmur Stefansson, *Unsolved Mysteries of the Arctic* (New York, 1939), p. 136. The record of the expeditions is contained in Thomas Simpson, *Narrative of the Discoveries on the North Coast of America effected by the officers of the Hudson's Bay Company during the years 1836–9* (London, 1843).

42. HBCA, PAM, A.10/42 FOS 557-557D, Christina Anderson, Lerwick, to William Smith, Secretary of the Hudson's Bay Company London, 22 December 1857.

43. *OSA*, vol. XIX (Orkney and Shetland), pp. 166–7 (Orphir); ibid., p. 135 (Kirkwall and St Ola); ibid., pp. 93–4 (Firth and Stromness).

44. Charlotte Erickson, *Invisible Immigrants: The Adaptation of English and Scottish Immigrants in Nineteenth-century America* (Ithaca and London, 1972), pp. 371–2, 375–6, 378.

45. PP 1873, X (313), *Select Committee on the Coal Industry*, Q. 4637. See also Q. 4634; R. T. Berthoff, *British Immigrants in Industrial America, 1790–1950* (Cambridge, Mass., 1952), pp. 51–2; Gordon M. Wilson, *Alexander McDonald, Leader of the Miners* (Aberdeen, 1982), pp. 111–13.

46. *Boston Post*, 1 September 1885, quoted in *Aberdeen Journal*, 29 September 1885.

47. William Barclay, 'Barre's Scotch Population – a history of the immigrants who came here in the years 1880–1889' (unpublished paper, 1936, Aldrich Public Library, Barre, Vt), pp. 1–2.

48. *Granite Cutters' Journal*, vol. I, no. 9 (January 1902), p. 2. The author of the article was an Aberdonian resident in the USA.

49. NAC, MG29/C/39, reminiscences of James Gordon, 1889.

50. 28 October 1907.

51. *Aberdeen Journal*, 30 October 1907; *Evening Express*, 1 November 1907.

52. Quoted in Lee Olson, *Marmalade and Whiskey: British Remittance Men in the West* (Golden, Colo., 1993), p. 18.

53. Quoted in Ferenc M. Szasz, *Scots in the North American West, 1790–1917* (Norman, Ok., 2000), p. 131.

54. The Marquis and Marchioness of Aberdeen, *More Cracks with 'We Twa'* (London, 1929), p. 72.

55. NRA(S), Survey no. 0055, Haddo House Muniments, Tarves, Aberdeenshire, item 10 in tin trunk, Private Journal of Lady Aberdeen, 27 June 1887.

56. Ibid., 3 July 1887.

57. The Marquis and Marchioness of Aberdeen, *'We Twa': Reminiscences of Lord and Lady Aberdeen* (London, 1925), p. 293.

58. David Mitchell and Dennis Duffy (eds), *Bright Sunshine and a Brand New Country: Recollections of the Okanagan Valley, 1890–1914* (Victoria, BC, 1979), p. 12.

59. Estelle Tinkler (ed.), *Archibald John Writes the Rocking Chair Ranche Letters* (Burnet, TX, 1976), p. 5.

60. 'As Manager of Rocking Chair Ranch Honorable Archie was a Good Dog Fancier', *Fort Worth Star-Telegram*, 15 July 1923, p. 8.

61. Tinkler (ed.), *Archibald John Writes the Rocking Chair Ranche Letters*, p. 16, Archie to Byron Jones, merchant, Memphis, Texas, May 1892, Rocking Chair Ranche Letters Miscellaneous.

62. Aberdeen, *'We Twa'*, pp. 90–91.

63. *South African Scot*, vol. 1, no. 1 (15 November 1905), p. 24.

Chapter 9: Issues of Identity

1. Ellis Island Immigration Museum, Oral History Project, E1-440, Margaret Jack Kirk, interviewed 25 February 1994.

2. Frederick Niven, *The Flying Years* (London, 1935), p. 19.

3. Margaret Bennett, 'Folkways and Religion of the Hebridean Scots in the Eastern

Townships', in Laurel Doucette (ed.), *Cultural Retention and Demographic Change: Studies of the Hebridean Scots in the Eastern Townships of Quebec* (Ottawa, 1980), p. 51.

4. Napier Commission, Appendix A, pp. 166, 169, 172; Angus Young to Donald Young, 23 October 1851; emigrants' statement quoted in Rev. John Milloy to A. C. Buchanan, 21 March 1864; John Macdonald to Sir James Matheson, 21 February 1866.

5. John J. Mullowney, *America Gives a Chance* (Tampa, 1940), quoted in Margaret Bennett, *Oatmeal and the Catechism: Scottish Gaelic Settlers in Quebec* (Edinburgh and Montreal, 1998), pp. 145–6.

6. Napier Commission, Appendix A, p. 135, Report of Angus MacCormic in 'Reports on the Crops grown in North-West Canada, by Emigrants from the Long Island', December 1883.

7. NAC, MG 27, C-1352 1L 1B5, The Journal of Lady Aberdeen (unpublished), 7 October 1890.

8. D. Campbell and R. A. Maclean, *Beyond the Atlantic Roar. A Study of the Nova Scotia Scots* (Toronto, 1974), pp. 113, 179.

9. PP 1841 (182), VI, 1, *First Report from the Select Committee on Emigration (Scotland) together with minutes of evidence and appendix*, Q. 189.

10. Ibid., Q. 2034, Hon. Christopher Alexander Hagerman, Justice of Queen's Bench in Upper Canada.

11. *Cuairtear nan Gleann*, vol. 2 (1840), p. 31, quoted in Sheila M. Kidd, 'Caraid nan Gaidheal & "Friend of Emigration": Gaelic Emigration Literature of the 1840s', *Scottish Historical Review*, vol. LXXXI, no. 1, 211 (April 2002), pp. 52–69.

12. Robert MacDougall, *Ceann-Iuil an Fhir-Imrich do dh'America Mu-Thuath (The Emigrant's Guide to North America)* (Glasgow, Oban, Inverness and Dingwall, 1841), translated and edited by Elizabeth Thomson (Toronto, 1998), p. 64.

13. Ibid., p. 22.

14. Michael Kennedy, '"Lochaber No More": A Critical Examination of Highland Emigration Mythology', in Marjory Harper and Michael E. Vance (eds), *Myth, Migration and the Making of Memory: Scotia and Nova Scotia, c. 1700–1990* (Halifax, NS, and Edinburgh, 1999), pp. 268–9. Kennedy's translation from Margaret MacDonell, *The Emigrant Experience: Songs of Highland Emigrants in North America* (Toronto, 1982), p. 80.

15. Kennedy, '"Lochaber No More"', p. 269, Kennedy's translation from MacDonell, *The Emigrant Experience*, pp. 88–90.

16. Rusty Bitterman, 'On Remembering and Forgetting: Highland Memories within the Maritime Diaspora', in Harper and Vance (eds), *Myth, Migration and the Making of Memory*, pp. 253–65.

17. Ibid., pp. 30–31; Kennedy, '"Lochaber No More"', p. 271.

18. 'From the Gaelic', *Blackwood's Edinburgh Magazine*, vol. XLVI (September 1829), p. 400.

19. Kennedy, '"Lochaber No More"', p. 274.

20. Alexander MacKenzie, *The History of the Highland Clearances* (Inverness, 1883), p. 13; Donald McLeod, *Gloomy Memories in the Highlands of Scotland: versus Mrs Harriet*

Beecher Stowe's Sunny Memories in (England) a Foreign Land: or a faithful picture of the extirpation of the Celtic Race from the Highlands of Scotland (Toronto, 1857), pp. 211–12,

21. MacKenzie, *The History of the Highland Clearances*, pp. 259–60, quoting *Dundas Warden*, 2 October 1851.

22. MacKenzie, *The History of the Highland Clearances*, pp. 391, 395.

23. Ibid., p. 313.

24. Ibid., p. 307.

25. Ralph Connor, *The Man from Glengarry: A Tale of Western Canada* (London, 1901), p. 5, and *Glengarry Days* (London, 1902), p. 11.

26. Hugh MacLennan, *Each Man's Son* (Toronto, 1951), pp. vii–viii.

27. Margaret Laurence, *The Diviners* (London, 1974), pp. 41–2.

28. PP 1841 (182) VI, 1, *First Report from the Select Committee on Emigration (Scotland) together with minutes of evidence and appendix*, Q. 2036, Hon. Christopher Alexander Hagerman.

29. SCA, George Hay to John Geddes, 11 November 1770, quoted in J. M. Bumsted, *The People's Clearance: Highland Emigration to British North America, 1770–1815* (Edinburgh, 1982), p. 69.

30. Ibid., pp. 73, 110–16, 138–9.

31. Rev. G. Patterson, *History of the County of Pictou* (Pictou, 1916), p. 199.

32. *Report of the Baptist Home Missionary Society for Scotland* (1831), p. 6, quoted in D. E. Meek, 'Evangelicalism and Emigration: Aspects of the Role of Dissenting Evangelicalism in Highland Emigration to Canada', in Gordon W. MacLennan (ed.), *Proceedings of the First North American Congress of Celtic Studies* (Ottawa, 1988), pp. 28–9.

33. Ibid., p.16; *Glasgow Constitutional*, 17 July 1852, quoted in Eric Richards, Alexia Howe, Ian Donnachie and Adrian Graves, *That Land of Exiles: Scots in Australia* (Edinburgh, 1988), p. 75.

34. J. S. Marais, *The Colonisation of New Zealand* (London, 1968), pp. 304, 347.

35. NRA(S), North-East Survey, no. 1345, John Fletcher to Charles Farquharson, 29 January 1863. See also pp. 85–9.

36. Meek, 'Evangelicalism and Emigration', pp. 27–8, 29–30; D. E. Meek, '"The Fellowship of Kindred Minds": Some Religious Aspects of Kinship and Emigration from the Scottish Highlands in the Nineteenth Century', in *Hands Across the Water. Emigration from Northern Scotland to North America* (Proceedings of the Sixth Annual Conference of the Scottish Association of Family History Societies, Aberdeen, 1995), p. 28; Laurie Stanley, *The Well Watered Garden: The Presbyterian Church in Cape Breton, 1798–1860* (Sydney, Cape Breton, 1983), pp. 134–6. MacFadyen also served as a minister in Montreal and among Tiree emigrants in Brock Township. The Tiverton congregation had been established after the Tiree Baptist Church lost two-thirds of its membership to emigration between 1846 and 1850.

37. Public Archives of Nova Scotia, RG 1, vol. 326, no. 171, 'Miscellaneous papers relating to Cape Breton, 1780–1809', quoted in Stanley, *The Well Watered Garden*, p. 44.

38. NAS RH4/80/5. George Forbes to John Forbes, Pittelachie, Tarland, 21 June 1846.

39. SCA, BL3/452/9, Rev. Roderick MacDonell, Culachie, near Quebec, to Bishop Geddes, Edinburgh, 1785. Thanks to Dr Christine Johnson for this and the following references from the Scottish Catholic Archives. See also A. I. Macinnes et al. (eds), *Scotland and the Americas, c. 1650–c. 1939: A Documentary Source Book* (forthcoming).

40. SCA, BL3/45/10, Captain John MacDonald, London, to John Geddes, Coadjutor Bishop of Lowland Vicariate, Edinburgh, 8 January 1785.

41. SCA, Preshome Letters, PL3/6/10, Rev. Angus MacEacharn, St Andrews, PEI, to Alexander Cameron, Coadjutor Bishop of the Lowland Vicariate, Edinburgh, 14 December 1807.

42. SCA, BL5/59/7. Rev. Angus MacEacharn to Alexander Cameron, 3 December 1819; SCA, BL5/81/18, Rev. Angus MacEacharn to Alexander Cameron, 23 June 1820.

43. SCA, DA9/44/1, Rev. George Corbett, parish priest, St Andrews, Ontario, to Bishop Angus MacDonald, Oban, 19 March 1884.

44. SCA, DA9/44/5, Alexander, Archbishop of St Boniface, Manitoba, to Bishop Angus MacDonald, Oban, 18 May 1844.

45. SCA, DA9/44/8, Rev. David Gillies, Villa Maria, Wassilla, North West Territories, to Bishop Angus MacDonald, Oban, 19 June 1886.

46. Inverness-shire Archives, D122/129, Glasgow Colonial Society, Eighth Annual Report, 1835, extract of letter from Rev. P. McIntyre, 7 March 1834.

47. Stanley, *The Well Watered Garden*, p. 122.

48. 'The Scotch Church at Chascomus, South America', *The Church of Scotland Home & Foreign Missionary Record* (1 November 1862), p. 210.

49. Frederick Stewart Buchanan, 'The Emigration of Scottish Mormons to Utah, 1849–1900' (MSc thesis, University of Utah, 1961), p. 50, quoting from *The Millennial Star*, vol. XXIII, p. 156.

50. Ibid., p. 18, quoting Alexander Wright's Journal, 17 July 1842.

51. Utah State Historical Society Archives, Salt Lake City, J. Mackintosh, Lochgilphead, to Daniel Mackintosh, Salt Lake City, 2 January 1851.

52. Buchanan, 'The Emigration of Scottish Mormons to Utah', pp. 37, 79.

53. Ibid., p. 133, quoting from 'Utah Scottish Bagpipe Band, suggestions for a meeting to be held Sunday, February 19, 1939'.

54. Norman Mackenzie to his brother, 1 February 1866; John Macleod to Sir James Matheson, 23 February 1866, both quoted in Napier Commission, Appendix A, pp. 174, 173.

55. Bennett, *Oatmeal and the Catechism*, pp. 16–17.

56. Sir Andrew MacPhail, *The Master's Wife* (Toronto, 1977 edition), pp. xi, 101–2.

57. MacLennan, *Each Man's Son*, p. viii.

58. MacDougall, *The Emigrant's Guide to North America*, p. 19.

59. Bernard Aspinwall, *Portable Utopia: Glasgow and the United States, 1820–1920* (Aberdeen, 1984), pp. 43–85.

60. MacPhail, *The Master's Wife*, p. 119.

61. Eric Richards et al., *That Land of Exiles*, pp. 101–11.

62. Marais, *The Colonisation of New Zealand*, pp. 349–50.

63. Tom Brooking, '"Tam McCanny and Kitty Clydeside": The Scots in New Zealand', in R. A. Cage (ed.), *The Scots Abroad: Labour, Capital, Enterprise, 1750–1914* (London, 1985), p. 184. See T. M. Hocken, *Contributions to the Early History of New Zealand (Settlement of Otago)* (London, 1898), p. 132, for comments on emigrants' indifference to education.

64. *Reports on the Schemes of the Church of Scotland, with the Legislative Acts passed by the General Assembly, Colonial Committee Report, 1920.*

65. *The South African Scot*, vol. 1, no.1 (15 November 1905), p. 2.

66. Bitterman, 'On Remembering and Forgetting', p. 260.

67. Richards et al., *That Land of Exiles*, p. 39.

68. *Wilmington Gazette*, 4 December 1800.

69. Quoted in Richards et al., *That Land of Exiles*, p. 114.

70. Gerald Redmond, *The Sporting Scots of Nineteenth Century Canada* (East Brunswick, 1982), p. 20.

71. *Inverness Courier*, 13 July 1842, quoted in Macinnes et al. (eds), *Scotland and the Americas*. Thanks to Dr Hugh Dan Maclennan for this and the following reference.

72. *Kingussie Record*, 2 May 1903, quoted ibid.

73. *Celtic Monthly*, vol. I, no. 11 (August 1893), p. 166.

74. *Falkland Island Magazine*, August 1892, quoted in Macinnes et al. (eds) *Scotland and the Americas*. Thanks to Jane Cameron, Falkland Islands Archivist, for this reference.

75. Wilfrid Campbell, *The Scotsman in Canada* (London, 1911), pp. 421–3.

76. Angus MacKay (Oscar Dhu), *By Trench and Trail in Song and Story* (Seattle, 1918), p. 116, quoted in Doucette (ed.), *Cultural Retention and Demographic Change*, p. 148. See also Bennett, *Oatmeal and the Catechism*, p. 45.

77. See above pp. 29–30.

78. William Bell, *Hints to Emigrants* (Edinburgh, 1824), pp. 103–4.

79. *Inverness Advertiser*, 16 March 1852.

80. Henry G. Dalton, *The History of British Guiana*, 2 vols (London, 1855), vol. 1, pp. 306–7. Thanks to Dr Roderick McDonald and Dr Douglas Hamilton for this and the following two references.

81. *Lady Nugent's Journal of her Residence in Jamaica from 1801 to 1805*, edited by Philip Wright, (Kingston, 1966), p. 29.

82. AUA, MS 602, The Journal of John Anderson, St Vincent Special Magistrate, 1836–9, p. 79.

83. Frederick S. Cozzens, *Acadia: or a month with the Blue Noses* (New York, 1859), pp. 150, 199, quoted in Harper and Vance (eds), *Myth, Migration and the Making of Memory*, p. 29.

84. Wayne Norton, *Help Us To A Better Land: Crofter Colonies in the Prairie West* (Regina, Sask., 1994), p. 47.

85. Ibid., p. 36, from NAS AF51/198/514, T. J. Lawlor to Sir George Trevelyan, 21 January 1895.

86. *Dundas Warden*, 2 October 1851, quoted in MacKenzie, *The History of the Highland Clearances*, p. 260.

87. A. M. Burgess to Hon. E. Dewdney, 18 July 1889, quoted in Kent Stuart, 'The Scottish Crofter Colony, Saltcoats', *Saskatchewan History*, vol. XXIV, no. 2 (Spring 1971), p. 47.

88. E. J. Cowan, 'The Myth of Scotch Canada' in Harper and Vance (eds), *Myth, Migration and the Making of Memory*, p. 62.

89. Ibid., p. 65.

90. Robert Louis Stevenson, *From Scotland to Silverado* (Cambridge, Mass., 1966), p. 211.

91. Cowan, 'The Myth of Scotch Canada', p. 59.

92. Samuel Johnson, *A Journey to the Western Islands of Scotland* (London, 1875), edited by R. W. Chapman (Oxford, 1924), pp. 86, 119–20.

ACKNOWLEDGEMENTS

This book could not have been completed without assistance and encouragement from a number of sources. At an institutional level, I benefited greatly from an extended period of study leave awarded by the Arts and Humanities Research Board under its Research Leave Scheme (RLS-AN 2017/APN 13372). As I have travelled throughout and beyond Scotland in pursuit of research materials, I have received generous and enthusiastic help from an army of librarians, archivists and museum curators at the McCord Museum, Montreal, the National Archives of Canada, Ottawa, the University of Cape Town Library, the Cape Archives Depot and the National Libraries of Australia, New Zealand and South Africa. A special tribute should be paid to the meticulous research of the late Claire Laburn of Cape Town, whose studies into Scottish settlement in Eastern Natal were cut short by her untimely death in 1991, but whose working papers are held in the Manuscripts and Archives Department of UCT Library. I drew heavily on Claire's notes, particularly when investigating the activities of John Walker.

Closer to home, Kevin Halliwell of the National Library of Scotland and Jane Brown of the National Archives of Scotland drew my attention to previously unused material, while George Dalgleish and David Forsyth of the Museum of Scotland International alerted me to relevant illustrations. It was a pleasure to revisit Quarrier's Village, where I was made so welcome by Bill and Helen Dunbar, and I have benefited from the advice and expertise of archivists at Stirling Council Archives and Shetland Archives, from where Angus Johnstone kindly sent me a large file of material relating to emigration from the Northern Isles. I am grateful to Mrs F. E. Young of Tomintoul for allowing me to use the correspondence of the Galbraiths of Tauranga, as well as to Len Gray of Auckland and the Sangster family for copies of the diaries of Mrs D. Bonthrow and George Sangster respectively.

Colleagues in my own institution and in other universities have given invaluable advice and support. Eric Richards of Flinders University, South Australia, has cheerfully and fully responded to my many requests for obscure references to Scots in Australia, and Susie Zada, President of the Bellarine Historical Society, provided invaluable information on Anne Drysdale. I am indebted to Lucille Campey for material on Highland emigration agents, while Philip Goldring and Judith Hudson Beattie supplied much of the evidence about Scots in the Hudson's Bay Company. Conversations and correspondence with Marilyn Barber, Bruce Elliott, Charlotte Erickson, Philip Girard, Dougie Hamilton, Sheila Kidd, Donald Meek, Katie Pickles, Ferenc Szasz, Margaret Connell Szasz and many others, have given me fresh insights and an awareness of the bigger picture in migration studies.

The greatest debts have been incurred closest to home. As always, the staff of Aberdeen University Library have offered unfailing support. Myrtle Anderson-Smith, Iain Beavan, Michele Gale and Jane Pirie in the Department of Special Libraries and Archives, along with Noreen Wilson and her colleagues at Inter-Library Loans and the Faculty Librarian, Gilian Dawson, have been particularly helpful. Donald Meek, formerly of Aberdeen University, now of the University of Edinburgh, kindly supplied me with a copy of J. Mackintosh's letter to his Mormon nephew. Colleagues in the School of History and History of Art have been steadily supportive: David Ditchburn and Andrew Mackillop in particular supplied me with very helpful references to European and Indian material respectively. I am immensely grateful to Tom Devine, Director of the Research Institute for Irish and Scottish Studies at the University of Aberdeen, for encouraging me to undertake the project, reading the first draft of the manuscript and spearheading an exciting and multi-faceted programme of diaspora studies through the Institute and the Arts and Humanities Research Board Research Centre in Irish and Scottish Studies. Stimulating seminars and conferences organized by the Institute constantly expand my horizons and fire my enthusiasm, and I have much appreciated the advice and support of those connected with RIISS, including John MacKenzie, Angela McCarthy, Enda Delaney, Steve Murdoch, Alexia Grosjean and Andrew Walls.

Special thanks go to my husband, Andrew Shere, not only for his constant support but also for sacrificing four days from a Cape Town summer to labouring in the archives on my behalf.

SELECT BIBLIOGRAPHY

In the first half of the twentieth century the standard general work on British emigration was W. A. Carrothers, *Emigration from the British Isles, with Special Reference to the Development of the Overseas Dominions* (London, 1929). Modern quantitative evaluations include Dudley Baines, *Migration in a Mature Economy: Emigration and Internal Migration in England and Wales, 1861–1900* (Cambridge, 1985) and *Emigration from Europe, 1815–1930* (Basingstoke, 1991). Charlotte Erickson's many pioneering studies of British emigration include *Leaving England: Essays on British Emigration in the Nineteenth Century* (Ithaca, 1994). The most recent short overviews are by James Horn, 'British Diaspora: Emigration from Britain, 1680–1815' in P. J. Marshall (ed.), *The Oxford History of the British Empire, vol. II, the Eighteenth Century* (Oxford, 1998), pp. 28–52 and Marjory Harper, 'British Migration and the Peopling of the Empire' in Andrew Porter (ed.), *The Oxford History of the British Empire, vol. III, the Nineteenth Century* (Oxford, 1999), pp. 75–87. The British perspective is also addressed in Eric Richards, *The British Diaspora* (forthcoming).

Gordon Donaldson, *The Scots Overseas* (London, 1966) provided the first basic overview of Scottish emigration. Throughout the 1970s and 1980s the emphasis was on the Highland exodus, explored in Eric Richards, *A History of the Highland Clearances*, 2 vols (London, 1982 and 1985), recently republished in a single volume, *The Highland Clearances: People, Landlords and Rural Turmoil* (Edinburgh, 2000). Emigration was also a major theme in T. M. Devine, *The Great Highland Famine: Hunger, Emigration and the Scottish Highlands in the Nineteenth Century* (Edinburgh, 1988) and *Clanship to Crofters' War: the Social Transformation of the Scottish Highlands* (Manchester, 1994). The focus of Scottish studies was extended beyond the Highlands in Malcolm Gray, *Scots on the Move: Scots Migrants 1750–1914* (Edinburgh, 1991), T. M. Devine (ed.), *Scottish Emigration and Scottish Society* (Edinburgh, 1992) and Jeanette Brock, *The Mobile Scot: A Study of Emigration and Migration 1861–1911* (Edinburgh, 1999).

An overview of British settlement in Australia in the mid-nineteenth century is given in Robin F. Haines, *Emigration and the Labouring Poor: Australian Recruitment in Britain and Ireland, 1831–60* (Basingstoke, 1997). Our understanding of Scots in Australia has been advanced by Malcolm D. Prentis, *The Scots in Australia: A Study of New South Wales, Victoria and Queensland, 1788–1900* (Sydney and London, 1983) and Eric Richards, Alexia Howe, Ian

Donnachie and Adrian Graves, *That Land of Exiles: Scots in Australia* (Edinburgh, 1988). Their role in both Australia and New Zealand has been explored by Jim Hewitson, *Far Off In Sunlit Places: Stories of the Scots in Australia and New Zealand* (Edinburgh, 1998) and their influence in New Zealand specifically by G. L. Pearce, *The Scots of New Zealand* (Auckland and London, 1976).

Emigration to North America in the colonial period is examined in Bernard Bailyn, *Voyagers to the West: Emigration from Britain to America on the Eve of the Revolution* (London, 1987). The Scottish experience in the American colonies is singled out in David Dobson, *Scottish Emigration to Colonial America 1607–1785* (Athens, Ga, 1994) and Anthony W. Parker, *Scottish Highlanders in Colonial Georgia: The Recruitment, Emigration and Settlement at Darien, 1735–1748* (Athens, Ga, 1997). Aspects of British settlement in the United States are analysed in Charlotte Erickson, *Invisible Immigrants: The Adaptation of English and Scottish Immigrants in Nineteenth-century America* (London, 1972) and William E. Van Vugt, *Britain to America: Mid Nineteenth-century Immigrants to the United States (*(Urbana, Il, 1999) while the role of Scots in the USA is the subject of Jim Hewitson, *Tam Blake & Co. The Story of the Scots in America* (Edinburgh, 1993) and Ferenc M. Szasz, *Scots in the North American West 1790–1917* (Norman, Ok., 2000). Scots in South America have received little attention, with the exception of Greta Mackenzie, *Why Patagonia?* (Stornoway, 1996) and Iain A. D. Stewart (ed.), *From Caledonia to the Pampas. Two Accounts by Early Scottish Emigrants to the Argentine* (Phantassie, East Linton, 2000). Scottish experiences in the Caribbean have been evaluated by Alan Karras, *Sojourners in the Sun. Scottish Migrants in Jamaica and the Chesapeake, 1740–1800* (Ithaca, NY, 1992) and their role throughout the American continent in L. G. Fryer, M. D. Harper and A. I. Macinnes (eds), *Scotland and the Americas 1650–1930: A Documentary Source Book* (Edinburgh, 2003).

Among many writings on the Scots in Canada are J. M. Bumsted, *The People's Clearance. Highland Emigration to British North America, 1770–1815* (Edinburgh, 1982), Marianne McLean, *The People of Glengarry:Highlanders in Transition, 1745–1820* (Montreal, 1991) and Marjory Harper and Michael E. Vance (eds), *Myth, Migration and the Making of Memory: Scotia and Nova Scotia, c. 1700–1990* (Halifax, NS and Edinburgh, 1999). Perceptions of Scottish identity in Canadian literature can be found in the novels of a number of writers, including, most recently, Alistair MacLeod, *No Great Mischief* (London, 2001).

Child migration policies have been subject to frequent scrutiny in recent years. The Scottish perspective is examined in Anna Magnusson, *The Village*

(Quarrier's, 1984) and Lynn Abrams, *The Orphan Country. Children of Scotland's Broken Homes from 1845 to the Present Day* (Edinburgh, 1998) and the Canadian experience in Joy Parr, *Labouring Children: British Immigrant Apprentices to Canada, 1869–1924* (London and Montreal, 1980). Female emigration has been analysed in a number of studies, though not from a specifically Scottish perspective, the most recent publication being Jan Gothard, *Blue China. Single Female Migration to Colonial Australia* (Melbourne, 2001). The issue is also addressed in Marilyn Barber, *Immigrant Domestic Servants in Canada* (Ottawa, 1991) and Cecillie Swaisland, *Servants and Gentlewomen to the Golden Land. The Emigration of Single Women to Southern Africa, 1820–1939* (Oxford, 1993).

Transatlantic and Antiopdean passages are examined in Terry Coleman, *Passage to America. A History of Emigrants from Great Britain and Ireland to America in the Mid-Nineteenth Century* (London, 1972) and Helen Woolcock, *Rights of Passage. Emigration to Australia in the Nineteenth Century* (London, 1986), while passengers' diaries are discussed in Andrew Hassam, *Sailing to Australia. Shipboard Diaries by Nineteenth-century British Emigrants* (Manchester, 1994).

INDEX